SUSPECT FREEDOMS

CULTURE, LABOR, HISTORY SERIES

General Editors: Daniel Bender and Kimberley L. Phillips

Suspect Freedoms

The Racial and Sexual Politics of Cubanidad
in New York, 1823–1957

Nancy Raquel Mirabal

NEW YORK UNIVERSITY PRESS
New York

NEW YORK UNIVERSITY PRESS
New York
www.nyupress.org

References to Internet websites (URLs) were accurate at the time of writing. Neither the author nor New York University Press is responsible for URLs that may have expired or changed since the manuscript was prepared.

Library of Congress Cataloging-in-Publication Data
Names: Mirabal, Nancy Raquel, 1966- author.
Title: Suspect freedoms : the racial and sexual politics of Cubanidad in New York, 1823-1957 / Nancy Raquel Mirabal.
Description: New York : New York University Press, [2016] | Series: Culture, labor, history series | Includes bibliographical references and index.
Identifiers: LCCN 2016023908| ISBN 978-0-8147-6111-3 (cloth : acid-free paper) | ISBN 978-0-8147-6112-0 (paperback : acid-free paper)
Subjects: LCSH: Cubans—New York (State)—New York—History—19th century. | Cubans—New York (State)—New York—History—20th century. | Immigrants—New York (State)—New York—History. | Exiles—New York (State)—New York—History. | Cubans—New York (State)—New York—Ethnic identity—History. | Blacks—Race identity—New York (State)—New York—History. | Race—Political aspects—New York (State)—New York—History. | Sex—Political aspects—New York (State)—New York—History. | New York (N.Y.)—Ethnic relations—History. | New York (N.Y.)—Race relations—History.
Classification: LCC F128.9.C97 M57 2016 | DDC 305.8009747—dc23
LC record available at https://lccn.loc.gov/2016023908

New York University Press books are printed on acid-free paper, and their binding materials are chosen for strength and durability. We strive to use environmentally responsible suppliers and materials to the greatest extent possible in publishing our books.

Manufactured in the United States of America

10 9 8 7 6 5 4 3 2 1

Also available as an ebook

For Melba Alvarado, who believed and understood.

And for Servelio and Delia Mirabal, for encouraging me to write,

be in spirit, and live a life of my own making.

CONTENTS

ACKNOWLEDGMENTS

I have been thinking about, researching, and writing this book for close to twenty years. It has taken many forms, but never a book, until now. I thank all of those who traversed these seemingly impractical and distracted roads with grace, kindness, and humor. I want to thank Earl Lewis and Robin D. G. Kelley for their encouragement and support. Their ability to envision this project as an integral part of a larger hemispheric and transnationalist history made all the difference. I am indebted to Ruth Behar, Elsa Barkley Brown, Eileen Boris, Lisa Brock, Sandra Cisneros, Arlene Dávila, Anani Dzinzeyo, Juan Flores, Donna Gabbacia, Farah Jasmine Griffin, Jennifer Guglielmo, Nancy Hewitt, Miriam Jiménez Román, Diana Lachatanere, Velora Lilly, Agnes Lugo-Ortiz, Diane Milioties, Premilla Nadasen, Suzanne Oboler, Annelise Orleck, Silvia Pedraza, Louis A. Pérez, Jr., Gerald E. Poyo, Barbara Ransby, Juana María Rodríguez, George Sánchez, Aldo Lauria Santiago, Rebecca Scott, and Vicky Ruiz, for publishing articles, offering invaluable advice, pointing out critical sources, writing (countless) letters, and teaching important lessons.

This book could not have been completed without the support of friends and colleagues who read drafts, offered suggestions, invited me to give talks, provided needed distractions, tolerated my attention to detail, and made the research and writing so much better. Thank you to Rosio Alvarez, Nancy Bercaw, Maylei Blackwell, Mary Pat Brady, Luz Calvo, Laureen Chew, Kathleen Coll, Eduardo Contreras, Raúl Coronado, Wei Ming Dariotis, María De Guzmán, Sergio De la Mora, Dawn Elissa Fischer, Aurelia Flores, Ester Hernández, Philip Jackson, Félix Kury, Carmen Lamas, Leslie Larson, Rodrigo Lazo, John Jota Leaños, Ricardo Lemvo, Katynka Martiñez, Lourdes Martiñez Echezábal, April Mayes, John McKiernan-González, Claudia Milian, Kristin Naca, Marcia Ochoa, Ariana Ochoa Camacho, Ricardo Ortiz, Naomi Quiñones, Isabelle Pelaud, Alaí Reyes-Santos, Roberto Rivera, Tamerra Roberts,

Ana Patricia Rodríguez, Merida Rua, Catriona Rueda Esquibel, Tania Triana, Carla Trujillo, Diana Valle, Deborah Vargas, Carmen Whalen, and Nataly Zaragoza. Thank you to Karina Lisette Cespedes for being my Cuban co-conspirator, and to the incredibly generous Gema Guevara for reading chapters, providing critical feedback, sharing invaluable sources, and being brilliant in so many ways. Thank you to Juana María Rodríguez for inspiring me to be a better writer and thinker. I deeply appreciate your feedback and assistance over the years. I am so grateful to my sister-friend Andreana Clay for showing unlimited kindness, humor, and love. I also want to thank her and Joan Benoit for inviting me to be part of Otis's life as one of his godmothers and many adoring tias.

Thank you to the participants of Tepoztlan for reading and critiquing my work at a pivotal juncture. I especially want to thank Jossianna Arroyo, David Sartorious, Yolanda Martínez-San Miguel, Robin Lauren Derby, Nicole Guidotti-Hernández, Lawrence LaFountain Stokes, and to Frank Andre Guridy who invited me to apply and opened a whole new world of collegial possibilities. From 2001 to 2003, I was awarded a Chancellor's Post-doctoral Fellowship in the Ethnic Studies Department at the University of California, Berkeley. I want to thank José David Saldívar for serving as my faculty advisor, and to Laura Pérez and Norma Alarcón for kindly inviting me to be part of conferences, workshops, and writing groups. In 2003 I was awarded a Social Science Research Council International Migration Post-doctoral Fellowship funded by the Mellon Foundation. The fellowship funded research trips and provided the time necessary to rethink and redraft this project. In 2012 I was awarded the Scholar in Residence Fellowship at the Schomburg Center for Research in Black Culture, funded in part by the National Endowment for the Humanities. The fellowship was a turning point in my research, career, and life. And for that I am forever grateful. I am deeply thankful to Farah Jasmin Griffin, Steven Fullwood, Antony Toussant, and Mary Yearwood, as well as to the many librarians and archivists, for helping me locate precious documents, research materials, and photographic images. I am especially indebted to Diana Lachatenere whose belief in this research has been invaluable. I am so grateful for her insights, patience, brilliance, and friendship. I want to thank all of my colleagues who were part of the Scholar-in-Residence Fellowship for reading drafts and offering needed critiques. In particular, I want to thank Miriam Jiménez Román, David Goldberg, Marisa Reese Fuentes, Anthony Foy, Kevin Meehan, and Jim DeLongh for their smart and thoughtful suggestions on the manuscript, and to Naomi Bland and Jadele McPherson for assisting me when I needed it most. Many thanks to the staff at the Center for Puerto Rican Studies, who were extremely helpful in locating important documents and ensuring that I received resources in a timely manner. I especially want to thank Pedro Juan Hernández and Yosenex Orengo for their assistance. My deepest gratitude to Eduardo Contreras, Arlene Dávila, Zaire Dinzey-Flores, Juan Flores, Miriam Jiménez Román, Arnaldo Cruz-Malavé, John Arenare, Jadele McPherson, Jo-Ana Moreno, Yesenia Selier, Pamela Sporn, Pablo Foster, Premilla Nadasen, Pamela Calla, Wendy Susan Walters, and Dan Charnas for providing community and making me feel at home while in New York. It made all the difference.

I would never have been able to spend an academic year at the Schomburg Center without the efforts and generosity of my colleagues in the College of Ethnic Studies at San Francisco State University. Thank you to Teresa Carrillo, former chair of the Latina/Latino Studies Department, Laureen Chew, former Associate Dean, and Kenneth Monteiro, Dean of the College of Ethnic Studies, for your assistance and support.

In 2014 I accepted a position in the American Studies Department and US Latina/o Studies Program at the University of Maryland, College Park. I am so thankful to Nancy Struna, Psyche Williams-Forson, Julie Greene, and Ira Berlin for being so kind and helpful as I transitioned to the University of Maryland and Washington, DC. I would also like to thank my wonderful colleagues in the American Studies Department and US Latina/o Studies Program for being so welcoming. I am particularly grateful to Betsy Yuen and Julia John for their gracious assistance.

Mil gracias to Mercedes Rubio (la comadre), Nicholas Saunders, Nico, and Jackson for being my DC family and generously giving me a place to stay and write while my furniture traveled across country. I am so grateful to Kimberley L. Phillips and Daniel Bender, who as series editors believed in this project early on and welcomed me with open arms. Thank you to my editors at New York University Press (past and present), Eric Zinner, Deborah Gershenowitz, Clara Platter, Constance

Grady, Amy Klopfenstein, and Alexia Traganas for their enthusiasm, expertise, and unlimited patience.

This book would not have been possible without Melba Alvarado. Her conviction that this book needed to be written and that I should be the one to do so made all the difference. I am deeply honored to have conducted oral histories and interviews, archived documents, and worked closely with her for more than twenty years to piece together a history that, in her words, "needed to be told." In working with Alvarado I learned the value of being invested in community and part of what she called "something bigger." She revealed a great deal to me, years of pain and struggle, but more importantly her tenacity, strength, humor, and love for her community. She is, and will always be, one of my greatest inspirations.

I am so thankful to the members of El Club Cubano Inter-Americano, in particular Jo-Ana Moreno, for inviting me to give a talk at the Cena Martiana, making sure that I got free tickets to La Fiesta del Mamoncillo, and for allowing me to assist her in organizing the 70th anniversary of El Club Cubano Inter-Americano at the Schomburg Center for Research in Black Culture. You have no idea how exciting this has been for me. Thank you to Lydia "Tata" Caraballosa, "my tia," for allowing me to interview her and learn more about her experiences in New York during the 1940s, and for being such a loving and strong spirit. And to my other "tia," Olga Marten, who for more than forty years lived in a rent-controlled apartment on 72nd Street and Broadway above the Ortiz Funeral Home. Olga graciously let me stay with her whenever I wanted and for as long as I needed, to conduct research and finish the writing. She never wavered in her curiosity, always asking me what I found in the archives and listening to the stories about "los cubanos en nueva york." Excited that I would be writing the history of "los cubanos de color," she died suddenly and tragically before the completion of this book. It was too soon, and I miss her.

I am forever grateful to my older brother George Mirabal for always being there for me, no matter what, and to Filomena Sofia and Finn Magnus for literally being at my side as I wrote and rewrote chapters of this book. Thank you to my great-aunt Josefina Hentschel and madrina Raquel Lavernia for their care during a critical moment in my life. Finally, I dedicate this book to my parents Servelio and Delia Mirabal,

Cuban immigrants who met and married in New York and moved to Southeast Los Angeles (South Gate and Huntington Park) where I was born and raised. It was their stories, experiences, hardships, and humor that from the very beginning shaped and influenced the direction of this book. They have never wavered in their support and love. And I love them dearly for that. Thank you for seeing what I had yet to see.

Introduction

Diasporic Histories and Archival Hauntings

Bueno mi'ja, apúrate con este trabajo, con estas entrevistas, porque nos estamos poniendo viejos, unos cuantos ya se han muerto. Y la historia, bueno ¿qué puedo decir? La historia se nos vá.
Melba Alvarado[1]

How can the negro be remembered when such speeches are not to be found in the National Library?
Richard T. Greener, 1882[2]

A colored woman, Juana Pastor was a noted poetess in the last century. Unfortunately, the present generation is unable to judge her work, as it was never printed. According to a good authority, she was the first in Cuba to write poetry.
New York Times, 1900[3]

I used the term haunting to describe those singular yet re-petitive instances when home becomes unfamiliar, when your bearings on the world lose direction, when the over-and-done-with comes alive, when what's been in your blind spot comes into view. Haunting raises specters, and it alters the experience of being in time, the way we separate the past, the present and the future.
Avery F. Gordon[4]

In 1995, on a very hot summer day in *el club cubano del* South Bronx, I interviewed Melba Alvarado for the first time. I wanted to learn about her activism, politics, and work. I wondered how it felt to be one of the first female presidents of El Club Cubano Inter-Americano (CCI), an Afro-Cuban social club founded on September 17, 1945 and led primarily by men.[5] At the time I had no idea that I would interview Alvarado for decades and that my ensuing relationship with her would so dramatically change my thinking and writing. But it did. Alvarado's recollections opened a needed dialogue into the complicated, difficult, and often painful discussions on memory and the politics of belonging within the Cuban diaspora in New York.

It would be years before I fully understood what Alvarado meant when she told me to hurry with this work, with these interviews, because *they* were getting older and some, as she put it, had already died. And our history, what can I say, "Our history leaves us." This quote has never left me. I use it often. It both haunts and forces me to understand the power and urgency of historical work and the precariousness and ephemerality of a history that doesn't always fit traditional historical narratives. What did it mean to write a history so shaped by impending death, fragmented collective memories, and dissoluble archives that it could "leave us"?

My initial interview with Alvarado spanned two days, with the last session held at El Club del Desfile de la Hispanidad located at 174 Fifth Avenue in Manhattan. It didn't surprise me that both interviews took place in social clubs. Club life defined Alvarado. She devoted most of her time to club activity, including organizing El Festival del Mamoncillo, an important music and community festival that was held in the "salónes y parques del Bohemian Hall" in Astoria every second Sunday in July.[6] It was through these early interviews that I first learned about El Club Julio Antonio Mella. For years, El Club Julio Antonio Mella was simply an intriguing reference to a club that Alvarado's uncle Manuel Delgado, a musician who played saxophone and clarinet, had joined when he first arrived to New York. Except for Alvarado's words, the club had yet to feel real. It remained a historical haunting pivoted in the imagination and memories of others, what Nicole Guidotti-Hernández writes are the "historical traces that are clearly there but not allowed to be heard, seen or experienced."[7]

It wasn't until I located the photo of members of El Club Julio Antonio Mella, the one that graces the cover of this book, that I finally understood why Alvarado mentioned it so often in her interviews. The photo was misfiled. I found it by chance. Had I not interviewed Alvarado for so many years, and scribbled the name El Club Julio Antonio Mella countless times followed by numerous question marks, I too would have put the photo back in the wrong file and moved on. Yet, there in the archive, surrounded by scraps of papers, endless files, and piles of books, I instantly recognized the name of the club. I looked closely at the black and white photo and heard Alvarado's words ringing in my ears. "There was a racially mixed club called El Club Mella. The members were exiled for political reasons. Women were also members, and the club was on Fifth Avenue."[8]

Pieces of her collective memory fell into place as I looked closely at the different faces of the members, sitting side by side at long narrow tables dressed with white tablecloths and flowers, celebrating the inauguration of El Club Julio Antonio Mella. In this one photo, with the inscription "Recuerdos de la inauguración de la logia 4763 Julio A. Mella I.W.O. 1500 5th Ave Oct. 2, 1938 N.Y.C.," the vague reference to a club that her father frequented, but never belonged to, was no longer a fleeting comment. There, in the faces of the members, were well known individuals, like the Puerto Rican activist and labor organizer Jésus Colón, and a founder of El Club Cubano Inter-Americano Pedro Millet, and others not so well known (at least to me). I wondered who these people were and why they joined El Club Mella. I tried to imagine the different conversations and debates that took place within the club, and if the women seated at the long tables were also members of El Club de Damas, a women's club that was an integral part of El Club Mella. What I didn't expect to see was that the club was part of the International Worker's Order (IWO). This took my research into completely different directions, revealing historical contradictions and requiring further questioning. It also allowed for uneasy continuities and dislocated connections between and among different historical periods and moments. Until recently, and only when shown the photo and confronted with questions about the club's relationship with the IWO, did Alvarado reluctantly mention that El Club Mella was socialist. Alvarado's unwillingness to divulge anything having to do with the club's politics is symptomatic of a larger historical depoliticizing and silencing of this period; a long-standing policy of convenient contradictions.

To understand where El Club Mella fit within the historical trajectory of Cuban diasporic politics, one that rarely looks at the history of Afro-Cuban intellectual production, it was important to look at how earlier nineteenth-century *independista* and revolutionary clubs influenced the formation of El Club Mella. Was this club a result and outgrowth of the ideas, thoughts, and writings of New York–based nineteenth-century Cuban and Puerto Rican revolutionaries Rafael Serra, Eugenio María de Hostos, Inocencia Mártinez, Arturo Schomburg, Ramón Emeterio Betances, Teófilo Domínguez, and Sotero Figueroa Hernández, to name a few, or was it an altogether different club shaped by the racial, diasporic, and labor politics of early twentieth-century US diasporic communities? Or was it a combination of the two?

There were similarities. Nineteenth-century Cuban and Puerto Rican political and revolutionary clubs cultivated transnationalist and hemispheric spaces where exiles and migrants incorporated nationalist desires with labor interests into their organizational platforms. This combination, while necessary, was not always seamless. By the early twentieth century, Cuban diasporic politics shifted. The end of the Spanish-American War and the subsequent US intervention and occupation of both islands led to the dissolution of early Cuban and Puerto Rican political and revolutionary activity in the United States. Within a year almost all clubs organized around independence, including the Partido Revolucionario Cubano (PRC), had been disbanded. Labor unions, however, grew stronger, and Cubans and Puerto Ricans who had been involved in the revolutionary movement and opted to stay in New York were now, more than ever, involved in labor unions. With the emphasis on labor organizing and unions it was no coincidence that El Club Julio Antonio Mella was a branch of the IWO, a Communist Party–affiliated insurance and mutual-benefit organization founded in 1930 and disbanded in 1954 as a result of legal action taken by the state of New York in 1951.[9]

El Club Mella, as the name suggests, was not focused solely on labor issues and the members were not simply interested in being another branch of the IWO. In naming the club after Julio Antonio Mella, the members deliberately echoed the hemispheric positions and Cuban-centered politics of nineteenth-century clubs while at the same time re-configuring notions of diaspora to reflect the evolution of Cuban politics in New York during the early twentieth century. Moreover, by naming the club after Mella, the members made public their support of communism, labor, and ending racial inequality and poverty.[10] By the early 1930s, the members expanded their scope to include the economic and political problems of the hemisphere, internationalism, and the Spanish Civil War. Along with the Lincoln Brigade, members of El Club Mella went to Spain to fight in support of Republican forces.

A co-founder of the Cuban Communist Party, Julio Antonio Mella was one of President Gerardo Machado y Morales' most vocal critics. A charismatic labor organizer and activist, Mella, who at the time was a student at the University of Havana, challenged Machado's oppressive and authoritarian policies, including his unwavering support of growing US economic and political control. In 1925 Mella was expelled from the University of Havana for his anti-government activities. After traveling throughout Central America he settled in Mexico, where he continued his efforts to overthrow President Machado. On January 10, 1929, Mella was assassinated in Mexico City.

Cubans who left for New York during this period did so for two fundamental reasons: their political opposition to the policies and actions of President Machado; and escape from the harrowing economic conditions of the depression. The migrations included a steady stream of Afro-Cubans who arrived in New York in the late 1920s and 1930s. In 1930, close to 19,000 Cubans migrated to the United States, an increase from 14,892 who migrated in 1920. Of that number, census records and data, suggest a third were Afro-Cuban.[11]

A racially integrated and inclusive club, El Club Julio Antonio Mella was a place "where black people," as Alvarado explained, came together "with whites" to practice "their politics." Although Alvarado remembered little concerning the club's logistics and structure, she considered El Club Mella "proof that Cubans of color" were not only politically active, but authors of their own political agenda, production, and action. According to Alvarado, "at that moment there was no racism."[12]

The process involved in locating, remembering, and historically contextualizing El Club Julio Antonio Mella within the larger historiography is a central metaphor for this book. A rarely discussed part of Cuban migrant, political, and labor history, it was only through Alvarado's te-nacious memories and one photographic image that such an "unthink-able history," to quote Michel Rolph Trouillot, emerged to complicate, haunt, and eventually force a rethinking of Cuban diasporic history in New York.[13] *Suspect Freedoms* subverts familiar and traditional notions of historical processes, narrative, source, and location. It argues that the questions of blackness, the problems of whiteness, and the implausibil-ity of the places in between figured in all aspects of Cuban diasporic history, regardless of what has been documented. It examines the legacy of diasporic narratives on race that would lead Alvarado to associate temporary integrations with a momentary lack of racism, and why we deliberately forget that multiple communities have always moved, have always reasserted and renegotiated borders and spaces, even in times of violence and disenfranchisement. It challenges normative masculini-ties and problematizes their use in discourse and self. Finally, it asserts that Afro-Cuban migrants have a long and varied political and intel-lectual history and existence in New York, one rooted in defining and fighting for their freedom. Rarely credited for their efforts and involve-ment, Afro-Cuban migrants were some of the most incisive, powerful, and radical voices in the exile nationalist movement, so much so that by the mid- to late nineteenth-century, meanings of Cubanidad were inextricably tied to ending slavery, racial equality, and a promise of enfranchisement.

This does not mean, however, that notions of Cubanidad were intact and flawless. They were not. It was precisely due to their imperfection, opportunistic evolutions, and problematic promises that Cubanidad was both integral to the nineteenth-century nationalist movement and a postwar burden. So seductive were the possibilities of an inclusive Cubanidad that it haunted the diasporic Cuban community years after the war, and years into US colonialism and control. For members of El Club Cubano-InterAmericano the haunting revealed itself in the never-ending celebrations of José Martí and Antonio Maceo, in their portraits, along with those of George Washington, Abraham Lincoln, and Simón Bolívar lining the walls of the club, and finally in the tireless, heartbreak-ing, and failed effort to build a public memorial of Antonio Maceo to complement or at the very least balance the historical primacy and im-position of José Martí memorials in New York.

Scripting Temporality: Dislocated Nations and Diasporic Desires

Cubans who left for the United States during the nineteenth century had little choice but to invest in a politics of spatial inquiry, reinvention, and fiction. It was precisely because the Cuba that Cuban exiles and migrants so longed for did *not* exist that exiles and migrants narrated and argued themselves into revolution and nation-building, and where Cuba, as *nation becoming*, operated in the realm of possibility and desire. It is in these moments of potential, temporality, and the becoming that most defines early Cuban diasporic politics, what Gayarti Gopinath has observed are diasporas and diasporic subjects that can "be seen as part of the nation itself," which in turn "allows the nation to be rewritten into the diaspora."[14]

For Cubans in New York City this meant scripting nation as artifact and spectacle. Cubans conceived, stitched, and first flew what would be known as the Cuban flag (Cuba Libre) on the balcony of the *New York Sun* in 1850, eight days before it ever flew on Cuban soil. It was in New York where the official Cuban Republic at Arms and the Partido Revolucionario Cubano were both headquartered—providing legitimacy to a provisional Cuban government and to the most powerful exile revolutionary organization. It was where Cirilo Villaverde completed the most Cuban of novels, *Cecilia Valdés o la loma del ángel*, where José Martí transitioned into the revolutionary architect of the Cuban War for Independence, where Afro-Cuban writer Eloisa Piñeiro migrated so she could write without restriction, and where countless newspapers, journals, poems, novels, and essays were published.[15]

So prodigious was the output that it is rare to find early Cuban diasporic sources, writings, and documents that were *not* written, published, disseminated, or otherwise produced in New York. As literary scholars have documented, New York's prominence as the center of knowledge production attracted its fair share of Cuban writers, journalists, and poets looking to be published. In fact, as Richard Newman, Patrick Rael, and Philip Lapsansky have written, by the 1850s nearly four times as many daily newspapers circulated throughout the country as there had been two decades earlier, while at the same time "the costs of production had plummeted by 600 percent."[16] These factors led to a boom in the publication and dissemination of printed media, especially among African Americans and immigrant communities in New York. Cuban exiles and migrants followed suit, publishing and disseminating hundreds of newspapers, pamphlets, journals, and speeches. The Afro-Cuban independista Martín Morúa Delgado declared exile revolutionary newspapers the "greatest wonder of all inventions throughout the ages." There was no other tool as effective in transmitting democratic ideas to the popular masses. For Morúa, they were critical in elevating "principles of freedom" and individual consciousness.[17]

Written in Spanish, the revolutionary newspapers, pamphlets, and other printed media were meant to travel beyond US borders. Designed to elicit a sense of nationalist exclusivity and hemispheric belonging, they established a shared revolutionary narrative in other countries, namely Jamaica, Haiti, Venezuela, Nicaragua, Dominican Republic, and Mexico, where revolutionaries had formed political clubs. Transporting them to Cuba, however, was not easy. Strict censorship laws limited the circulation of revolutionary newspapers in Cuba, and anyone found with one could go to jail. The editors of the pro-annexationist newspaper *La Verdad* publicly criticized the "island press" for not publishing what Cuba thinks and suffers, "except in such terms as the royal censors direct."[18]

The extensive publication and circulation of text, the mobility of bodies, particularly black bodies, and the determination to re-script nation and experience at all times, shaped a fleeting and subjective Cuban diasporic imagining of nation that was continually open to revision. In her invaluable analysis of José Martí, Lillian Guerra writes that in the process of conducting research in the Cuban archives, "breathing in the emotions that produced the personal and public testimonies," she realized that "Cubans seemed to talk past each other, toward a truth they imagined differently and remembered differently. This truth, by their own account was the nation." Guerra conceived of the nation much as her archival sources indicated they had conceived it. That is, "the nation was nothing more and nothing less than the mental location of liberation in the form of political entity and community yet to be achieved."[19] Pivoted in temporality and longing, it is in those theoretical sites and crevices of a community "yet to be achieved" that this book ruminates and dwells.

If, as this study argues, the Cuban nation was scripted in the diaspora, then to what extent did the diaspora influence meanings of freedom, revolution, and nation? Throughout the book I have consciously used the terms diaspora and diasporic as well as exile and migrant to trace the unevenness of movement and the imprecise processes involved in shaping a Cuban diasporic consciousness and community. The aim is to denote temporality and complication as well as acknowledge that communities do not act alone and are influenced by the actions and beliefs of other communities, what Earl Lewis sees as the "reminders of the diversity of black life" and what Brent Hayes Edwards calls the "differences within unity."[20]

In framing the diaspora as a dislocated and impermanent site, we are left with the inevitable question of diasporic imaginings as part of a larger fiction, one that, while meaningful at the time, could be discarded when no longer needed. If so, can diasporic revolutionary and nationalist thinking ever be transferred back to the island, despite the privileging of the diaspora? Or are they, by their very nature, only viable as diasporic constructs steeped in nostalgia and meaningful only within and among the diaspora? In the end, are diasporic constructs of nation and nationalisms inextricably tied to those moments, to those colonial contexts when, to quote Michelle Stephens, "the state seems furthest out of reach"?[21]

As a space posited and directed on possibility, returns, and the *future*, the Cuban exile and migrant community was always in transition, what Avtar Brah writes is the "processes of multi-locationality across geographic, cultural, and psychic boundaries."[22] For early Cuban exiles and migrants the diaspora was a site of temporary belonging, of a nationalist exclusivity that could be suspended with their eventual return to Cuba. It was also a space of multiple reinventions; a messy and conflicted site defined by what Brah calls the "politics of location as locationality in contradiction."[23] Within this narrative, Cuba was characterized as unfinished and in need of the diasporic community to evolve and complete its transformation from colony to independence. A familiar and oft-used narrative, Cuba was cast as a perpetually fragmented island that could only be reinvented and "put together" from the outside. In a speech given in 1891, José Martí illustrates the peculiars of exile nation-building when he tells the audience filled with Cuban revolutionaries and cigar workers that it is "*allí* (in Cuba) where the island falls to pieces (*se cae en pedazos*)" while "*aquí* (in the United States) it rises (*se levanta*)."[24] Perhaps the ultimate function of diaspora is a restless imagining that makes it easy to dwell on the unfinished, the desired, and of course the poetics of belonging. If the Caribbean, as Antonio Benítez-Rojo contends, is perpetually in chaos, and seeking to be controlled by the other,[25] then maybe the diaspora is the opposite; a place of order, albeit artificial, where exiles and immigrants can conjure the unthinkable, while always longing to be something and somewhere else.

De-Territorialized Historiographies: Framing the Study

Unlike other studies that focus on either the nineteenth *or* twentieth century, *Suspect Freedoms* looks at those periods in Cuban diasporic history that tend to be under-studied: the period before the Ten Years' War, the transitional period between both centuries, and the period before the Cuban Revolution of 1959, in an effort to provide contextual cohesiveness. The aim is to understand and privilege those moments of rupture, chaos, and historiographic silences, and their impact on shaping Cuban diasporic history. Often these periods have gone without study because the assumption is that "nothing really happened," or there were too few Cuban migrants to justify a thorough study. Maybe. But to my way of thinking, there are always fragments of experiences, of histories that lead to those moments where something supposedly "happened." Nothing occurs in a vacuum. There are hints, signposts, and clues that ultimately prove to be the most interesting and provocative.

At its core, *Suspect Freedoms* explores how race as construct, rhetoric, theory, and imaginary affected political doctrine, revolutionary thought, community formation, and the meanings of nation and freedom within the diaspora. It argues that Afro-Cuban exiles and migrants were authors of their own experiences and published newspapers, gave speeches, and founded important exile and political revolutionary clubs. It examines what it meant for free people of color from Cuba to move during a period of slavery, empire, and colonialism, and how narratives of mobility informed ideas of revolution, independence, and visibility. At the same time, this study looks at how Cuban diasporic notions of race contested, were informed by, and at times accommodated US racial definitions, laws, policies, and practices. Cubans did not live in isolation from other groups—the hundreds of immigrants arriving daily into New York, the wealthy elite, or the long-standing African American community—and their actions and philosophies reflected the politics of the period, often challenging the ideas they arrived with from Cuba.

In writing such a history certain questions are invariably posed: How did African American thinking and writing on race, especially with regard to slavery, emancipation, and enfranchisement, influence how Cubans in the diaspora thought about their own freedoms? Did the growing interest in hemispheric thinking—one intent on connecting African peoples and reconfiguring independence and freedom through *territoriality* to redefine blackness—change how Cubans articulated and organized around race, independence, and location? How did the discourse on shared masculinities and the subsequent erasure of female bodies from such a narrative influence the way power, geography, and the exile movement were chronicled and remembered?

The book steadfastly questions conceptions of masculinity and problematizes their uses in the patriarchal distillations of power. Nineteenth-century revolutionary clubs did not offer women formal membership. Instead, they were expected to form auxiliary clubs, where their power was controlled and limited. Organized as spaces where the wives of prominent members and revolutionaries served the movement, the auxiliaries supported the larger all-male clubs. Women were responsible for raising funds, cooking and serving food, disseminating materials, and working closely with their husbands to support independence.

For some, participation in the auxiliary clubs was the only way to be involved in the movement, for others it was a social outlet, and yet for others, it was a waste of time. Some, like Carolina Rodríguez and Paulina Pedroso, preferred to work independent of auxiliary clubs. Others, such as Señora Agüero y Ricardo, were involved solely in the war effort, transporting arms in a trunk and sewing bullets in the lining of her dress.[26] While for Emilia Casanova de Villaverde and the Puerto Rican activists Inocencia Mártinez and Lola Rodríguez del Tió it was through the different auxiliaries, including Las Hijas de Cuba, El Club Mercedes Varona, and El Club de las Hermanas Ruiz Rivera, that they rose to prominence within the movement. The newspaper *La Discusión* commented on how El Club de las Hermanas Ruiz Rivera "greatly assisted in a financial and propagandist capacity."[27] It also didn't hurt that both Casanova de Villaverde and Martínez were married to powerful men active in the exile revolutionary movement.

Outside of Paulina Pedroso and La Señoras de la Liga, an auxiliary club of La Liga sociedad de instrucción y recereó, there are few sources that speak directly to Afro-Cuban women's activism. Yet, as Carmen Montejo Arrechea and Gema Guevara have documented, the publication of *Minerva*, a magazine written by and for Afro-Cuban women that first appeared in 1888 in Havana, had a major impact on the Afro-Cuban exile and migrant community in New York and Florida. The magazine named several Afro-Cuban men living in the United States as "agents" responsible for distributing *Minerva*. With that in mind, this study employs *Minerva* as an important archive for documenting Afro-Cuban female intellectual production in New York and argues that despite the lack of source, Afro-Cuban women actively supported women's rights and publicly articulated a discourse on enfranchisement and liberation.[28]

Unfortunately, the involvement of a wide spectrum of women did not translate into a feminist vision within the exile nationalist movement. The political platform of the Partido Revolucionario Cubano made no references to women or to women's rights. The scripting of nation, as M. Jacquie Alexander, Hazel Carby, Carol Boyce Davies, Ginetta Candelario, Maylei Blackwell, Michelle Mitchell, April Mayes, and Michelle Stephens have so well argued, is a masculinist act that expunges female bodies from a nationalist rhetoric embedded in patriarchal discourses on nation and power.[29] If the nation and the nation-building project are inherently masculinist projects, how did women negotiate power within a movement intent on oppressing and silencing them? Emilia Casanova de Villaverde, for one, used text to script her way into the movement, redefining herself and historically intervening into future historical narratives and sources. Others, like Carolina Rodríguez, who were not married or wealthy, paid a heavy price for their commitment to revolution.

Lauded for her tireless political activism and fund-raising, Rodríguez, who earned the epithet *la patriota*, was mistreated by the men in the movement, who did little for her when she became gravely ill and succumbed to dire poverty. After the Cuban War for Independence, Rodríguez, destitute and ill, returned to Cuba and died.[30] As Rodríguez's example reminds us, not all white Cuban women who were involved in the movement were from the elite classes or married to powerful men. There was a large female working class, black and white, that worked in the cigar factories and related industries, as well as in domestic work, as boarding house managers, and as cooks. There is also strong evidence that nineteenth-century Cuban women were involved in labor unions and went on strike. In addition to integrating the history of Cuban exile and migrant women, this work disrupts the uses of masculinist rhetoric and gendered conceptions of power to define nation within the émigré community.

In positioning this work as part of a larger US hemispheric and transnationalist historiography, I am left with an indelible question: Where exactly does this work fit within the historical imagination of the United States? Theoretically, there is a fictive and transient character to the writing, where historical source, or more accurately my reading of source, is in a place of potentiality and the future. One can't help but acknowledge the ongoing references to possible freedoms and sovereignty, and to the fears such promises bring. Yet, to write such a history—one pivoted on a connective and speculative model that blurs geographic borders and names their artificiality—it was imperative to configure a changing US historical terrain influenced by larger hemispheric and geographical forces, analyses, and the enduring problems of the unfinished and the imprecise. Much like the nineteenth-century Cuban exile and migrant community, who used the term *destierro* to define themselves and their work, the United States was also part of *destierro*, a deterritorialization that fueled its own never-ending desire to assert and control geographic completion.

Although *Suspect Freedoms* follows a recognizable chronology, it is not wedded to a strict periodization. The dates, nonetheless, have meaning. I begin in 1823 to mark a period that witnessed both the Monroe Doctrine and the exile of Father Félix Varela y Morales—two events that influenced early Cuban diasporic politics. The Monroe Doctrine opened the hemisphere to US intervention, initiating a narrative on expansionism that shaped the relationship between the United States and Cuba for generations. The exile of Father Félix Varela cast the United States as a necessary site for organizing against Spanish colonial rule and building nation. After years of criticizing Spanish colonialism, advocating revolution, and supporting the gradual abolition of slavery, Varela was forced into exile. Singled out by José Martí as the person who taught "Cubans how to think," Varela first moved to Philadelphia and later New York, where he founded and wrote for a series of Spanish-language newspapers and pamphlets, including *El Habanero* (1824–1826) and *El Mensajero Seminal de Nueva York* (1829–1831). In 1837 he was named the Vicar General of the Catholic Diocese of New York and remained active in a number of Catholic charities and published and wrote for two more newspapers, *The Protestant Abriger* and *The Annotator*. In 1853 he died in Saint Augustine, Florida.[31]

Varela has been credited, and rightly so, as the first to establish a Cuban exile political identity in the United States.[32] He was also the first to connect anti-slavery and anti-colonial politics with a Cuban exile nationalist rhetoric, a project taken up by the Partido Revolucionario Cubano (PRC) decades later. His thinking shaped generations of scholars and philosophers who grappled with the contradictions of emancipation and freedom in a period of empire and slavery. Yet, as Gema Guevara so well argues, Varela represents selective historical remembering. He was an enigmatic figure who was silenced by subsequent Cuban exiles and migrants who vehemently disagreed with his radical views on abolishing slavery and promoting freedom.[33]

Citing the relatively few numbers of Cubans who arrived to the United States before the Civil War, scholars have focused on the period during and after the Ten Years' War (1868–1878), when large numbers of Cubans, including Afro-Cubans, left for the United States. This makes sense. The Ten Years' War was bloody, chaotic, and forced thousands to leave the island. It was the major impetus for the relocation of the Cuban cigar industry to the United States and for changing the nationalist discourse to one that was inextricably tied to ending slavery and enfranchisement Yet, as this book contends, it was the pro-annexationist and pro-slavery politics of the pre–US Civil War period that most influenced how subsequent migrations responded to the annexationist, expansionist, and divisive racial politics of earlier migrations.

Early Cuban migrants were entrenched in and defined by transgeography and territoriality. Pro-annexationist Cubans reinvented spatial geographies to justify expansionism and annexation. At the same time, the Haitian Revolution, the Aponte Rebellion, and La Escalera, along with slave revolts in the British Caribbean and Southern United States, were constant reminders of the limits and consequences of slavery, realities that were not only cause for concern, but an obsession. By the same token, Cubans who left during this period would have experienced the end of slavery in New York,[34] the New York legislature and Wall Street's celebratory response to the Fugitive Slave Act (1850), and the impact of the Dred Scott decision.[35] They would have lived among "one of the largest free urban black communities in the North" and witnessed the "massive exodus of black people from Manhattan" as a result of the Draft Riots of 1863.[36] Cubans were aware of African mutual aid societies, anti-slavery societies, and the black press, including the *Freedom's Journal* (1827–1829), the *Weekly Advocate* (1837), the *Colored American* (1837–1841), the *North Star* (1847–1851), the *Frederick Douglass' Paper* (1851–1859), and the *Weekly Anglo-African* (1859–1860), as well as the rise of an African American hemispheric discourse on race and slavery.

The first chapter of *Suspect Freedoms* explores these contradictions and investigates how hemispheric and racialized imaginings of space were translated and understood among Cuban exiles and migrants involved in translocal political activity. It argues that race, in particular whiteness, was embedded within territoriality, complicating and asserting annexation as a racialized project that allowed for the possible expansion of US slavery to Cuba.

An important yet under-studied aspect in the discourse on geography and expansionism were the diasporic practices of whiteness. The politics of whiteness, whitening, and white supremacy, what I call a *diasporic blanqueamiento*, traveled north, shaping the annexationist movements and establishing the rhetorical conditions for expanding slavery to Cuba. It also provided the necessary fodder for an alternative independista rhetoric that connected diasporic blanqueamiento with potential US economic and political interests on the island. Pro-annexationists in New York wrote essays promoting white migration to the island and warned that Cuba would soon turn into "another Haiti" if Cubans did not significantly alter the racial composition of the island, especially after emancipation. They published and promoted the writings of Cuban philosopher José Antonio Saco, who advocated for the abolition of slavery and the whitening of the island.

Concerned with the disproportionate number of Afro-Cubans, free and enslaved, Saco argued that the racial configuration of the island needed to be balanced to ensure that white Cubans remained in power. He regarded the close proximity and the large African descended populations in Haiti, Jamaica, and the Southern United States as detriments, and supported the importation of European migrants as a solution for whitening the island. Saco, however, was against the annexation of Cuba to the United States, and in his extremely thorough treatise *Contra la anexión*, warned of the dire consequences of being annexed to the United States. His writings did not endear him to the Spanish colonial authorities, and he was exiled to Paris and London for much of his adult life. Saco also fell out of favor with pro-annexationist exiles who, on the one hand, supported his calls for whitening, but on the other disagreed with his views on abolition and total independence.[37]

The heavy emphasis on blanqueamiento and annexation inspired a backlash. As concerned slaveholders expanded slavery and supported annexing the island, Cuban anti-annexationists published and disseminated anti-slavery and independista newspapers in New York, including *El Mulato*, which garnered the attention of African American anti-slavery activists and the early black press. Frederick Douglass and Martin Delany routinely protested what they saw as the "summa of Africanization fears," and the overt, almost public declaration of slave expansionism to Cuba. They questioned William Walker's "relegalization" of slavery in Nicaragua and connected US imperial designs to the nascent federation of slave states in Central America, Cuba, and "possibly Mexico."[38]

In 1868 Cuban insurgents rebelled. El Grito de Yara, that is, the Ten Years' War, captivated the imagination and interest of African Americans, who followed every battle, skirmish, and development in the local New York newspapers. They supported the rebels, knew of the mambises who fought in the war, and followed the exploits of the Afro-Cuban general Antonio Maceo. African American leaders Henry Highland Garnet, Samuel Scottron, Peter W. Ray, Philip A. White, and Charles E. Pindell, to name a few, considered the Ten Years' War a catalyst for expanding and reframing African American abolitionist politics, one that included a discourse on enfranchisement and civil rights.

In 1872, these same leaders founded the Cuban Anti-Slavery Society in New York. The second chapter unravels the history of the Cuban Anti-Slavery Society and traces the creation of a transnationalist articulation of revolution, independence, shared masculinities, and freedom. Intrigued by the Ten Years' War and the accompanying nationalist rhetoric that privileged blackness as part of the nation-building project,

African Americans called for the end of slavery and the liberation of their "brethren" during a period marked by the end of the Civil War, as well as the passage of the Reconstruction Amendments. The articulation, however, was uneasy and problematic. African American leaders touted their notions of freedom to enslaved Cubans, while struggling to reconcile their own suspect and limited freedoms in the United States. Within a few years the Cuban Anti-Slavery Society was reorganized into the American Foreign Anti-Slavery Society, which expanded its scope to Brazil and Africa. Interestingly enough, by the turn of the century, many of the same men who pushed for abolition and independence now applauded the United States' colonial policies in Cuba.

In 1878, Cuban rebel leaders reluctantly signed the Pact of Zanjón, effectively ending the insurgency and ceding power to the Spanish. A year later, in what Cubans called La Guerra Chiquita, insurgents once again rebelled and lost. Chapter 3 examines the postwar discursive evolution of race, labor, and nation in New York. Focusing on the period after the Ten Years' War and before the United States' intervention in the Cuban War for Independence, chapter 3 argues that the politics of nation, race, and revolution were now more complicated than ever. Several factors led to the raveling: the Cuban cigar industry in New York; the increase in the migration of Afro-Cuban men and women; growing support for labor, socialism, and anarchism; challenges to traditional separatist politics; and the rise of Afro-Cuban intellectual and revolutionary thought and writing. Combined, these factors changed the direction and meaning of the exile separatist movement.

The changes were not always welcomed. The rise of labor unions was at odds with the interest of separatist leaders who owned cigar factories. Rarely discussed within the context of early Cuban diasporic history in New York, labor played a significant role in the politics of disunity. Cuban cigar workers joined unions, challenged the separatist platform, published pro-labor newspapers, and pointed out the limits of Cuban republicanism. No longer willing to toe the nationalist line, Cuban cigar workers challenged traditional separatist thinking, prompting divisions among the exile and migrant community. Separatist leaders struggled to find ways to keep the movement intact. They expanded the separatist and nationalist agenda by incorporating race, equality, enfranchisement, and now labor into its platform. They also chose to focus solely on independence, at the expense of other pressing issues and matters. The short-term solution worked; however, the process was riddled with problems and dissensions. The long-term effects of such decisions proved disastrous.

Unlike in the past, Afro-Cuban revolutionaries were now at the forefront of scripting new readings of blackness and enfranchisement within the diasporic nationalist agenda. Rafael Serra, Martín Morúa Delgado, and Teófilo Domínguez edited newspapers, wrote essays, and published biographies. They established Afro-Cuban and Puerto Rican collectives in New York and formed organizations that catered to black Cuban and Puerto Rican men. One in particular, La Liga sociedad de instrucción y recreó, educated men of color from Cuba and Puerto Rico and was an example of post–Ten Years' War rethinking on race. Traditionally chronicled as an apolitical space where classes were taught and young men of color were afforded an opportunity to elevate their status, chapter 3 argues that La Liga was in fact a radical site for articulating an alternative and complicated politics on blackness, masculinity, and power. In addition, Serra considered La Liga a training ground to prepare young men of color to also be part of the nation-building project in Cuba. He, like most of the leadership of La Liga, understood that Afro-Cubans held a precarious position within the nation-building project, and that there were few if any guarantees that Afro-Cubans would play a significant role in establishing the Cuban Republic. The question of visibility informs and grounds this chapter. Afro-Cuban migrants were aware of their tenuous visibility and impending erasure within that nationalist movement. This self-awareness and acknowledgment is evident in the publications of Afro-Cuban male biographies and essays following the Spanish-American War, when Afro-Cuban diasporic revolutionary thought was most at risk of being silenced.

On December 10, 1898, delegates from Spain and the United States met in Paris to "transfer" the remaining Spanish colonies to the United States. The United States' intervention in the Cuban War for Independence was brief and lucrative, prompting the Secretary of State John Hay to remark that the Spanish-American War was "a splendid little war." The ensuing US occupation and the tense passage of the Platt Amendment to the Cuban Constitution in 1901 all but cemented US control of the island. On December 21, 1898, weeks after the Treaty of Paris had been signed, Tomás Estrada Palma, the past president of the Partido Revolucionario Cubano and the soon to be first president of Cuba, heralded the end of the Cuban exile and migrant political community. Writing in the soon to be defunct exile newspaper *Patria*, Estrada Palma declared that since "Cuba has ceased to be Spanish and is independent, the Cuban Revolutionary Party has finished the mission it undertook. From this day on the clubs, the boards of directors and the agents abroad have no reason to exist."[39]

For Cubans in New York, this was a mixed blessing. On the one hand, Cuba was free from Spanish colonial rule; on the other, the future of the exile and migrant community was now more uncertain than ever. Within months the Partido Revolucionario Cubano as well as a number of Cuban political and revolutionary clubs in New York, Florida, New Orleans, Philadelphia, and Washington, DC were dissolved. The revolutionary silence was so deafening that it prompted the Puerto Rican activist and labor organizer Bernardo Vega to observe in his memoirs that "Once the thunder of revolutionary struggle against Spain had subsided in the Antilles, the Cuban and Puerto Rican emigrant community in New York fell silent."[40]

The early twentieth century was a transitional period when past notions of Cubanidad gave way to the "realities" of building a republic in Cuba, one that, despite decades of intellectual and political activism, failed to fully enfranchise Afro-Cubans. Some Afro-Cuban exile and migrant male leaders, including Rafael Serra, Martín Morúa Delgado, and Juan Bonilla, returned to Cuba with mixed results. Faced with conditions and realities that differed greatly from their past envisioning of republic and nation, some attempted to make changes from the inside, working closely with Tomás Estrada Palma and serving in administrative posts and legislative positions. Others challenged the US-dominated provisional government from the outside, publishing articles and writing essays that questioned decisions and called for the end of racism and discrimination.

For Afro-Cubans who stayed in the United States, this meant reconstituting community outside of the rhetoric of potentiality. With the end of the separatist and nationalist movement, Afro-Cubans were now left with configuring a black immigrant identity that was both tied to and severed by the nascent Cuban nation-building project. It was a period that witnessed the radicalization of Cuban migrants, the formation of socialist organizations, the racial separations of Cuban social clubs, and the formation of one of the most important and longest-standing Afro-diasporic Cuban clubs in New York, El Club Cubano Inter-Americano.

This period has not received the same attention as that of the nineteenth century. Nineteenth-century Cuban exiles and migrants published a great deal, leaving a vast archive of written work. The early twentieth century, on the other hand, is quite the opposite. While sources do exist, they are not always what you might expect. In researching the last chapters of *Suspect Freedoms*, I depended heavily on club records, oral histories, newspapers, testimonials, census data, and biographies to write a history that examines postwar community formations, changing politics, and diasporic reinventions. In the process I have been part of a collaborative effort to establish and expand archives. It is curious, but not unfamiliar, to be both documenting and creating archives at the same time.[41]

Writing the last two chapters I now understand why so many scholars have either ended their research in 1898 or begun it in 1959; revolutions and wars generate much source material and provide effective context. Yet, if willing to take theoretical and methodological risks, it is possible to see that despite the gaps in historiography and analyses, Cubans continued to migrate, produce texts, and form communities in New York. This period might just be one of the most distinctive and revealing in early Cuban diasporic history.

Chapter 4 looks at how the impending US colonialism in Cuba shaped postwar Cuban migrant political activity in New York. Employing what Ann Laura Stoler writes is the "familiar, strange, and unarticulated ways in which empire has appeared and disappeared from intimate and public spaces in United States history," this chapter argues that it was in those "ambiguous zones of empire,"[42] one translated and rearticulated within the diaspora, that led to both the formation and historical silencing of El Club Julio Antonio Mella as a pivotal site of Cuban diasporic history in New York. As such, this chapter positions the club squarely within the larger Cuban migrant historiography. The intention is to avoid categorizing the club as artifact and outlier, and instead to see it as part of a larger evolution of Afro-Cuban diasporic political and intellectual formation: one that connects nineteenth-century revolutionary thought with early twentieth-century political organization. El Club Julio Antonio Mella, as noted earlier, was one of many clubs organized under the International Worker's Order. Members were involved in labor unions, the Communist Party, and critical of the United States' policies in Cuba. They were also committed to anti-racism, internationalism, ending fascism and, much like the anti-slavery clubs of the mid-nineteenth century, they hoped to expand their political scope and influence to the hemisphere. The members also worked closely with the New York–based El Club José Martí and the Organización Revolucionaria Cubana Anti-imperialista (ORCA) to organize Cuban and Puerto Rican migrants in Harlem, support labor unions, protest US imperialism, and send members to fight against Franco's forces in the Spanish Civil War.[43] El Club Mella did not last long. By 1940 the club disbanded.

It was not until after World War II that Afro-Cuban migrants once again organized a club. Convinced that "they needed a club like this one," Afro-Cuban migrants founded El Club Cubano Inter-Americano on September 17, 1945 at the home of Julio and Francisca 'Paquita' Cardenal in Harlem.[44] Intent on being as expansive as possible, while at the same time privileging Cuba and their own brand of Cubanidad, the members deliberately included the terms Cubano and Inter-Americano when naming the club. The club's open and inclusive policy was a clear and public statement against the covert and informal discrimination and exclusion among the Cuban exile and migrant community during the 1940s. It was a painful and problematic practice that was deeply felt and resented by Afro-Cuban migrants who grew weary of the constant machinations designed to exclude. This chapter examines the diasporic workings of racial separations among Cuban migrants, and argues that it shaped early twentieth-century definitions of Cubanidad. It looks at how Afro-Cubans reconfigured blackness to suit both Cuban and United States' racial, economic, social, and cultural conditions. At the same time, the chapter interrogates why the club's founders prohibited members from discussing politics and religion while in the club. The club was not allowed to formally endorse or support any political movement, position, event, or politician. So adamant were the founders concerning these prohibitions that the first articles in El Club Cubano Inter-Americano's bylaws forbade any discussions of politics and religion.

And yet, if one looks closely at the archive, the club and club members were indeed political. The early club leadership cultivated close relationships with politicians, social activists, academics, labor organizers, and were publicly aligned with labor unions, the Socialist Party, the Catholic Church, and local botanicas. Several of the founders of El Club Cubano Inter-Americano were members of El Club Julio Antonio Mella. Moreover, their decision to not be political was not a new practice. La Liga sociedad de instrucción y recreó also declared itself to *not* be political. Yet, they too were very political and worked closely with the independence movement and were sympathetic to labor. Even the cultural events, which were the CCI's hallmark, could be read as political. The CCI was one of the few places where Afro-Cuban musicians performed to an Afro-Cuban audience. It was also one of the few clubs to routinely honor Afro-Cuban musicians, writers, poets, scholars, journalists, and sports figures. The public celebrations were part of a larger politics of black visibility that disrupted the racism that kept Afro-Cuban artists, athletes, and performers from being recognized by the general Cuban public.

In researching and writing a book that examines the workings of race, diaspora, politics, and nationalism during such a long historical period, I have faced many of the same challenges shared by colleagues: the tensions among racial categories, archive, and use. How does one write about race in a manner that is consistent with the archive, while at same time remaining malleable enough to convey change, spirit, struggle, agency, pain, and power? In writing a history that seeks to move past the comparative to multiple productions, meanings, as well as constructions of race, gender, self, movement, and territoriality, there needs to be recognition that racial categories are by their very nature imprecise and incapable, yet critical to understanding historical actions, ideas, and thoughts. In short, racial hierarchies, categories, and white supremacy defined, and continue to define, and influence how people live. The archive, however, is messy and inconsistent. There are no satisfactory solutions, simply acknowledgment that racial categories and hierarchies not only existed, but had meaning, and grave consequences. To pretend otherwise is not the answer. I have done my best to write a book that engages the archive, denotes fluidity, and explores the workings of race, masculinity, and power, while at the same time providing consistency in narrative and form.

The Unfinished

In 1995, El Club Cubano Inter-Americano celebrated its fiftieth anniversary. It was a bittersweet occasion. The program for the commemorative is full of precious photos and well wishes from local businesses, politicians, labor unions, individuals, and other Cuban and Puerto Rican clubs in New York. There are poems written *by* Martí and *for* Maceo. I still remember Melba Alvarado handing me a copy of the program as I sat with her in the club, talking and reminiscing. Surrounded by boxes, endless files, and folding chairs lining the wall, I couldn't help but notice the familiar busts of Martí and Maceo gathering dust in the corner. The program, memories, and artifacts could not belie the fact that the club had been in decline.

Seen as a relic, younger generations were no longer interested in belonging to a club favored by their parents. At the same time, older club members had retired and moved to Florida. By the late 1990s and early 2000s, the club lost more than half of its membership to retirement. As the dues-paying members left, making the rent was close to impossible. In the mid-2000s, Alvarado, one of the last full-time members, packed up the club's records and photos and put them in her basement.[45] El Club Cubano Inter-Americano was now officially closed.

The closing of El Club Cubano Inter-Americano has ironically led to its resurgence. Jo-Ana Moreno, whose parents were members of the club, has initiated a network that consists of the "Children of El Club Cubano Inter-Americano" and has reignited La Fiesta del Mamoncillo and La Cena Martiana. Moreno has done the seemingly impossible: She has kept the club relevant for past, present, and future generations. In many ways the recent experiences and history of El Club Cubano Inter-Americano is an apt and powerful symbol for the research and writing of this book. It has been difficult to close the door on this research, to ignore the fragmented archives and documents that inform and shape this history. What I have learned—perhaps my greatest lesson—is that surviving source and documentation do not tell the whole story; really, they were never meant to. The archive offers little solace. From my experience, it has been the crevices, the unexpected historical figures, the events and moments that go without notice or study, the haunting, unthinkable, and uncanny that reveal the most, whether we like it or not.

1

Rhetorical Geographies

Annexation, Fear, and the Impossibility of Cuban Diasporic Whiteness, 1840–1868

The Queen of Spain and the marquis of Havana will prick up their ears when they are told, upon the authority of a New York Newspaper that the civilization of the Western Hemisphere depends upon a few Cuban negroes, and that the little Island which they hold under their thumb is the pivot of our future destiny.
New York Daily Times, 1856

The writers for the *Empire* evince great concern for the few misgoverned white people of Cuba; but no one speak of sympathy for the 600,000 down-trodden African slaves who are oppressed by those few whites notwithstanding they know perfectly well that the Yankees wish to acquire Cuba to extend and perpetuate slavery. They ought also to know, as they meddle so much with Cuban affairs, that the chance of those 600,000 slaves becoming freed, under Spanish rule, is tenfold to which it is under that hypocritical Republic.
Provincial Freeman, Toronto, June 12, 1855, "A Descendent of the African Race"

We consider a Cuban every person born in Cuba and what we wish is that white people be born by thousands every hour.
La Verdad, New York City, 1848

Hemispheric Longings: Cuban and US Expansionist Designs, 1823–1865

On December 3, 1856 the *New York Daily Times* published a scathing critique of the *Day Book's* support of slavery in both the South and in Cuba. The *Daily Times* ridiculed the *Day Book* and claimed that it had more in common with the pro-slavery politics of the *Charleston Mercury* or the *Southside Democrat* than with the newspapers published in New York. While it questioned the *Day Book's* standing among the "press of New York," it reserved its most fervent attacks for the argument against emancipation in Cuba. Mocking the newspaper's claim that emancipation would make Cuba like Jamaica, "a colony of emancipated slaves," the *Daily Times* argued that such an event "had as much probability as Jefferson Davis becoming a Garrisonian Abolitionist." It went on to question the *Day Book's* contention that Cuba was "the turning point of the future and the battlefield of our destinies." According to the *Day Book*, Cuba could not "remain Spanish, it must not be African, for that would be the destruction not only of New Orleans but of American civilization."

Equating emancipation in Cuba with the destruction of American civilization inspired perhaps the strongest attack against the *Day Book*. According to the *Daily Times*, American civilization rested "on a more stable basis than the negroes in Cuba, whether they be free or slave." The *Day Book's* insistence that the racial politics in Cuba were critical to the United States' success in the hemisphere reveals how racial politics both in New York and on the island were conflated to express hemispheric desires and longings.

Despite the different arguments and positions, both newspapers reflect an ambivalent commitment to Cuba as hemispheric potential. As long as Cuba's future could be negotiated and ultimately changed to suit the interest of the United States, it remained an accessible and tangible reality wrapped in fiction. Renegotiated and reassessed time and time again, Cuba as diaspora, as expansion, as part of a larger national and geographic potential would, for most of the early to mid-nineteenth century, prompt the United States to reconfigure itself and its future through a recreated Cuban imaginary. For some, Cuba represented a hemispheric yearning for expansion and power; it was, as the *Day Book* argued, the "battlefield of our destinies." For others, as the *New York Daily Times* reiterated, Cuba was nothing more than "a little island" with no sway over the future of US politics.

Driving much of the argument were contradictory opinions concerning Cuba as a racialized hemispheric presence. For the *Day Book*, the problem with Cuba was the large number of free people of color and enslaved Africans that, if freed, could change the dynamics of slavery, independence, and colonialism. Because Cuba was located close to Jamaica and Haiti, both contested and feared sites of revolution and power, newspapers wondered aloud what would happen to Cuba if slavery were abolished. Would Cuba turn into another Haiti, or as the *Day Book* warned, into another Jamaica made up of "a colony of emancipated slaves"? Or would it evolve into an altogether different society where, as the *New York Daily Times* contended, a "few Cuban negroes" couldn't possibly decide the fate of the hemisphere?[1]

The specter of an available Cuban nation inspired US newspapers to ruminate on the future destiny of Cuba and the impact such destiny would have on US expansionist and political designs. Unlike other Latin American countries during the nationalist movements of the early nineteenth century, Cuba did not end Spanish colonial rule, thus earning the epithet "the ever faithful isle." As a colonial possession of Spain, Cuba remained an attractive option to US slaveholders and expansionists who were confident they could wrestle it from Spanish domination. Located less than a hundred miles from the shores of Florida and close to the Southern United States, Cuba was coveted as a necessary strategic gateway to the rest of Latin America. The proximity of the island inspired an imagined and entitled geography that shaped the politics of physical distance between both countries—countering whether it was possible to be so close to the United States and *not* be a possession.

While the discussions and writings concerning independence, slavery, abolition, and annexation differed, they were all informed by race and its impact on labor, society, and politics. In 1855, the *Journal of Commerce* complained that "Nearly half of the Africans in Cuba are free already." According to the *Journal*, the "great scarcity of labor" led Cuban planters to look toward "over-peopled Asia for a supply of labor from her most degraded classes." The importation of Chinese workers, or what the *Journal* called "hired Coolie labor," was seen as a serious threat that signaled the end of slavery in both Cuba and the hemisphere.

> It is not easy to see in the very fact of the substitution of free Asiatic for African slave labor in Cuba, an evidence and an acknowledgement that Slavery is about to die out in Cuba; when it dies, will it not die everywhere? Or will it be uprooted there only to be replaced elsewhere?[2]

The *Journal*'s anxiety over Chinese workers hastening the end of slavery in Cuba, and leading "either by a legal or natural process," to its demise in the United States, illustrates how notions around slavery, race, and labor—in this case, the importation of Chinese workers—traveled beyond ever-changing national borders and expectations. For the *Journal* and other newspapers of the period, Cuba's fate was inextricably linked to that of the United States.

At the root of such fears was the lingering belief that the emancipation of slaves in Cuba, or, as the *Journal* put it, "the loss of slave products in Cuba," concentrated "American Slavery in those regions which are productive of cotton and sugar, particularly in Texas and Louisiana." The concern about sugar trade in 1855 was indeed warranted. In the early nineteenth century Louisiana plantations could only accommodate one-third of the national demand for the product. While trade between Cuba and the United States had declined after the War of 1812, it remained strong from 1835 to 1865, making the United States dependent on shipments of Cuban sugar. The increase in trade was important not only to the question of slavery, but also to the economics of Northern states and cities where it had been abolished. The trade rise contributed significantly to the commercial growth of New York City, which along with other Eastern cities "became a center for sentiment favoring the annexation of the island."[3]

The move toward annexation was an outgrowth of New York's close relationship with the Southern cotton economy. Following the War of 1812, as Ira Berlin and Leslie Harris have documented, New York became the primary port for the shipment of raw cotton from the South to the textile mills of Europe. New York bankers, merchants, insurance brokers, and financiers bankrolled the Southern cotton economy, and made it possible for slaveholders to purchase more crop land and buy the slaves needed for the increasing acreage. New York businessmen sold the tools for harvesting cotton, the clothes worn by slaves, known as "negro cloth," the dresses worn by plantation mistresses, and even the whips used by overseers to punish slaves. Interestingly, slavery was ending in New York, but "New York's links to—even dependence upon—slavery grew."[4]

New York's relationship to slavery and the South was not solely economic, but also ideological. Though the city outlawed slavery in 1827, many businesses, political and otherwise, continued to support it and formed alliances with slaveholders and Southern businesses. Antebellum New York was a stronghold for the Democratic Party, whose members assured "Southerners of New York's reliability on the question of slavery."[5] Through networks that linked Northern commercial interests with those of Southern slaveholders, pro-slavery Cuban exiles in New York organized for the annexation of Cuba and the expansion of North American slavery to Cuba. This insured that Northern states would be implicit in the slave system, regardless of their slaveholding status.

A prominent strategy was the idea that expansionism or, in the case of Cuba, annexation, could solidify the US political and economic position within the hemisphere. The Monroe Doctrine of 1823 formalized as US foreign policy an ongoing reinvention of the Americas. By declaring that the United States would protect the Americas from foreign or, better put, European invasion, the Monroe Doctrine attempted to reposition colonial power over and control of Latin America by putting it in the hands of North Americans. Initiated in a speech given by President James Monroe, the doctrine was an exercise in rhetorical geographies, where expansion, acquisition, control, and power could be scripted and made part of a larger geographical imaginary, regardless of political and social realities. But here too, Haiti and the Haitian Revolution posed problems. The doctrine was a catalyst, if not a justification, for US intervention in potential hemispheric and specifically Caribbean revolutions. A corollary to the principles of the Monroe Doctrine was the preservation of the "special relationship" the United States had with Cuba in terms of commerce and strategy. Fearing Great Britain's involvement in Cuban affairs, the United States wanted to protect its varied interests, including slavery. The doctrine was also used to restrict French intervention in Haiti and other parts of the Caribbean. While the Monroe

Doctrine cast the French, Spanish, and British as rivals to the United States, they were nonetheless united in their fear of another Haiti.[6]

Years after the Monroe Doctrine, Cuba continued to figure in the politics of expansionism. In October 1854, with the support of President Franklin Pierce, members of the European and United States diplomatic corps convened in Ostend, Belgium and presented Spain with what would become known as the Ostend Manifesto, an offer to purchase Cuba for $130 million. This was not the first time the United States offered to purchase Cuba. President James K. Polk, emboldened by the massive territorial expansion resulting from both the US-Mexican War and the Treaty of Guadalupe Hidalgo, set his sights on Cuba in 1848, offering Spain $100 million for the island.[7] Spain refused both offers.

What was most telling about the Ostend bid was not Spain's refusal—no surprise there, but the Manifesto's words and presentation. The document called for military force if the United States did not get its way, a controversial directive that would later be rejected by the US Congress. Using the language of "self-preservation" the Ostend Manifesto made it clear that if Spain "seriously endangered The United States' internal peace and the existence of our [the United States'] Cherished Union" the United States would go to war.[8] At the same time, it provided a set of compromises to gather support in Congress and entice Spain to sell Cuba. Those provisions included the suppression of the African slave trade, commercial advantages to both Spain and the United States, and the acquisition of Cuba, an island the United States considered necessary to control Latin America.

The rhetoric of US expansionism vacillated between the threat of war and compromise; between entitlement and negotiation. It was a racialized discourse that centered on questions of immigration, labor, and slavery, with the potential for abolishment stirring fears of a racial majority. It was also, without a doubt, an exercise in preserving and extending notions of US white supremacy. So critical were these issues that in 1829 the Mexican government abolished slavery to, among other reasons, stave off US slaveholders and sympathizers seeking to push slavery west of the Texas territories. The anxiety was justified. The United States' move west toward the Mexican territories was a major impetus for the Texas Revolt and US-Mexican War. The expansionist and colonial designs on the Mexican territories and Cuba were so closely allied that annexationists consistently referenced Texas and Mexico when promoting the acquisition of Cuba.

In 1855, lawyer, journalist, and filibusterer William Walker invaded Nicaragua. His early success caught the attention of Cuban expansionists, who tried to convince him to do the same in Cuba. Invited by the Nicaraguan liberals, Walker's army defeated the conservative's forces. By 1856, Walker had declared himself president, raised the US flag, and initiated an Americanization program that made English the official language in Nicaragua. With the urging of pro-slavery politicians, including the Louisiana-born minister to Spain Pierre Soulé, Walker reinstituted slavery in a nation that had already abolished it in 1824 during the creation of the United Provinces of Central America. The reestablishment attracted more than a thousand US citizens who sought to further expand slavery into Central America.

Shortly after President Franklin Pierce formally recognized Walker's government, in 1856, the Cuban general and filibusterer Domingo Goicuría went to Nicaragua to help Walker enlist recruits, stabilize the nascent Walker government in Nicaragua, and plan an invasion of Cuba. Named brigadier general of the Nicaraguan army, Goicuría proved to be more of a problem than a solution to Walker, who grew increasingly frustrated with Goicuría's insistence on mounting a Cuban invasion. Admittedly, the mission was of greater interest to Goicuría than Walker, who found it difficult to stay in power in Nicaragua, let alone plan an invasion of Cuba.

Goicuría did not stay in Nicaragua long, parting ways with Walker and traveling to Louisiana to work in "mercantile pursuits."[9] By 1857 Walker had little choice but to surrender to the US Navy and be repatriated. The Cuban exile newspaper *La Verdad* followed Walker's pursuits in Nicaragua and supported his cause. *La Verdad* anointed Walker the legitimate president, and published the number of Cubans who were killed in Nicaragua (seven); who returned to the United States (six); who stayed with Walker (three); and who joined Goicuría in leaving Walker behind (fourteen).[10] Three years later, after writing *War In Nicaragua*, a book chronicling his experiences, Walker disembarked in Honduras and attempted to regain control of the region. This time his ambition was thwarted. After being delivered to Honduran authorities by the US Navy, Walker was executed by a firing squad in September 1860.

A familiar figure in exile politics and filibustering campaigns of the 1840s and 1850s, Goicuría worked closely with the Venezuelan-born General Narciso López to organize and raise money for his ill-fated campaign to invade Cuba in August 1851. Goicuría was notorious for getting wealthy Cuban women to donate their jewelry to the cause.[11] However, he did not accompany López to Cuba. Like many Cuban émigrés, he stayed behind. Interestingly enough, the majority of men who joined López in his various campaigns and expeditions to Cuba were not Cuban. They were mostly paid mercenaries, veterans from the US-Mexican War, and pro-slavery advocates who supported both the preservation of slavery in Cuba and the expansion of US slavery into Cuba. Of the four hundred men who accompanied López on his last expedition to Bahia Hondo, only forty-nine were Cuban.[12]

The September 1851 firing-squad execution of López did not deter Goicuría from continuing to plan expeditions to Cuba. With the assistance of General Quitman, Gustavus W. Smith, Mansfield Lovell, and George B. McClellan, Goicuría raised funds and developed strategies to end Spanish colonial rule on the island. Suddenly, however, and without much explanation, Goicuría abandoned his plans to invade Cuba. Seeing the Civil War as another opportunity to recoup López's dream of a Cuba free from Spanish control, he moved to Louisiana and restarted his career in trade and transportation, making the contacts necessary to plan another invasion while refusing to take part in the battle.

A few years after the end of the Civil War, Goicuría traveled to Mexico, where he landed a job in 1867 as a commercial agent of the Vera Cruz liberal regime. Forging a close relationship with Benito Juárez, Goicuría brokered deals to intervene in and colonize parts of Mexico on behalf of the US government. Juárez was not amused by his actions. When questioned, Goicuría acknowledged that he had no "real" ties to Mexico and that his ultimate goal was to finish the work López had begun sixteen years earlier, work that had been left for the former governor of Mississippi, General Quitman, to complete.[13]

After years of planning, Goicuría's single-mindedness bore fruit. On October 10, 1868, the Ten Years' War broke out in the eastern provinces of Cuba. Again, he planned and managed a number of expeditions, primarily from Louisiana to Cuba, but this time, he joined them. Once in Cuba his fate took a tragic turn. Invited to visit an insurgent camp in Havana, he was arrested and taken to a prisoner camp where he was court-martialed before being executed at Principe Fort in Havana on May 7, 1870.[14]

Although well known in the Cuban exile insurgency and filibustering drama, Goicuría is often mentioned only in passing. Yet, he represents the type of mobility and hemispheric imagining common among Cuban émigrés during this period. Goicuría, much like other expansionists, embodied a belief and practice that territories were always in flux and subject to change and control. Passing and moving through Nicaragua, Mississippi, Louisiana, New York, and, ultimately, Cuba, expansionists sought to redraw fluid and changeable geographical and spatial delineations. Spaces were conceived as malleable entities open to change and reconfigurations, and so too were exile politics.

Born in Havana on June 23, 1801, Goicuría was educated in London and spoke several languages fluently. Influenced by the work of the nineteenth-century Cuban historian Miguel Estorch y Siqués, a strong advocate of blanqueamiento on the island, he returned to Cuba in 1840. There he met Cirilo Villaverde and became involved in transporting Spanish migrants to "whiten" the Cuban population. A few years later, Goicuría migrated to the United States where he joined his old friend Villaverde. Involved with both La Junta Patriótica de Nueva Orleáns and El Club de la Habana in New York, Goicuría was an early supporter of using annexation as a strategy for maintaining white supremacy.[15] Despite being an unabashed expansionist, he did not support extending US slavery to Cuba. Similar to Villaverde, Juan Clemente Zenea, and Miguel Teurbe Tolón, Goicuría changed his mind concerning annexation and later argued that it was antithetical to wealth and independence. His shift in thought and practice represents the complicated and often contradictory politics of slavery and territorial expansion that were part of the larger filibustering campaign.

Influenced by the writings of Lorenzo de Allo y Bermúdez, a lawyer, professor of Political Economy in Cuba, and one of the founders, along with Carlos de Colins and Juan Clemente Zenea, of the anti-slavery exile newspaper *El Mulato*, Goicuría published Allo's speech on the impracticality of slavery and then facilitated the English translation of Allo's speech to his "American friends in their own language" in January 1855.

Entitled "Domestic Slavery in Its Relations with Wealth: An Oration," and first printed in Spanish "for the purpose of free circulation in Cuba," the treatise leaves little doubt concerning Allo's position on slavery. The speech, given at the Cuban Democratic Athenaeum of New York on January 1, 1854, was separated into three parts.[16] The first argues that slavery is antagonistic to wealth; the second refutes arguments in support of slavery; and the third details the means by which slavery should be abolished in Cuba.

While Allo was fundamentally concerned with pushing Cuba toward modernity and capital, he believed "that Cubans thoroughly comprehend that labor depends on intelligence, that our want of workshops and our industrial backwardness proceed solely from slavery," and professed that progress required Cuba's independence from Spain. "In Cuba there will be slaves as long as there is a Spanish government; and I abhor that government, because I desire the benefits of liberty for the inhabitants of Cuba—be they Creoles or Peninsulars [sic] and for all men." His solution was to make Cuba a Republic with "a popular government, with liberty of the press, of commerce and of worship," and if so necessary to "assure her well-being and safety by becoming allied or annexed to the United States."[17] Although publicly aligned with the anti-annexationist movement in New York, Allo was careful not to alienate pro-annexationist Cubans and North Americans. Instead, he crafted a space for contemplating US collaborations and if necessary, interventions. The shape and meanings of those interventions, however, are never made clear within the text.

Allo's speech was reprinted a number of times, excerpted in countless exile and migrant newspapers, and circulated widely among North Americans. The speech follows traditional arguments common to social reformist ideologies in Cuba. Combining Christianity with capital and morality, Allo fashioned an argument designed to specifically speak to the Cuban exile community, which according to him had yet to fully embrace the abolition of slavery in Cuba. Allo makes two major points that influence the direction of his thinking: without "morality there is no prosperity," and "slavery, wherever it exists, destroys morality." Since slavery "corrupts the soul of society," slavery as a labor practice cannot be sustained over time.[18] Allo's ideas would have been very familiar to the Cuban exile community. He borrowed heavily from the writings of Father Félix Varela, and his analysis reflected Varela's own belief that "the enslavement of African peoples meant the enslavement of whites."[19]

This was no coincidence. Allo attended the San Carlos Seminary in Havana and was a student of Varela. Early in his career, however, Allo deviated from Varela's teaching and supported the annexation of Cuba to the United States, publishing pamphlets and writing articles for the expansionist newspaper, *La Verdad*. Yet, he changed his mind, like many of his contemporaries, and questioned the viability of maintaining a slave system within a free and independent Cuba. The two, he would later admit, were simply incompatible. In 1852, two years before giving his speech, Allo traveled to Saint Augustine, Florida to visit with his old mentor, who was ill at the time. Varela's death, in 1853, deeply affected Allo. Soon thereafter he wrote a letter, which was made public in Havana that openly lamented the fact that most of Varela's students, himself included, had abandoned their mentor and rejected his teachings.[20]

Influenced by Varela's discourse on the spiritual and moral consequences of slavery and its impact on slaveholders, Allo was also concerned with the *capital* annihilation of slaveholders. "The arguments that are alleged in favor of slavery are nothing more than simple sophistries against Christianity, against morality, and against political economy."[21] Allo's emphasis on free trade and strengthening the Cuban political economy is strangely reminiscent of the writings of the Cuban economic reformer and philosopher Francisco Arango y Parreño, who argued that it was in the island's political and economic interest to take advantage of the successful slave revolt in Haiti to expand Cuba's sugar industry. As Dale Tomich writes, Arango was acutely aware "of the ways United States independence, the French Revolution, and the Haitian slave insurrection were restructuring the Atlantic economy," and had a "profound understanding both of the possibilities that this political economic conjuncture opened up for Cuba and of what was required for Cuba to take advantage of these conditions."[22] For Arango, this meant significantly increasing the numbers of slaves on the island. The call to take advantage of the revolt in Haiti, and the Spanish Crown's 1789 decree declaring the free slave trade throughout the empire, led to a massive importation of slaves to Cuba. From 1790 to 1820, no less than 300,000 slaves entered Cuba. From 1816 to 1867 more than 595,000 Africans arrived in Cuba. In 1846, 36 percent of the population lived in bondage and 17 percent were free people of color. Compared to the

United States, which imported roughly 523,000 slaves over its entire history, the expansion of slavery and free people of color population in Cuba dramatically changed and influenced all levels of its society, economy, politics, and culture.[23]

Allo too wanted to expand and strengthen Cuba's economy. But for him, slavery was no longer a sustainable spiritual or economic practice, especially in regard to independence. Returning to the ideas and politics of the reform movement that championed the abolition of slavery in the 1830s, Allo argued that Cuba needed to end slavery in order to be independent. The question, then, was how to end Spanish colonial rule, strengthen Cuba's economy, and successfully transition slave labor into free labor without losing productivity, capital, and control of the work force. The solution, at least for Allo, was to emphasize the ideological, spiritual, and material benefits of free rather than enslaved labor. "Some believe that slavery, supposing it to be morally right, contributes to the production of wealth; a most fatal error since political economy would not be a true science if it were not based on morality."[24]

Ultimately concerned with redefining the concepts and uses of labor, Allo interpreted slavery as an inherently flawed system that causes slaves to be less productive than free laborers, since a slave "does not devote his mind to work, but to avoid work." In one of the more indicative passages, Allo correlated economic incentive to intelligence, in contrast to prevalent biological constructions of racial inferiority employed to justify enslaving African peoples. Here, it was not race that determined intelligence, but instead the African's position as free laborer. According to Allo, a free laborer "keeps in his view his fortune, his family, his future: he studies, economises [sic], undertakes, improves, invents, and overcomes all obstacles." The slave, however, expects nothing from his toil; "for him there is no stimulus but the whip; and he has not before him any scheme for his own and his sons' future. He is consequently idle, insensible; his very intelligence is his worst enemy, since it only serves to point his misfortune."[25]

In his broader analysis on the familial consequences of slavery, Allo provided an intriguing and revealing discussion of both enslaved and free women. He acknowledged the difficult and compromising positions of Cuban women who, without the protection of men, are left impoverished and desolate. "Among those persons without capital stand in the first rank women, particularly those who have lost parents, husbands, and brothers." When discussing enslaved women, Allo employed a language of respectability, sexuality, and morality to illustrate the cruel nature of the slavery.

> In connection with slavery, virtue is no longer a virtue. For a slave woman to marry a slave and preserve her conjugal fidelity, is to condemn herself and her children to slavery; and for that slave woman to surrender herself as libertine, is to aspire to her own freedom and to the freedom of her children. This truth is seen in every slave country, a sad truth [*sic*], which is confirmed by the extraordinary number of children born of slave women out of the bonds of matrimony.[26]

Allo uses the bodies of enslaved women to reject the institution of slavery and to make a case not only for freedom, but, more importantly, *free labor*. For him, it was the material productions of free labor that ultimately proved redemptive:

> In a free country, as in New York for instance, there are for these women, workshops, manufactures [*sic*] and every sort of occupation. In a land of slaves, as in Cuba, there are no workshops, and poor women are in want of the necessaries of life, because they have no business to apply themselves to.[27]

Unlike his analysis of enslaved women, the passages referring solely to "women" makes no mention of sexuality, fidelity, marriage, or race. Allo also avoided any treatment of race or social position among white women and free women of color in Cuba even though these factors dictated every aspect of their lives. He suggested only that these women were free to exercise their labor capacity—an exercise that was their ultimate salvation. The conflation speaks to Allo's determination to polarize and simplify the discourse between slavery and freedom. In his argument there is no room for problematizing or differentiating freedoms within Cuba's strict racial and gendered social hierarchy. Yet, as Luz Mena has documented, free women of color used their mobility to "stretch the limits of gendered and racialized spaces," filling the streets and plazas much more than white women and integrating themselves into almost every aspect of daily life in Havana. Free women of color contributed greatly to the city's local economy as teachers, midwives, merchants, and artisans.[28]

Throughout the speech, it is evident that Allo was aware that his work would circulate widely among North Americans. He knew his audience well and took a distinctly self-interested capitalist approach to convince Southerners to forsake slavery.

> But the southern States of America, as well as the northern States are interested in behalf of Cuba; not because she may or may not have slaves, but that they may establish in Cuba new markets, new branches of business, new sources of wealth, and that they may export from the mouth of the Mississippi, and from other centres [sic] of trade, their products into the adjacent points of Cuba.[29]

At the same time, he attempted to quell the fears of emancipation in both the United States and Cuba, by arguing that the North has "great numbers of free negroes and they have schools, churches, societies of various kinds and even military companies, without their being that identification which it is pretended to dread." He later reassured his readers that free people of color have not demanded equality or enfranchisement, even though they have established community.

Regarding the South and Cuba, Allo directly confronted the question of whiteness and racial mixture: "In the southern States, as well as in Cuba, there are very many free negroes, and there does not exist any such mixture with the whites. Laws are one thing and customs another." He further acknowledged the politics of whiteness when he pointed out that his close friend Goicuría, and "other good Cubans, have solicited permission to introduce white laborers, and have presented projects and means for carrying out their idea, and the Spanish Government has always repulsed them, that it might continue the African-slave trade." Allo was very careful not to cast the importation of Spanish workers as party to a larger policy of whitening the island, but instead as a challenge to enslaved labor. He noted that Cubans prefer free laborers, "because they understand the civilization of the nineteenth century, a civilization which point the harmonies [sic] existing between wealth, intelligence, and the doctrines of morality."[30]

Allo's speech is a call for rethinking notions of labor, capital, and modernity while maintaining a structured racial and sexual hierarchy where white Cuban men remain in power. It is clear from his gaze, perspective, and language—a discourse that both absolves the audience and alleviates its fears. By using virtue, capital, and morality as cornerstones of his speech, Allo avoids directly discussing the inherent cruelty of slave institutions, the culpability of slaveholders who have supported, reinforced, and greatly benefited from such a violent system, and the social, political, and economic consequences of slavery, especially for racial and sexual hierarchies and power relations. Moreover, there are no directives on how to incorporate recently freed slaves into the republic. Instead, he presents them as free laborers, whose position as workers in the free market is what ultimately saves them.

Allo's strategy foregrounds the making and future trajectory of a nuanced, circuitous, and tenuously inclusive exile independence and nationalist movement that would eventually aspire to appeal to as many people as possible. The gist of his approach: As long as Cubans denounced slavery and Spanish colonial rule, then the details of emancipation and enfranchisement could be worked out later when the republic was built. This tack, though it boosted the viability of the movement, would prove to be its undoing.

On March 18, 1854, *El Mulato* reported on Allo's untimely death, lamenting the loss of such a "virtuous and just man." The following day a large number of New Yorkers, "of all nationalities" but primarily "Cuban residents of New-York," met at the Cuban Democratic Athenaeum on 600 Broadway Street, where Allo had given his speech a few months earlier, to honor and pay tribute.[31]

La Verdad and the Politics of Slavery, Annexation, and Locative Whiteness

Before publishing and circulating Allo's speech, Goicuría was a member and treasurer of El Club de la Habana,[32] a powerful pro-annexationist club in New York with direct ties to El Club de la Habana in Havana. In January 1848, with the financial support of wealthy pro-annexationist Cuban planters and sympathetic US expansionists and investors, the members of El Club de la Habana launched *La Verdad*, one of the longest running and most influential exile newspapers in New York. This Spanish-English bimonthly was distinctly anti-Spanish, pro-slavery, annexationist, and rooted in a transnational and collaborative politics between the United States and Cuba.

The idea for this New York-based club and newspaper—and for a Cuban junta, which served as the executive and representative council—came a year earlier, when members held a meeting at the estate of Miguel de Aldama in Havana to devise strategies for promoting the annexation of Cuba to the United States. The meeting included other wealthy Cuban landowners Cristóbal Madan, José Antonio Echevarría, and José Luis Alfonso, as well as US expansionists and journalists Moses Yale Beach, editor of the *New York Sun*; John O'Sullivan, Madan's brother-in-law who coined the term "Manifest Destiny"; and John S. Thrasher, editor of the pro-annexationist business newspaper *El Faro Industrial*.[33]

At the center of the debate was whether slavery could be preserved in Cuba without Spanish governmental and colonial control. This was no small issue, considering slaveholders' anxiety over the public discourse on revolution and freedom together with the growing support for the abolition of slavery in Cuba. The British and North American abolition movements along with the increase in anti-slavery sentiment among Cuban exiles and migrants led pro-slavery annexationists to wonder whether slavery and independence could coexist and thrive on the island. This became a transgeographical dilemma that pitted questions of independence, power, and control against the campaign to end slavery in the hemisphere. It was no accident then that Cuban elites would settle on annexation as the perfect solution. Annexation signaled a reassertion of territoriality based on a shared interest in expanding slavery and controlling blackness. By annexing to the United States, a partly slaveholding nation, pro-slavery Cuban elites believed they could gain independence from Spain, strengthen slavery, foment nation, preserve the power of the white Creole elite, and still be part of a larger modernizing project.

For the United States, annexation meant expanding US slavery, influence, capital, and empire. As an advisor on Latin American affairs to President James Polk, Beach considered annexing Cuba a logical next step after the US-Mexican War and the Treaty of Guadalupe Hidalgo.

Once in New York, Beach agreed to mount an editorial campaign in the *New York Sun* to promote the annexation of Cuba and to assist with the creation and publication of *La Verdad*. He provided financial support, offered the *Sun's* printing presses, and ensured that the offices of *La Verdad* be located across the street from the *Sun's* headquarters at 89 Nassau Street. Beach later selected Gaspar Betancourt Cisneros, a rich Cuban cattle rancher and writer, and journalist Jane McManus Storms, who used the alias Cora Montgomery, to head the newspaper. Beach also had a hand in promoting Cuban diasporic nationalist iconography.

A critical strategy in scripting nation in the diaspora was the creation of an oppositional nationalist discourse, replete with a flag stitched and flown in New York. There are several accounts of the flag's origin, each with its own plot and cast of characters. Like all nationalist imaginings, these versions are surrounded by myth and numerous retellings, some more fantastical than others. The details that have remained constant, whether they are true or not, are that the flag was designed by Narciso López in 1849, stitched by a woman in a boarding room in Manhattan (perhaps one located on Warren Street between Church Street and College Place), and flown for the first time on May 11, 1850.[34] On that date Beach hoisted and flew the flag of Cuba Libre on the top floor of the *New York Sun's* headquarters. He also made sure to publish an article in the *Sun* introducing the flag to their readers: "High above is the flag of free Cuba. There is the flag which sooner or later [*sic*] will float over the Morro." Beach's prediction was soon realized. Eight days later, on May 19, 1850, López landed at Cardenas, Cuba and carried the flag with him into his second unsuccessful battle. There and then, the flag was flown for the first time in Cuba. It would not be seen publicly in Cuba for another seventeen years. In 1867 General Manuel de Céspedes carried the flag of Cuba Libre while fighting in the Ten Years' War. In 1895, during the Cuban War for Independence, the flag was again flown in Cuba.[35]

The flag, as an icon and symbol of nationalist desire, could not erase the questions surrounding slavery, the fear of slave revolts, and the ambivalent politics of annexation. The specter of past, recent, and future revolts, along with the possibility that Spain would yield to British abolitionist demands, convinced the early members that they must take action soon or fall victim to their greatest fear: a massive slave revolt in

Cuba.[36] This urgency was magnified in December 1843 when a planter uncovered a supposed slave conspiracy in Sabanilla, the sugar district of Mantanzas, and alerted General Leopoldo O'Donnell. In response, O'Donnell initiated a year-long campaign of terror, imprisonment, exile, and executions—*La Escalera*. O'Donnell quickly surmised that the conspiracy included a coalition of British abolitionists, anti-slavery Cuban whites, free people of color, and slaves. The former British consul to Havana David Turnbull was convicted in absentia and two of Cuba's leading liberal intellectuals, Domingo del Monte and José de la Luz y Caballero, were implicated. Both would eventually be absolved. Del Monte, however, would never again return to Cuba.[37]

Those most greatly affected by La Escalera, so named for the use of ladders to bind and punish victims before interrogation, were free people of color and slaves. The persecution and violence was a severe blow to the intellectual, creative, and cultural authority of free people of color, and demonstrated the suspect relationship among mobility, access, and blackness in Cuba. In 1844 the famous poet Gabriel de la Concepción Valdés, better known as Plácido, was executed for his rumored role in leading free people of color and slaves to revolt. To date, there is no conclusive evidence that he was involved in organizing a revolt. The conspiracy itself remains largely speculative.

Plácido's execution reverberated throughout the hemisphere. Different abolitionist campaigns in North America and Britain took up his case and used it to strengthen their fight against slavery. What distinguished Plácido was that his story and poetry "traveled," making him, as Ifeoma Kiddoe Nwankwo writes, both a threat to the Cuban government and "part of the discourse of the Atlantic World."[38] The black press in New York followed every detail of La Escalera, local pamphlets published Plácido poetry, and nineteenth-century African American writer William Allen compared him to Toussaint L'Ouverture. Perhaps the most famous narrative use of Plácido was as a central figure in Martin Delany's novel *Blake; or the Huts of America*. In Delany's hands, Plácido represented an uncompromising blackness, a Pan-Africanism that moved beyond the geographical confines of Cuba to represent a larger, almost transgressive reading of blackness.[39] Delany's casting of a Cuban literary figure to articulate ideas and notions of blackness reveals what Nwankwo has asserted is a hemispheric consciousness of blackness, a consciousness allowing Delany to confront "issues that a Cuban race man may have to deal with that he, Delany, or an African American race man might not have to engage."[40] The complication was necessary in establishing a black radical consciousness that acknowledged the different meanings of blackness.

Yet, as Sibylle Fischer explains, Plácido was a "troubling" and "ambiguous" figure whose life was both resistant and open to interpretation. He did not fit the Cuban liberal elite's anti-slavery narrative; rather, as one of the first Cuban poets to make a living from his writings, he ingratiated himself to the very people who would later call for his execution. It was precisely the ambiguity, the unknowing, and the multiple meanings attached to Plácido's life and death that most defined La Escalera and rendered it such power and resonance within and among the hemisphere. As Fischer writes, "The violence of his death, the unresolved questions that surround his life and work, and the fact that Plácido, more than anyone else in the nineteenth century, embodied the uneasy relationship between antislavery and anticolonialism have produced what can only be called a traumatic memory."[41] The relationship between antislavery and anticolonialism in Cuba was indeed uneasy and fueled the move toward annexation. The deep and abiding anxiety among slaveholders that revolts were imminent and that Cuba would soon become another Haiti filled the pages of La Verdad. In one of the earlier editions the editors referred to it as "the conspiracy of slaves of 1844" and claimed that a great part of the problem "was witchcraft and the superstitious practices among slaves."[42]

For La Verdad slavery, revolts, independence, and the future of "whiteness on the island" were all-consuming topics. In one of the first editions, the poet Pedro Santacilia wasted little time in calling for the US government to annex Cuba. In an article entitled "A los habitantes de Cuba," Santacilia makes a case for annexation.

> That Cuba annexed to this strong and respected nation whose interests in the South would be identified with hers, would secure her tranquility and her future fate; she would increase her wealth, the value of her plantations and slaves being doubled and that of her territory tripled it would give freedom to the individual action and banish that "odiour" and pernicious system of restrictions which paralyzes commerce and agriculture.

He went on to assert that if the Spanish or any other nation should intend to emancipate the slaves, "then all patience will be at the end, as well as all faith, and we shall rebel, and throw ourselves in the strong arms of the generous American nation." Santacilia equated the success of Cuban independence from Spain with that of the Southern United States, thereby privileging the slaveholding community as the saviors of Cuban liberty and freedom. Aware of United States, British, and Cuban liberal campaigns to end slavery in Cuba, Santacilia warned his readers that Cubans would have little choice but to rebel and align themselves with the United States if slavery were to be abolished.

Santacilia used the fear of Cuba becoming another Haiti to solidify the pro-slavery contingent in the diaspora and to enlist support from US sympathizers. Only through "the union of the whites" will Cubans "prevent the island from becoming another Santo Domingo,"[43] he contended, applying both the fear of blackness and the exclusivity of whiteness to unify a community whose fundamental connection was preserving and expanding slavery in Cuba. Within this context, to be white not only meant *not* being black; it also meant supporting slavery and annexationism, thereby excluding abolitionists, anti-expansionists, and anyone who did not accept such politics. Santacilia articulates a situational, almost convenient political definition of whiteness that appeals to and includes US slaveholders, pro-slavery expansionists, and annexationists.[44]

In 1849, the editors of La Verdad published a "Series of Articles on the Cuban Question." The pieces were printed in earlier editions of La Verdad that focused on Cuba "becoming a free and independent nation," as well as being "annexed to this Confederation." The articles are not authored or dated, and are arranged into distinct sections that respond directly to slavery, annexation, and expansionism. Printed in English, they are designed to appeal to US audiences. The first section begins with a question deliberately posed to US readers: "Will the annexation of Cuba add to our strength as a Nation?" The "our" in the subtitle refers to the United States. The rhetorical question is answered a few sentences later with the de facto claim that the annexation of Cuba is "written on the map of North America and in the last ten years of her history."[45]

Throughout the text are familiar tropes that are continually discussed and incorporated into the larger narrative: the fear of slave revolts and in particular, the Haitian Revolution, the commercial and geographical advantages of annexing Cuba to the United States, the conditional uses of whiteness to justify annexation, and the need to eliminate British influence from the hemisphere. Early on, the authors make a case against emancipation in the South and in Cuba, "To those who argue that emancipation is too slow in the States, I will not reply, it can move no faster." But the discussion of emancipation's impact on Haiti and Jamaica proves to be the most revealing.

> In Hayti the negroes have had unlimited power, as in Jamaica they have had unlimited equality, and what advance have they made in happiness or civilization? In the plenetude of their undisputed sway, they have murdered, insulted it; and driven out the whites in St. Domingo, and no authority prevented; they have governed themselves, and no man has said them nay, yet in the mad, unchecked animality of their untaught, untamed masses, they have heaped upon each other more sufferings, more bloodshed, more tortures, and even in that beauteous island of plenty, more downright want and misery among their populations of 780,000 than could be inflicted on our thrice that number of slaves in the presence of a white community.[46]

The main objective here is to associate blackness and emancipation with the inability to self-govern. Because these islands had captured the imagination of abolitionists, enslaved, and free people of color populations, it was critical that they be dismissed and undermined. So determined was La Verdad to invalidate and refute any promise of Haiti and Jamaica that it discussed little or none of the island's colonial rules, policies governing manumission and abolition, or conditions for revolution and emancipation. The need to equate blackness with chaos, freedom with unworthiness pervades the text despite confusing moments of ambiguity and imprecision. This ambivalence is most evident when the authors write that the instability in Haiti "does not prove that slavery is good, or that the race is incapable of better things, but it does prove by conclusive evidence of experiment, that hasty emancipation has its evils for the unprepared Africans, even though we refuse to count for anything that befalls whites."[47]

By casting free people of color and previously enslaved Africans as chaotic and unpredictable, the creole elite further appealed to white Cuban exile anxiety concerning the changes in Haiti and Jamaica, as well as to US slaveholders who too had experienced their share of slave uprisings in the South. The Southern revolts, including Gabriel Prosser (1800), Chatham Manor (1805), Denmark Vesey (1822), and Nat Turner (1831), cast a long shadow, reminding slaveholders that control was impermanent and that slave revolts were not only possible, but inevitable. Yet, these uprisings are never discussed in *La Verdad*. Neither are the Aponte Rebellion (1812) nor La Escalera mentioned by name. While there are references to "conspiracies" and "secret inquisitions set afoot in Matanzas,"[48] the authors instead focused on Haiti and Jamaica, setting up cautionary tales regarding Cuba falling into the hands of the British. "If England settles the destiny of Cuba, her lot is read in the story of Jamaica, Hayti, and Martinica." Here, too, *La Verdad* employed a discourse on whiteness—in particular, white superiority—to extol the "superior intelligence" of the outnumbered white population in Cuba.

> If she becomes really independent the whites who are but little inferior in numbers to the black, will maintain the ascendency by their superior intelligence, and slavery will probably be abolished by slow degrees. Britain remained a powerful colonial and abolitionist presence in the Caribbean and their influence was not lost on the editors of *La Verdad*, who warned readers of British designs on Cuba.[49]

One can read the anxiety over expansionism and slavery in how the British are presented as obstacles to US political furtherance and economic trade, "This simple geographical fact constitutes Cuba the key of the gulf and it would be felt if it passed into the grasp of a strong and jealous rival," while the United States' desire to expand and annex Cuba is both normalized and revered, "It will not be denied that its purchase would be an economy, and its admission a rich gain to our republican strength and majesty."[50]

One of the more pressing questions facing the United States during this period was whether newly acquired territories would be slave or free. The dilemma shaped US politics for most of the early to mid-nineteenth century, leading to the Missouri Compromise of 1820, which regulated slavery in the Western territories, including the Louisiana Purchase. In 1854, the pro-slavery Kansas-Nebraska Act repealed the Missouri Compromise. Between 1820 and 1854 important agreements dictating the terms of slavery and expansionism were passed, most notably the Wilmot Proviso of 1849 and the Compromise of 1850, the latter including the controversial Fugitive Slave Act. Recognizing the potential ramifications of the 1850 agreement born of a four-year negotiation to regulate the slave and free status of the territories newly acquired through the Treaty of Guadalupe Hidalgo, *La Verdad* cites the Compromise of 1850 to refer to annexation. "The fate of Cuba with her million souls and boundless hereafter, may be submitted to the verdict of our people before 1850 has run its last sands, and a just, wise and magnanimous nation would not willingly meet unprepared this momentous question."[51] Aware of the intense and brutal battles over the rights of slave and non-slave states, the editors assuage anti-slavery advocates by claiming that Cuba as an annexed territory—not a state—would have little influence in US electoral politics. "The non-slaveholding States would show a most ungenerous sectional spirit if they object to the addition of Cuba to the political weight of the South, for her vote will not give the South an even, much less a controlling Voice."[52]

The constructed and conflicted relationship between slavery and expansionism characterizes much of the argument and narrative in the text. The editors reference the recent acquisitions of Mexican territories and applaud the actions of the US government. "We broke forever her [Britain] closer and stricter circle, when we annexed Texas, obtained California, and removed her from Oregon claims far North of Columbia River." At the same time, it argues that the US government did not go far enough with the Treaty of Guadalupe Hidalgo signed on February 2, 1848. "The omission to secure the right of way across the Isthmus of Cortes, and to carry our southern boundary so far south as was needful to open a fair and practicable [*sic*] land route on our own soil to the Pacific, was a stupid and disgraceful lapse in those who signed a peace with Mexico."[53] *La Verdad* positioned Cuba as the next important acquisition, one that matched if not surpassed the territorial spoils of the US-Mexican War.

Racialized Spaces: The Black Press's Response to Cuban Annexation and Expansionism

Mr. Editor—I wish through the columns of your valuable paper to caution all persons of color to beware of the Island of Cuba.
Colored American, September 1837

Surely this talk about the acquisition of Cuba is nothing other than talk about stealing Cuba.
Frederick Douglass Monthly, March 1859[54]

Unfolding in the pages of the early black press were the various expansionist schemes and dramas, including what one newspaper called "The Cuba Question." The newspapers reported at length on the various excursions, policies, and bills designed to extend US territorial influence and control. *The Frederick Douglass' Paper* described the Ostend Manifesto as a "deep plot to gain possession of Cuba, either by a bribe of a hundred and twenty millions of dollars, or by the dearer cost of war." Much like other African American newspapers, pamphlets, and journals, the *Frederick Douglass' Paper* was severely critical of Cuban annexation and the growing alliance between Southern US and Cuban slaveholders whose "avowed purpose to acquire Cuba by purchase or by force, in order to prevent emancipation in that island, must shock the moral sense of every true American. Our peace is imminently threatened by these machinations." Connecting the plight of enslaved populations in Cuba with those in the United States, the paper warned its readers to "be on the alert" and "to counteract these base maneuvers of the Slaveocracy and its tools."[55]

From the early to mid-nineteenth century no fewer than twelve black newspapers were published in New York, including the nation's first black newspaper, *Freedom's Journal* published on March 16, 1827, the same year that slavery was abolished in that city. Conceived at the home of M. Boston Crummell at 139 Leonard Street in Manhattan, and published out of the Zion Church located at 152 Church Street, *Freedom's Journal* was launched to respond to the white press's attacks on free people of color and to advocate for abolition. Frederick Douglass, alone, was involved in no fewer than five newspapers published before the Civil War, from 1846 to 1860.[56]

While the publications ranged in thought, politics, and intention, they were united in challenging US expansionism and ending slavery. Newspapers such as the *Colored American* edited by black abolitionists Samuel Cornish, Philip Bell, and Charles B. Ray and run from 1837 to 1842 were committed to a hemispheric perspective that linked all African peoples and sought to create a larger diasporic thinking and identity. The pages of the *Colored American* detailed events and movements in the Caribbean, from civil society in Jamaica to the economy in Haiti. It published articles on the emancipation of slaves throughout the British West Indies, South Africa, and Latin America: discussing the end of slavery in Chile, Colombia, and Mexico, and emphasizing that "in all of these cases, not one instance of insurrection or bloodshed has ever been heard of, as the result of emancipation."[57]

In a letter to the editor entitled "A Caution to Travelers in general," William A. Gibbs writes of his most recent visit to Cuba, where he stayed for five weeks. The letter is a powerful testament to African American mobility. While on the one hand, the letter signals the movement of free black bodies within and among the hemisphere, on the other, it chronicles the unspeakable violence and terror African Americans faced when they traveled. The possibility of African American mobility was enough to signal suspicion and conspiracy. Perceived by colonial authorities as a threat to the institution of slavery, Gibbs chronicles the experiences of Mr. George Davis: "a colored citizen of the United States and a tailor by trade, was suspected of being an abolitionist." According to Gibbs, he was soon arrested and locked up in prison, and his trunk searched, "wherein were found several abolition books and papers." Davis was given no trial and instead, was executed, being "screwed to death, a most inhuman torture." Gibb provides another example of a supposed abolitionist, "a white man who was called a missionary, but who proved to be a book agent from the United States." After finding a few abolitionist papers on him, he was arrested and awaiting trial. The mobility of black bodies is so dangerous that "no colored seamen are allowed to come to the Island [*sic*] from the United States." If they do, Gibb writes, they are sent to prison, executed, or "sold into perpetual slavery." Even the mere mention of abolitionism in public or in letters to friends on the island "will seal a man's doom forever."[58]

The interest in slavery, abolitionism, and insurrection in Cuba extended to 1840, when the *Colored American* featured a column devoted to slavery in Cuba. It put the population of slaves at "about one million," and assessed that slave mortality was "very great—owing chiefly to their being excessively overworked." The column listed the harrowing conditions; "Slaves are badly fed in Cuba. They have no ground to cultivate for themselves. They are shut up nights [*sic*] promiscuously in large enclosures called Baracoons, having no roofs. Much of the whipping is for scaling walls." A year later, the paper reported on a "rumored insurrection that broke out in Trinidad de Cuba." The revolt was no rumor. Although not as widespread as La Escalera, the inability of the Spanish troops to squash the insurrection terrified Cuban slaveholders, who publicly questioned the effectiveness of the Spanish colonial government.[59] The *Colored American's* powerful response to the revolt reflects the early New York African American position on slavery in Cuba. "Whether this is anything more than rumor or not, we are not able to say, but one thing, in the nature of things seem to threatened that Island; [*sic*] either they must relinquish their hold upon these poor victims of their rage, or their Island will at no distant day be deluged in blood, as a judgment from Heaven."[60]

Holding slaveholders and slave institutions responsible for the violence, the *Colored American* refused to play into the public discourse on black transgression, undermining, and fear. This does not mean, however, that it supported slave revolts. Much of the paper's language is motivated by the move toward nineteenth-century ideologies of racial uplift and moral reform, including articles in support of temperance and on "the evils of tobacco." African American women were expected to be pious and upstanding.

Samuel Cornish, one of the founders and editors of the publication, was also the founder of the First Colored Presbyterian Church and served on the executive committee of the interracial (but mostly white-led) American and foreign anti-slavery societies. Promoting his version of acceptable behavior for the African American middle class caused tensions between the working and middle classes, as well as among the abolitionist factions that opposed incorporating religion and morality into political activism. While Cornish sought the end of hemispheric slavery, he was ultimately committed "to the radical abolitionist tenet of nonviolence" and was unwilling to advocate for any form of violence, even in the name of emancipation.[61]

The *Colored American* published a number of pieces extolling the virtues of islands such as Trinidad and Guyana, noting that "the numerical superiority of the negroes in the West Indies is great." Notices from government agents of Trinidad seeking "free industrious persons of color of good character" who wanted to "emigrate to the British Island of Trinidad"[62] also appeared. At the same time, the paper reflected Cornish's position against emigration colonization schemes. For example, the "Immigration Question" began with the unequivocal announcement that the *Colored American* has "taken a decided stand against Trinidad and Guiana emigration, and in fact, all emigration to the West Indies under the present system." The main problem was that the British possessions in the West Indies were "cursed with slavery," making it difficult to believe that employers could truly change their behaviors and treat free people of color with dignity. "With respect to the treatment of the laboring class, an entire set of habits has been formed in the employers, deeply injurious and absolutely intolerant to persons accustomed to freedom."[63] Before the *Colored American*, Cornish edited the *Freedom's Journal*, with John Brown Russwurm. Within six months the two had a falling out over the American Colonization Society's desire to colonize African Americans to Liberia. Cornish soon left the newspaper, leaving Russwurm in charge. Two year later, in 1829, Russwurm resigned as editor and departed for Liberia.[64]

The emigration of African Americans out of the United States was a controversial proposition that divided the African American leadership in New York. Some, like Henry Highland Garnet, who was closely associated with the *Colored American*, considered emigration a necessary strategy for black empowerment. Garnet founded the African Civilization Society, which according to Joel Schor was not the equivalent of the American Colonization Society as Garnet's critics alleged at the time. Garnet was against the involuntary emigration of African Americans and did not believe that free people of color should leave against their will. At the same time, Garnet understood how important it was for African Americans to have the *right* to leave oppressive conditions if they chose to. Garnet's thinking concerning emigration was further complicated by his belief, as Schor writes, that African Americans had intermixed too deeply with whites to be forcibly emigrated abroad. "Garnet's inescapable conclusion was that this western world is destined to be filled with a mixed race."[65] Others, namely Frederick Douglass, believed that African Americans needed to see themselves as rightful citizens of the United States, and under no conditions should they leave. Martin Delany, who was selected by Douglass to edit the *North Star*, but did not share his politics, considered emigration a voluntary form of resistance. It is important to note that, while elite African American men debated the merits of emigration, traveling and mobility were a harrowing and daunting prospect for most African Americans.

When it came to the annexation of Cuba, the racial politics of expansionism, and slavery, Garnet, Douglass, and Delany were all in agreement. They, like most of the black press in New York, questioned the US government's involvement in the US-Mexican War and their obsession with annexing Cuba. For many, the war and the Compromise of 1850 were proof that the federal government was indeed dominated by slaveholding interest. In 1840, the *Colored American*, aware of the expansionist desires to institute slavery in Texas, ironically noted that "some of the Spaniards think our countrymen are emigrating to Cuba with a view to take ultimate possession of Texas." Almost a decade later, in 1849, Delany published "Annexation of Cuba" in the *North Star*, where he wrote of a "deep-concerned scheme" to annex Cuba to the United States.[66]

After the passage of the Kansas-Nebraska Act, the *Frederick Douglass' Paper* explained the tensions between territories and slavery by blaming both the North and the South for the untenable situation.

> Obliged of course, to suffer to obtain Oregon, and Minnesota, the black Power is very anxious to preserve its equilibrium; or in other words, counting these future Free States, by making a Slave State of Kansas, dividing California setting new States off from Texas, annexing Haiti and Cuba etc. it will be able to maintain its ascendancy.[67]

As this quote illustrates, territories were conceived as malleable sites that could be divided, "set off," and annexed at will. Because slavery was so embedded within the language of territoriality, African American leaders used fragmented territorialities and geographies to script an oppositional discourse on space and meaning.

In questioning the reasons behind annexation, the black press also challenged the diametrically opposed roles that Cuba and Haiti played in the ongoing hemispheric drama and were quick to criticize and, in some instances, satirize the greatest fears of pro-annexationist Cuba émigrés: Haitian control of Cuba. One of the more dramatic and revealing pieces was a letter published in the *Freedom's Journal* in 1827. Addressed to the editor, who at the time was most likely Russwurm, and sent to the newspaper's headquarters at 6 Varick Street in lower New York City, the letter commends the Haitian Revolution and warns that it is only a matter of time before the "whole of the West Indies" followed suit, causing "our southern planters" to anticipate that "their trial is drawing near." The author makes references to Cuba and how the "slaveholders of Cuba tremble whenever a fleet is descried from their shores."

> In this respect, their fears are not groundless, the awful realty to them is near, their crimes have nearly reached their climax, their cup is nearly full, the day of retribution is at hand—the hands which now hold the reins so tight, and embrace the lash . . . will find their nerves unstrung and a final overthrow of that tyrannical power at present used, will be realized.[68]

The letter to the editor indicates that such a dialogue was indeed taking place in New York. Although the author is not named, the letter was published and its circulation among African Americans in New York demonstrated that these ideas, opinions, and thoughts were part of a larger African American public discourse.

Years later, in 1852, Frederick Douglass would take up the question of Haiti and the fear of slave revolts in Cuba. This time, however, Douglass satirized what was clearly an ongoing concern among slaveholders and pro-annexationists. In this piece, Douglass cites reports from the *New York Courier* and *Enquirer*, which claim that the US "government is now convinced that Cuba is lost forever to the Spanish crown," and that the "Spanish navy" will carry "The Haytien army to Cuba" where the slaves will be emancipated and "the island given to the Haytiens."

Douglass ends the piece with a sentence that "the statement lacks confirmation."[69] By including this one last sentence, Douglass reveals his intent. He is not interested in confusing or misinforming the public, but instead in disrupting the racist public discourse that used Haiti to justify slavery in Cuba and within the hemisphere. A year later, in 1853, in an article entitled "The Africanization of Cuba," Douglass questions the constant rumors of a conspiracy "between Spain and Great Britain to fill Cuba with African apprentices, to the manifest danger of liberty in the United States." Calling it "humbug" and a "hoax," he challenges the uses of blackness for political gain, and directly correlates it with the US government's intent on "wresting Cuba" from Spain.[70]

El Mulato and the Dislocation of Cuban Diasporic Blackness

In March 1854 the *Frederick Douglass' Paper* briefly mentioned the publication of the "Spanish journal *El Mulatto* [*sic*]" and noted receiving the "fourth number." It applauded the publication of the newspaper and hoped that its success may "help extricate Cuba from the thralldom by which she is bound," and allow it to "take her stand among the nations of this continent."[71] A few weeks later, on April 25, *El Mulato* published a critical response to Martin Delany's letter in the *Alienated American*, a black newspaper published in Cleveland and edited by William Howard Day, Samuel Ringgold Ward, and J.W.C. Pennington.[72] According to *El Mulato*, Delany's letter contained "a tissue of invectives directed against Mr. Colins the Editor of this journal." The response to Delany was swift and firm. While it did not publish Delany's letter nor provide any insight into what Delany may have written, it made sure to note that his comments were "false" and that "the reputation of Mr. Colins reposes [*sic*] on too firm a pedestal to be affected by Delany; and that he, Delany, and his remarks, Mr. Colins [*sic*] can treat with the most sovereign contempt."[73]

It's not clear from the brief response published in *El Mulato* what Delany wrote that so offended the newspaper and its founding editor, Carlos de Colins. What is evident is that in its brief tenure, *El Mulato* garnered the attention of not only the Cuban exile and migrant community, but also the black press and the African American leadership in New York, who, at least from Douglass' mention of the newspaper and Delany's criticism of de Colins, received the newspaper with mixed emotions.

Unlike other Cuban exile newspapers, *El Mulato* did not have a long run. It lasted no more than a year.[74] A departure from the pro-annexationist and pro-slavery discourse that dominated Cuban exile and migrant political activity, *El Mulato* was founded in part by past members of El Club de la Habana and the Cuban Junta, who were now challenging the very movement they helped to establish. The first editor of the newspaper Carlos de Colins and one of its more prolific writers, Francisco Agüero y Estrada, both white Cubans and recent arrivals to New York, used the newspaper to advocate for the gradual abolition of slavery in Cuba, the extension of universal rights to slaves, the complete independence of Cuba, and the rewriting of a nationalist dialogue to include and incorporate all Cubans, regardless of race.[75] Their position did not endear them to the pro-annexationist creole elite who from the onset publicly challenged the publication of such a newspaper.[76]

Founded in 1854, the same year the Kansas-Nebraska Act was eventually passed, *El Mulato* advocated against what it called that "iniquitous and demoralizing measure, the 'Nebraska bill.'" It reported on the delaying tactics of certain members in the House of Representatives who, in an effort to kill the bill, sent it to the committee on the whole on March 21, 1854, where it was listed as the last item on the calendar, by supporting the "hesitancy which is manifested by the members of the House of Representative" to thwart "the nefarious designs of its author to disseminate the contaminating and pestilential seed (slavery) in one of the fairest parts of this continent." The brief article ends with a melodramatic scene. If the bill is killed, the editors note, then the memories of those politicians who fought against the bill "will be revered and honored . . . and every colored mother will teach its infant offspring to lisp the names of its benefactors."[77]

The optimism was short-lived. Demanding that the act be passed at all costs, President Franklin Pierce strongly encouraged Democrats to find the votes necessary to pass the act. After a number of debates on the floor of the House of Representatives, members narrowly passed the Kansas-Nebraska Act by a vote of 113 to 100. On May 30, Pierce signed it into law. *El Mulato* was deeply disappointed by the passage of the act and considered it a *mancha negra*, a black stain on US policy. For the newspaper, the passage of such an openly pro-slavery law "went against the interest of humanity and the United States."[78] It also went against the interest of anti-slavery Cubans. If Congress could dictate the future of slavery in recently incorporated territories, especially in such partisan terms, then what did the future hold for Cuba?

Such questioning influenced the writing and perspective of *El Mulato*. In addition to the Kansas Nebraska Act, *El Mulato* also reported on the "Black Warrior Affair," on the contested political and economic relationship between the United States and Cuba, the future of slavery, events in Mexico, the Dominican Republic, and Europe. It also published a serialized anonymous novel, *El negro mártir: Novela cubana* (Black Martyr: A Cuban Novel) which according to David Luis Brown was one of two Cuban anti-slavery texts to "endorse slave rebellion as the basis for republican freedom."[79]

What most distinguished *El Mulato* from other exile newspapers was that it cast racial mixture as a cornerstone of Cuban revolutionary and nationalist thinking in the diaspora. In naming the newspaper *El Mulato*, the founders, editors, and writers consciously privileged racial mixture within the discourse of revolution and independence, dismantling what Brown calls "the Negrophobic logic of Cuban exile nationalism as pro-slavery annexationism."[80] Considering the uses of whiteness and white superiority so common in *La Verdad*, the émigré annexationist movement, and in many of New York's mainstream newspapers, *El Mulato's* position was transgressive, especially within a diasporic context, but no real surprise. The politics and rhetoric of racial mixture, or mestizaje, was a familiar and complicated strategy promoted by early nineteenth-century Cuban creole writers and intellectuals to whiten the Cuban population. The belief was that sexual relationships between European immigrant men and free women of color and enslaved women would whiten the population to a point where there would be no racial distinction. It was a practice, as Vera M. Kutzinski writes, embedded in the fear of slave revolts and the "anxiety about ethnic, particularly black enclaves that could (and did) threaten the cause of Cuban national unity."[81]

But for this to succeed, there also needed to be a deliberate practice of forgetting blackness and the horrors of slavery. Miscegenation, as a tool for moving Afro-Cubans toward whiteness, was also a strategy for reinforcing white supremacy and patriarchy, and for dismantling the possibility of post-emancipatory enfranchisement and equality, a position that ultimately benefited white Cubans, regardless of a racially inclusive nationalist identity. The historical complications and fissures surrounding racial mixture shaped how *El Mulato* scripted blackness and nation. While on the one hand, *El Mulato* was intent on undermining the workings of whiteness among pro-annexationist Cubans, on the other, its reading of blackness, of its desired role within the anti-slavery nationalist movement, was designed to ultimately appeal to white Cubans. In short, Afro-Cubans had little to do with *El Mulato*'s articulations of racial mixture or blackness.

In an article published on April 17, 1854, Agüero uses his personal relationships with Afro-Cubans to denounce the rampant racism within the diasporic community.

> Well then, there are mulattoes in my land and blacks also, that I have always respected due to their honesty and other worthy endowments that distinguished them: loyal friends, capable of the most noble self sacrifice, to whom I would constantly entrust my most dear interests, better than many whites that prize themselves with an ancient nobility, and of whom character and public and private conduct made them worthy of the most precise blasphemy. I know mulattoes and blacks also, who have rendered their notable services to the cause of our liberty.[82]

In highlighting the positive and noble character of "mulattoes in my land and blacks also," Agüero both contests and assuages the fears of Cuban blackness among whites in the diaspora. He reminds his readers that Afro-Cubans are loyal and "capable of the most noble self-sacrifice," thereby making them deserving of freedom and a shared nationalism. At the same time, he questions white Cubans who "prize themselves with ancient nobility," but whose private conduct makes them "worthy of the most precise blasphemy." This passage, albeit brief, foreshadows much of the nationalist rhetoric common to the late nineteenth century: a paternalistic scripting of blackness shaped by a white gaze. In personalizing his reading of blackness, Agüero deems Afro-Cubans worthy of freedom and a shared nationalism, while at the same time, much like his mentor Lorenzo Allo, refrains from any concrete discussion of enfranchisement and equality. The sympathetic reading of blackness used to convince white Cubans to change their political views and actions would be echoed by José Martí and the Partido Revolucionario Cubano more than thirty years later.

A further significant element in Agüero's quote is that he refers to Afro-Cubans on the island and *not* in the diaspora, thereby dislocating blackness within the diasporic imaginary. This is a common theme throughout the newspaper. While it is arguable that the lack of discussion of Afro-Cubans in the diaspora can be attributed to the relatively few numbers of Afro-Cubans who migrated to New York before the Ten Years' War, there is a disconnect, a detachment from Afro-Cubans as equal partners in the making of a shared Cuban nation. Within the pages of *El Mulato*, a newspaper pivoted on racial mixture, blackness figures primarily as an oppositional trope in the ongoing narrative against slavery.

The Enduring Drive for Annexation

An annexed race is an absorbed race.
Eugenio María de Hostos, *La Revolución*, 1869[83]

The hemisphere loomed large among Cuban exiles and migrants in New York during the early to mid-nineteenth century. The Haitian Revolution, La Escalera, the different Latin American independence movements, the US-Mexican War and the persistent call for the annexation of Cuba to the United States were all part of how Cuban exiles and migrants mediated the hemisphere and their place within it. As one of the last countries to abolish slavery and end Spanish colonialism, Cubans were deeply aware, if not anxious, of their position within the larger hemispheric modernizing project. Some feared becoming the next Haiti, others privately agonized over their growing dependence on the United States, and still others worried about Cuba's readiness for independence. Cubans, however, did not have a monopoly on hemispheric thinking. African Americans in New York continuously wrote about their place within the hemisphere. They complicated African American mobility and emigration, challenged annexation as a strategy for expanding slavery, decried the passage of acts insuring slavery in "new territories," and used the hemisphere to articulate alternative and varying definitions of blackness. In so doing, African Americans subverted the discourse on territoriality and slavery; location and race.

In 1865 the Civil War ended. Three years later, Cuban insurgents incited a revolt that led to the Ten Years' War in Cuba. While both temporarily hastened annexation as a viable option, it did not eliminate it as a strategy for building empire. In November 1869 a "grand banquet" was given by the Cuban Club of Kingston Jamaica in "commemoration of the declaration of Cuban Independence." Invitations were handed out to Jamaicans, and a large, enthusiastic crowd had assembled to celebrate the one-year anniversary of the beginning of the Ten Years' War in Cuba. At the event, a "Cuban gentleman of influence" toasted the United States and remarked that so much had that great country improved "that Europe was jealous of America." After extolling the virtues of the United States, Aaron Gregg, US consul, rose to give a brief speech encouraging Cubans "that as sure as tomorrow comes, Cuba would be free." He assured the members of the Cuban Club and their guests that the first act of the US Congress "will be the recognition of the independence of Cuba." Before ending his speech, however, Gregg made a point to remind the guests that, "if the Cubans should gain their independence without outside aid, and then thought it to incorporate their star with the thirty-seven of the American constellation, the American people would gladly receive them." This comment, according to the *New York Times*, received the loudest applause of the evening.[84]

2

"With Painful Interest"

The Ten Years' War, Masculinity, and the Politics of Revolutionary Blackness, 1865–1898

The Colored People of the United States, who have so recently been invested with the rights of citizens of our Republic, have very naturally, from our own experience of the evil effects of slavery in this country, been particularly interested in the condition of five hundred thousand of our brethren, now held as slaves in the Island of Cuba, and have watched with painful interest, the struggle that has been going on in the Island [*sic*] during the past four years, between the Cuban patriots and the Spanish Government.
Notice and Invitation to the Cuban Anti-Slavery Society
Meeting, December 13, 1872[1]

I see before me to-night [*sic*] many native Cubans, who, driven by the fierce fires of Spanish oppression, have sought and found shelter in our free land. Permit me to assure you, my exiled friends, that I know that I am justified in saying to you that this meeting, and millions of American citizens, bid you God speed in your noble cause; and in their behalf I extend to you my hand, pledging ourselves to stand united with you in your efforts for the promotion of the interests of liberty, and the universal brotherhood of man.
Henry Highland Garnet, 1872[2]

We are driven to the irresistible conclusion that the interests of humanity are inseparably connected with the cause of the Cuban patriots.
Samuel Scottron, 1872[3]

The Cuban Anti-Slavery Society and "The Rights of Freemen."

On a cold December evening in 1872, hundreds of African Americans and "a few foreign negroes" attended a meeting organized by the newly formed Cuban Anti-Slavery Society.[4] There, inside the Great Hall of the Cooper Institute, also known as the Cooper Union, Samuel Raymond Scottron called the meeting to order and welcomed the audience who had gathered that evening to hear Reverend Henry Highland Garnet speak on slavery and insurgency in Cuba. The organizers, who were all men, were impressed by the large turnout and especially with the number of reporters from major New York newspapers who attended the event, including correspondents from the *Evening Mail*, the *New York Sun*, and the *New York Herald*. The reporter for the *New York Times*, however, was not as impressed; in a brief column entitled "The Cuban Negroes–An Enthusiastic Meeting of the Cubans Last Night," he observed that the meeting "was not largely attended, with less than 300 persons being present."[5] For Samuel Scottron, however, the fact that close to three hundred "colored citizens" braved the cold night to protest slavery in Cuba was extraordinary.[6]

The meeting took weeks to plan. Concerned that Cuba was one of the last countries to abolish slavery and determined to rally support for the Ten Years' War, the founding members Samuel Scottron, Peter W. Downing, J. C. Morel, John Peterson, Philip A. White, John Zuille, David Rosell, and T.S.W. Titus circulated a call in early December inviting "the Colored Citizens of the United States" to attend a meeting protesting slavery and supporting the Cuban Patriots who "have already decreed and put in practice the doctrine of the *equality and freedom of all men.*" The call authored by some of New York's most respected African American abolitionists, newspaper reporters, inventors, and business owners implored their fellow "colored citizens" to view "with abhorrence the policy of the Spanish Government during the past four years in the island, both, [*sic*] for its unnecessary and inhuman butcheries that have taken place under its rule, and for the tenacity with which they cling to the barbarous and inhuman institution of Slavery."

Before introducing Reverend Garnet, Scottron appointed members to committees and nominated Brooklyn resident Dr. Peter W. Ray, a physician and well-known editor of *The Colored American*, as chairman, and Charles E. Pindell of Boston as secretary to a committee entrusted to expand and publicize the work of the Cuban Anti-Slavery Society.[7] After securing the nominations, Scottron read resolutions calling on the US Congress to demand the end of slavery in Cuba and "accord to the Cuban Patriots that favorable recognition that four years' gallant struggle for freedom justly entitles them to." Convinced that slavery would finally be abolished if the Spanish were defeated, the members watched with deep interest "the struggle going on in the island for the past four years between the Cuban patriots and the Spanish government."[8]

The resolutions that Scottron read that evening were remarkable in how they directly connected the plight of *free* African Americans with enslaved Cubans. Well aware of their status as "colored citizens of the United States," the members used their "rights of freemen" to advocate for Cubans who are "now in a state of slavery, undergoing the same sad experiences of ourselves in the past." Based on an extracted memory of hemispheric slavery, one that recalled "full well the cruelties of family separation, of the lash, constant toil and pain, of inequality before the law," the resolutions echoed the stirrings of an Afro-diasporic imaginary rooted in notions of a shared experience of slavery, violence, injustice, and belonging.[9] They also signaled, albeit not in text or procedure, a larger and difficult dialogue on the meanings of freedom, revolution, and civil rights during a period defined by post–Civil War policies, Reconstruction Amendments, and the Ten Years' War in Cuba.

Why would African American men, "so lately possessed of their liberty," organize around slavery and insurgency in Cuba? To what extent did their reading of freedom reveal masculinist desires and longings to destablize and reimagine the self, while attempting to define the other? In a speech the *New York Times* deemed "of considerable length,"[10] Scottron spoke to the evolving discourse on civil rights, hemispheric freedoms, and nineteenth-century diasporic politics. Departing from past abolitionist rhetoric, which cautioned against supporting slave revolts and anti-colonial revolutions, he reminded the audience that there "may be those perhaps, [*sic*] who are opposed to introducing anything of a political nature in connection with that of emancipation," hinting at both the legacy of African American involvement in anti-slavery societies and the recent passage of the Thirteenth, Fourteenth, and Fifteenth

Amendments. Aware of how the newly passed Reconstruction Amendments influenced the way African Americans viewed their place in the United States during the post–Civil War period, Scottron argued that since "our race enjoy all the rights of freemen in our Republic and, as a consequence, are respected as men everywhere . . . we should use all our efforts to ameliorate the condition of our brethren in other lands and endeavor to destroy slavery wherever it exists." Conscious that the task before them was "weighted with difficulties," especially since those "whom we propose to free are not within our grasp," Scottron nonetheless affirms that such difficulties can be successfully surmounted.[11] While directing their gaze toward Cuba as symbol and narrative was not new, this time around African Americans were constitutionally free, and for men like Scottron this meant putting those freedoms into practice. Grounded in a long history of African American leadership and participation in transamerican anti-slavery societies, the Cuban Anti-Slavery Society was the first organization founded by African American men in New York to focus primarily on supporting insurgency and ending slavery in Cuba.

Missing from the resolutions and speeches, however, were the uneasy workings of nineteenth-century freedoms and enfranchisement. Scottron expressed his own ambivalence on the future of such freedoms and the viability of granted rights when he exalted "the rapid strides made by our Government toward human equality in the past few years, and the gradual extinction of caste prejudice necessarily concomitant of the institution of slavery." On the other hand, he conceded that there was indeed a "time when it was necessary for other men to hold conventions, appoint committees and form societies, having in view the liberation of four million among whom were ourselves."[12] The ambivalence was palpable. While the resolutions and speeches speak to the intense disenfranchisement, brutality, and cruelty of slave institutions in both countries, they say little concerning the violence that erupted as African Americans asserted their rights in the United States. In one of the few references to the Civil War, Henry Highland Garnet connected the "terrible ordeal" of the Civil War with the African American community's "hearty sympathy" for Cuban insurgency.

> We who have passed through the terrible ordeal of the struggle for freedom and equal rights which [sic] in 1861 brought the two divisions of our

country into deadly conflict, and animated in the complete overthrow of despotism in the United States are in hearty sympathy with the patriots of Cuba.[13]

Implicit in Garnet's assertions is a reading of connection and mutuality that translated into a larger Afro-diasporic politics of equality and civil rights. In equating the slaveholding states and interests in the United States with those in Cuba, Garnet establishes a transnational critique of Spanish and US empires from the perspective of African peoples in the diaspora. It was more difficult, however, to articulate the changing meanings of hemispheric freedoms and civil rights, meanings that members of the Cuban Anti-Slavery Society were themselves grappling with.

This sentiment was not limited to New York. On March 10, 1873, a "convention of colored men" met at the Fifteenth Street Presbyterian Church in Washington, DC to express their views on the subject of Cuba. During the meeting George Downing, a businessmen and civil rights leader from Massachusetts, called on Congress to pass a supplemental civil rights bill that would provide the "full measure of civil rights to which the colored people are entitled." In the same speech, Downing also "denounced the barbarity of Spain in the continued enslavement of its negro population." Although seemingly disparate, the two, as the Honorable N. P. Banks from Massachusetts noted, "really constituted but one subject." According to Banks, there was "only one question with colored men in this country and the colored men in Cuba, and that was civil rights."

Later that year, on November 18, the "colored citizens of the District of Columbia" again held a mass meeting and invited Frederick Douglass to address the members.[14] Banks' emphasis on civil rights as the signature issue that tied both African Americans and Afro-Cubans was an important development in the articulation of hemispheric anti-slavery politics. First, it shifted the political narrative to one that included equality and civil rights as a unifying theme in building community among African peoples in the United States and Cuba. Second, it privileged blackness and masculinity as major tropes in the redefinition of transnationalist and diasporic meanings of freedom.

The belief that African American men were in a position to insure the freedom of "all men everywhere" meant recasting definitions of freedom that echoed their own constructed sense of empowered hemispheric black masculinities. This allowed them to not only project ideas of black manhood *in the making*, but also to universalize and conflate them to reflect what they believed were Puerto Rican and Cuban nationalist ideas of manhood. The display of hemispheric black masculinities is threaded throughout the minutes of the meetings and in the different resolutions passed that evening. In one particular passage Scottron reifies abolitionism in Puerto Rico and Cuba as a distinctly masculinist project.

> The gallant Cubans, who have battled heroically under a banner [*sic*] which is the symbol of manhood equality, have for more than a quarter of a century, insisted upon the abolition of slavery both in Cuba and Porto Rico.[15]

In casting abolitionism in Puerto Rico and Cuba as "a symbol of manhood equality," members of the Cuban Anti-Slavery Society adjusted their uses of modernity as one partly informed by hemispheric promises of protection, uplift, power, and a constructed, if not hoped for, belief in a larger and collaborative Afro-diasporic transnational community.

In her work on the masculine global imaginary of Caribbean intellectual men in the United States, Michelle Ann Stephens argues that uses of masculinities and masculine discourses were created to fit the needs of a "new and modern black male subject entering onto the stage of world politics." She further argues that as they sought to imagine a form of racial sovereignty for a disenfranchised and still colonial world population, "they drew key elements of imperial discourse along in their wake, racialized and gendered elements of empire and nation that would shape their own visions of the black state in the twentieth century."[16] Stephens' analysis of black masculinist subjects also pertains to the mid- to late nineteenth century when African American and Afro-Cuban men tested and negotiated multiple meanings of revolution, liberation, and black masculinity during a period of chaotic and violent freedoms. In his analysis of black masculinity, Maurice O. Wallace argues that African American men during the colonial and nineteenth centuries developed tools and technologies needed for "masculine authentication."[17] Although Wallace primarily focuses on the process of defining black masculinities among free men of color, he is cognizant of the problems and paradoxes of sex and gender inherent in black enslavement. Citing George Cunningham's assertion that "within the domain of slavery, gender or culturally derived notions of man- and womanhood do not exist,"[18] Wallace questions to what extent constitutional freedoms can ever fully eradicate the historical erasure of proscribed and commodified sexualities during slavery. In short, to what extent were their definitions of freedom defined and haunted by slavery in the United States and Cuba? As both Stephens and Wallace point out, the politics of black masculinity reveal the consistent and pervading tensions between unfinished freedoms and the desire for autonomy and self-definition. These tensions would soon be put to the test.

On April 8, 1870, African Americans commemorated the passage of the Fifteenth Amendment with a parade down Broadway. From Thirty-fourth Street to Union Square, the streets were "lined with the colored people of both sexes," who were there to celebrate the "elevation of black men to equal citizenship." African Americans carried signs with mottoes reading, "Now we have peace and equal rights through the Fifteenth Amendment"; "We ask nothing but a fair race in life"; and "Give us the rights of education without distinction of color."[19] Some, like the abolitionist Wendell Phillips, invoked a masculinist narrative when he suggested that African American voters put their newfound rights to work by "keeping out of the streetcars anyone who voted against the black man. They might forgive him in their prayers, but never in the voting-room."[20] Puerto Rican and Cuban revolutionaries were familiar with Phillips and knew his speech on Toussaint L'Ouverture quite well. Given in December 1861 and translated into Spanish and French by the Puerto Rican revolutionary Ramón Emeterio Betances in 1869, Phillips famously called L'Ouverture "one of the most remarkable men of the last generation."[21]

Although New York was one of the first states to ratify the Fifteenth Amendment in 1869, the amendment was controversial and New York state legislators fought to rescind the ratification. This proved to be a moot point. By March 1870 enough states voted for ratification, thereby formally amending it to the Constitution of the United States. The effort to rescind the Fifteenth Amendment echoed the precarious racial conditions in New York. The end of slavery did not necessarily translate into voting and equal rights. As the nation undertook the difficult and violent steps toward Reconstruction, African Americans continued to struggle with economic and political disenfranchisement, as well as the horrific aftermath of the Draft Riots of 1863.

One of the most violent riots in New York history, the Civil War Draft Riots began on July 13, 1863 and lasted five days. Initially, rioters targeted military and governmental buildings, "symbols of the unfairness of the draft." They soon turned their attention to African Americans and attacked them, as well as anything that was symbolic of black political, economic, and social power.[22] Rioters burned down African American–owned businesses, homes, and organizations, including the revered Colored Orphan Asylum. The blaze left more than two hundred children homeless. As night fell, racial assaults worsened. African American women were beaten and raped. African American men were sexually mutilated, stabbed, drowned, and lynched. Whites who attempted to intervene and stop the brutal attacks were severely beaten. In the end, eleven African American men had been lynched and hundreds were forced out of New York City, virtually emptying the downtown waterfront of African Americans.[23] The locative displacement was so extensive and long-standing that, by 1865, the African American population in Manhattan "plummeted to just under ten thousand, its lowest since 1820."[24]

The passage of the Reconstruction Amendments did little to ease the racial tensions that plagued the city. African Americans lost their jobs, were excluded from unions, and all traces of working-class alliances, which had existed before the Draft Riots, were erased. Even the Fifteenth Amendment, which provided the coveted right to vote, needed to be protected by a series of Enforcement Acts passed by the US Congress in 1870 and 1871. New York, as Leslie Harris so well surmised, "had never unified to overcome the problems of racism and fully embrace black freedom; neither would the nation."[25]

It was under these conditions and within this context that African American men formed the Cuban Anti-Slavery Society in 1872. It was no surprise then that during a period of intense violence, displacement, and disenfranchisement in New York, African Americans would look to Cuba and the dramatic events surrounding the Ten Years' War. The war was an ongoing insurgent drama that filled the local newspapers and spread quickly throughout the African American community. It was, as Lisa Brock has written, the African American community's "first act of international solidarity as free men and women. Unlike any episode since Haiti, Cuban freedom fighters aroused the 'revolt' sensibilities in most African-Americans."[26] Aware of the rebellion's impact on the black revolutionary imaginary, Scottron, to "great applause," informed the audience that the Cuban Republic's first official act was the "unconditional emancipation of the slaves within its jurisdiction and to make constitutional promises that all inhabitants of the Republic are absolutely free." Using "authentic and reliable sources," Scottron asserted "that an actual state of freedom exists among all classes." He went on to cast Cuban insurgents as purveyors of modernity. "God grant it may be our province to divest her (Spain) of this portion of her little greatness, and she be made to respect the spirit of the age, which can tolerate nothing but liberty."[27]

Scottron's claim that "an actual state of freedom" existed among all classes was not necessarily the case. On the morning of October 10, 1868, Carlos Manuel de Céspedes, a slaveholder and sugar planter, famously gathered his slaves around him, addressed them as "citizens," informed them that they were now free, and invited them to fight for Cuban independence. The call to fight against the Spanish resulted in a disproportionately large number of previously enslaved and free men of color fighting in the war. The visibility and authority of Afro-Cuban male bodies in battle did not go unnoticed by Scottron, who made a point to tell the audience that "the colored inhabitants of Cuba battle side by side with the white, holding the rank of officers, and in numerous instances, colored officers commanding white troops." The belief that all slaves had been freed as a result of the Grito de Yara was a familiar public discourse. Two years earlier, in July 1870, the New York Times reported that Cubans had "inaugurated their movement for national independence by a manumission of all of their slaves, which they confirmed in their constitution." Covering a meeting held in Brooklyn to support the Ten Years' War, the Times reported that "Negroes have not only been set free, but have been allowed the equal political rights and privileges with whites wherever the patriot cause has prevailed." Invoking nationalist and racialized masculinities, the Times also noted that Afro-Cubans had "fought manfully side by side with white men."[28]

The large number of Afro-Cuban men in battle was seen as a necessary justification for ending slavery, the price to pay for abolition. And yet, abolition was not the formal policy of the new movement.[29] While the Cuban constitution written in Guáimaro in 1869 declared all Cubans free, the legislative chambers enacted labor laws to control the emancipation process. In was not until 1886 that slavery was formally abolished, eight years after the end of the Ten Years' War. But what the war did do, and do quite well, was to establish a nationalist rhetoric that emphasized Cuban nationalism over race. Such a language, although pivoted in the future and suspended in possibility, established a discourse of black citizenship during a period of revolutionary wars, slavery, and nationalist imaginings. In addition, as Ada Ferrer writes, "black insurgents and citizens now had a powerful language with which to speak about race and racism within the rebel polity—a language, with which to show that the transcendence was yet to occur."[30]

African Americans had no promise of a language or doctrine of racelessness they could use to assert their place within the nation, especially one emerging from the Civil War. There was no space for conjuring rhetorical possibilities of nationalist racial unity or even a potential transcendence "yet to occur." But they could, as Scottron's speech demonstrates, be seduced by the promises made to *other* nations and claim them as their very own. Once Scottron ended his speech the members adopted the different resolutions, and the audience "evinced their sympathy by prolonged cheering."[31]

After the speech, Scottron introduced the current president of the Cuban Anti-Slavery Society, the Reverend Henry Highland Garnet. Choosing Garnet to be the evening's keynote speaker made sense. A Presbyterian minister, author, and anti-slavery activist, Garnet had been involved in either forming or participating in the most important abolitionist campaigns and organizations in New York, including as one of the founding members of the American and Foreign Anti-Slavery Society of 1840. Born into slavery on December 23, 1815 in Maryland, Garnet's family escaped after receiving permission to attend a family funeral and failing to return. Garnet's family settled in New Hope, Pennsylvania, and then moved to New York City in 1825. A year later, Garnet entered the African Free School, an abolitionist-sponsored school for African Americans, where he met and befriended Alexander Crummell, Samuel Ringold Ward, Ira Aldridge, and Charles Reason, friends who greatly influenced his intellect and ambitions.

Early in his career, Garnet worked closely with the abolitionist William Lloyd Garrison. However, by the mid- to late 1840s Garnet broke with Garrison and his emphasis on moral reform, and moved toward direct political action. He urged slaves to revolt, supported the black emigration movement, and in 1843 gave a historic speech that publicly formalized his break with Garrison. The speech, "An Address to the Slaves of the United States of America," was given at the National Negro Convention in Buffalo, New York. It is best remembered not only for Garnet's bold remarks, but also for Frederick Douglass' attempts to silence Garnet and erase him from the public record. A staunch supporter of Garrison, Douglass successfully lobbied to have the speech edited from the published proceedings of the meeting. His actions initiated a long and tense rivalry between both men and within the African American abolitionist movement. Douglass' efforts at silencing Garnet proved futile. Not only did Garnet eventually publish his speech, he did so in conjunction with David Walker's *Appeal to the Coloured Citizens of the World*, a direct and public challenge to both Douglass and Garrison. Published in 1829, Walker's *Appeal* was a call for slaves to rebel against their condition and "cast off their chains."[32] *Appeal* went out of print soon after Walker's untimely death in 1830. Determined to preserve Walker's legacy, Garnet, who had never met Walker, reprinted the pamphlet and secured its dissemination among future generations.[33]

In 1848, Garnet gave a speech to the Female Benevolent Society, in which he discussed the slave trade, "which is carried on briskly in the beautiful island of Cuba." Referencing the illegal slave trade in Cuba, which according to Garnet went unchecked, he informed the audience that a few years ago he "witnessed the landing of cargo of slaves, fresh from the coast of Africa, in the port of Havanna, in the presence of the Governor, and under the shadow of the Moro Castle, [*sic*] one of the strongest fortifications of the world."[34] Garnet's actions and speeches sealed his reputation as a radical thinker, activist, and abolitionist. By the time Garnet had been asked to serve as president and the keynote speaker at the first mass meeting of the Cuban Anti-Slavery Society, his position on slavery and anti-colonialism was widely known.

Unlike Scottron, Garnet spoke directly to the Cubans in the audience. He told the audience of his travels to Cuba, where he had "witnessed the horrors of slavery."[35] He assured them that Cubans had the sympathy of the African American community and that although the members "cannot give you the material aid we would wish to afford you," they would "create a public sentiment to this land that will urge our government to acknowledge the belligerent rights of the patriots of Cuba." He reminded them that the US government was indeed strongly in favor of Cuban liberty and when the time comes and "in conformity with international law they can render Cuba the aid she needs." But there were limits to the United States' support for Cuba, and Garnet understood the contradictions of US foreign policy. Disappointed that the US government refused to pressure Spain to end the slave trade, Garnet noted that "our government holds diplomatic relations with Spain. I would prefer that we had none."[36] Garnet was not alone in his ambivalence. After the meeting, members collected more than 5,000 signatures on a petition demanding that the US government formally recognize the insurgency in Cuba.[37] A few months later, President Grant met with a delegation from the Cuban Anti-Slavery Society and expressed his concerns about slavery. Grant referred the matter to his Cabinet, where it lingered and was eventually forgotten.[38]

Toward the end of the speech Garnet invoked two major tropes signaling Caribbean revolutionary blackness: Plácido and Haiti. Almost thirty years after his execution by the colonial government in Cuba, Plácido remained a revered figure within the African American abolitionist movement. But he was also, as Garnet knew full well, an important revolutionary symbol among Cubans in the diaspora. "You cannot forget, Cubans, the immortal mulatto poet of your country, the brave and heroic Placido." Amidst "long continued cheers," Garnet noted "Like yourselves, you know that he loved liberty, and freely offered himself on her sacred altar. He was accused of being concerned in an attempted insurrection, and was condemned to die the death of a traitor."

Garnet's comments were met with "great excitement among the Cubans, and loud cheers." Garnet concluded his speech by connecting the Haitian Revolution with the ongoing Ten Years' War. Once Haiti "disenthralled herself," the strong arm of the tyrant's power was "broken." Garnet remarked incorrectly, but nonetheless dramatically, that once Cuba abolished slavery, "the last foul blot of slavery will be removed from our portion of the globe."[39]

In acknowledging blackness and revolution *within* the Cuban diaspora, Garnet's speech complicates nineteenth-century African American political activity and thought. No longer simply part of a detached Caribbean imaginary, Garnet's reference indicates both recognition and acknowledgment of an Afro-Cuban diasporic presence in New York. Unlike in the past, when Cuba and Afro-Cubans operated as metaphors for establishing a larger Pan-African community, Afro-Cubans were present at the meeting and arguably involved in producing diasporic revolutionary thinking.

And yet, their place within the Cuban Anti-Slavery Society, at least in terms of historical production and archive, is unclear. Outside of Garnet's reference to Cubans in the audience, there is no record in the official proceedings of how many Cubans attended the meeting that evening, their role in the Cuban Anti-Slavery Society, if they held positions of power and influence, whether they gave speeches that evening, or if the Cuban Anti-Slavery Society had any relationship with Cuban revolutionary clubs in the city. Yet, according to the *New York Times*, a large number of "Cuban Negroes" attended that meeting. The article goes on to cite that a number of speeches were given that evening, including one by "Señor Felix Fuentes, and others."[40]

An active member of the Cuban exile and migrant revolutionary and nationalist movement, Félix Fuentes was involved in the formation of several important political clubs, including the Asociación Cubana de Socorros. According to his fellow Afro-Cuban revolutionary Teófilo Domínguez, Fuentes was a close friend of Rafael Serra and one of the more eminent Afro-Cuban revolutionaries living in New York during the mid- to late nineteenth century.[41] If, as the *New York Times* article noted, Fuentes gave a speech that evening, why did it not appear in the Cuban Anti-Slavery Society's official records of the first meeting? Were there other speeches, events, and spaces where Afro-Cubans spoke or participated that were left out of the published historical narrative? What does it ultimately mean that African Americans failed to include Afro-Cuban voices and bodies in their own attempts to produce historical source and archive?

Two years later the members of the Cuban Anti-Slavery Society "extended its scope" and renamed their organization the American Foreign Anti-Slavery Society. Moving beyond the "Cuba question," the letterhead of the newly formed American Foreign Anti-Slavery Society proclaimed that, "Slavery is a crime against humanity, and it is the duty of nations and individuals to interfere for the liberation of the enslaved wheresover held."[42] The reconstitution allowed members to expand the society's geographic reach to slaveholding countries such as Brazil, and to include labor and labor organizing into their political platform. For Scottron, in particular, the decision to reorganize the Cuban Anti-Slavery Society was a "moral force" necessary to the "extinction of slavery in Cuba and Brazil, and the slave trade in the Soudan [sic] Africa." In terms of orga-nizational structure, little changed. The society remained in contact with the British Foreign Anti-Slavery Society, Garnet was named president, and Scottron was secretary.[43]

The inclusion of labor into the platform made sense. The Wall Street Panic of 1873 and the policies of Reconstruction had, as Nell Irving Painter writes, "destroyed the order of things."[44] The Panic of 1873 was the first major crisis of industrial capitalism in the United States and it changed the discourse on political ideologies and labor rights, includ-ing the workings of freedom and the sustainability of the Reconstruc-tion Amendments. Between 1873 and 1878, close to eighteen thousand businesses failed and the unemployment rate was at its highest, reach-ing almost 14 percent. The economic crisis and loss of jobs resulted in labor strikes, social unrest, and increased class and racial tensions. The panic and ensuing chaos made it nearly impossible to discuss the abolition of slavery in Cuba without also considering empire and the future of newly emancipated African peoples as waged laborers. This more than anything else influenced how members of the American Foreign Anti Slavery Society, namely Garnet and William Butler, de-veloped and promoted strong critiques concerning US capital and empire-building in Cuba, analyses that would not endear them to the increasingly reformist and annexationist Cuban exile community in New York. And yet, despite their fundamental disagreements, Garnet, Butler, and Scottron forged connections and cultivated temporary al-liances with politically connected and wealthy Cuban exiles, all in the name of ending Spanish colonial rule and slavery in Cuba. What this would entail, especially with regard to Afro-Cuban enfranchisement, had yet to be determined.

Unmanned Nations and Revolutions: Las Hijas de Cuba

In January 1870, the state of New York formally recognized the Cuban exile government under Carlos Manuel de Céspedes and acknowledged those offices as the seat of the Cuban government. This made it possible for leaders of the American Foreign Anti-Slavery Society to forge links with official representatives of the Cuban government, as well as the more wealthy and elite segments of the Cuban diasporic community who filled and dominated those positions. Samuel Scottron, for instance, elicited funds from privileged white Cuban exiles and migrants, including José Manuel Mestre, a lawyer, reformist, and advocate of gradual emancipation and annexation. Mestre arrived in New York at the request of José Morales Lemus, who in 1869 was made the official envoy and representative of the exile Cuban republican government and president of the Junta Revolucionaria de Cuba y Puerto Rico. With Morales Lemus' urging, Mestre moved to New York, where he served as a diplomat and representative of the revolutionary Cuban government. A year later, Morales Lemus died and Mestre, along with Miguel de Aldama and José Antonio Echevarria, continued their work in support of the revolutionary government, including publishing articles in the exile newspaper, *La Revolución Cuba y Puerto.*[45]

The problem was that Scottron established relationships with representatives of an exile government considered suspect by Cuban independistas in New York.[46] One of the more vocal critics was the influential Emilia Casanova de Villaverde, who founded the first all-woman political society in exile, La Liga de las Hijas de Cuba, in January 1869. Formed by elite women for the sole purpose of raising funds to support the Ten Years' War, La Liga de las Hijas de Cuba consisted of fourteen Puerto Rican and Cuban women committed to the independence of both islands. The members held their first meeting on February 6 at the St. Julien Hotel located near Washington Square.[47] By the time Casanova de Villaverde established La Liga de las Hijas de Cuba, her reputation as a strong, outspoken, and powerful activist was well known. Born to a slaveholding family on January 18, 1832 in Cardenas, Cuba, Casanova de Villaverde left Cuba for New York in 1852 with her father Inocencio Casanova Fagundo. While still in her teens, Casanova de Villaverde was already involved in the effort to liberate Cuba, and had pledged her support to Narciso López. Her actions and public rebuke of the Spanish colonial authorities garnered untold enemies in Cuba and solidified her exile. By 1854 the entire family moved to Philadelphia, and later New York. While in Philadelphia, Emilia Casanova de Villaverde met and married the Cuban writer Cirilo Villaverde, who was twenty-one years her senior. The couple moved to New York to be directly involved with the Cuban revolutionary movement. Casanova de Villaverde wrote letters to the *New York Herald* challenging the Spanish authorities and helped to establish La Sociedad Republicana de Cuba y Puerto Rico in 1866.[48]

But it was as the founder and secretary of La Liga de las Hijas de Cuba that Casanova de Villaverde made the most impact. She wasted little time in publicly accusing the members of the Junta Revolucionaria de Cuba y Puerto Rico of "annexationist maneuvers and betrayals." Despite their frequent denials, Casanova de Villaverde was not far off. In 1874, the same year that the American Foreign Anti-Slavery Society was founded, Carlos Manuel de Céspedes was captured by the Spanish and killed. His death was a blow to the émigré community and magnified what had been brewing for years: a deep fragmentation among Cuban exiles and migrants. Hastening those divisions were the never-ending questions surrounding the possible annexation of Cuba to the United States; questions advanced by social reformists who left Cuba during the Ten Years' War and now filled the ranks of the Cuban republic-in-arms.

The period after the Civil War and during the Ten Years' War witnessed a resurgence in pro-annexationist literature and politics. No longer associated with expanding slavery or advancing the interest of slaveholders in the South, annexation was now seen as an option for securing postcolonial stability on the island. This did not mean, however, that race no longer played a role in the reemerging politics of annexation. On the contrary, in 1869 Plutarco González, a ranking member of the Junta Central's leadership, authored a pro-annexationist pamphlet entitled, "The Cuban Question and American Policy in the Light of Common Sense." Published in New York and approved and financed by the Junta, the pamphlet uses racism, stereotypes, and fear to argue for annexation. Echoing the familiar concerns of landholding Cuban elites, the pamphlet warns that even the most "docile of negroes" are "ignorant and capable of fearful excesses as was seen in San Domingo [sic], when aroused by suffering or wicked leaders." Sixty-five years after the Haitian Revolution, González connects the United States and Cuba's future with Haiti's past, writing that "passions which revolution lets loose would find their vent, probably in a war of races and factions and we might see the horrors of San Domingo [sic] revived. The Richest [sic] and most productive country in the world would be utterly ruined and left a pretty [sic] to frightful disorder and carnage."[49]

The post–Civil War period not only summoned possible freedoms, it also revealed persistent anxieties among those who considered such freedoms to be a threat to white supremacy, landholding interests, capital, and political control in both the United States and Cuba.[50] The reconfiguration of annexation as a possible option, along with the invocation of the oft-used, yet still effective black fear narrative, were part of a larger strategy in hemispheric empire-building. No longer able to use slavery as a catalyst for colonial expansionism, annexationists refashioned a discourse that positioned fear, blackness, and unreachable modernities as a warning against *total* independence in Cuba.

The racial politics of post–Civil War annexation did not go unnoticed by prominent US journalists, politicians, writers, and social reformers who in March 1869 signed a letter calling for the continued support for Cuban independence. Exhibiting a different approach and strategy than the supporters of annexation, the undersigned, William Cullen Bryant, Henry Ward Beecher, George William Curtis, Charles A. Dana, George Wilkes, John K. Porter, and Silas M. Stillwell, to name a few, invited the public to a meeting at Steinway Hall to confer upon matters connected with the present condition in Cuba. Fully satisfied that "the present struggle of the Cubans for independence is based upon principles of eternal justice," the signatories made a point to publicly express "their sympathies for a people living on our very borders and almost a part of us, who are pledging their fortunes and lives to obtain rights long unjustly withheld from them."[51] The meeting was one of many held in New York to support independence, all carefully orchestrated rebukes of the government's attempts to build empire in Cuba. Frustrated with the United States' unwillingness to formally declare support for independence, the signatories, many of whom were reformers opposed to annexation, wanted to publicly embarrass the US government over their inaction with regard to Cuba.

The idea of annexation as a strategy for post-independence Cuba was anathema to independistas like Casanova de Villaverde who believed in nothing less than total independence and sovereignty. Devastated by the deaths of both Céspedes and Morales Lemus, Casanova de Villaverde was convinced that the Junta was taking advantage of the loss of both leaders to advance their annexationist agenda. On September 28, 1874, Casanova de Villaverde published "una hoja," a sheet, entitled "A los cubanos," in which she criticized the members of the Junta Revolucionaria de Cuba y Puerto Rico for failing to "even raise their voices" in protest against Céspedes' assassination, and for supporting exile newspapers that "do not publish the truth." In a remarkable passage, Casanova de Villaverde conflates the move toward annexation with what she sees is the widespread silence among the men, in particular the leadership of la Junta. Her solution lies with the women, who unlike the men are not afraid to speak out. The pamphlet begins with a powerful indictment of the men in the leadership.

> Compatriots! Enough time we have remained silent. Enough time we have kept within our chest our indignation for the iniquities of which was victim Carlos Manuel de Céspedes: but since men are silent, strength is that women speak.[52]

Casanova de Villaverde does not end there. She adds insult to injury when she writes that while members of La Sociedad de Artesanos de Nueva Orleans have energetically protested against the overthrow of the first president of Cuba, compatriots in New York "have not even raised one voice to echo such dignified protest."[53] In depicting the men in the movement as silent bystanders, and the women as the ones courageous enough to speak out, Casanova de Villaverde employs the politics of voice to subvert male authority. By accusing the male leadership of being silent, she renders them powerless, ineffective, and disloyal to the revolution. Their unwillingness to speak, an inherent male privilege, is for her, the ultimate betrayal.

Casanova de Villaverde's reading of voice as a gendered strategy extends to the publication of the pamphlet "A los cubanos." The pamphlet lists twenty different demands, including calls for the Spanish authorities to take full responsibility for their mistreatment and assassination of Cespedes. It challenges the leadership of Miguel de Aldama, Juan Clemente Zenea, Juan Manuel Macias, José Manuel Mestre, José Antonio Echevarria, and of affiliated agents and commissioners for their betrayal of Céspedes and the exile independence movement, and questions those exile newspapers that publish "nothing but lies." "A los cubanos" is one of the most strongly worded public rebukes of la Junta so far recovered. Not only does it name names, it publicly shames and accuses powerful male figures in the exile independence and nationalist movement of supporting annexation, and even worse, of being autonomist, "willing to fly the Spanish flag."[54]

Although the pamphlet is from La Liga de las Hijas de Cuba, the only signature that appears is that of Emilia Casanova de Villaverde, who served as the permanent secretary. As evident from her past writings, the pamphlet reflects much of Casanova de Villaverde's own political views. Notorious for pushing her agenda, refusing to ask permission, or to reach a consensus with other women in the group, Casanova de Villaverde had a difficult time working with many of the women in the organization and overall movement.[55] But she had an even more difficult time working with men. Outspoken and unafraid, Casanova de Villaverde consistently questioned the agenda, motives, and politics of the Cuban exile leadership. Exhibiting little patience with propriety, Casanova de Villaverde was not always well liked or understood by the men in the movement, even though she was one of the most effective revolutionaries in exile. In a letter dated April 1, 1871 and written to her dear friends Filomena and Caridad Callejas, she complained about not having enough time to meet her "domestic obligations," and dealing with people who did not give women enough credit to think for themselves.[56] In the same letter, she challenges the Junta Central, arguing that Cuba would soon be free if the men of the Junta Central "do not take over the management of the affairs of this country." Listing the men by name, "Los Morales Lemus, los Aldama, los Cisneros, los Mestres, los Fesser, los Martín Rivero," Casanova de Villaverde accuses them of "entering into the revolution to railroad and sabotage, not to support its triumph."[57]

Casanova de Villaverde's frustration with the Junta stemmed from her unshakeable and polarizing belief that Juan Clemente Zenea was intimately involved in Céspedes' assassination. So convinced was Casanova de Villaverde of Zenea's guilt that on February 4, 1871, the same year Zenea was shot to death by Spanish troops as he attempted to return to the United States, the members of La Liga de las Hijas de Cuba passed multiple resolutions condemning Zenea as a traitor and "upholding him to the execration of mankind."[58]

Producing Visibility: The Deliberate Archive of Emilia Casanova Villaverde

In the first place, the data provided to us was very scarce; secondly, we had to acquire them without the knowledge of the heroine.
Apuntes biográficos de la ilustre cubana Emilia Casanova de Villaverde (1874)[59]

The same year that Emilia Casanova Villaverde disseminated the pamphlet "A los cubanos," her biography, *Apuntes biográficos de la ilustre cubana Emilia Casanova de Villaverde*, was published in New York. Authored by "un contemporaneo," it is common knowledge that it was her husband Cirilo Villaverde who wrote the book.[60] A positive and uncritical look at her life, *Apuntes biográficos* deliberately positions Casanova de Villaverde squarely within the exile revolutionary movement. Considered by the author to be an important intervention in the history of "nuestra patria," the biography, or better the biographical notes, has for years served as a foundational text documenting Casanova Villaverde's role within the exile nationalist movement in New York. Few studies of the Cuban exile revolutionary movement, including my own, have *not* used *Apuntes biográficos*. The problem is not the use of the biography as historical text and source, but the lack of analysis with regard to its production. It is by examining the production of the *Apuntes biográficos* that we understand how the text operates as a gendered and deliberate production of knowledge and historical source designed to privilege the life and exploits of one particular white, elite Cuban woman. At the same time, a closer look renders insight into why certain elements of the exile revolutionary movement were included, and why others—notably race and slavery—were left out in the making of a future historical narrative.

The *Apuntes biográficos* is a powerful testimony of the workings of masculinities in historical imaginaries, masculinities that Casanova de Villaverde both challenged, and as a result of her wealth and access, employed to her fullest advantage. The text both disrupts and replicates masculinist archival desires. On the one hand, it inserts Emilia Casanova de Villaverde within a male-dominated narrative, while on the other, it uses the very tools and strategies adopted by men to dominate and control historical source and analysis. Unlike the men in the movement, Casanova de Villaverde was not formally recognized during her lifetime as a poet, a novelist, or a journalist. Yet, she wrote. And much like the men, she wrote often, self-consciously, and with purpose. However, it would be through the *Apuntes biográficos* that Casanova Villaverde—with the help of her husband—willed herself into history. As someone who was married to a writer, translator, editor, and journalist, Emilia Casanova de Villaverde fully understood the power of printed media and producing one's own historical record. Highly educated and fluent in English, Casanova de Villaverde was afforded extraordinary access to political and literary figures in the United States. She traveled to Washington, DC, where she routinely met with senators, lobbyists, and government officials, and according to her biography, met with President Grant on more than a few occasions. Casanova de Villaverde disseminated countless pamphlets, wrote letters to the editors of major newspapers, and published articles in the exile press, including in *El Espejo*, a separatist newspaper founded by her husband in 1874. Despite her writings and activism there are few if any guarantees that she would have been remembered had the *Apuntes biográficos* not been published. Outside of the *Apuntes biográficos*, there are scant sources detailing her life and work. There are even less that suggest that she had any real and lasting power in an exile revolutionary movement controlled by men.[61]

As production, the *Apuntes biográficos* seeks to both remember and recover Casanova de Villaverde. It affords visibility and voice to a woman, who like so many in the exile community, could easily have been erased had source not been created. There are no illusions that it is meant to be an accurate historical study of the period: the fickle dating, the inclusion

of letters over biography, and the feigned detachment and supposed anonymity of the author. Instead, it reads as one that is pivoted in the future;
a corrective to a potential historical record where Casanova de Villaverde
may not appear. Early in the book the author emphasizes Casanova de
Villaverde's "distinguished patriotism and service to the causes of liberty
and independence," implying that she has yet to be given credit for her
achievements and activism.[62] Perhaps true. The tricky part is that Casanova de Villaverde was still active in the exile revolutionary movement
when the biography was published. She was at the height of her career
and there was still sufficient time to proffer credit.

The use of biographies to create archive is nothing new. During the
nineteenth century, as Scott E. Casper writes, biographies were not only
used to produce archive, but to define the meanings of nation and self.
The reading public was fascinated with the private lives of public figures,
and the demand for biographies grew exponentially. They were so plenti-
ful that they evolved into one of the most popular genres of the period.
As Casper documents, the subjects and constructions of biographies expanded and changed to appeal to an ever-growing audience. Along with
biographies of eminent politicians and artists, there were also biographies
and memoirs of the not so famous, of laborers, and of the everyday people that were published and read widely. It was common for biographies
to be written with the cooperation of the subject at hand, to refuse to be
locked into any set dating or periodization, and to employ an expansive
if not reworked narrative.[63] Biographies, to cite Roland Barthes, are fictions and productions used to create distinct and alternative realities.[64]
Their uses were multiple, often having little to do with historically nar-
rating or contextualizing one's life. According to Casper, much of the lure
pertained to the idea that biographies allowed North Americans to articulate for themselves what it meant to be an "American." It was through
biographies that the public debated the changing meanings of a distinctly
"American character," especially during a time of civil war, massive immigration, economic depressions, labor unrest, and industrialization.

The *Apuntes biográficos* operated similarly. It allowed Casanova de
Villaverde to position herself squarely within the exile revolutionary
movement, guaranteeing that her political thoughts, ideas, activism,
and perspective would survive, regardless of possible competing and
varied sources and records. In recasting her as a central figure in the

movement, the text attempts to redefine the parameters of revolutionary thinking. Taking its cue from nineteenth-century biographical genre
and form, it also sought to reconfigure historical memory and narrative,
creating a space for an alternative reframing of experience.

Set during the Ten Years' War, the *Apuntes biográficos* is an unabash-
edly nationalist text. It emphasizes the years that Casanova de Villaverde
was involved in the exile revolutionary and nationalist movement. Ironically, the dating here is problematic. The publication date of the manuscript is 1874. Yet, as Ana Cairo has noted, it was probably published ten
years later, in 1884.[65] The bulk of the biography consists of letters that
Casanova de Villaverde wrote and received from distinguished figures
in the movement during the Ten Years' War. Here too there is a problem.
While the publication date of the biography is 1874, the section devoted
to the many letters is dated 1869–1876.[66] The random dating has meaning. In 1874 Carlos Manuel de Céspedes was killed. By dating the book
1874, Casanova de Villaverde signals that she is perhaps more interested
in marking a specific experience and moment than in providing an accurate publication date.

Further distinguishing the text is the lengths to which Villaverde goes
to create an air of detachment, independence, and objectivity. In a section that introduces the book, entitled "Advertencia," which translated
means "comment," "observation," or even "warning," Villaverde informs
the reader that the book was written anonymously and without Casanova de Villaverde's knowledge or cooperation. Yet, he is able to procure
"a copious extraction of her large correspondence with diverse and notable people." It is not clear whether at the time that the *Apuntes biográficos* was published Villaverde's authorship and Casanova de Villaverde's
possible cooperation were open secrets, as was the case with biographies
published during this period. The ambivalent authorship of biographies,
however, did not diminish their value or popularity. Supposed anonymous biographies continued to be sold and read by the wider public in
large numbers.[67]

Unlike most biographies, the bulk of the *Apuntes biográficos* consists
of letters written by and addressed to Casanova de Villaverde. The biographical narrative is only thirty-six pages. The correspondence, however,
extends to more than a hundred pages with letters from and by José Morales Lemus, Manuel Quesada, and General Garibaldi. Although fewer in

number, there are letters from women in the movement, including Concepción C. de López and Asunción Adot de Miranda. The inclusion of so many letters is no accident. Authored by some of the more powerful men in the movement, the letters laud her achievements, detailing how they sought her advice and considered her integral to the exile independence movement. The letters read as a masculinist spectacle of acceptance, revealing a curious interplay between gender and authority, narrative, and power. In using their words to highlight her accomplishments and thinking, Villaverde positions herself as their equal and in some instances, a leader among the *men* in the exile revolutionary community.

Missing from the narrative and letters is any discussion of race and blackness, of Afro-Cuban activism in New York, and the role of US antislavery movements supporting Cuban insurrection. Except for a brief passage in the introduction that associates Casanova de Villaverde's opposition to slavery with her hatred of Spanish tyranny, the *Apuntes biográficos* is devoid of any concrete discussion of slavery, abolition, and the future of emancipation in Cuba. Considering that the *Apuntes biográficos* is regarded as a significant and powerful representation of exile insurgency and revolution, the elimination of race from the exile nationalist platform is troubling and revealing.

Historians and literary scholars have depicted Casanova de Villaverde as a staunch advocate of ending slavery in Cuba. She has been credited with convincing her husband Cirilo Villaverde to change his position from supporting slavery and annexation to emancipation and independence. She has also been cited as the person who most influenced Villaverde to be more forceful and incisive in his treatment of slavery in his famous anti-slavery novel, *Cecilia Valdés*. The novel, which first appeared in Havana in 1839 when Villaverde still lived in Cuba, was, after countless revisions, finally published in New York in 1882.[68] Yet, none of Casanova de Villaverde's anti-slavery activism is evident in the *Apuntes biográficos*.

The questionable absence of blackness and nation in the *Apuntes biográficos* has seldom, if ever, been discussed. This is a fundamental problem that speaks to the historical negation of blackness as a central intellectual and political trope within the exile and migrant Cuban community, and moreover in the case of the *Apuntes biográficos*, historical remembering. The erasure of blackness, of Afro-Cuban women and men, has meaning. There is a reason for it. It is often assumed that blackness does not enter the exile nationalist discourse or become part of the nationalist ethos until the late nineteenth century with the rise of the Partido Revolucionario Cubano. Yet, if the Cuban Anti-Slavery and American Foreign Anti-Slavery Societies are any indication, there already existed a public discourse that merged blackness with Cuban independence and nation in the diaspora. Articulated by African American anti-slavery activists, Cuban exiles and migrants were nonetheless well aware of it and some, like Mestre, supported and funded the work of the American Foreign Anti-Slavery Society.[69]

The *Apuntes biográficos* represents a dilemma in nineteenth-century biographical historical source. One would be hard-pressed to write a history of the nineteenth-century New York Cuban and revolutionary diaspora without including it as part of the historiography. An important intervention in the diasporic history of elite white Cuban women in New York, it is one of the few sources that focus on women, even if its emphasis is primarily on Casanova de Villaverde. Yet, the gaps, logistical lapses, and silences are hard to ignore. If the *Apuntes biográficos* is to be read as a deliberate attempt at creating archive, then we must contend with the fact that blackness, slavery, and emancipation were for the most part eliminated from the production of a future historical narrative. If we are to believe that the authors understood the power of biographies and text in creating archive, then we must at the very least question what they intended to be remembered, to be forgotten, and why.

Prelude to Empire: Abolitionism and the Problems of Annexation

The recent news of the spread and successes of the insurrection has greatly elated the spirits of the Cuban citizens among us. They have unbounded faith that Cuba will soon become independent and finally annexed to the United States.
New York Times, 1869[70]

In December 1874, the very men that Casanova de Villaverde had attacked months earlier attended the funeral of Gerrit Smith, one of the most powerful, wealthy, and well-connected white abolitionists in

New York. A delegation from the Republican Central Junta of Cuba and Puerto Rico, which included José Antonio Echevarria, General López de Queralto of the Cuban Army, and "three distinguished citizens" eulogized Smith as the advocate of free Cuba in heart and soul and requested permission to present a floral wreath and send a committee of three to accompany the body to Peterboro, Smith's hometown in upstate New York. Also in attendance were African American abolitionists Henry Highland Garnet, Dr. Charles B. Ray, J. W. De Mulford, and Peter S. Porter.[71]

Known for his public and generous support of Cuban independence, Smith worked closely with Miguel de Aldama and, according to his biography, donated a thousand dollars to the Junta.[72] In a speech given on July 4, 1873 in Syracuse, Smith outlined what was already a familiar response to Cuban slavery and independence among abolitionists in New York. Using the Fourth of July celebrations as a springboard, Smith argued for the expansion of the "grand doctrine" that all men are created equal to push for the "deliverance of four million of our countrymen from the yoke of slavery."[73] In a rhetorical statement he asked the audience, "Now, why, in the light of these facts, should we not sympathize with Cuba, and make this fourth of July [sic] beautiful and blessed by expressing our sympathy with her?" Throughout the speech Smith expounds on the philosophical and political ideas previously expressed by the members of the Cuban Anti-Slavery Society, most notably, the belief that free people have a duty to extend those same rights and privileges to enslaved populations. This was no coincidence. Smith had close ties to the Cuban Anti-Slavery Society and in a letter addressed to the leaders in 1873, reiterated his support for African American abolitionists organizing around Cuba.[74] Echoing the ideas of the Cuban Anti-Slavery Society, Smith emphasized the close proximity of Cuba to the United States. Noting that the "island of Cuba is less than a hundred miles from us," Smith makes a case for not only protecting Cuba, but casting the people and island as an inalienable part of the United States. "Cuba, by force of geographical position and indissoluble commercial ties, is part of our country." He goes on to tell the audience in no uncertain terms that the Cuban is "our countryman."[75]

Despite their close ties, Smith and the members of the Cuban Anti-Slavery Society disagreed over the question of annexation. Interestingly enough, at a meeting held to commemorate the ninth anniversary of the beginning of the Ten Years' War, Smith's early biographer Reverend Octavius Brooks Frothingham spoke of Smith's "proposition to annex Cuba to the United States 25 years ago." The idea was that once slavery ended in the United States, an annexed Cuba "would share in the blessing." The problem, as Frothingham acknowledged, was that Smith was the only abolitionist at the time "who wanted it done."[76] While abolitionists were at odds with Smith's logic, his view on annexation resonated with members of the Cuban Junta who pushed for annexation as a postwar solution for ending slavery, and more importantly, for securing economic and social protections in Cuba.[77]

At the same meeting, the members of the American Foreign Anti-Slavery Society met to reinforce their commitment to insurgency and to again challenge the United States' position on slavery in Cuba. Held at the Cooper Institute on October 24, 1877, the meeting was crowded to "its utmost capacity," with a third of those present being African American and with "many ladies in the audience and on the platform." Reverend Henry Highland Garnet, president of the Society, chaired the meeting and Reverend William Butler, second Vice president, read a series of resolutions denouncing the continued existence of slavery in Cuba and told the audience in no uncertain terms that "the only hope for the final liberation of the slaves is the success of the Cuban patriots." In an impassioned speech, Butler disclosed what had been an open secret: that despite the end of slavery in the United States, many US citizens "are owners of slaves and of estates worked by slaves in Cuba." Seeing this as both the height of hypocrisy and deeply dangerous to the future of liberation in the hemisphere, Butler demanded that the United States pass laws prohibiting US citizens from having any economic investment in slave property, and called on the government to place a duty on all products made from slave labor in Cuba, since according to Butler it was the "low price of slave labor that motivated Cuban planters to hold so tenaciously to their slaves." Butler's revelation was not new. African American abolitionists, including the members of the American Foreign Anti-Slavery Society, were aware of the United States' slave interest on the island and for years had campaigned against it.[78]

The problems of slavery and empire were on Garnet's mind when he gave a speech that evening. Concerned over whether the proposed

Cuban Republic could effectively enfranchise Afro-Cubans and secure post-revolutionary civil rights, Garnet exhibited a rare public display of uneasiness with the "Cuban question." After the members passed several resolutions calling for the end of slavery, including stricter controls on US citizens profiting from slavery in Cuba, Garnet urged Cubans in the audience "to accept no terms except for freedom in conformity with the Cuban Constitution of the Cuban Republic for black and whites alike."[79] Garnet's warning is telling. In past speeches, Garnet rarely, if ever, differentiated between white and black Cubans, especially in regard to freedom and nation-building in Cuba. He was not one to caution against the pitfalls of freedom. However, as the Ten Years' War neared its end, guarantees of equality and enfranchisement proved fleeting.

On June 6, 1878, less than a month after the war ended, General Antonio Maceo was the guest of honor at a reception given by Henry Highland Garnet at his home on 102 West Third Street in New York. In attendance were members of the American Foreign Anti-Slavery Society, including Samuel Scottron who met with Maceo a day earlier. While it is not clear what exactly was said at the reception, there is no doubt that slavery was discussed at length. In a letter addressed to General Antonio Maceo and published in the independista newspaper *La Verdad*—not to be confused with the pro-annexationist newspaper of the late 1840s and 1850s—Scottron congratulated Cubans for demanding "the immediate abolition of slavery as a price for your allegiance."[80] The immediate abolition of slavery, however, would have to wait. In 1878 the rebel leadership in Cuba signed the Pact of Zanjón, which ended the Ten Years' War. The pact did not abolish slavery nor give Cubans their independence. Antonio Maceo, for one, denounced the pact and refused to sign.[81] A year later, Cuban rebels mounted what turned out to be an unsuccessful second attempt at independence. Known as La Guerra Chiquita, the war lasted no more than a year and further delayed full emancipation.

Garnet's concerns over slavery were warranted. Despite years of working with the Cuban Anti-Slavery Society and the American Foreign Anti-Slavery Society, he did not live to see the end of slavery in Cuba. On February 12, 1882 Garnet died. Named US Minister to Liberia in 1880, he was given a state funeral by the Liberian government as well as several formal sermons and eulogies in the United States, including one given by his close friend, Alexander Crummell, in Washington, DC and another at the Cooper Union in New York. In attendance that evening was the Cuban poet and revolutionary José Martí who had arrived in New York two years earlier.[82]

The memorial service at the Cooper Union was particularly impressive for the number of African Americans who attended, the distinguished religious and political leaders seated at the platform, and the uncompromising eulogy of Richard T. Greener, past dean of Howard University law school, who reminded the audience of Garnet's many accomplishments and the lack of recognition he received outside of the African American community. He spoke of Garnet's early enslavement, difficult childhood, and struggle to be educated. In addition, Greener made a point to mention that Garnet's speeches had not been archived in the National Library, and therefore not worthy of historical memory. "I went to the Congressional Library yesterday and was unable to find a copy of the speech delivered in the Capitol by Dr. Garnet in 1865. How can the negro be remembered when such speeches are not to be found in the National Library?" Greener left his sharpest comments for the end. Noting that the Republican Party and the city of New York did little to acknowledge Garnet's many accomplishments, Greener declared that "Dr. Garnet's services in behalf of his party were not thought worthy of reward until the last moment, and then from a wing of the Republican Party with which he had not an avowed sympathy." He concluded his speech by reminding the audience that "New York was always proud of her adopted son, but its politicians took care not to weigh him down with too many honors." The ceremony ended with a benediction from Reverend Dr. Deems.[83]

In December 1883, more than a year after Garnet's death, the members of the American Foreign Anti-Slavery Society met in Brooklyn at the home of the First Vice President Charles Dorsey. Called together by Greener, the members agreed that the best way to honor Garnet's legacy was to continue with the American Foreign Anti-Slavery Society. The members had not met since Garnet's death, and even though only a few attended the meeting, it was agreed that there still needed to "be more earnest action" in the campaigns "against slavery in Cuba, Brazil, and the slave trade in Africa, which appears from the latest accounts to be more active than it has been for a few years past." Greener singled out the Moret Law as a major problem facing slaves in Cuba. Approved in Spain on July 4, 1879, the law, which was intended to provide gradual emancipation, did not, as Greener noted, "give the speedy relief that the cause of humanity demands." While it secured a few "their nominal freedom," the Moret law left "the freemen worse off than before."[84] Seen by the Spanish colonial government as the logical outcome of the Ten Years' War, the Moret Law only granted freedom to children born of enslaved mothers, slaves born after September 17, 1868, to those who served in the Spanish army, to those over sixty years of age, and to those who were owned by the Spanish government. These freedoms, as Rebecca Scott writes, were "limited, compromised, and, in many cases, quite illusory."[85]

The Moret Law was reason enough for the members of the American Foreign Anti-Slavery Society to continue to advocate for the suppression of the slave trade, and pressure the US government to "lend the weight of its moral influence to the cause of humanity." The members also put pressure on the Cuban Junta, who they believed were simply not doing enough to end slavery on the island. In August 1883, a few months before the meeting, Samuel Scottron wrote a letter to Colonel Fernando López de Queralto calling attention to the Moret Law. Published in the *New York Globe*, Scottron stressed the disappointment of those "who have watched and waited for substantial results from these latest measures of the Spanish Government for the abolition of slavery and the slave trade." In a comment reminiscent of his earlier work with the Cuban Anti-Slavery Society, Scottron invokes the African American community support for freedom in his reading of emancipation in Cuba.

> Considering how hopeless seems the cause of liberty in Cuba, that human slavery there will ever end except by violent means, any light, however feeble, that arises and gives promise of the desired end must be heartily supported and welcomed by the colored people of the United States, and by the lovers of freedom everywhere.

López de Queralto did not respond to Scottron. Instead, he had General Ramón Leocadio Bonachea, who was traveling in New York and Philadelphia raising funds for the third attempt at independence, write a letter reassuring Scottron that the decree "abolishing slavery in Cuba, will be not only respected, but enforced." Bonachea's guarantee proved ephemeral at best. Despite his promises, it would take another three years before slavery ended in Cuba.[86]

Toward the end of the evening the members revealed another major reason for calling the evening on such short notice: to honor and pay "the respect due to the memory of the late President, Reverend Henry Highland Garnet, D. D." The members had done little to recognize Garnet's critical role in the society and decided to draft resolutions commemorating his service to the American Foreign Anti-Slavery Society, "even at so late a date, to make this public acknowledgement of his great services in the cause for which this Society was organized." After adopting the resolutions, the acting President Charles A. Dorsey set their next meeting for the first week in January 1884 in New York City.[87]

The American Foreign Anti-Slavery Society continued to meet, albeit less frequently. By the late 1880s, the society eventually disbanded. This did not mean, however, that African Americans were no longer involved in hemispheric racial politics. By the turn of the century, some of the members, most notably Samuel Scottron, shifted their focus to the Spanish-American War and US colonial policies in Puerto Rico, Cuba, and the Philippines, to curious effect.

The Curious Politics of Samuel Scottron

His [African-American] home is wherever the American flag is unfurled and he will cheerfully give his whole self to the development of every inch of territory acquired by his government.
Samuel Scottron, 1899[88]

On October 5, 1900, at a reception held at the Henry Highland Garnet Colored Republican Club located on Fulton Street near Lewis Avenue in Brooklyn, Samuel Scottron was invited to give a speech. His appearance that evening evoked great applause, and it was several minutes before he could begin to speak. Scottron was now in his late fifties and since 1894 had served on the Brooklyn board of education, the only African American appointed to it.[89] But on this evening Scottron harkened back to what he considered to be "one of the greatest national campaigns since the Civil War"—the campaign to acquire and control Spain's last territorial possessions. In a speech where he warned those in attendance to "not be deceived by the cries of the Democratic party that we are denying liberty to Cuba, Porto Rico and the Philippines," Scottron characterized President McKinley as a wise and thoughtful man who is "pursuing a course in the interest of the people of these islands."[90]

Scottron, it appeared, had a change of heart when it came to Cuban self-determination and governance. "They are not ready yet; they are not quite intelligent enough to appreciate a government of their own. It will not be long before they will have reached the stage of intelligence and then they will be given the reins of government in their own hands."[91] After years of tirelessly supporting the Cuban insurrection, Scottron now believed that Cubans, Puerto Ricans, and Filipinos were "not quite intelligent enough to appreciate a government of their own." It is not exactly clear why Scottron changed his mind about Cuba. He gives no explanation of the sort. What is evident is that his involvement with the Republican Party and close relationship with Booker T. Washington influenced his view of the "races of men that the fortune of war has placed under our care."[92]

By the turn of the century Scottron had become a controversial figure known for his writings condemning uncouth and "ill-bred" African American migrants who moved to New York from the South. He used his position as the sole African American member on the Brooklyn school board to argue for the importance of public education in assimilating and "polishing" a population that he argued had added to "our troubles." Scottron, as Craig Wilder writes, "typified the elite people of color, who reacted to the advent of two-tier democracy by trying to define themselves as a distinct social group worthy of greater liberties." He was part of an African American community that was loyal to the Republican Party, conscious of their past in the city, anti-immigrant, and "careful stewards of colored institutions." But he was also, as Wilder observed, part of a community that "championed the cause of people who were stripped of political power; paradoxically, doing so while seeking social distance from the group."[93]

Samuel Raymond Scottron was born free in 1843 in Philadelphia. Six years later his family moved to New York, and in 1852 to Brooklyn, where he lived for the rest of his life. He married Anna Maria Pellet, fathered six children, and moved into a tall, narrow brownstone on the corner of Stuyvestant Avenue and Monroe Street in the well-to-do neighborhood of Stuyvestant Heights. The Scottrons, as Gail Lumet writes, were among the "first fifty black families to settle there."[94] Scottron garnered much attention for being a prolific inventor and entrepreneur who secured a number of patents for his many inventions, insuring his eventual wealth. The most famous were the adjustable window cornice (1880), a curtain rod (1892), supporting bracket (1893) and what came to be known as Scottron's adjustable mirror, which he invented while working as a barber to help his customers better see the sides, rear, and top of their heads.

In 1904, the *Colored American Magazine* featured his adjustable mirrors, writing that the mirrors were arranged opposite each other to "give the view of every side at once." The mirrors were so successful that it allowed him to open a new firm at 658 Broadway Street in New York City under the name of Pitkin and Scottron. Over the next twenty years Scottron established a number of businesses with different partners. He worked as a traveling salesman, general manager for an export-import business, and always, as an inventor. He continued to secure patents for his inventions well into his late fifties.[95]

Although he spent most of his time in New York, Scottron did travel to South Carolina in 1863, and then a year later to Florida to assist freed men to vote during the first general election. In 1865 he represented the African American residents of Fernandina, Florida at the National Colored Convention held in Syracuse. By all accounts his time in the South was short-lived. Yet, his experiences proved to be a defining moment.[96] After returning to New York, Scottron became involved in the African American anti-slavery movement. In May 1875, three years after co-founding the Cuban Anti-Slavery Society, Scottron graduated from the Cooper Union, with a degree in Algebra.[97] He was also, like many of his contemporaries, a Freemason. In 1879, he was elected Secretary General of the Freemasons, and was a thirty-third-degree Mason, belonging to a temple founded in pre-Revolutionary Boston.[98] Through his involvement with Freemasonry, Scottron established close relationships with a number of African American Freemasons, including Garnet, Crummell, and Booker T. Washington. In fact, according to Joanna Brooks, almost "every free black male political leader of the nineteenth century, with the notable exception of Frederick Douglass, was also a Prince Hall Freemason."[99] Scottron was also known among Afro-Cuban Freemasons, such as Rafael Serra, who published a brief account of Scottron in his collection of political essays.[100]

Scottron's friendship with Booker T. Washington ran deep. In *The Negro in Business*, Washington devoted an entire chapter to Scottron's life and career. Entitled "Samuel Scottron, Inventor, Manufacturer, and Friend of His Race," Washington begins the chapter by writing that "Perhaps no man of the Negro race has shown such versatility in the field of invention as Mr. Samuel R. Scottron of Brooklyn, New York." He highlights his many inventions, and interestingly enough, gives credit to his wife and two daughters for their role in his success. In explaining his 1894 invention of "porcelain onyx," a process to make glass look like onyx, Washington writes that it was Mrs. Scottron and their two daughters that "superintend and actively do the secret work in the process of manufacture [*sic*] of artificial onyx."

Washington also mentions that Scottron is a writer and speaker of "force and acumen" upon subjects connected with "the welfare of his race," not only in this country, "but elsewhere, in the West Indies and in Africa." Although Washington cites Scottron's transnationalist and global activism, including the founding of both anti-slavery societies, he is most interested in his post–Spanish-American War writings. Washington points to the articles published in the *New York Age* and one in particular, written to the *Boston Herald* in 1890, challenging the editorials for unfavorably comparing "the Negro to the Chinese as American citizens." The article, Washington asserts, "was very much quoted, and is, to use Mr. Scottron's words, [*sic*] 'the one thing that I should like to see perpetuated in some form.'"[101]

The writings that Scottron's desired to see perpetuated, and that Washington endorsed, reveal a man who, despite his past involvement to liberate Cuba from Spain, was uneasy with the manifestations and workings of sovereignty and self-government. The articles were part of a series that ran under the heading "Mr. Scottron's Views," and published in the *Brooklyn Eagle*. In it, Scottron ruminates on how the "newly acquired territories" will impact the African American labor force and challenge the idea, perpetuated by the *Boston Herald*, of an "unsolved negro problem." Responding to critics who considered African Americans inferior to the newly arrived "Asiatic races," Scottron argued for "the nation's interest in the disposition of or employment of the negro."[102]

In a section entitled "Chinese Versus Negroes," Scottron, who admitted to writing "from memory," questions the articles published in the

Boston Herald that cast the Chinese as "an ancient race with a civilization antedating our own," and the African American as "a barbarian, a slave, mean of intellect and of forbidding mien with thick lips, black face, flat nose and woolly hair; who has not in the interval time shown the high capacity of the Caucasian for improvement." Explaining that his fundamental interest was to support asylum for Chinese workers—thereby challenging the Chinese Exclusion Act—Scottron calls for the end of the act, "Were the fears which moved the American people in the past to exclude Asiatic races justified, or have we seen a new light?" At the same time, he makes a case for African American workers by employing a discourse on African American citizenship and cultural relativity.

> Since the negro is already admitted to citizenship guarded by constitutional enactment, and whatever may be the difference of opinions as to his mental capacity, as compared with Caucasian or Asiatic, there nevertheless remains the gratifying fact that no one has attempted to prove that his presence is in the least threatening to our Christian institutions.[103]

Scottron's uses of citizenship here are markedly different than the ones employed to justify African American support for Cuban insurrection. In the past, Scottron used citizenship and the "rights of freedom" to inspire African Americans to fight against slavery in the hemisphere. By the turn of the century, Scottron used African American citizenship and the ability of African Americans to "assimilate into the body politic," to advocate for their employment and, moreover, distinguish them from the thousands of immigrants arriving every day to New York. "The negro came with his mind blank, with no preconceived opinions as to forms of government, no attachment to a foreign flag or institutions. No flag, only the American flag; no home save America."[104]

Despite its brief tenure, the Cuban Anti-Slavery Society illustrates the possibility and limits of African American hemispheric political organizing and thinking during the nineteenth century, what Earl Lewis writes is the need to move past one's historical imagination. At the same time, the Cuban Anti-Slavery Society demonstrates the workings of suspect and complicated freedoms and the desire to resolve and translate them outside of the self. In choosing to organize around Cuban insurgency, members of the Cuban Anti-Slavery and American Foreign Anti-Slavery Societies sought to both transfer their anti-slavery politics and redefine the discourse on hemispheric and local civil rights. They also intended to create an expansive African diasporic identity and community. Unfortunately, there were limits. By the turn of the century the radical pro-independence discourse so common to African American men changed. The public articulation of a shared African diasporic political reality dissipated as men like Scottron, fought, with painful interest, to enfranchise and empower African Americans within a nation that wanted little to do with them.

3

In Darkest Anonymity

Labor, Revolution, and the Uneasy Visibility of Afro-Cubans in New York, 1880–1901

Many of the figures that helped found The Cuban Revolutionary Party remain in the darkest anonymity today; relegated there by a bourgeois historiography, which does not find it convenient to highlight the vanguard role of the working-class, cigar-workers, typographers, and workers from the masses of emigrated revolutionaries from Tampa, Key West, and New York.
Josefina Toledo[1]

Socialism is the leveling, not of riches, but of the rights of man to acquire them, to possess them, to enjoy them. It is not equality of fortunes, no, it is individual equality to gain access to them.
Martín Morúa Delgado, 1884[2]

New York is becoming a vortex: whatever boils over anywhere else in the world spills into New York.
José Martí, 1883[3]

Every whiff, then, of cigar smoke blown in New York from a Cuban cigar made here, means so much powder and ball to be sent to the island for its emancipation.
New York Times, 1871[4]

On August 5, 1883, a group of Cuban migrants "composed principally of cigar-makers, many of whom are negroes," met in the basement of Clarendon Hall in New York City to "perfect its organization." Settling on the name El Club de los Independientes No. 1, the members elected Cirilo Pouble, the editor of *El Separatista* and current treasurer of El Comité Revolucionario Cubano, its first president and created a Board of Trustees that included Justo Lanigua, Martín Morúa Delgado, Rafael Serra, and Vicente Diascosmas, some of the most important pro-independence and pro-labor revolutionaries in the city. That evening the members, which included Leandro Rodríguez and Juan Beldeido de Luna, listened to Martín Morúa Delgado read a paper describing the current condition in Cuba, which according to him "was ripe for revolution." Morúa Delgado, who had arrived a year earlier, in 1882, explained that the veterans of the last revolution who had seen ten years of service in the field, were anxious to again "raise the standards of liberty." With that, the members recognized General Ramón Leocadia Bonachea as a "true Cuban patriot" and pledged the club's funds and support to him, and to the revolutionary effort in Cuba.[5]

A general in La Guerra Chiquita, the failed second attempt at liberation, Bonachea met with key figures in the movement, including the members of El Comité de Nueva York. He wrote editorials, gave speeches, and did everything possible to raise money and gather support from the New York Cuban exile community. By the end of the year Bonachea was in Jamaica, meeting with Cuban revolutionaries living and organizing in Kingston.[6]

Bonachea's decision to go to Jamaica made perfect sense. In addition to clubs located in the United States, there were Cuban revolutionary clubs in Haiti, the Dominican Republic, Venezuela, Panama, Nicaragua, Mexico, and Costa Rica. In 1892 there were five clubs in Haiti alone, including El Club Hijas de Martí and El Club Guarionex y Hatuey.[7] Their importance was not lost on the newly elected president of El Club de los Independiente No. 1, Cirilo Pouble, who discussed his own recent travels to Vera Cruz, where he met with members of El Club Político Cubano Bartolome Masó, which counted Rafael Serra as one of its honorary members, and with the all-female club Máximo Gómez, who sent "greetings to their fellow countrymen in this city."[8] By the time Pouble traveled to Mexico there were already a large number of Cuban revolutionary clubs located throughout the hemisphere. As early as 1873, the *New York Times* reported on the "Cuban exile societies" with branches in Jamaica, Brussels, Paris, London, and in "many places in South America."[9] These clubs were part of a circuit of information, mobility, and knowledge designed to expand the movement's political scope and organize the large number of Cubans and Puerto Ricans who left the island, but did not move to the United States. Through printed media, temporalities, and constructed nationalist desires, Cuban and Puerto Rican revolutionaries cultivated a shared nationalist discourse that not only traveled but was also recognized and used to cultivate a larger hemispheric belonging.

By end of the Ten Years' War a number of Afro-Cuban men moved throughout the Americas on behalf of different New York revolutionary organizations. Afro-Cuban members of El Club de los Independientes No. 1, Rafael Serra and Martín Morúa Delgado, traveled throughout Latin America disseminating El Plan Gómez-Maceo (1884)—which called for another attempt at revolution—meeting with revolutionaries, and forming clubs. Some, like Serra, took the opportunity to write and reflect on his experiences living outside of Cuba and the United States. After leaving Panama, Serra arrived in Kingston in 1885 and published "Ecos del alma, Ensayo literario," which he dedicated to Antonio Maceo's wife, María Cabrales de Maceo. Years later, in 1894, the Afro-Puerto Rican revolutionary Sotero Figueroa spent time in Central America "completing urgent tasks."[10]

In addition to their activism, Afro-Cuban migrants wrote continuously and published often. They authored critical and incisive texts on race, enfranchisement, labor, civil rights, and the meaning of nation. While in New York, Morúa Delgado wrote for *El Pueblo* and *La República*.[11] In 1886 Serra published one of his earlier pieces, *Ideas y pensamientos, Album poético, político y literario* and, in 1892, *Ensayos políticos*. Three years later, in 1895 he founded and edited two major newspapers: *La Doctrina de Martí: La República con todo y para todos* and *La Verdad*. Headquartered at 122 West 33rd Street, the newspapers circulated throughout Mexico, Central America, and the Caribbean. Emiliana Bravo, secretary of Hijas de Martí in Port au Prince, thanked Serra "with all the effusion of my soul" for sending her copies of *La Doctrina de Martí*. Serra's old friend Dr. José A Malberti, president of the El Club Político Cubano Bartolome Masó based in Mexico, wrote to thank him for publishing such "an important newspaper for all Cubans," while María Cabrales de Maceo wrote from Costa Rica to wish the newspaper "much life."[12]

The period after the Ten Years' War and before the Cuban War for Independence was a prolific period for Afro-Cuban activism and intellectual production in New York. The final end to Cuban slavery in 1886 along with the rise of the labor movement in New York created a powerful space for Afro-Cubans to organize around independence, equality, and the future of wage labor in Cuba. An implicit element in the remaking was mobility, intellectual thought, social justice, self-expression, and control over their labor. Although rarely articulated, the discourse on labor was directly correlated to securing social and economic enfranchisement within an imagined post-slavery society in Cuba. Afro-Cuban migrants envisioned a world without slavery, one they were determined to name and dictate.

Such ideas, however, were not always palatable to white Cuban separatists. The growing prominence of Afro-Cuban writers, editors, activists, and labor organizers did not sit well with white Cuban separatist leaders and elites who were accustomed to dealing with race as metaphor and argument. White Cuban separatist leaders were not ready or willing to accept Afro-Cuban visibility and intellectual authority on their own merit. It was left up to white Cuban sympathizers, José Martí, Enrique Trujillo, Benjamin Guerra, and Juan Fraga, to translate and articulate Afro-Cuban experience and thought within the separatist and revolutionary movement. But this proved more difficult and complicated than expected.

Afro-Cuban men who migrated during this period were, as F. V. Domínguez explained, not only "looking for work," but also had a great desire to rupture "the irons of domination." They were, as Domínguez continued, determined to end the legacy of slavery, oppression, and create a world of their own making.[13] Yet, the idea of a racially enfranchised nationalism remained a vague and problematic premise that had more to do with convenient, momentary promises than with concrete solutions. Widely credited for integrating blackness into the Cuban exile nationalist movement, José Martí was nonetheless conflicted and equivocal when it came to discussing and solving the "race problem."

In examining Martí's "circuitous writing and contradictory discourse," what Lillian Guerra writes is the "dissonance between his private and public correspondence," Guerra found that no such terms as "racial equality" or "social equality" ever appeared in his writings, speeches, or correspondence (whether public or private). As Martí famously extolled the impossibility of race and racial hatred in his writings and speeches, he silenced what Guerra calls the persistent racial hatred that "remained primary obstacles to both social unity and social peace." Her findings on Martí are particularly revealing considering that black intellectuals close to Martí did not hesitate to use such direct terminology in their own writings. And yet, Martí continued to have the broad support of Afro-Cubans on the island and among émigrés.[14] Given the circumstances, another reading is that Martí actively cultivated an alliance with Afro-Cubans to assist with mediating larger tensions and disputes with regard to labor. As long as he had the full support of Afro-Cubans, many of whom were cigar workers and advocates of Cuban independence and labor rights, he could neutralize the growing labor conflicts and divisions within the separatist movement.

When Martí arrived in New York in 1880 the revolutionary movement was in crisis. Martí knew that unless the separatist leaders expanded the movement's platform to include race and labor, they would be rendered irrelevant. In a speech given in 1888 at the Masonic Hall on 23rd Street and 6th Avenue, Martí expressed his dissatisfaction with the current direction of the separatist movement. He told the audience gathered that evening that there was only one "aristocracy; that of the workers; and that there was only one color: those of honorable men who love freedom."[15] Four years earlier, General Máximo Gómez also commented on the growing class division and resentment among Cubans. In 1884, in a letter he addressed to Juan Arnao, treasurer of El Club de los Independiente No. 1, Gómez wrote that the movement was made up of two sections: "one aristocratic and the other democratic." Knowing full well that the movement could not count on the aristocratic, he argued that the rebellion would have "to depend on the poor class, the people, always the people." They, Gómez asserted, are the ones "that will give us powder and bullets so we can take the field."[16]

The rise of labor and the ensuing challenges to traditional exile separatist politics almost derailed the exile independence and nationalist movements. The proliferation of Cuban cigar factories in New York, along with the increased migration of Afro-Cubans to work in those factories, unleashed a crisis of consciousness, a rethinking if you will, on the meanings of enfranchisement, labor, and the future role of Afro-Cubans in the republic.[17] Some Afro-Cubans who worked in the cigar industry, like Margarito Gutíerrez, a labor organizer, translator, and union delegate for Cuban cigar workers in New York, believed that labor, unlike the separatist movement, better represented the concerns of Afro-Cuban immigrant workers.[18]

From Martí's perspective, Gutíerrez posed a grave threat. He represented exactly what Martí hoped to avoid. In an effort to ensure that Afro-Cubans did not abandon the separatist movement, Martí included economic enfranchisement within a racially inclusive nationalism. The reinvention of an expansive nationalism signaled an important shift in the exile and immigrant movement. The leaders of the separatist and nationalist movements could no longer solely cater, at least in terms of rhetoric, to the interest of the elites in exile. The needs of a fast-growing working-class and poor Cuban exile and migrant community in New York had to be addressed. If not, the movement risked a complete unraveling.

By the late 1880s the relationship between the Cuban working class and the independence movement in New York and Florida was, as Gerald Poyo writes, "not always cordial."[19] In fact, it was hostile. Workers were deeply frustrated with a separatist leadership that supported manufacturers over workers, and suspected that "cigar capitalists" manipulated the patriot movement to their advantage; "that is, they used it to suppress strikes in the name of Cuban independence."[20] By 1875, tensions were brewing between the separatist movement and Cuban cigar workers in New York. That year, cigar workers staged a series of strikes challenging the conservative faction of the separatist movement led by Miguel de Aldama. They rejected Aldama's call for a gradual end to slavery, and instead supported General Manuel de Quesada's demand for revolution and an immediate end to slavery, cementing the relationship among labor rights and abolitionism within the radical separatist movement.[21] As the divide between the two sides grew, workers openly questioned the viability of the Aldamista-led junta, which supported manufacturers over workers, challenged labor demands, and called for quick settlements of disputes, often at the expense of workers. The tensions between the Aldamistas and Quesadistas led to the dissolution of several clubs, including the Sociedad de Artesanos de Brooklyn and the Sociedad de Artesanos Cubanos. In turn, the Quesadistas founded the Sociedad Independencia de Cuba in 1873; and later, the Sociedad Caja de Ahorros de los Tabaqueros de New York.[22]

In 1883, the same year that El Club de los Independientes No. 1 was formed, one of its members, Martín Morúa Delgado, published "La cuestión obrera." The article, which examined the labor movement in the United States and within the Cuban exile and migrant community, encouraged the rise of local and international labor unions, and employed a theoretical reading of labor as intrinsically tied to character and honor. Morúa Delgado supported the eight-hour workday, declaring that "eight hours of work is enough," and predicted that the working class would "soon be free," making social revolution "inevitable." He challenged manufacturers who took advantage of workers and who planted anti-labor articles designed to undermine labor unions and strikers.[23]

Although Morúa Delgado was sympathetic to labor, he did not idealize all workers. In a related piece he discussed the strikes taking place in April 1883 in the Bowery among what he called the irregular and regular. "I said regular and irregular because around here there are two types of cigar makers; those who come together to defend themselves from the dominion or the devil of capital; and others who have decided to not come together." According to Morúa Delgado, those who do not come together are content to continue working under unfair conditions, with no change in sight.[24] That same year, Cuban cigar workers formed La Unión de Torcedores (the Cigar Maker's Union), an organization with ties to the separatist movement. Although tensions existed, workers were not ready to leave the separatist movement, especially if there was a chance they could be part of the labor movement and still support Cuban independence. The challenge was how to negotiate the demands of cigar manufacturers and capitalists with the call to end Spanish colonialism on the island.

Despite their efforts, the relationship between workers and management reached a boiling point three years later when eighty-three Cuban cigar makers went on strike. The response of the separatist leadership was quick and ruthless. They labeled the strikers unpatriotic and denounced them for going on strike. La Unión de Torcedores, which portended to have a civil relationship with manufactures, responded by printing a manifesto declaring the separatist leadership "hostile to labor."[25] Previous attempts to merge labor and separatist politics under the banner of Cubanidad had failed. Cuban labor organizers and anarchists criticized the exile separatist movement for being insular and irrelevant. In turn, separatist leaders refused to include labor or workers' rights into the separatist agenda, wrongly assuming that the struggle for Cuban independence was enough to insure unity, regardless of the social and economic inequities among Cuban exiles and migrants.

What the leadership failed to understand was that workers were looking past independence toward enfranchisement and nation-building. Workers wanted a stake in defining and establishing nation and republicanism, even if it meant dismantling it. It was with this in mind that José C. Campos, a white Cuban cigar maker, printer, and leader of the Unión de Torcedores, organized workers against the separatist leadership. Campos was angry at the leadership for using exile newspapers to smear workers who made labor demands. Their actions were especially egregious considering that most, if not all, of the official separatist newspapers were financed by cigar makers' continuous donations. As Joan Casanovas writes, Campos argued that "workers felt betrayed," and urged cigar workers to stop "financing periodicals that insulted them." The answer, according to Campos, was to form separate organizations "to preserve their freedom."[26]

The claim that the separatist leadership restricted the freedom of workers and independistas was serious. This caused workers to question the intentions and motives of the leadership, particularly with regard to independence. Labor unrest and tensions continued throughout most of the 1880s, with some Cuban cigar workers looking to the Knights of Labor for support.[27] The Chicago Haymarket Strike of May 4, 1886 proved to be the catalyst needed for Cuban workers to distance themselves from the separatist movement, and, as Gerald Poyo writes, be "more receptive to anarchist ideals."[28] In July 1887 immigrant workers in New York, including Campos, founded an anarcho-collectivist group. Campos would later become the New York correspondent for El Productor of Barcelona, the most important anarchist periodical in Spain between 1887 and 1893. In 1891, Campos founded an anarchist weekly in New York, El Despertar (1891–1902), with "the collaboration of several separatist workers."[29]

Cuban workers were now publicly questioning the very premise and utility of the exile separatist movement. For Martí personally, the Haymarket Strike and the ensuing trial would be a turning point. Shortly after the strike and during the early stages of the trial, Martí published an article in *La Nación*, expressing "little or no sympathy for the anarchists and no doubt at all about their guilt."[30] As he learned more about the strike he changed his mind. Less than a year later, Martí wrote an essay sympathetic to both the strike and the anarchists who were sentenced to die for their actions. He singled out the factory owners who "threw out the workers who came to present their demands as if they were mangy dogs to be kicked into the street," and challenged the harsh sentence levied against the eight anarchists, with seven condemned to death. In an impassioned defense of not only the anarchists but the future of labor and worker's rights in the United States, Martí wrote that "Their anarchy was government by order, not by force, their dream a new world without misery or slavery, their sorrow the belief that selfishness will never yield to justice by peaceful means."[31] For Martí, there was no going back. Labor, whether the separatist leadership liked it or not, needed to be part of the independista and nationalist discourse.

It was within this context that La Liga sociedad de instrucción y recreó (1890) and the Partido Revolucionario Cubano (1892) were formed to solidify a movement that was unraveling. It was no coincidence that blackness as trope and metaphor entered the exile nationalist discourse precisely at the moment when the movement was at its most precarious. As theory and rhetoric, a sanctioned definition of blackness proved to be an effective tool in cultivating unity, lessening the urgency of labor, silencing the legacy of slavery, and dulling the growing controversies surrounding wage labor in Cuba.

The "Cuban Quarter": The Cuban Cigar Industry in New York

Cuban cigars made in New York are greatly in demand, for if not superior to imported, they are, at least on an average quite as good as those made in Havana and why should they not be, some of the very best of the Cuban workmen have left the island.

New York Times, 1871[32]

The rise of the Cuban cigar industry in New York was swift and impressive. As early as 1871 the *New York Times* reported on the recent popularity of Cuban cigars and the dramatic increase in the migration of Cuban workers to the city. After "somewhat careful estimation," the *Times* reported that close to 5,000 cigar workers arrived in the United States to work in factories located in Charleston, Baltimore, Philadelphia, New York, and Boston, with the "largest factory in New York where some sixty find employment." Before the Ten Years' War cigars made in New York were, in the words of the *New York Times*, "execrable." "Five years ago if told by an honest vendor that the cigar was made here, we would have turned up our noses at it."[33] Revolution it appears had been good to New York City cigar smokers. In 1885, there were close to 800 factories in Brooklyn alone. A year later, in 1886, there were more than 1,800 cigar factories in Manhattan, surpassing the number in Florida.[34]

The growth of the Cuban cigar industry in New York was directly related to the violence and chaos of the Ten Years' War. During the war, tobacco plantations burned and factories were destroyed, leaving the cigar industry in ruins. Manufacturers relocated their businesses to the United States. Cuban workers who moved to New York labored in the Spanish- and later Cuban-owned factories on Maiden Lane, Pearl, Nassau, and Water Streets. By 1894, there were no less than nine Cuban-owned factories on Pearl Street, with the popular López Havana Cigar Company located a few blocks away on 86 Maiden Lane.[35] Cubans worked in factories situated on the upper end of Maiden Lane, where they "sit up in high lofts and shake out the odors of tobacco rare and stupefying to intoxicate the passengers who go up and down Pearl Street on the elevated railroad." It was in these "aerial factories" that Cubans, described as "small, slender, sallow, black-eyed men," prepared, sorted, and compacted "the dry nicotinum."[36] In one cigar store in Nassau Street, "already celebrated for its Cuban cigars made in the city," Cuban cigar makers were famous for "raising the cigars to their ears to see, or rather, hear how dry it was before handing them to their customers," all the while informing them that if the cigar was too dry, "it would snap."[37]

Highlighting the exceptional skill of Cuban cigar workers, the *New York Times* compared them unfavorably to German and North American cigar makers, who were far too "helter-skelter" in their methods. Cubans, on the other hand, lay their "pieces of leaf in the bunch side by side, so as to assure the burning of it evenly." Detailing all aspects of the cigar making process, the reporter commented on how Cubans "smoke cigars as they make them," and were so exact to the size, that very little trimming of the square end of the cigar is necessary. Nothing "could exceed the skill of these workmen."[38]

Taking note of the seemingly unified support for Cuban independence, the New York Times reported that, "To a man, all Cuban cigar makers in the United States are patriots, and bitterly opposed to Spain. From their wages they contribute largely to the cause of Cuban liberty."[39] As one of the more rebellious elements of Cuban society, cigar workers brought their politics, ideologies, and activism to New York. In addition to forming labor unions, they helped to fund and organize the radical independence movement, challenged the rise of capital and industrialism, and went on strike. Because cigar work was, for the most part, an economically stable job, cigar makers were called on to donate to revolutionary clubs, mutual aid societies, labor unions, and the war effort. Cigar workers were so faithful and generous that Cuban military leaders and politicians made a point to visit the many New York cigar factories in search of funds. Few left empty-handed.

The Spanish- and Cuban-owned cigar factories in New York were racially integrated, with black and white Cuban men sitting next to each other at the long wooden tables rolling cigars. Cuban cigar workers exerted an inordinate control over their time, labor, and production. Workers moved freely throughout the factory, selecting and weighing tobacco leaves, drinking Cuban coffee, smoking cigars, and talking with other workers. The freedom of movement and control over production made the factory floor a politically and intellectually engaged space perfect for organizing. It was no surprise then that workers seriously questioned the exile separatist movement and merged their alternative readings of revolutionary Cuban politics with critiques of capital and industrialism.

One of the more coveted traditions brought to the United States was the reader, "el lector," who read to the workers several hours every day in Spanish and "was paid for his services."[40] The lectores read newspapers, journals, and pamphlets, including works by Marx, Bahktin, Plutarch, as well as popular novels of the period, such as those authored by Hugo and Dumas.[41] The workers voted on what would be read, how it *should* be read, and by whom. They registered their delight by clapping, whistling, or hitting the *chaveta* against metal plates. Just as easily, cigar workers heckled and demanded that lectores be fired. Responsible for their salaries, cigar workers were quick to replace anyone who did not measure up to their standards.[42]

The factories were highly masculinist sites that prohibited women from certain trades. Cuban women were given the least skilled jobs: tobacco leaf stemmers, bunchers, and floor sweepers. Some women operated independent cigar stands known as chinchalles or buckeyes, where they sold surplus cigars at a cheaper price. In the chinchalles, women rolled cigars and sold them directly to customers. It was not uncommon for Cuban women to work out of crowded tenement apartments making cigars and caring for their families.

Prohibited from male-dominated networks in the factories, Cuban women were nonetheless active in strikes, political action, and establishing their own labor unions. Stemmers organized a union, "un gremio de despalilladores," and went on strike with the men. Demanding an increase in pay, women held meetings, distributed materials, raised funds, attended rallies, and were involved in organizing other women in the community.[43] Afro-Cuban women also worked as laundresses, domestic workers, dressmakers, and boarding-house keepers.[44] Margaret Murdoch left Cuba in her late teens to work as a servant, while Ms. Rose, already well into her forties, migrated from Cuba to work as a cook. A number of women listed in the 1860 census as "negro" and Cuban have English and French last names, indicating that they were children of Jamaican, Haitian, as well as other British and French colonial West Indian parents who settled in Cuba to work in the sugar industry. As free Caribbean migrants they had the mobility necessary to migrate during the 1860s, before and during the Ten Years' War.[45] These were the women who initiated political networks and were instrumental in assisting Afro-Cubans who arrived in the 1880s with finding housing, work, and building important social connections within the larger Afro-Cuban and West Indian community. As Irma Watkins-Owens has documented, there was an effective and powerful network among different Afro-diasporic women and men in New York, despite the differences in language and culture.[46]

The growth of the cigar industry spurred the development of immigrant enclaves in the downtown and waterfront areas. Afro-Cuban migrants, men and women, worked in the restaurants that filled the "Cuban quarter." Built to feed the hungry cigar workers, the restaurants remained empty until noon when suddenly, they were crowded and filled with hungry workers from Cuba, the Philippines, Mexico, Venezuela, Costa Rica, Colombia, Paraguay, Brazil, Portugal, and China. Within minutes, smells of "garlic, tobacco leaves, and pimentos" enveloped the restaurants. A typical menu included white rice and black beans, arroz amarillo, arroz con pollo, fried liver, chopped kidneys, and bacalao. For dessert no Cuban restaurant was "ever quite complete" unless they served the small wooden boxes "containing the paste and the jelly of guava."[47]

One restaurant, "The House of Biscay," hired Afro-Cubans, expatriated Haitians, and Dominicans as waiters and cooks. In discussing what must have been a large number of Afro-diasporic workers cooking, cleaning, and serving clients, the New York Times used racist language replete with African stereotypes to describe a typical meal at the House of Biscay, what the Times called the "cordon bleu" of Cuban food. In the process, the reporter singled out one worker for particular vitriol.

> This is undeniably a cannibal of the Congo with his teeth filed till his mouth looks like the maw of a reptile, his hair bound with brass wire into little black and gold spikes that stick out all over his round cranium like quills upon a new variety of porcupine, the black face of the quality of shark skin gashed with Obeah scars. Altogether a savage and uncanny creature, he bends over his pots and pans, glistening with sweat, baring his alligator fangs and crooning in a mystical minor some legend of African mythology.[48]

The use of violent and degrading African imagery illustrates the reporter's inability to read diasporic and foreign blackness outside of the purview of savagery and the uncivilized. There is little if any indication of a larger hemispheric understanding of blackness that did not include racism, and stereotypes of Africa and being African.

Afro-Cubans, along with Haitians, Dominicans, Jamaicans, West Indians, and other black immigrants, experienced a great deal of discrimination and segregation. In a letter written to Tomás Estrada Palma in 1890, Rafael Serra commented on the difficulties of living in New York as a man of color. He spoke of the discrimination he experienced when looking for employment and adequate housing. He noted how few landlords rented to families of color, and when they did find housing, it was very expensive and located "muy arriba de la ciudad," away from the city center. The discrimination and racism in New York troubled Serra. He complained bitterly to friends, family, and colleagues. For Serra, it was only the "glorious hope of the triumph of the Cuban cause" that kept him going.[49]

Serra's experiences while living in New York, which included working in the cigar factories, attending regular meetings at the Masonic lodge, hearing lectures at the Cooper Institute, and visiting fellow Cubans throughout Manhattan and Brooklyn, reinforced what he believed was a deep and abiding racism in the United States. He questioned whether North Americans could ever transcend their racism, and was concerned that they would bring their brand of discrimination and prejudice to Cuba. This, more than anything else, is why he opposed the annexation of Cuba to the United States. Citing a long history of racism in the United States, he warned against annexation, especially for Afro-Cubans. "Once blackness enters the discourse, justice, humanity, and consciousness cease to exist for Americans."[50]

At the same time, Serra was aware of the racism within the Cuban exile and migrant community. He referred to it in his writings and chastised white Cuban migrants who practiced such divisiveness, considering it a betrayal to Cuban nationhood. In a letter to Martí he complained of the racism and prejudice he encountered as he struggled to form La Liga sociedad de instrucción y recreó. Martí's response is telling. He advised Serra to stop thinking about so many "injustices," and instead to rise above and act as though racism "didn't exist."[51] Martí's advice can be read in multiple ways. On the one hand, it is a call for Serra to remain focused and not be distracted by the discrimination, segregation, and exclusion experienced by Afro-Cuban migrants. On the other, it reflects Martí's tendency to minimize racism within the Cuban community in order to insure unity at all costs, even if it meant silencing the ever-present undercurrents of racism within the exile and migrant community.

Serra understood full well the complicated and contradictory racial and political relationships among Cubans in the diaspora and on the

Rafael Serra, 1907. Photographs and Prints Division, Schomburg Center for Research in Black Culture, New York Public Library, Astor, and Tilden Foundations.

island. Ideological and philosophical, he was nonetheless a realist when it came to working with white Cubans. He recognized that there were white Cubans who "in their noble efforts towards the independence of Cuba have proven themselves to be deserving of the trust of black Cubans." But he was also clear that white Cubans were not off the hook, especially when it came to independence. As Serra would later write, white Cubans "will acquire more love from their compatriots the day that in Cuba brotherhood and justice reigns for all."[52]

It was under these circumstances that Serra, along with small group of black and white Cuban and Puerto Rican men—José Martí, German Sandoval, José C. López, Juan Bonilla, and Enrique Trujillo—founded La Liga sociedad de instrucción y recreó. Designed to "elevate the character of men of color born in Cuba and Puerto Rico,"[53] La Liga was a diasporic experiment, one with roots in Cuba, but intended to meet the educational needs of black Cuban and Puerto Rican men in New York. In the words of Pedro Deschamps Chapeaux, La Liga was "a long time in coming." On October 10, 1888, at an event commemorating the beginning of the Ten Years' War, Serra publicly introduced the idea of a "sociedad de instrucción" for black Cuban and Puerto Rican men. Held at the Masonic Hall, he explained to the audience that he wanted to form a club that emphasized education, discussion, and community. Modeled after La Armonía, a club in Matanzas, he enlisted José Martí's help in organizing the club.[54] Less than a year later, Martí acknowledged Serra's difficulty in establishing the club and agreed that La Liga needed to be built "immediately." Finally, on January 22, 1890, the founding members of La Liga sociedad de instrucción y recreó held their first official meeting.

The creation of La Liga was a radical act. Not only was it a place where young men of color could take classes and learn, it was also an intellectual and political training ground where they were taught the finer points of working toward social justice, equality, and labor rights, what Martí called "una sociedad reparadora," a restored society.[55] Despite the obvious political activism and work done at La Liga, Serra went to great lengths to insure that it was "far from being a political center," and instead, characterized it as a patriotic benevolent brotherhood with "no religious predispositions."[56] Serra's hesitations, although curious, make sense. He understood that creating a space where poor men of color were encouraged to reach "their highest class position" was potentially threatening to white Cuban separatists.[57] Although open to all races, the founders had to be careful to not alienate white Cuban independistas. It was a delicate balance. Afro-Cuban political and intellectual production was necessary and integral to expanding the diasporic nationalist movement. Yet, their demands and ideas could be seen as a threat to the very movement they sought to influence and integrate. How to speak to blackness, and address the needs of black Cubans and Puerto Ricans without alienating potential allies, was a constant concern for the founders and members of the club.

Another concern was the future of Afro-Cubans within a newly independent Cuban republic. Serra ruminated publicly over whether the changes he and others worked so hard to secure would result in what Martí called the "triumph of a sincere and just Republic."[58] For Serra the only way to guarantee that Afro-Cuban men would fare much better once they returned to Cuba was to educate, train, and mentor them while in New York. "In Cuba we have a great problem that needs to be resolved. The problem is economic. Through no fault of their own, Afro-Cubans remained the poorest and most uneducated element of Cuban society." These problems were further exacerbated, as Serra wrote, by the growing threat of government-sponsored European migration to whiten the island. If the Cuban government were to underwrite these migrations, Afro-Cubans would find it even more difficult to secure employment and elevate their social and political status in Cuba.[59] The future, Serra warned, did not bode well for subsequent generations of Afro-Cubans in New York and Cuba who were not prepared, educated, or politically connected.

Our Collective: *La Liga sociedad de instrucción y recreó*

This city is so big and the Cuban-Puerto-Rican community is so dispersed! And, moreover, they are poor workers who must earn their daily wage and some have families; but they all know their way to La Liga, 74 West 3rd Street.
Manuel De J. González, 1899[60]

¡Black Race Elevate!
Minerva, 1888[61]

La Liga sociedad de instrucción y recreó was like no other Cuban club in New York. Located "on one of the poorer streets facing the Washington Square Arch," it was, as José Martí wrote, "el corazón de Rafael Serra," where "blacks and whites sit together." According to Martí, Rafael Serra "fue el creador," the one most responsible for creating, organizing, and sustaining La Liga.[62] In writing about La Liga, Teófilo Domínguez claimed that no other organization "ever had the same moral reach."[63] The club's primary objective was to educate poor young men of color and help them secure a "respectable station in life."[64] The founders established an educational salon where members as well as the public gathered to share ideas, organize cultural events, raise funds, and support similar clubs known as sociedades idénticas in the Antilles.[65] The club, however, would prove to be much more than simply a place to meet and take classes.

Unlike other clubs, the black Cuban and Puerto Rican male members of La Liga were seen, without question, as intellectual authorities and producers. It was a rare space where immigrant and working-class men of color occupied positions of institutional, intellectual, and social power in New York. While white Cubans José Martí, Manuel Barranco, Enrique Trujillo, B. H. Portuondo, Benjamin Guerra, and Gonzalo de Quesada taught courses and were credited with being socio-fundadores and, in Martí's case, honorary president, it was the black Cuban and Puerto Rican men, namely José C. López, the brothers Juan and German Bonilla, Manuel de Jesús González, Pedro Calderín, Sixto Pozo, Santos Sánchez, Sotero Figueroa, Justo Castillo, Olallo Miranda, Aquiles Brane, Fernando Vásquez, Isidoro Apodaca, Luís Valet, Enrique Sandoval, Juan Román, Eligio Medina, Pastor Peñalver, and Rosendo Rodríguez, who served in leadership positions. They were the presidents, vice presidents, secretaries, and treasurers of the club. Many taught courses, and like their white counterparts, were referred to as professors.[66]

The first president of La Liga, German Sandoval, embodied what Serra admired most. Respected among the Cuban community, Sandoval lived in New York for three decades and was active in North American clubs and societies, including the prestigious West India Society and the San Felipe Episcopalian Congregation, which included "the most aristocratic elements of the community of color in New York." Sandoval was also a Mason. He was, as Serra observed, "the soul" of the San Manuel

Lodge of the Order of Odd Fellows.[67] In writing about Sandoval, Serra revealed quite a bit about what he valued and considered important. He described Sandoval as someone who was "not a politician, nor desired to be one. He was not rich, not a writer, not a scientist, but instead, someone whose character and organizational abilities were unparalleled." He was the moral authority and head of what Serra called "our collective in New York for twenty-nine years."[68]

Serra's reference to "our collective" speaks to a long history of an Afro-diasporic political, social, and cultural community and movement in New York. This included the existence of other black Cuban and Puerto Rican clubs, such as the Directiva del Club Guerilla de Antonio Maceo, which was organized after 1888 and founded by José C. López, Augusto Benech, and Pedro Calderín, all future members of La Liga. Similarly, Las Dos Antillas, founded in 1892, counted Sotero Figueroa, Modesto Tirado, Arturo Schomburg, Augusto Benech, Silvestre Pivaló, and Isidoro Apodaca, as members. Both Guerilla de Maceo and Las Dos Antillas lasted well into 1895, and, as in the case of La Liga, were part of the Partido Revolucionario Cubano.[69]

Serra's use of the term "our collective" to refer to an extensive Afro-diasporic intellectual and political community challenges the common practice of positioning Afro-Cubans as an auxiliary to white Cuban activism. By asserting and acknowledging the existence of a black Cuban and Puerto Rican collective of migrants who were politically involved, Serra renders visible black Cuban and Puerto Rican activism. Moreover, he provides an effective context for understanding the founding and evolution of La Liga, and its place within the diasporic migrant community. In other words, La Liga was not a phenomenon or an outlier. It was also not a center founded solely by Martí to help Afro-Cubans. On the contrary, it was a by-product of an already established and long-standing collective of black Cuban and Puerto Rican thinkers, writers, and activists. The idea, as Serra stressed repeatedly, was to expand concepts and notions of the political, to include black Cuban and Puerto Rican intellectual production, authority, and mentorship.

Every Monday, "after a tiring day at work," members Manuel de Jesús González, Manuel Barranco, B. H. Portuondo, Rafael Serra, Enrique Trujillo, Benjamin Guerra, José Martí, and Gonzalo de Quesada taught evening courses at La Liga.[70] The students arrived around eight thirty, ready to begin their courses in literature, science, math, history, and art. Their professors, however, were often delayed up to an hour. It was not uncommon for instructors to work several jobs. Martí, for instance, translated texts and taught courses on the Upper West Side, "en la parte alta de la ciudad," to make ends meet. Some members who taught, lectured, or worked at La Liga were paid a modest sum, while others volunteered their time. Funding came primarily through donations. The most consistent funders were cigar workers. Since many of the members were themselves cigar makers, they turned to their fellow workers for support. Cigar workers routinely donated a portion of their salaries to cover tuition, meals, and other costs needed to keep La Liga afloat. Students, accustomed to waiting for their professors, used the time to finish their assignments, discuss the readings, and play the piano. Students formed friendships and created informal social networks that would ultimately be part of "la colectiva." Tuition for La Liga was modest. Students who could pay, did so. Those who could not were still welcome to attend classes, lectures, and be part of La Liga. No one was turned away.[71]

When class was over students, professors, and their families were invited to enter one of the bigger rooms and listen to lectures on philosophy, history, and politics. In an essay on La Liga, one of the founding members, Manuel De Jesús González, described the large and spacious rooms where the Monday night lectures were held. He notes the sketches of Martí and Serra that line the walls, the painting loaned by Martí of an Afro-Cuban man guarding the door of his home in Cuba, and on the opposite wall, between two doors, a framed image of Central Park in the winter. He mentions the glass doors covered with white curtains, a jug of water with cups on one of the tables, a desk, a bookshelf filled with books, a heated stove to warm the room, seats organized in a semi-circle, and to the left a piano. He points out the doors that connect the various rooms, and how those doors are only opened on Mondays, "cuando La Liga está de fiesta."

In a room with golden gas-lit lamps and furniture the "color of light," the members gathered to speak openly about their hopes, fears, desires, and disappointments. It was one of the few places where "the sons of both islands" could express themselves without retribution.[72] Open to the public, these lectures highlighted current events, revolution, racism, and the future of independence in Puerto Rico and Cuba. The discussions were highly political and the public was welcomed to join in the "meaningful discussions." On one evening in November 1892, both salons were full of people debating the "particular problems in Jamaica, Haiti, and Santo Domingo." At the center of the discussion were the inescapable "problems of race," the politics of each country, and the limits of culture. In one specific exchange, the members singled out the "books and men of Haiti," and elaborated on their significance in defining patriotism and the future of politics for men of color.[73]

At other times, the members, students, and their families would stay late into the evening listening to musicians play the piano and poets recite "poetry of the soul." As one of the few places where Afro-diasporic migrants gathered, it was important that it be a safe place to exchange ideas, provide opinions, and look each other in the eyes without "being humiliated," interrupted, or disrespected. La Liga was especially sensitive to "workers of color," who because of their current circumstances were unable to receive an education, but nonetheless wanted to learn. A pronounced theme in many of the written accounts of La Liga was the call to remain modest and humble; to refrain from embarrassing others less educated and knowledgeable and instead to "lift all" through kindness, education, and access.[74]

Few historical accounts and primary sources mention emotional safety and acceptance as much as those that discuss La Liga. Despite their efforts to create a different diasporic reality, Afro-Cubans could not escape an undercurrent of racism within the exile community, what Deschamps Chapeaux writes consisted of "the old prejudices born of Spanish colonialism."[75] In his writings on La Liga, Teófilo Domínguez briefly mentions the tenuous position of La Liga, writing that it did not have "the expected results, even though one can not deny the impact it had on community like ours: so in need of education."[76] Despite lauding the efforts of La Liga, there is a sense from Domínguez's writings of unfinished businesses, of work yet to be done.

There are scant records of women taking classes, teaching courses, or giving lectures at La Liga. We know, for instance, that Rafael Serra's daughter Consuelo Serra gave such an impressive lecture on the evening of July 1, 1893, that she "garnered the best applause."[77] Women, however, were more likely to be invited to the public lectures, educational salons, and events open to families held on Monday evenings. The sources that *do* speak to women and their involvement within the club position them as performers in service to the club's nationalist ideals or as auxiliaries to male-dominated political activism. There is mention of María Mantilla playing El Moujik on the piano,[78] Mariana Calderín singing "La Bayamesa," the national anthem of Cuba, María Mori accompanying several men on the piano,[79] and América Fernández, "Beneche's companion," performing poetry.[80]

Similar to most clubs of the period, La Liga had a women's auxiliary club, La Señoras de la Liga. Except for Carmen de Miyares, one of Martí's closet allies and friends,[81] and Candelaría de Graupera, one of the first to financially support La Liga, the club consisted of all Afro-Cuban women, many of whom were married to the founding members. These women included Ana M. de Benavides, Dionisia Apodaca de Bonilla, Josefa Blanco de Apodaca, Lorenza Geli de Courouneau, Isabel V. de Bonilla, Mariana Rivero de Hernández, Josefa N. de Cárdenas, and Pilar de Pivaló.[82] While there are sources that list Afro-Cuban women membership and discuss minimally their role within auxiliary clubs, few, if any detail the political and intellectual lives of these women outside of male-dominated sites. Existing sources reveal little concerning what took place in the different comités de damas, especially those consisting of Afro-Cuban women.

And yet, as Carmen Montejo Arrechea and Gema Guevara have demonstrated, this was a rich period for Afro-Cuban female political writing and activism in Cuba and abroad. The publication of the first edition of *Minerva: The Biweekly Magazine for the Woman of Color* on October 15, 1888 in Cuba, was a turning point for Afro-Cuban female intellectual and political production. According to Montejo Arrechea, it was the first known magazine in Cuba devoted to black women. *Minerva* proved to be a pivotal vehicle through which Afro-Cuban women on the island could be linked "to black Cuban women in the United States and in the Caribbean."[83] Considering that the 1888 edition lists Juan Bonilla, a founding member of La Liga, its agent in New York, it is almost certain that Afro-Cuban women in New York read and disseminated the magazine. It is likely that they discussed many of the same issues concerning revolution, independence, and respectability in their Comité de Damas meetings, at the public lectures given at La Liga every Monday night, and of course, privately among themselves, and in their homes.

Along with Bonilla, *Minerva* named Joaquin Granados in Key West, and Primitivo Plumas in Tampa, as their agents in the United States.[84]

The majority of articles and essays published in *Minerva* are by Afro-Cuban women. Yet they did feature writings by Afro-Cuban men living abroad. The magazine published essays, commentaries, and poetry by Rafael Serra, Martín Morúa Delgado, and Joaquin Granados. Granados, in particular, played a large role in the magazine. In addition to his many articles, the editors frequently referred to his many involvements as "proyecto Granados" and he is commonly singled out as their "illustrious collaborator" in Key West.[85]

Minerva received financial support from Afro-Cuban migrants and African American women who promoted and circulated the magazine outside of Cuba. Many of them sent in articles, poetry, and essays to be published. *Minerva*, as Montejo Arrechea writes, was determined to echo "all black women's concerns and to address women in general who identified with their struggles and who suffered similar kinds of affronts arising from the inferior status from which they were assigned."[86] As such, *Minerva*—as a transnationalist text designed to travel outside of Cuba and within the diaspora—expands our use and understanding of what constitutes diasporic archival source. As a text that moved and was purposefully disseminated, *Minerva* allows for historical examination and speculation on the range and possibility of Afro-Cuban female intellectual production and political activism in the United States, even though published in Cuba.

On January 17, 1887, a few years before the founding of La Liga, Martín Morúa Delgado convened a conference on women's rights in the club El Progreso located in Key West. Two years later, he wrote an essay under the heading "La mujer–Sus derechos" condemning the ongoing racial and sexual violence endured by women in Cuba, calling it a "horror," and demanding that Afro-Cuban women be treated fairly.[87] In the accompanying column, "Reflexionemos," a title signaling an unapologetic and public assertion for Afro-Cuban women to speak for themselves, Africa Céspedes comments on Morúa Delgado's essay, the conference in Key West, and her own analysis on the present conditions of women of color in Cuba. Powerful and direct, Céspedes criticized the exploitation of women, labeled "each man an enemy," and accused Cuban society of being cowardly for not speaking the truth, "el lenguaje de la verdad." Toward the end of her essay, Céspedes includes excerpts of the poem "Queredlas cual las hacéis o hacedlas cual las buscais," or

Senator Martín Morúa Delgado with his daughters, Arabella and Vestalina, 1907. Photographs and Prints Division, Schomburg Center for Research in Black Culture, New York Public Library, Astor, and Tilden Foundations.

"Hombres necios," authored by the sixteenth-century nun and scholar, Sor Juana Inés de la Cruz, to further make her point. Considered to be one of her most famous poems, "Hombres necios" challenges patriarchy and the subservient role of women in colonial Mexico. It is a powerful indictment and commentary on sexism and male authority. After citing several key verses, Céspedes concludes by declaring that the only thing "women want is justice, but justice in all matters."[88]

Céspedes was by far the most radical and confrontational of all writers published in *Minerva*. She challenged the legacy of slavery in Cuba and demanded that Cuban society change and treat Afro-Cuban women fairly and with respect. In an article simply entitled "A Cuba," Céspedes writes that it is a "dream that social codes have erased the word slavery substituting it for the word freedom." She extols the political changes that have provided "the black race their alienable rights," which for so long have been denied. Céspedes further argues that black families need to be compensated, in the form of reparations, for the "heroic sacrifices of blood of so many martyrs" in the name of Cuban liberation during the Ten Years' War.[89]

In addition to Céspedes' bold and uncompromising essays, there are pieces authored by Felicia Váldes, Ursula Coimbra de Valverde (Cecilia), Lucrecia González, America Font, Cristina Ayala, and Natividad González that discuss the role of black families, the importance of education, the politics of female enfranchisement, the demands of work, the need to change sexual dynamics in Cuba, and even the history of the women's movement in Europe.[90] At the same time, there is a consistent and parallel theme of uplift and the uses of marriage to legitimate Afro-Cuban sexuality that runs throughout *Minerva*. Marriage and family were seen as strategies for eliminating the persistent colonial images of Afro-Cuban women as sexually promiscuous and available to white men. The writings are a curious and powerful mix of personal responsibility and respectability with political commentary and analysis. In one piece entitled "La felicidad del hogar," V. Kop y Torres urges women to be educated so they can in turn teach their children and make their families stronger. "La Lección," authored by Lucrecia González, asserts that we "love to study, love lessons. We are not looking for pointless distractions." González further writes that women "cannot live in the inaction. We are the heroines of our sex, liberating ourselves from the yoke of ignorance."[91]

Most of the women who wrote for *Minerva* used pseudonyms, as in the cases of Africa Céspedes and "Cecilia." Some signed "anonymous," while others used the term "incognitus."[92] There was a reason why Afro-Cuban women did not sign their names. It was dangerous to express their views openly in such a public medium. The women who wrote for *Minerva* were harassed, intimidated, and threatened with jail and exile. The colonial Spanish government did not take kindly to the public critiques of slavery, racism, and the demands for Cuban independence, especially from Afro-Cuban women. The magazine was often read in secret and smuggled out of the country. On May 30, 1889, in the section labeled "Administración," the managing editor Enrique Cos wrote that as a result of financial stress, intimidation, and lack of resources, the newspaper was at risk of folding. Listing concerns and worries, including threats and continual attempts by the Spanish colonial authorities to shut down the newspaper, Cos ended the brief column with the fateful sentence, "God willing this will be the last jeremiad." It was not. The last known edition of the early versions of *Minerva* was published on July 19, 1889.[93]

Necessary Alliances: The Making and Unmaking of the Partido Revolucionario Cubano

In anticipation of another Cuban revolution the Cuban revolutionary party has been formed in the United States, Jamaica and Mexico. They declare that they want liberty for all inhabitants of the Island-Spaniards and Cubans [*sic*], negroes and white men.
Chicago Daily Tribune, 1892[94]

President Fraga of the New York Club opened the meeting amid such a storm of applause that for several minutes he had to stand in silence and wait till the handclapping and shouting had subsided.
New York Times, 1895[95]

On October 10, 1895, an "enormous crowd" of Cubans "surged through the doors" of Chickering Hall on Fifth Avenue to commemorate the beginning of the Ten Years' War in 1868. As the throng of Cubans walked down the aisles to take their seats "a band of drums, fifes, harps, and violins discoursed stirring and patriotic music." The stage was decorated with Cuban flags and photos of Carlos Manuel Céspedes and José Martí, who had been killed less than six months earlier on May 19th. The speakers spoke "only in Spanish" and were greeted with "tremendous applause" every time the word "patria" was mentioned. One of the most popular speakers that evening was Juan Fraga. Interrupted several times by applause, Fraga stepped back from the podium and waited for the cheers to subside before resuming his speech.[96]

Modest, unassuming, and relatively unknown in comparison to other historical figures of the period, Fraga was revered among the Cuban émigré community. He was one of the founders and architects of the Partido Revolucionario Cubano (PRC), delegate to the Cuerpo de Consejo—the highest authority of the PRC in each community, a supporter of labor rights, and founder and president of one of the most influential political clubs in the city, El Club Los Independientes.[97] However, unlike others in the movement, Fraga would not serve in the nascent Cuban government or be involved in forming the republic he fought so hard to manifest. His participation in this meeting, despite the applause and recognition, would not even be mentioned in *Patria*, the official newspaper of the PRC.[98]

Fraga did not live long. On May 2, 1899, he died at the French Hospital on 34th Street, penniless and forgotten by his friends and colleagues, especially those who returned to Cuba. However, he did live long enough to witness the US intervention and the beginning of US political and economic influence and control of the island. In a letter he penned to his good friend Rafael Serra, Fraga expressed feelings of betrayal and isolation.

> The war has ended and I am left ruined. I live off the hundreds of cigars that I personally make everyday and with that I support my sick and widowed sister. But what hurts me the most is that all of my friends have forgotten me. Not even a kind word have I received from the many who have left to Cuba. I am thankful that you count on me even though I'm not worth much. I have included a dollar for a copy of your book.[99]

It is hard to *not* read Fraga's words as testament to his broken heart and spirit. As he himself writes, the end of the war was "his ruin." The postwar period was difficult for those who had opposed US intervention and postwar colonial policies, including the renewed call for annexation. For Fraga, who had dedicated most of his life to the struggle for Cuba's independence, this period was particularly disheartening.

In many respects, Fraga's experiences represent the dilemma of geographic dislocation and the tyranny of returns. Like many who chose to stay, Fraga was left to negotiate postwar temporality as loss, fragmentation, and dismissal. In examining Fraga's experiences before and after the war we are faced with a pivotal question that often goes unanswered: What did it mean to stay? How did Cubans who were so invested in revolution and nation reconcile their place in New York during a period of US empire-building? This, as Fraga's letter reveals, was not easy. The shift was dramatic. Seemingly overnight, Cubans went politically and metaphorically from being exiles to immigrants; from being relevant to forgotten.

The United States' intervention in 1898, the Treaty of Paris (1898), and the Platt Amendment (1901) further complicated the process of postwar diasporic Cubanidad. Not only did such policies circumscribe the Cuban nation, they also changed the perception of the United States as a liberatory space grounded in possibility. For some, the work had been done, and the promises fulfilled. For others, like Fraga, there was still work to do. The question this time around was how to do it. How would Cuban migrants organize around labor, sovereignty, equality, and racial enfranchisement now that Cuba was independent from Spain? Would the divisions and tensions, which had haunted the movement for years, plague the political and intellectual migrant community now that there was no longer a common goal?

Like many of his contemporaries, Fraga migrated to the United States during the Ten Years' War.[100] Unlike other Cuban migrants, he eschewed Manhattan and moved to Brooklyn, where he settled and operated a small tobacco shop at 839 Fulton Street.[101] While most Cubans lived in Manhattan, a growing number moved to Brooklyn. Some worked in the cigar factories dotting Fulton Street, including those owned by J. M. Agüero, F. Bentacourt, and R. C. Galindo. They stayed at boarding homes, like the one run by Señorita Estenoz located only two blocks from the newly built Brooklyn Bridge at 32 Poplar Street. Estenoz served Cuban food, offered "trato Cubano," and had fairly priced rooms.[102]

Outside of making and selling cigars, Fraga spent the bulk of his time organizing revolutionary clubs and raising money to fund a second and third attempt at independence. A working-class white Cuban cigar worker committed to labor rights and racial equality, Fraga worked closely with Rafael Serra, Sotero Figueroa, and Juan Gualberto Gómez, the PRC delegate in Cuba, to include both race and labor into the PRC's political agenda and platform.

On June 16, 1888, in his tobacco shop in Brooklyn, Fraga and Raimundo Ramírez founded El Club Los Independientes, one of the most powerful revolutionary clubs in New York and precursor to the PRC. Concerned over the polarization of the separatist movement and its possible impact on the war effort, Ramírez and Fraga formed a club that would both unify independistas and privilege labor and race as central principles of the movement. At their first meeting, Fraga was elected president; Ramírez, vice president; Rafael Serra, secretary; and Juan M. García, treasurer. The club lasted almost eleven years with Fraga serving as president for most of those years.[103]

A month later, on July 15, Fraga, along with Afro-Cuban general Flor Crombet, Teodoro Pérez, and José Martí attended a public meeting at the Pythagoras Club in New York. Forty people attended the meeting devoted to finding ways to finance a third attempt at revolution. Three days after the meeting, Fraga sent a letter to Enrique Trujillo of *El Avisador Cubano* expanding on the "intentions of the founders," and what had been ultimately decided at the meeting. The idea, according to Fraga, was to centralize the power and financial interests of the revolutionary movement into one club and eventually, one bank account. This would make it easier and faster to respond to insurgents in Cuba. Within a year *El Avisador Cubano* published an advertisement stating that club funds had been deposited into the Brooklyn Savings Bank.[104] In 1893, *Patria* highlighted Fraga's skill at raising money among the "destierro" and financially stabilizing the movement.[105]

The meeting at the Pythagoras Club initiated El Club Los Independiente as the umbrella organization of independistas throughout the city. Considered to be a man of great integrity, "sin mancha,"[106] Fraga was determined to be inclusive and worked tirelessly to solidify the movement at all costs. His skill at mediating the various factions was singled out by Martí in a speech he gave at Hardman Hall on June 16, 1890.[107]

The following year, when Néstor L. Carbonell, president of El Club Ignacio Agramonte, invited Martí to visit Tampa and initiate the early stages
of the PRC,[108] he asked Fraga to accompany him as part of the New
York delegation. This was a smart choice. Respected and discreet, Fraga
was entrusted to serve as the intermediary between Martí and Máximo
Gómez. This was not easy. Martí and Gómez did not get along, and it
was up to Fraga to insure that both were informed, in agreement, and
ready to move forward in mounting a successful revolution.[109]

It was during this period that Sotero Figueroa migrated to New York
with his wife Inocencia Martínez, who would later organize El Club
Mercedes Varona. After arriving in July 1889, Figueroa immediately
made contact with Fraga, and joined what he considered to be the "only
revolutionary club in the city: El Club Los Independiente."[110] For almost
ten years, Figueroa remained an active member of the club. The same
year that he joined El Club Los Independiente, Figueroa formed El Club
Borinquen. Determined to form a club that represented the interests
of Puerto Ricans in New York and the future of Puerto Rico, Figueroa
organized close to two hundred Puerto Rican residents in New York
and held the first official meeting at their headquarters on West 25th
Street. Figueroa was elected president and Ramón Emeterio Betances,
who had been living in exile in France, was named honorary president.
The club was racially integrated and welcomed Cubans as members and
as part of the leadership. El Club Borinquen, as Josefina Toledo writes,
was the model and rationale for the Puerto Rican section (La Sección
Puerto Rico) of the PRC. During the early stages of the PRC's ratification in March 1892, Fraga and Figueroa demanded that there be a section devoted to Puerto Rico. The members agreed and asked Figueroa
to head La Sección Puerto Rico of the PRC, insuring that Puerto Ricans
would be an integral part of the PRC. In addition to El Club Borinquen,
Figueroa was also a member of La Liga sociedad de instrucción y recreó,
Las Dos Antillas, and editor of both *La Ilustrada Revista de Nueva York*
and *Patria*.[111]

Shortly before traveling to Tampa, "Cuban residents in New York" celebrated what the *New York Times* wrongly called the "anniversary of the
Declaration of Independence in their country." According to the *Times*,
close to "six hundred men, women, and children filled Hardman Hall on
Fifth Avenue and Nineteenth Street" to celebrate "Cuba's Independence

Day." It was, in fact, both a celebration of the start of the Ten Years' War and a rally to support the third attempt at independence. If there were indeed so many people in attendance that evening, the show of support was staggering. That evening Enrique Trujillo, Rafael Serra, Castro Palomino, Benjamin Guerra, and of course Martí all gave speeches. Also on stage were the widow, son, and daughter of Ignacio Agramonte, a military hero who had been killed in 1873. The first speaker of the evening, Gonzalo de Quesada, was interrupted several times by "long bursts of applause" as he "called on the young men to prepare to go to Cuba if needed, to defend their country, to speak against the vicious attacks of the Spaniards, and help set it free." García Laroge, who had recently left Cuba, told the audience that Cubans were desperate and that the "country was on the verge of ruin." Singling out Cubans in the United States, "where so many now live," Laroge invoked blessings on this government, "which allowed Cubans and all others to celebrate the memory of their heroes."[112]

The meeting at Hardman Hall could not have come at a better time. It provided the economic and political support the New York delegation needed as they planned their trip to Tampa. Tensions between the New York and Florida revolutionary communities boiled over in 1878 when Calixto García organized La Guerra Chiquita in New York under the central junta who, as Poyo writes, "did not consult with other centers in confirming García's leadership." To add insult to injury, the junta's bylaws declared all other centers "subservient to New Yorkers."[113] The tensions between New York and Florida simmered throughout most of the 1880s, especially when it came to labor and working-class issues. Cubans in Florida publicly accused the New York junta and exile community of supporting the interests of the elites, and sought to establish their own movement and leadership separate from New York. It was this more than anything else that prompted the New York delegation to travel to Tampa to establish an organization that would encompass and solidify a broad section of revolutionary centers in the United States.

Late in the evening on November 25th, the New York delegation arrived in Tampa in a torrential rainfall. It was a well-orchestrated visit. Cognizant of the ongoing labor and racial problems in Tampa and Ybor City, Martí and the delegation met with individual cigar workers, gave impromptu talks at different factories, and at every turn thanked the workers for their support. This, however, was not a goodwill tour. Martí, who was already familiar with defusing labor and racial tensions in New York, knew exactly what to say and what to do during his visit. He spoke of the need to transcend the divisions that plagued the exile and migrant community, and assured workers that they were integral to the success of the revolutionary movement.[114] Martí was also fully aware of the political and economic power of cigar workers. By the 1890s, cigar workers in Florida surpassed those in New York when it came to financial support and the formation of revolutionary clubs. The number of clubs in Tampa and Key West outnumbered those in New York by a large margin. Even the members of the New York–based Club Las Dos Antillas admitted that patriots in Florida "often times donate half of their salaries to the cause."[115]

Intent on cultivating relationships with Afro-Cubans, Martí requested meetings with Afro-Cuban independistas. Martí, as Susan Greenbaum writes, was interested in the "symbolism of his association with Afro-Cubans, and in mobilizing their collective support for the movement."[116] Martí first met with Cornelio Brito, a successful businessman, who was among a select group of men invited to welcome him to Tampa. According to a number of sources, during their first meeting Martí took Brito aside and encouraged him to organize a Tampa branch of La Liga sociedad de instrucción y recreó. Brito wasted little time and on that same day founded a branch of La Liga at his home.[117]

Not everyone was so quick to embrace Martí. Persuaded by Cornelio Brito to host a luncheon in his honor, Ruperto Pedroso a cigar worker and his wife Paulina Pedroso were initially reluctant. Paulina Pedroso, as Greenbaum chronicles, was a "fanatical follower of Maceo and Gómez," thereby contradicting Martí's form of activism, which was considered passive and detached. Eventually, Paulina Pedroso agreed to invite Martí to her home and was so impressed by him that both Ruperto and Paulina Pedroso became life-long supporters.[118]

Soon after returning to New York, Fraga held a series of meetings to discuss the visit, explain the organizational structure of PRC, and ratify the bylaws. It took almost four months and endless hours of discussion to finally get the New York contingent on board. The first meeting, held on January 24th at the offices of Barranco and Cia, was primarily for the members of El Club Los Independientes. Fraga wanted the membership to be the first to ratify the resolutions, bases, and platform before it was presented to the wider public. This allowed members to register their opinions before presenting the resolutions to the broader public. Once the members were in agreement, it would be easier to persuade others in the exile and migrant community to follow suit. A few weeks later, on February 13, club members met again in Hardman Hall to finalize and consolidate their membership and to support José Martí as the first president of the PRC.[119]

Less than a month later, Fraga called a meeting at the Military Hall on 193 Bowery Street to amend and ratify the bylaws of the PRC. Fraga, who represented El Club Los Independiente, invited Figueroa of El Club Borinquen, Martí of El Club José Martí, and Frederick Sánchez of Nuevos Pinos so they could work "in harmonious action with the other Cuban clubs in the city." Together they negotiated and agreed on the preliminary ratification of the bases and resolutions.[120] The members of the women's auxiliary club were not invited to the meeting. Instead, they met "uptown" far away from the men and even farther away from the decision-making process. [121]

It was not until March 26 that the wider Cuban community ratified the PRC's bases and resolutions. At this meeting the Puerto Rican section was officially included as part of the PRC, and New York was chosen as its headquarters. For the New York community this was an easy sell. The Key West contingent, however, was not so quick to ratify the PRC. After much deliberation, and a promise by Martí that General Máximo Gómez would lead the military contingent of the movement, the Key West revolutionary community agreed to ratify the PRC on March 26. On April 1, Martí received news by telegram that the Key West branch was on board and worked quickly to begin the process of electing delegates for the Cuerpo de Consejos.[122]

Two weeks later, on April 17, 1892 in Hardman Hall, the PRC was finally ratified and sealed in New York. Martí, who had been elected president a week earlier by members of twenty-four different clubs in New York, Tampa, and Key West, was now the official president of the PRC.[123] After four months of discussion, meetings, and votes, the PRC was set up as a two-tier organization that allowed for grass-roots, democratic participation at the local level, and a centralized authority dedicated to the immediate revolutionary activities at the national level. While the local level was democratic and inclusive, the national level was highly centralized and exclusive. In other words, despite the show of inclusivity, the real power rested in the hands of the few. This was most evident in the way the PRC elected leaders and issued directives. One of the more powerful decision-making bodies of the PRC was the Cuerpo de Consejo. The members of the Cuerpo de Consejo were presidents of the different local clubs with at least twenty members who accepted the PRC's charter. The members voted for the party's national officers known as the delegados. According to Poyo, the delegados enjoyed "absolute authority," demonstrating what he called the PRC's "conspiratorial character."[124]

Within months after the final ratification, Martí was in Haiti and later in South America urging Cuban revolutionaries to support the PRC.[125] While in Haiti, Martí met with members of the Cuerpo Directivo of El Club Guarionex y Hatuey, gave several speeches throughout the capital, was honored at a large banquet, and met with Cuban, Puerto Rican, and Haitian revolutionaries, including Rosendo Rivera, Juan Rodríguez, and his old friends José and Emiliana Brava Calderín.[126] A month later, on October 19, Martí was in Kingston meeting "with 250 revolutionists," to explain "the objects of the revolutionary organization, the present state of affairs in Cuba and what changes the Revolutionary Party, if successful, intended to bring about." The meeting ended with the Kingston delegation, led by Alejandro González, pledging their support to the PRC. That afternoon Martí returned to New York.[127] From the moment the PRC was ratified to the formal declaration of war in 1895, Martí never stopped traveling. He visited revolutionary centers in Philadelphia, New Orleans, Dominican Republic, Ocala, and Mexico, to name a few.[128] On a hot summer day in July, close to 1,500 people gathered in Jacksonville to hear Martí speak on "the exact situation in Cuba."[129] Martí was gone so often that when a reporter inquired about his whereabouts, Benjamin Guerra, the treasurer of the PRC, responded, perhaps protectively, that he was now "on the ocean, but I cannot tell you where he is going."[130]

By all accounts the PRC was successful. It raised money, unified a once fragile movement, and inspired the formation of countless local revolutionary clubs throughout the hemisphere. It was a turning point in exile revolutionary activism, a formal declaration of unity in a time of disunity. And yet, there was a certain restlessness that mired the PRC.

To sustain unity at all costs, issues of race and labor were minimized, even though black Cuban and Puerto Rican members continued to organize around race and labor. This, Lillian Guerra writes, was Martí's tendency to both "include socially marginal groups symbolically" and deny "openly radical black activists such as Rafael Serra from leadership in the movement." As Guerra argues, Martí did not imbue these groups with the same structural authority within the PRC that he offered their conservative, wealthier, and formally educated counterparts, such as Tomás Estrada Palma and Gonzalo de Quesada.

The Afro-Cuban members of the PRC were aware of Martí's willingness to "act the part of social democrat whenever the chance presented itself," and did their best to negotiate such tactics while emphasizing their own political demands and agenda. At the PRC meeting on April 17, Sotero Figueroa gave a speech where he emphasized the need to educate workers so they could "consciously move forward to securing their rights."[131] Members of La Liga, many of whom were involved with the PRC, continued to have meetings and hold lectures where they reaffirmed their commitment to racial and social equality. From 1894 on, the founders and editors of *La Verdad*, Rafael Serra, Juan Bonilla, and Rosendo Rodríguez, published articles on race, racial hierarchies, the impact of white immigration on the island, and problems of colonialism.[132]

Women and women's rights were nowhere to be found in the PRC's membership, agenda, bylaws, and platform. Women were never part of the leadership or elected to any positions of power. In fact, as mentioned earlier, women were excluded from all important and decisive meetings. It was never clear what exactly constituted women's rights within the PRC, since their activism was defined primarily by their involvement in El Club Mercedes Varona, the female auxiliary club of the PRC. The club was named after a spy and revolutionary in Cuba who took inordinate risks during the Ten Years' War. At only seventeen years of age, Varona was killed by the Spanish.

According to Josefina Toledo, the members of El Club Mercedes Varona had some power, even playing a role in voting for delegates to the Cuerpo de Consejo. However, because the club never reached the required number of twenty members, they had no voice. From the limited records, it appears that this was the only time that women in the

PRC were so close to voting for delegates. As Toledo notes, there is no indication that women exerted similar voting power in 1893 and 1894. However, in 1895 there was a subtle shift in power when the PRC rules governing club voting were amended to allow clubs that do not have twenty members, but are deemed "worthy patriotas," to still participate in voting for delegates.[133]

Although the bylaws promise to sincerely respond to "historical and political factors within and outside of the island," they do not mention race per se. Instead, bylaws, which were always printed on the first page of *Patria*, refer to "all honorable" men devoted to the independence of Cuba and Puerto Rico and highlight the desire to quell any and all divisions. In brief, the bylaws were written to represent the interests of all Cubans and Puerto Ricans, without distinction, both in- and outside of the island, and to create the necessary conditions for revolution and independence. The emphasis on a politics of mutuality and racelessness obfuscate what were still critical questions concerning race, labor, and postwar enfranchisement in Cuba. The lack of public discourse rested uncomfortably with the visible and prominent presence of black Cubans and Puerto Ricans in the PRC, including Sotero Figueroa, who was now secretary of the New York Cuerpo de Consejo and editor of *Patria*.

The calculated silences also filled the pages of *Patria*. There are a few articles on race and labor. There are even fewer that seriously consider gender. There is, however, mention of several revolutionary clubs in Haiti, the Dominican Republic, and Jamaica organized after the death of Antonio Maceo on December 7, 1896 that allude to blackness and the privileging of the Antilles as a site of racial empowerment. During a period when speaking openly about race could be seen as undermining the nationalist movement, Maceo's death was an acceptable conduit for disrupting the silences surrounding race and nation, prompting the formation of revolutionary clubs informed by hemispheric blackness.

Devastated by the loss, exiled Cubans and a large number of Haitians formed El Club Antonio Maceo, La Unión Cubano-Haitiana, and El Club Toussaint L'Ouverture in Port-au Prince shortly after Maceo's death in early 1897. In a letter to the editor Simon Poveda Ferrer, who was secretary of the Cuerpo de Consejo in Haiti, reflected on the impact, "el golpe," of Maceo's death on the exile community in Haiti. Ferrer conveyed how upon hearing of Maceo's death the president of El Club

Maceo made the hall available so Haitians and Cubans could mourn together. From that moment, Haitians and Cubans were united in fighting for Cuban liberation. That same year, in 1897, Dominican, Cuban, and Puerto Rican women in the Dominican Republic formed Hijas de las Tres Antillas in solidarity with Cuban migrants.[134] The death of Maceo also shocked Mexicans and Cuban migrants living in Mexico. A few months after Maceo was killed in battle, "El Club Morelos y Maceo" was formed in honor of José Mariá Morelos y Pavon and Maceo, both Afro-descendent revolutionary leaders.[135]

A notable exception to the brief articles and passages that referred to race was a lengthy article published in *Patria* on January 1, 1896 entitled "El negro cubano." Submitted by Wen Dilar, the director of El Continente Americano in Vera Cruz, Mexico. Dilar wrote the piece in response to C. Rubio's article in *El Nacional,* which argued that Afro-Cubans on the island were hostile to the concept of the Cuban republic and unwilling to be part of the nation-building project. Dilar's response is a mixture of condescension, paternalism, and support for Afro-Cuban equality and civil rights. Claiming that in Cuba "there exists few Africans," no more cabildos or "nañiguismo," Dilar asserts that Afro-Cubans have progressed, are civilized, and are above all now Cubans. Using race-lessness as a strategy for Cuban unity, Dilar reminds readers that, "as Cubans we should be of politics, not of color, unless we want to be part of the ridiculous farce of the enemies of our liberation." Dilar's article employs several familiar tropes and tactics common to discussing race among Cubans: the differentiation between the African and the Afro-Cuban; the use of nationalist discourse to subsume race and deny racism; and lastly, an appeal to white Cubans to, once and for all, relinquish their racism and fear, and see Afro-Cubans as their equal.[136]

Interestingly enough, the article was published after Martí's death and during Sotero Figueroa's tenure as editor of *Patria.* The piece can be read in multiple ways, especially when considering the politics of the period. It can be seen as a bold move on Figueroa's part to present a sympathetic, albeit problematic, appeal to support Afro-Cuban enfranchisement and integration within the nation-building project. It is also possible that Figueroa published the article to challenge racism within the separatist movement, and to establish a position on race within the PRC. At the same time, the tone and content of the article serve as a reminder that, despite the years of hard work and activism, Afro-Cubans still faced exclusion and discrimination, often by their own allies and counterparts.

Nothing symbolized the shift more than the election of Tomás Estrada Palma as president of the PRC shortly after Martí's death in May 1895. His presidency was met with mixed feelings. Estrada Palma was a wealthy, white Cuban exile who represented the conservative faction of the New York Cuban revolutionary community. He was a US citizen who spoke fluent English and lived in the United States for more than thirty years. Estrada Palma's election solidified the more conservative New York political community's hold on Cuban revolutionary and nationalist politics, to the detriment of Afro-Cubans and the more radical faction. Throughout the thirty years that Estrada Palma studied, lived, and worked in New York he rarely wavered in his support for US intervention in Cuba. During the mid-nineteenth century he advocated for annexation and expansionism, at times changing his position, but never fully convinced that Cubans could achieve or manage total independence.

For Cuban exiles and migrants committed to ending racism and supporting labor rights, the election of Estrada Palma was a blow. He signified what they had fought so hard against. Although Serra continued to have a respectful relationship with Estrada Palma, often exchanging letters and attending the same meetings, his response to the election was to publish *La Doctrina de Martí* in July 1896.[137] Much like Serra's other newspaper *La Verdad*, *La Doctrina de Martí* was a reminder of Martí's commitment to racial and social activism and change, which were "conveniently ignored" by the leadership and conservative wing of the PRC, represented and led by Estrada Palma.[138] Serra emphasized the politics of the radical faction of the PRC, reaffirming their commitment to labor and race, while at the same time denouncing those who sought to divide and polarize. He summarized these feelings succinctly, writing, "Cubans who share in the sacrifice, should also share in the benefits."[139] *La Doctrina de Martí* received wide support from the Cuban and Puerto Rican labor movement. The Key West labor newspaper, *El Vigía*, as Gerald Poyo writes, heralded *La Doctrina* for issuing the "'first alert' when the commitment to Martí's ideals had weakened in exile." In addition to *La Doctrina*, a series of pro-labor newspapers including *El Intransigente* and *El Yara* in Florida supported worker's rights.[140]

In April 1898 the United States militarily intervened in the Cuban War for Independence. Less than a year later on December 10, representatives from Spain and the United States met in Paris to sign the Treaty of Paris. Cuba, Puerto Rico, the Philippines, and Guam were now under US control. Less than two years later, on December 31, 1901, Estrada Palma was installed as the first president of the Cuban Republic. Despite becoming the first president, Estrada Palma waited until the very last moment to return to Cuba. He conducted his campaign from New York and arrived in Havana "only days before his inauguration."[141]

The events during and after the US intervention were a disastrous blow to Cubans committed to complete and total independence. Few would recover. It was no surprise to the radical faction of the PRC that Estrada Palma's presidency would result in the incorporation of the Platt Amendment to the Cuban Constitution as well as a renewed interest in the annexation of Cuba. They had their doubts from the very beginning. It was also no surprise that the promises made to create a more racially just and equal society would be delayed if not betrayed.

Archiving Visibilities: Postwar Afro-Cuban Male Imaginaries, 1899

It is not possible to understand the intimate history of a community or of a social class, if certain details are ignored, those that appear insignificant at first look.
Teófilo Domínguez[142]

In 1899, Teófilo Domínguez published a collection of seven biographical sketches of Afro-Cuban men active in the separatist and nationalist movement. Of the seven profiled, four—Rafael Serra, Juan Bonilla, Margarito Gutiérrez, and Manuel de Jesús González—migrated, lived, and worked in New York. The other three, Joaquin Granados, Emilio Planas, and Julian González, settled in Tampa. The history and experiences of these men reflect the trajectory of many Afro-Cubans, including Domínguez, who moved back and forth between New York and Tampa. By the time *Figuras y Figuritas* was published, Domínguez had moved from New York to Tampa, where he edited the newspaper *El Sport*.[143]

The publication year of *Ensayos biográficos: Figura y Figuritas* was not random. Disseminated during and after the Cuban War for Independence, the text is a conscious decision to build archive and insure Afro-Cuban male historical relevance and visibility within an exile and immigrant community that perpetually sought to diminish their intellectual and political contributions. As Reverend Pedro Duarte writes in the introduction, the book's objective is to "make the world aware of seven of our patriots . . . who out of nowhere have lifted themselves." The book, Duarte asserts, will "mentor future generations well."[144] Aware of the prodigious timing of its publication, Duarte situates *Figuras y Figuritas* during a period defined by the end of four centuries of Spanish colonialism and fifty years of revolution and battle, what he calls "a new phase" in Cuba's history. By contextualizing the book within such a transitional period, Duarte emphasized Afro-Cuban male political contributions and marked the period as both meaningful and transformational. According to the text, those selected were all upstanding men who had overcome incredible odds and barriers to reach their highest potential. The individual sketches promote certain Afro-Cuban men as thinkers and intellectuals worthy of remembrance. In short, they are examples of racial uplift. And yet, there are no guarantees that they, like so many others, will be remembered. Will Afro-Cubans be included within this "new phase"? Or will they be forgotten and replaced by more convenient historical narratives?

Duarte himself answers these questions by acknowledging that, although such a history may not reach the "aristocratic libraries," it will in the end reach the most noble and worthy of all readers, "the workers."[145] His conclusion is telling and sobering. On the one hand, he sees the history of Afro-Cuban men as one that belongs to the public, to the deserved workers. On the other, he understands full well the impossibility of blackness as official history, memory, and archive. Unless deliberately scripted and disseminated by Afro-Cubans, there is no place for blackness in the historical articulation of postwar Cuban exile and migrant communities.

In the case of Joaquin Granados, Domínguez emphasizes the importance of historical documentation and references the painful writings of the Cuban poet and slave, J. Francisco Manzano. He reminds the reader that had Manzano not written, not testified to his experiences as a slave, we would not be aware of such a history, nor understand the unfolding of Granados' life.[146] Born in 1856 to enslaved parents in Havana, his parents used "the law" to free their child. According to Domínguez, the decision would have grave consequences. Because Joaquin Granados was free and living under "different social conditions," he was prohibited from living with his parents and placed in the care of a poor family in Santiago de las Vega in Havana. Six years later, when his birth parents attempted to retrieve him, the "adopted" family refused to let him go. As a result, Granados was not raised by his birth family, and as Domínguez writes, was denied any sort of formal education. To avoid the chaos Granados turned to literature. He read voraciously and began writing for a number of newspapers in Cuba, and later the United States. By 1883, he had earned a teaching degree and soon thereafter migrated to Key West.[147]

At the other end of the spectrum is the biography of Juan Bonilla. Born and raised in Key West on June 24, 1869, Bonilla is the opposite of Granados: an Afro-Cuban man born and raised free in the United States. Yet, he was, as Domínguez acknowledges, part of a group of "young men born in this country—of Cuban parents—who have devoted all of their energies for the good of Cuba."[148] Bonilla represents the Cuban immigrant historical narrative that is rarely told: an Afro-Cuban man born in the United States during the mid-nineteenth century who crafted and lived an Afro-Cuban identity. Fluent in both English and Spanish, Bonilla moved to New York, where he wrote for newspapers, published essays, and like Granados, was involved with the newspaper, *Minerva*. Bonilla also translated texts, was a member of the "'San Manuel' Grand Order of the of United States Odd Fellows," and secretary of La Liga, "one of the best Cuban institutions that ever existed."[149]

It is clear from the different biographies and his own conclusion that Domínguez anticipated postwar racial exclusions and silences and sought to address those potential erasures by creating archive, publishing photos, and privileging Afro-Cuban male visibility within the Cuban nationalist discourse. During the same period of the book's publication, Domínguez was involved in a difficult episode in the history of the Afro-Cuban community in Ybor City.

Shortly after the war, Afro-Cuban members of the previously racially integrated club, El Club Nacional Cubano, October 10, were expelled.

On October 26, 1900, many of the same members who had been expelled attended the first meeting of the Martí-Maceo Society of Free Thinkers at the home of Ruperto Pedroso. There is no clear indication from the minutes of the meetings why the Afro-Cuban members were expelled. What is clear from the minutes of the first meeting is that Teófilo Domínguez, who had been a member of La Liga and was closely involved with La Colectiva in New York, stood up with a copy of the newspaper *El Pueblo Libre* in his hand and explained why it was necessary for "men of dignity" to form an independent institution similar to the one in Cuba known as the Antonio Maceo Free Thinkers of Santa Clara. Referring back to his experiences with La Liga in New York, Domínguez reminded the twenty-three men gathered that evening that the fundamental idea of the club should be to "help finish their intellectual education."[150] The Martí-Maceo Society of Free Thinkers eventually evolved into La Union Martí-Maceo, one of the oldest and most respected Afro-Cuban clubs in the United States. Although there is speculation, it is still not clear why the Afro-Cuban members were expelled from El Club Nacional Cubano, October 10 or what this would mean in terms of building a postwar Cuban immigrant community in Ybor City.

The period following the US intervention in Cuba was unpredictable and complicated. What did it mean to be black and Cuban during a time when it was no longer part of a nationalist strategy of Cubanidad? Like many in the Afro-Cuban immigrant community, Domínguez understood the consequences of the discursive unraveling of nation, blackness, equality, and social justice, and sought, through text and action, to render visible the efforts of Afro-Cuban male revolutionaries. It is clear that Domínguez intended *Figuras y Figuritas* to be an antidote to such deliberate forgettings, a stubborn reminder that Afro-Cuban migrants were and continued to be an integral part in articulating independence and building nation. Domínguez's intervention and archival desires proved to be more important than anyone ever imagined or expected. As Afro-Cuban leaders and revolutionaries returned to an island they had left years earlier, those who stayed were tasked with figuring out what it meant to be black, Cuban, and revolutionary in places and among communities that preferred to forget.

4

Orphan Politics

Race, Migration, and the Trouble with 'New' Colonialisms, 1898–1945

I ask where is the Cuban nation. There is no Cuba. There is [*sic*] no Cuban people. There are no freemen here to whom we can deliver this marvelous land.
New York Times, 1898[1]

If Independence is granted to Cuba, the gravest problem to be faced and solved will be the racial problem. The supremacy of the whites must be guaranteed. It should be borne in mind by the negroes that there can be no social equality at any time and no political equality until a considerable period has elapsed.
La Lucha, 1899[2]

The experiences of the blacks must be reckoned within every phase of the reconstruction of the island.
New York Tribune, 1901[3]

Now, the Cubans are all orphans.
Brigadier General William Ludlow, 1899[4]

On November 16, 1899, less than a year after the Treaty of Paris was signed and during the military occupation of the island, the governor of Havana, Brigadier-General William Ludlow, was invited to speak to the members of the Cuban Orphan Society in New York City. In his opening remarks General Francis V. Greene, the president of the Cuban Orphan Society, listed Ludlow's military and administrative accomplishments: military attaché to the US embassy in London, chairman of the Nicaragua Commission, and commanding officer at El Caney. That afternoon at the Chamber of Commerce on 32 Nassau Street, Greene introduced Ludlow by expressing his own colonial desires. "In our colonial systems, or whatever system our foreign possessions may come into, whether as colonies or as territories, if it is to be successful, it will be by the skill and untiring energy of such men as General Ludlow and General [Leonard] Wood."

The Cuban Orphan Society was founded to help "those poor little waifs who were left in destitution." That afternoon, there was little interest in the work of the twelve women who only a few months earlier traveled to Cuba to establish a home that catered to "four hundred children, who are there to be clothed, fed and educated."[5] Instead, Greene, the board of trustees, and the invited guests wanted to hear Ludlow discuss the political situation in Havana, "its past, present, and future." As provisional governor in Havana, Ludlow established and executed policies in Cuba. He instituted "white-only" policies barring Afro-Cubans from certain civil service and governmental jobs, and supported the adoption of racial segregation in public facilities and spaces. Ludlow's ideas reverberated throughout the United States and were integral to managing colonialist rhetoric and empire-building in Cuba during the turn of the century.

Ludlow began his speech by emphasizing the "conditions prevailing during the last year; what we did, how we found things, and about how things are this time."[6] He discussed the need for sanitation, infrastructure, housing, policing, health care, and education, all the while emphasizing Cuban frailty and the United States' postwar "responsibility" toward the Cuban people. "Cubans are to-day [sic] actually wards of the nation. The United States has made itself responsible for them; it has made itself responsible for the formation and maintenance of a government there."[7]

The reception tendered by the Cuban Orphan Society proved to be an ironically appropriate place, if not metaphorically, for Ludlow's speech. In his opinion, Cuba along with Puerto Rico, the Philippines, and Guam were territories that had recently been "orphaned" and in need of protection and governance. In explaining the current political and economic situation in Cuba, Ludlow described the Cuban people as a "weak race" with no discipline, no management, and "no comprehension of government."

> Now, the Cubans are all orphans. They had a rather tough domestic discipline, to be sure. The mother was what is popularly supposed to be a stepmother. She held them by the throat with one hand and robbed them with the other. To-day [sic], the Cubans are the most easily influenced I have ever seen.[8]

Ludlow employed an oft-used practice of casting colonized nations and people as children unable to govern themselves, let alone a nation. In this case, Cubans had been abused by their Spanish "stepmother," leaving them easily influenced and in need of protection. "They are like children in that respect—when they are frightened they are dangerous. They are suspicious. They have learned that from three or four centuries of Spanish rule."[9]

No doubt Ludlow's wrought metaphor on mothering and orphan politics was designed to appeal to those in attendance. It was, after all, the perfect metaphor for the perfect audience; one that achieved the colonial trick of eliminating all semblances of agency, power, and historical context. The erasure of context is most pronounced in Ludlow's refusal to mention the Ten Years' War, La Guerra Chiquita, the Cuban War for Independence, let alone the role of the Cuban exile and migrant community in fomenting revolution. Except for a brief reference, where he states that at "one period we are disposed to consider them martyrs and patriots struggling for freedom and entitled to all of our sympathies,"[10] there is little discussion of the Cuban struggle for independence. From Ludlow's vantage point, Cuba began the moment the United States intervened in 1898, rendering Cuba and the Cuban people *archival* orphans.

Much like his depiction of the intervention, the language used to discuss postwar Cuba is marked by the invisibility of the Cuban people and the hypervisibility of white US citizens. Ludlow's interest in erasing Cubans from historical relevancy is particularly evident when describing the early stages of US occupation. He eliminates all Cuban and Spanish experiential and historical traces as he tells the audience that on the "first January of last year, the flag was transferred and the American flag took its place." There is no mention of what flag was lowered and why. There is no acknowledgment of a Cuba Libre because for Ludlow, an independent and sovereign Cuba is simply unfathomable. "We have a suitable government there, peace has been established, the courts are open to any man, life, and property are secure."[11] When he does mention Cubans they are out of control and incapable of governance, "the average Cuban lacks the knowledge of how to administer a public office; and it is going to take him a long time to acquire it." Early into the speech Ludlow explained why it was so important for the United States to insure political stability on the island. "There are in Cuba some sixty or seventy millions of dollars in foreign investments. The Spanish have some, the Germans have some and the French and Americans also have some. The interests should be protected; the island could not be abandoned."[12] Ludlow's demarcation of the North/South is a territorial fiction that has fed into the myth of a hemispheric divide. As Román de la Campa writes, the divide "managed to demarcate a game of inflexible oppositions that still animates fables of identity and republican fictions. Civilization/barbarism, Anglo/Latin, North/South, capitalism/one-man-rule—thus went the cartography that followed these civilizing impulses."[13]

Ludlow's civilizing impulses were evident in his constant efforts to mark the United States as finished and Cuba as unfinished. Citing the high illiteracy rates among the Cuban people, "in the island of Cuba there is something like from 75 to 85 percent of illiteracy," Ludlow argues against universal suffrage. "To grant universal suffrage to such a population would hopelessly prejudice the entire future of the island." If Cubans were to be given the vote, then the United States would have no other choice, according to Ludlow, but to "leave it to-day [sic] and call it Hayti No. 2. The people of substance would be absolutely swamped and the entire situation destroyed."[14] In referencing Haiti, Ludlow issued a familiar and dangerous warning, one predicated on the fear of "people of substance," referring to whites, being "swamped" by Afro-Cubans. This, according to Ludlow, would not only destroy the burgeoning colonial project, but also the possibility of future modernities. To become like Haiti meant reaching the pinnacle of the unfinished. Once arrived, there would be no turning back.

The never-ending speculation of Cuba becoming another Haiti remained a familiar specter well into the twentieth century. The *New York Herald* and the *New York Times*, among others, published articles and editorials warning that Cuba could easily become another Haiti if the United States did not assume full control. On January 30, 1898, before the United States' formal intervention, the *New York Herald* reported that, "A free Cuba means another black Republic. It would be too close and we have enough with Haiti. If we are to intervene, it should be to insure that Cuba be part of the United States."[15] A year later, on August 7, 1899, the *New York Times* associated universal suffrage in Cuba with establishing a black republic. Citing what the newspaper called a "leading Havana merchant," it argued that the only way to prevent Cuba from becoming a "black republic in the near future" would be to incorporate "the island as a possession of the United States in the form of State, Territory [*sic*], or colony." Otherwise, Cuba is "doomed to become another Haiti."[16] The *New York Tribune*, on the other hand, disagreed with the other New York newspapers, writing that the "idea of a black republic in Cuba is un-thought of. The black population of Cuba can only be swelled by colonization or immigration on a colossal scale."[17]

By employing Haiti to project racialized fears of underdevelopment and the unfinished, the press situated Cuba within the precarious and the fallible, where anything could happen unless the United States made it "a possession." Moreover, since Haiti signaled locative disaster and danger before *and* after the war, it operated as a simultaneous justification for intervention, annexation, and in the case of Ludlow and the *New York Times*, preventing universal suffrage to all men regardless of color. The fear of Cuba or any island becoming another Haiti was so pronounced that anything associated with Haiti, including the right to vote and the power to administer one's own government, was immediately suspect. Less than three weeks later the *New York Times* published an article that correlated the fear of Haiti with the need to possess and annex the island. Claiming that Cubans were now in favor of annexation, it reported that "Only weeks ago it was considered almost treason on the part of a Cuban to say he was in favor of annexation, but now it is discussed by Cubans in clubs, in cafes, in the parks and squares, and on the streets." According to the paper, support for annexation among Cubans was so ubiquitous that "some of the most enthusiastic *independistas* now urge a continuance of the American occupation for at least a year or two longer."[18]

In February 1899, less than a year before Ludlow's visit to the Cuban Orphan Society, President McKinley gave a speech in Boston in which he reminded the audience that control of the Philippines, Cuba, and Puerto Rico was a "great trust" carried "under the providence of God and in the name of human progress and civilization." While the lasting implications of the relationship being forged were yet unknown, what was clear, especially to McKinley, was that it was imperative that the US government calm any fears the public may have concerning US influence in Cuba; "our priceless principles undergo no change under a tropical sun. They go with the flag."[19]

President McKinley's words and ideas evolved into a decades-long foreign policy that allowed the United States to expand and protect capital in Cuba. The hallmark was the incorporation of the Platt Amendment into the Cuban Constitution. Consisting of eight separate acts, this proposal required that the US government be given the right to intervene in order to preserve Cuban independence; to maintain a government adequate for the protection of life, property, and individual liberty; and to discharge the obligations with respect to Cuba imposed by the Treaty of Paris on the United States, now to be assumed and undertaken by the government of Cuba.[20] It protected the rights of the US military government, forbade the Cuban government from entering into any foreign treaties unless agreed upon by the US government, and lastly, allowed the United States to acquire and hold land titles and secure naval stations. Once drafted, Secretary of War Elihu Root presented the amendment to Senator Orville Platt of Connecticut and within months, it was ratified as the Platt Amendment.

From the beginning the Platt Amendment was controversial. Cubans protested, held rallies, marched through neighborhoods, and lodged formal complaints to the provisional government in Havana. The United States refused to budge. In a bold move, Root informed the Cuban government that the US military would not leave until the constitutional amendment was put into effect. In 1901, the Cuban convention adopted the Platt Amendment by a slim margin and incorporated it into the new Cuban constitution.[21]

In addition to facilitating US intervention and colonialism, the Platt Amendment navigated around the previously passed Teller Amendment, which was intended to protect Cuban sovereignty. A congressional resolution, the Teller Amendment was adopted by the US Senate on April 19, 1898, during the Spanish-American War. Named after the senator of Colorado, Henry M. Teller, it outlined the United States' intentions in Cuba *after* the war. Supported by the exile Cuban revolutionary community and the Anti-Imperialist League, the Teller Amendment recognized the right of the Cuban people to be free from Spanish colonial rule and US rule. In fact, according to Article IV of the Joint Resolution, once Cuban sovereignty had been established, the United States was expected to leave the government and control of the island to its people.[22] In other words, occupation was never meant to happen. For the Cuban exile and migrant revolutionary community, the Teller Amendment was a guarantee that the United States would *not* occupy or colonize the island. It was a legislative promise designed to calm the fears of those wary of US intervention. The passage and incorporation of the Platt Amendment broke those promises.

The United States' political intervention in Cuba was matched by its economic intervention. From 1899 onward, companies, including the Cuban-American Sugar Company, the Cuban Company, and the United Fruit Company, acquired vast amounts of land, equipment, and access to resources. The United Fruit Company alone purchased 250,000 acres of land. Within a short period, North American companies and investment groups single-handedly took over land, materials, labor, and production. The passage of the Foster-Cánovas agreement further facilitated US control of Cuban sugar when it allowed the United States access to sugar trade and production. A year later, the Cuban Company completed construction of a railway system, and in the process acquired close to 50,000 acres of Cuban land. In addition, individual investors flocked to Cuba to buy land. By 1905, US corporations and individuals owned 60 percent of rural property in Cuba, while Cubans owned only 25 percent of the land.[23] Afro-Cubans fared even worse. Between 1899 and 1931, black control over land decreased by 50 percent.[24] A year later, the Tobacco Trust, which controlled 90 percent of export trade of Havana cigars, bought acres of land used to grow and produce tobacco. So advantageous and lucrative was this period for investors and businesses that one US newspaper gushed, "everyone in Cuba is getting rich."[25]

One reporter who wrote on the changes taking place in Cuba was Dorothy Stanhope, the *New York Times* foreign correspondent stationed in Cuba during 1900. Observing that "Americans are in evidence" everywhere on the island, she aptly captured the chaos of an empire in the making.

> Cuba is simply over-run with Americans of all ages, of all conditions of life, of all professions and of no profession. From the gray-haired man, down to the newsboy selling his papers in the street. Americans are in evidence. Years ago the rush was to the west of the United States: now the tide has turned southward to Cuba, and when the Government shall have become settled it is expected, that there will be such an inflowing of immigrants as has not been exceeded anywhere in years.[26]

Stanhope illustrates the multiple processes at work in Cuba—from the expectation that the government will be "settled," making the island ripe for US investment and immigration to the island, to the acknowledgment that Cuba, like the western United States years earlier, is now part of a land rush designed to make Americans rich. At the same time, she warns her readers to be cautious before traveling to Cuba. "From appearances, many seem to think that they will find the streets here paved with gold to be had for the picking up, but this is far from being the case." She describes the jobs available for those arriving in Cuba during the United States' occupation. "There is work for the hundreds on the many roads that are being made and repaired; there is work on the electric railroad in course of construction, and there are other improvements which employ much labor."

Not all jobs were lucrative or high-status. The majority, as Stanhope explains, were back-breaking, menial jobs that paid little. In describing the conditions and jobs available in Cuba, Stanhope does what so many in the press do: she justifies the land rush and speculation by making those from the United States worthy of economic opportunities, and

Cubans, despite their years of struggle and sacrifice, unworthy. "There is scarcely an able-bodied American who refuses work of this kind rather than let his family starve, but many of the lower-class Cubans have no such scruples and if they cannot have comfortable and ornamental positions prefer to allow those dependent on them to starve or live on charity."[27]

Stanhope's overall description of postwar Cuba is predictable, propagandistic, and wrong. Cubans filled all types of positions. Afro-Cuban men and women, in particular, were over-represented in those jobs that Stanhope argues were filled by Americans. According to the 1907 census, Afro-Cuban men were employed as shoemakers, tailors, bakers, barbers, day laborers, and servants. Afro-Cuban women worked as seamstresses, laundresses, and servants.[28] Ironically, Stanhope says as much in an article published a few months later. "At present there are only a few negroes in Cuba holding responsible positions. There are some policemen, and I have heard that there are also a few mail carriers of this race, though I have not seen them. They are mostly seen in menial positions as porters, waiters, laundresses etc."[29]

What distinguishes Stanhope's article is that she is one of the few to document the experiences of white women from the United States in Cuba during this period. "Men are not alone in seeking their fortunes here. Many women have come also." She chronicles the problems of white women who migrated to Havana to work as governesses for wealthy Cuban families, the success of those looking for work as teachers, even though there is a "great danger of an oversupply of them," and the growing demand for stenographers. She writes of a young woman stenographer from New York who from "the first has met with marked success." In Cuba for more than a year, the woman now has an office in the busy part of town, although unfortunately in the district known as "the yellow fever zone." This, however, has not been bad for business. Unlike New York, where she earned a modest sum due to the competition, in Cuba the lack of stenographers allowed her to earn "an income of $200 to $400 a month." Such an income was indeed impressive and by reporting it, Standhope encouraged travel to Cuba. Stanhope ends her article by writing that "the needs here are legion." Yet, instead of arguing for better hospitals, schools, and housing, she contends that what Havana really needs is a good hotel to make up for the miserable Cuban hotels, which are the "laughing stock of everyone who comes to Havana," and a "large New York department store."[30] Like so many other reporters, Stanhope envisioned a Cuba, not for Cubans, but for US residents. Despite Stanhope's optimism, there is a major problem that stands in the way. In Cuba, as Stanhope reports, a large proportion of the population "belongs to the colored race."[31]

In "The Negro Race in Cuba," Stanhope is clearly disgusted by what she perceives as the lack of racial separation, and likens Havana to a Southern City in "our own country, but with a difference." In the South, the "race knows it place and keeps it; there is no attempt at familiarity with white persons." Stanhope criticizes intermarriages, blacks and whites living together in tenement houses, and black and white children playing together and sitting side by side in schools. She is also rather surprised that "Cubans of whatever color" look upon General Maceo, "a black man," as one of the "noblest of their countrymen."

When it comes to Afro-Cuban women, Stanhope is deeply problematic. In a troubling and racist passage, Stanhope acknowledges that "there are some very pretty women among both mulattoes and blacks." She mentions how they pay a great deal of attention to their appearance, and dress tastefully "as well as their means will afford."

> But some of the black women are very homely, and even more, they are, barbaric. Not long since I saw one on the street, who, with her wild expression and great hoops of earrings, would have been far more in keeping with the home of her ancestors in the wilds of Africa.[32]

By invoking a stereotypical image of Africa, Stanhope deliberately cast Afro-Cuban female bodies as savage and uncivilized; designating them as not only "unattractive," but unworthy of even being Cuban. In an earlier passage, Stanhope unfavorably compares Afro-Cuban women to white Cuban women, using the most recognizable of Cuban artifacts, cigars, to script gendered, racial, social, and class distinctions among the women.

> Almost without exception, colored women here, especially the older ones, smoke great black cigars, face and cigar all of one color. They never use a pipe like the Southern "mammy." They walk along the street smok-

ing just as a man would. White women of the lower class smoke also, but rarely cigars: they prefer cigarettes.[33]

Stanhope's dispatches on race, travel, gender, investment, and the future of Cuba were read widely. Published in the *New York Times* and reprinted in local newspapers across the country, her articles promoted themes of underdevelopment, inferiority, and spectacle, and were used to manufacture characterizations that were not only in keeping with US mores, but indicative of how the United States envisioned and cataloged Cuba.

African American reporters also looked to Cuba as a site of reinvention, but for altogether different reasons. Unlike Stanhope, African American reporters and writers applauded what they considered to be racial and social equality in Cuba. The island was lodged in the memory and imagination of African Americans who believed, as Booker T. Washington did, that Cuba had "surpassed the United States in solving the race problem in that they have no race problem." The idea that Cubans had somehow eradicated the race problem inspired African American writer John M. Cromwell to write that Cubans, both blacks and whites, "lived on terms of perfect equality."[34] There were two major events during this period that deeply influenced how African Americans viewed their place in the United States, Cuba, and within the hemisphere: the passage of *Plessy vs. Ferguson* in 1896 and the Spanish-American War. Within years of the *Plessy vs. Ferguson* Supreme Court decision legalizing racial separation in the United States, African American men were drafted to fight for a nation that had just deemed them second-class citizens.

The Spanish-American War was controversial and polarizing. It invigorated a decades-long discussion and thinking over citizenship, civil rights, and what it meant to be black within and outside of the United States. For some, the war represented long held promises, for others it stirred deep resentments. Booker T. Washington, as Frank Guridy writes, was a vocal supporter of the draft, joining "the chorus of African-American voices agitating for participation in the conflict after the explosion of the Maine." He lobbied for the draft, and used what Guridy calls the "racialist idea that black people could handle the tropical climate better than whites," to make his case.[35] Washington was not alone. Newspapers, including the *Cleveland Gazette*, encouraged African

Americans to support the war. "As citizens and patriots, let us be ready and willing to do our part, to do our full duty, and to do even more than others in the hour of our nation's peril."[36] By asking African Americans to do "more than others," the Cleveland Gazette repeated a commonly held belief among certain sectors that to secure rights at home they had to prove themselves on the battlefield. Others disagreed.

Less than a month later, the Kansas City American Citizen reminded its readers that African Americans were bearing the brunt of the war yet reaping few of the benefits. "Colored troops are moving to the front. They should remember the conditions of mankind are not equal in this republic and there will be no return for too strong a patriotic zeal."[37] The Indianapolis Freeman moved beyond the promises of patriotism and enfranchisement and linked the participation of African Americans with a call to end racial violence, presenting a vivid and painful description of the quotidian brutality and cruelty experienced by African Americans. "If the government wants our support and services, let us demand and get a guarantee for our safety and protection at home. We want to put a stop to the lynch law, the butchering of our people like hogs, burning our houses, shooting our wives and children and raping our daughters and mothers."[38] The Richmond Planet followed suit a few months later, questioning the true cost of United States' actions in Cuba. Noting that the war with Spain has cost "nearly a billion dollars," the paper wondered why the United States had not spent "a cent to put down lynching, cruelty, and outrages in the United States?"[39]

Unlike the mainstream press, the black press examined the war and its aftermath in terms of race, enfranchisement, and hemispheric realities and potentials. Some, like the Kansas City American Citizen, connected their plight in the United States with Afro-Cubans on the island, reporting that the "fear of Negro dominancy" was at the root of the United States' desire to annex the island.[40] Even the Cleveland Gazette, which tended to be more conservative, published the writings of Reverend C. C. Astwood, who was stationed in Santiago de Cuba during the war. Concerned over the impending racial segregation and violence in Cuba at the hands of the US military forces, Astwood observed that the "color line is being fastly drawn by our whites here, and the Cubans abused are Negroes." He went on to wonder if Afro-Cubans could ever escape US racism, violence, and mistreatment, especially once the United States controlled the island. "It has been found out at last, as I used to tell them in the United States, the majority of Cubans were Negroes; now that this fact has dawned upon the white brother, there is no longer a desire to have Cuban independence."[41]

Recognizing that annexation was a real possibility, Rafael Serra wrote an essay denouncing it. First published on July 16, 1899 in *La Doctina de Martí*, "La anexión" examined the racial and class politics of annexation and its potentially disastrous effects on Cuba. Serra called annexation a "horrible calamity" that would "in an instant, end the last vestiges of Cuban identity" and "Americanize" the island.[42] According to Serra, annexation would eliminate all traces of Cuban independence, self-government, and history. By severing Cuba from its own efforts at sovereignty, the US government, business interests, and allies created the necessary conditions not only for controlling the island, but for making it appear that such actions ultimately benefitted Cubans.

Unlike Ludlow and Stanhope, Serra's thoughts on the influx of US companies, investors, and workers were not positive. Deviating from the prevalent discourse of the period, Serra writes that Cuba excites "yankee greed," and that the United States' interest in Cuba is solely predicated on controlling important tobacco and sugar markets, and taking advantage of Cuba's strategic geographic position. He goes on to write that by occupying and eventually annexing Cuba, the United States stood to control the "key to America."[43] In one of the more perplexing passages, Serra argued that since African American migrants spoke English and were familiar with US culture and traditions, they would do better under annexation than white Cubans. "Black Americans for their part, tired of struggling in their country against so many obstacles would not hesitate in choosing to migrate to a nearby country under their same flag and climate."[44]

The problem with such an assertion is that Serra underestimates the damage of US colonial policies on all Afro-descended populations. There is very little to indicate that African Americans transcended their racialized conditions simply through the act of emigration, especially if they were moving to an island under US control. Yet, according to Serra, leaving the United States for Cuba was an easy decision for African Americans. Given the choice between migrating to Cuba or leaving the South where they are "cruelly lynched," and the North, "where they go hungry, since most jobs in the north close their doors," taking their chances and moving to Cuba was an easy one.[45]

Nonetheless, the discourse remained a powerful enticement to African Americans seeking to relinquish and forsake US racism, exclusion, and brutality. The same year that Serra published "La anexión," Captain John L. Waller founded the Afro-American Cuban Emigration Society with the purpose of resettling African Americans to Cuba. Inspired by Waller, W. L. Grant, a popular Kansas minister, proposed that the US Congress appropriate $100 million to settle 2 million African Americans not only to Cuba, but also to Puerto Rico, Hawaii, and Africa.[46] The idea of migrating to what many thought was a racial paradise was enviable. For African Americans, Cuba was not, as David Helwig explains, an "accessible holiday retreat for the wealthy or an outlet for investment," but instead a setting for an experiment in race relations "offering hope that former slaves and slave masters could live together harmoniously." Interest in migrating to Cuba quickly dissipated as African Americans realized that the drive for annexation was directly tied to whitening the island through white-only policies and imposed racial segregation.[47]

Rafael Serra, Martín Morúa Delgado, and the Problems of Exile Politics in Cuba

They [Afro-Cubans] say they have got beyond that stage; that during the war whites and blacks were known only as Cubans, and that such a thing as color was not thought of until after the war, when pale faced youths who fled to New York and other safe places in the United States while there was fighting to do returned to Cuba and took the offices which others [Afro-Cubans] who fought and suffered privations deserved.
New York Tribune, 1902[48]

In April 1899, Serra returned to Havana. Although he traveled to New York several times over the years, he settled in Havana and continued his political and journalistic work. He founded and edited *El Nuevo Criollo* (1904–1906), was appointed by Tomás Estrada Palma to a coveted administrative position in the post office, and was elected to Congress in

1904 under the more conservative National Radical Party. Estrada Palma also appointed Serra's close friend and La Liga colleague Juan Bonilla to a job in the department of public instruction. It was an appointment that provoked "the mass resignation of white clerks."[49]

The return of Afro-Cuban revolutionaries shaped and marked the early Cuban republic. As Aline Helg writes, the most prominent Afro-Cubans after 1898 were "not the mambises but the middle-aged intellectuals, already famous before 1895, who had spent the War for Independence in exile." The returned exiles had acquired new skills that "set them apart from those who remained on the island." These included men like Rafael Serra, Martín Morúa Delgado, Juan Bonilla, Manuel De J. González, who were involved with La Liga in New York, and the journalist Juan Gualberto Gómez, who spent most of his exile in France and Spain. Except for Gómez, few of these men experienced combat. Martín Morúa Delgado joined the rebellion in June 1898 to become, as Helg cited, "lieutenant without having held the machete . . . who spent his life in the camp's archives."[50] The more revered black military heroes and leaders, Antonio Maceo, Flor Crombet, and Guillermón Moncada, had died. Others, like Quintín Banderas, who was well into his sixties by the end of the war, had no land, formal education, or skills, and was left destitute. A member of the Asociación Nacional de Veteranos, he was nonetheless refused a position as janitor by the government, a denial that "deeply humiliated him."[51] The vacuum left by the death of Afro-Cuban military leaders along with the appointment of Cuban exile Tomás Estrada Palma elevated Afro-Cuban exile influence.

Not all black revolutionaries who returned to Cuba were welcomed with open arms. Like so many of his contemporaries, Sotero Figueroa moved to Havana to help build the republic. Interested in continuing to print and publish newspapers, Figueroa spent whatever resources he had left transporting his printing plant from Key West to Cuba. Although recommended by many of his peers, including Tomás Estrada Palma and Gonzalo de Quesada, Figueroa did not receive the support and protection he anticipated upon his return. After only a few months in Havana, Figueroa's business failed and his printing plant ended in the civil courts. According to La Discusión, Figueroa was left destitute and "unnoticed by those he had helped for free."[52] Figueroa remained active in politics, working with different commissions and organizations, including La Asociación de Revolucionarios Cubanos Migrantes formed in Havana to support the presidency of Estrada Palma and promote exile revolutionary politics in Cuba.[53]

The question facing Estrada Palma and his supporters was how to take those ideas born in exile and apply them to a nation in the making, a nation that outside of the imaginary few had experience building. The process was messy. While in New York, Serra and Figueroa challenged the conservative faction of the Partido Revolucionario Cubano headed by Estrada Palma. Once in Cuba, both openly aligned themselves with Estrada Palma and the Moderate Party. As one of the few to benefit from Estrada Palma's patronage, Serra's decision left him open to sharp criticisms. Some characterized it as a sign that he had abandoned his principles and acquiesced to the racist policies of the nascent republic. Others saw it as a clever strategy for tenaciously enfranchising Afro-Cubans from the inside.[54]

Serra's writings reveal a man who, although committed to social justice, labor, and racial equality, was confronting new realities in Cuba. In *El Nuevo Criollo*, Serra pointed out the lack of jobs for Afro-Cuban men and women. He denounced racism, rampant discrimination, and questioned the government's support of Spanish immigration, calling it "a means of destroying the blacks" through demography and low wages. He opposed the selling of Cuban lands and resources to the United States and other foreign powers, and criticized the dominant thinking on white supremacy. At the same time, he used *El Nuevo Criollo* to advance Estrada Palma's political agenda and promote values associated with racial uplift including marriage, steady employment, cleanliness, education, and chastity.

Serra's perspective on Afro-Cuban respectability echoed the familiar rhetoric espoused by Booker T. Washington. The two were politically aligned and Serra openly admired Washington and the Tuskegee Institute. He considered Washington a visionary with a practical plan for educating African Americans, a plan that Serra argued Cuba should consider emulating.[55]

Serra himself never lost sight of the benefits of US education and access. In 1905, *El Nuevo Criollo* published an article on the recent graduation of his daughter Consuelo Anacleta Serra Heredia from the New York Normal College and her subsequent return to Cuba. Written by

Miguel Gualba, director and editor of the newspaper *Redención*, the piece highlights her successes and makes a case for more Afro-Cubans to enter higher education in the United States with the goal of working in Cuba. In fact, Gualba concluded the article by adding that a degree from New York Normal College would be more than enough credentials to teach in Cuba.[56]

After living in New York for close to twenty years, it was not easy for Serra to relinquish his diasporic influences, ideas, and alliances. Most of his writings and publications reflect a distinctly diasporic directive shaped by narrative fictions and possibilities so common to diasporic longings. One of the most immediate and ongoing commitments was to José Martí. Not only did Serra name a newspaper after Martí (i.e., *La Doctrina de Martí*), he cited him in almost every article, journal, and essay he published in the United States and Cuba. In one of his last publications Martí appears throughout, and is employed as a morally authoritative voice and justification for Serra's own controversial political alliances; "as Martí would say, it is not important if some are liberals and others conservatives. What is important is to know if liberals or conservatives serve the nation."[57]

Serra's insistence on using Martí as symbol and trope represents what Lillian Guerra argues was a fascination, if not obsession, with "entombing" Martí as a universal sign of unity during the early years of the Cuban Republic. The liberal party, the different nationalist factions, and even the pro-imperialists all used Martí to promote their politics, ideas, and strategies. The pro-imperialist employment of Martí was especially egregious considering that Martí had been a vocal critic of the United States and US imperialism for most of his adult life. This, however, did not stop supporters of US imperialism who, in 1905 and 1906, presided over the "public unveiling of two nearly identical national monuments to Martí, the first in Havana Central Park and the second in Cienfuegos Central Park."[58]

It was through these narratives and public displays that, according to Guerra, Cubans created "a collective origin myth of social unity rooted in the messianic martyrdom of Martí." The problem with such pliable fictions is that different groups invoked his memory to either promote their interests or blame others for violating "the sacred standard of unity incarnated in Martí."[59] Martí was imbued with so many meanings that it was difficult to decipher which side he belonged to or what interpretations to accept. One writer, as Guerra documents, went as far as to identify Martí "with both the divinity of Jesus Christ and the delusional idealism of Cervantes' famous character of Don Quixote."[60] Martí lived, worked, and wrote in exile for more than fifteen years. Yet, he remained embedded within a Cuban nationalist and republican discourse that made little reference to his years lived in exile. As factions and groups in Cuba rushed to reclaim and reconfigure Martí for their own purposes, they failed to consider just how much of his thinking was influenced and shaped by living and working in the United States. Exiles and migrants, on the other hand, were already skilled in how to use Martí to promote contradictory politics and legitimize ideas that would never have been accepted otherwise. In short, he fit perfectly into the common diasporic parlance of temporalities, potential, and futures. By the time of his death, Martí had been elevated to the highest levels of migrant and exile moral, political, racial, and ideological symbolism.

Diasporic thinking also influenced Serra and Estrada Palma's relationship and their approach to Cuban politics. It allowed them to see themselves not as outsiders who spent most of their lives in exile, but as innovators unencumbered by past events in Cuba. Serra was not afraid of the United States or its immediate plans for the island. At times, he even considered the United States a stabilizing force. Yet, his confidence in the United States was measured. As he disclosed in a letter he published in New York in 1901, he was wary of the United States' racism and intervention. Published in *El Pueblo Libre*, Serra wrote of the conflicts surrounding the United States' intervention and the growing instability in Cuba. Claiming that he wanted the "yankee lynchers to go and leave us," Serra also worried about the consequences of political instability in Cuba, warning that "if tomorrow the interveners leave we know the lesson: the tyranny continues." Serra's letter reveals what for him was an ongoing dilemma concerning the US intervention, and occupation: To what extent was Cuban dependence on US investments, resources, and control a detriment to sovereignty? Could Cubans effectively govern without US intervention?

Despite his concerns, Serra benefited a great deal from his alliances with Estrada Palma and the Moderate Party. As Melina Pappedemos explains, Serra was a "black broker" who was expected to secure electoral outcomes and serve as a partisan spokesperson for the ruling party. In return, he was afforded power, influence, and the opportunity to shape the republic from the inside.[61] Serra was not the only one. By January 1901, citizenship rights and universal suffrage were granted to all men irrespective of color. This resulted in new political concerns taking hold among African-descended men who learned "how to participate fully in formal politics beyond the mere exercise of casting a vote." These rights and interests led to a postwar period defined by black patronage networks where almost all Afro-Cuban activists, "except for those who formed the short-lived PIC, joined the ranks of mainstream parties."[62]

The black patronage networks did not come without a fight. On May 20, 1902, Afro-Cuban veterans of the Liberation Army formed the Comité de Acción de los Veteranos y Asociaciónes de Color presided over by Captain Generoso Campos Marquetti to bring attention to the lack of jobs, resources, and economic access. Their concerns reached the *New York Tribune*, which published an article on the color line in Cuba. The reporter observed that, "Never before has the negro question been so important in this country as it is today. The 'Veteranos de Color' have issued a formal declaration of their intentions and aims."[63] Their aim was to pressure the provisional government to provide Afro-Cubans with more public jobs and to denounce racism and exclusion.[64] The Comité de Acción members were fully aware that Estrada Palma was politically vulnerable. His de facto support of the white-only policy instituted by Governor Ludlow and the overwhelming economic investment threatening the Cuban economy, made it difficult for Estrada Palma to convince the members present that he supported Afro-Cuban enfranchisement, regardless of Serra's support. A month later, members, including Julián V. Serra and Evaristo Estenoz, again met with Estrada Palma. The meeting degenerated quickly and the committee failed to secure promises or make any gains.[65]

When the Comité de Acción met again with the governor and mayor of Havana, they delivered a memorandum to the House of Representatives calling for the repeal of the whites-only policy. Afro-Cuban veterans joined the Comité de Acción in chastising white Cuban officials for their actions and accused them of betraying the racially enfranchised and inclusive definitions of nation so critical to the war effort and the struggle for independence. Protests, meetings, and memorandums eventually yielded some results. Afro-Cubans were granted low-level posts in different public offices and government administrations. However, while the president and the House of Representative delivered on their promises to provide employment, they, as Pappedemos points out, "failed to institute the more far-reaching legislative reforms necessary to satisfy the demands of black and mulatto veterans and clubmen or fully ease tensions."[66]

The distrust, anger, frustrations, and feelings of betrayal reveal a deeply conflicted postwar period in Cuba. In addition to the exclusions and lack of opportunities, definitions of blackness and its uses within Cuban society were under intense scrutiny. On the morning of April 22, 1900, *Diario de la Marina* released figures from the 1899 census showing that a third of the population was of color and that overall the Cuban population had declined. This numeric significance did not translate into power and access for Afro-Cubans. Instead it signaled a dangerous situation "for the white race," one that, according to the *Diario*, needed to be rectified once again, through the importation of Spanish workers to whiten the island and provide cheap labor.[67] The support for Spanish immigration was a direct threat to Afro-Cubans who, despite their involvement in a long and protracted struggle for independence, were now competing with Spanish immigrants for jobs. The competition would not end there. Years later, the Cuban government would import workers from Jamaica and Haiti, further debilitating the Afro-Cuban labor force.[68]

At the same time, Afro-Cubans were being pressured to move past any identification with blackness to a larger "race-less" nationalist identity. The idea, as Helg writes, was to foment a nationalist strategy and discourse used by "foreign powers and ruling white Cubans" to deny the existence of racism and to justify the current social order.[69] In doing so, the government and elites conveniently placed the blame on Afro-Cubans for their continual subordination and lack of opportunities, deeming any discussion concerning racism, disenfranchisement, and exclusion unpatriotic.

Afro-Cuban intellectuals, veterans, and activists challenged the provisional government's position on race, which called for them to remain silent and grateful, and demanded that there be a public acknowledgment that racism was indeed a problem in Cuba. They used the dispro-portionately high level of Afro-Cuban involvement in the revolutionary wars to claim their right to the republic and reject the belief that black enfranchisement was a white concession. The *New York Tribune* cited an Afro-Cuban veteran who connected the postwar plight of Afro-Cuban veterans with their involvement in the war.

> But the colored veteran is not getting justice here, and we have decided to adopt quiet but effective measures to improve this condition. The whites themselves cannot deny that we fought the hardest for Cuban indepen-dence. Ten colored soldiers died in the revolution to one of the white. Can you blame us for complaining?[70]

Furthermore, they argued that their massive participation in the wars made "la patria possible." This argument, as Alejandro de la Fuente explains, was used by members of the Partido Independiente de Color (PIC) who set black participation in the war "at 85 percent," and made it a cornerstone of the "radical interpretation of Cubanness."[71]

In a disputed election, Estrada Palma defeated the Liberal Party can-didate José Miguel Gómez to become president for the second time in 1905. Less than a year later, members of the Liberal Party, which in-cluded a large number of Afro-Cubans, rebelled against Estrada Palma, labeling the elections and his presidency corrupt. The insurgency, known as the August Revolution, resulted in a second US military oc-cupation of the island from 1906 to 1909. During the second occupation and under the supervision of the United States, José Miguel Gómez was elected president in 1908. That same year on August 7, the Agrupación Independiente de Color, later known as the Partido Independiente de Color (PIC), was founded under the leadership of Evaristo Estenoz. The PIC was a culmination of almost a decade of struggle, protests, and de-mands for Afro-Cuban economic and political enfranchisement. Two years later the PIC would be banned as a result of a law authored by the Afro-Cuban exile Martín Morúa Delgado.

Like his colleague Rafael Serra, Morúa Delgado left New York and moved to Havana after the war. Unlike Serra, he did not support Es-trada Palma or the Moderate Party. Aligned with Gómez and the Lib-eral Party, Morúa Delgado had been appointed president of the Senate by Gómez and remained an integral part of his cabinet. This fact was not lost on the *New York Times*, who reported on Morúa Delgado's multiple appointments, writing that he was "the first negro to receive a portfolio."[72] While serving as president of the Senate, Morúa Delgado introduced a bill that banned the formation of political parties based on a single race or color. Designed to prohibit any form of racial exclusion and separation, Morúa Delgado justified the amendment as one that promoted inclusion at all costs. Yet, as historians have argued, the Morúa Amendment had more to do with preventing the PIC from taking votes away from President Gómez and the Liberal Party than insuring racial equality.[73] Ironically, the Gómez administration was now confronting many of the same criticisms leveled at Estrada Palma and the Moderate Party, including the lack of jobs and government appointments for Afro-Cubans.

On October 24, 1909, Rafael Serra died. Although he lived most of his adult life in exile, he was officially mourned by the Cuban nation. The vice president of the Republic, Alfredo Zayas, led his funeral procession. A year later the newspaper *Minerva* honored his legacy: "Today Cubans cry in remembrance of this sad anniversary." Preceded by a quote by José Martí, it mentioned his friendship with Martí and championed his work as a poet, journalist, and activist. Oscar P. Alacán depicted Serra as a good, honorable, and cultured man who was committed to putting theory into practice, especially in defense of the "beloved Republic." He also referenced the posthumous publication of Serra's last work, "La república posible," as proof that despite his continual alliances, he was committed to building a republic for everyone, especially for "the poor and the working-class."[74]

Published shortly after his death, "La república posible" is one of Serra's most telling texts. It is thoughtful and troubling. He expresses both sadness and measured optimism as he warns readers of the dangers associated with a republic in the making. In admitting that the Cuban republic is "not perfect," Serra isolates two major problems that need to be addressed if the republic is to heal and "be made possible": the "economic question," and the lack of harmony among the different "ethnic elements of the country."[75] The text is not without controversies. In it, he acknowledges the August Revolution, reaffirms his commitment to Estrada Palma and the Moderate Party, and questions whether the Liberal Party "will resolve the problem." He also expressed support for the appearance of the illustrious newspaper, *Previsión*, the official newspaper of the PIC edited by "the distinguished Evaristo Estenoz."[76] Serra's support of the PIC is not altogether surprising considering that Pedro Ivonnet, one of the leaders of the PIC, had also supported Estrada Palma and was a member of the Moderate Party. Like other Afro-Cubans who supported Estrada Palma, Ivonnet was rewarded with a government job as a veterinarian in the rural guard.[77] Ivonnet's distrust of the Liberal Party was further solidified with the drafting and support of the Morúa Amendment of 1910.

Martín Morúa Delgado never witnessed the repercussions and brutal consequences of the amendment he authored and advocated. On April 28, 1910, he died. He too would be mourned by the nation as President Gómez headed his funeral procession. Similar to Serra, *Minerva* dedicated a memorial page to his writing and political activism a year after his death. The page applauded Morúa Delgado's accomplishments, his labor activism, and documented his unwavering and singular influence on the burgeoning republic, declaring that Morúa was "in peace," what "Maceo, Crombet, and Gómez were in war." Longer and more effusive than the one published on Serra a year earlier, there is an unmistakable patriotic zeal that runs throughout the article honoring Morúa Delgado. Labeling him a "patriot," the essay placed him in the same company as Martí, Maceo, Aguilera, Agramonte, and even Ben Franklin. The author, who is unnamed, refused to accept Morúa Delgado's political and theoretical death, writing that "men like you do not die." Instead, they exist "as guides" to direct future generations "towards peace and progress."[78] By the time *Minerva* published the memorial in 1911, Morúa Delgado was one of the most controversial figures in Cuba and among the Afro-Cuban community. The Morúa Amendment had effectively banned the formation of organizations based on race, notably the PIC, which by 1911 boasted a membership of close to several thousand members. Yet, the memorial reveals little of the chaos brought about as a result of the Morúa Amendment.

After ending its run in 1889, *Minerva* resumed publication in 1910. The second phase, which lasted from 1910 to 1915, was significantly different than the first phase. During the second phase *Minerva*'s commitment to feminism, racial enfranchisement, and maintaining diasporic connections changed dramatically. The later editions of *Minerva* focused on the nation, racial uplift, and empowerment through elections. Since only men were granted the vote, women were excluded not only from electoral gains, but from the very narrative of civil rights and equality. Despite past commitments to empowering Afro-Cuban women, *Minerva*, like the republic itself, pushed Afro-Cuban women to the political, social, and economic margins.

The later editions of *Minerva*, which were renamed *Minerva Revista Universal Ilustrada*, deemphasized race and gender, and according to Gema Guevara, privileged national identity "over any other competing construct." *Minerva*'s writers and editors included mostly men and went from being concerned with the ramifications of slavery and targeting women as agents of social change, to advocating for political enfranchisement and electoral gains for Afro-Cubans. *Minerva*'s resurrection in 1910 coincided with the intense national debates on race and politics, the mass arrests of black activists, and what Pappedemos writes was the "vigorous black electoral activism, primarily from the PIC."[79]

At the same time, as Guevara points out, the fear of reprisal during a period of political instability motivated *Minerva*'s editorial board to issue a statement clarifying that *Minerva* was a magazine for all Cubans and as such, "not dedicated to political parties nor to race." *Minerva* did admit that it "might show preference" to "the color element" in Cuba whose aspirations it "tends to champion." The articles published in the magazine did not always follow such rhetoric. As Guevara demonstrates, editors and writers of the magazine including Juan Gualberto Gómez, who served on the first editorial board, were quick to criticize articles that failed to confront racism in Cuba. Gómez in particular believed that *Minerva* needed to take more risks and be a site for experimentation of ideas and collaborations among men and women.[80] In addition to the customary pieces that emphasize nationality over race and gender, there were those that took risks and directly challenged the "white danger," the problems of classifying race, and the future of race in Cuba. There were, as expected, critical editorials written by Juan Gualberto Gómez, Miguel Espinosa, and even a letter by G. Campos Marquetti to José del C. Poves, president of "la Sociedad Unión Fraternal," where he argues that "equality and civil and political rights are intangible. Without them who could explain the existence of our Republic."[81]

Although *Minerva* continued to be sold as a magazine for women, the writings by and on women declined.[82] There are few if any pieces that discuss the future of Afro-Cuban women in politics and the nation. Not only did *Minerva* tolerate patriarchy during the second phase, it was more focused on the "inclusion of the black middle class into the business of nation."[83] This was indeed the case in a brief article on the "Club Feminista Minerva" in the Paginas Feministas section of *Minerva*, which cast Afro-Cuban women as "elegant ladies" interested in the arts, literature, and sports, and noted that the Club Feminista Minerva rivaled any women's club in Europe.[84]

The business of nation so dominated *Minerva*'s second period that the magazine barely cultivated diasporic connections with Cubans living abroad. Unlike the first phase, there were no agents who sold copies of *Minerva* in the United States, there were only a few published pieces written by migrant Cubans, and the editorial board consisted solely of Cubans on the island. Simply put, Cuban migrants were no longer seen as powerful figures critical in articulating the future of the Cuban nation. The articles that did mention the United States varied widely in terms of politics and insights. "La crónica neoyorquina," for instance, was a tourist account that highlighted the Statue of Liberty, Central Park, and the Brooklyn Bridge. Others, like the one written by Facundo Ación y Naranjo titled "De Tampa," is a powerful meditation on racism, work, and the pain of "having to abandon one's homeland." He writes of "the disgrace of having to live in a strange land where the color of one's skin impedes access to everything and to all places." He singles out certain barbershops, cafes, and La Union Martí-Maceo as the only places in town "that welcome men of color."[85] Published a few weeks after the revolt against the Morúa Amendment, Ación y Naranjo's was likely influenced by the political chaos leading up to the revolt. Although he does not mention the revolt per se, it is one of the more politically and racially charged pieces published in and on the diaspora.

On May 20, 1912, ten years after the official formation of the Cuban Republic, the PIC and hundreds of its sympathizers organized an armed protest. The Cuban government under Gómez reacted by labeling the protest a "race war" and by sending military troops to Oriente to quell the protests. The government also requested and received support from the United States, who sent military reinforcements to subdue the protesters. Thousands of PIC members and supporters were killed or jailed. On June 27, Evaristo Estenoz was shot. Less than a month later, on July 18, Pedro Ivonnet was killed in Oriente while trying to escape. His lifeless body was paraded through the streets of Santiago de Cuba before being buried in a common grave.[86]

The killings of Estenoz and Ivonnet along with the death and imprisonment of thousands of Afro-Cubans across the island ended the revolt and silenced dissent. What began as protest, ended in massacre. The *Chicago Defender, Washington Post,* the *Crisis,* and the *New York Times* reported on events in Cuba before and after the revolt. The *New York Times* even published editorials written by President José Miguel Gómez in which he assessed the current situation, blamed Afro-Cubans for the revolt, and affirmed his control of the government. "I expect to have under control within a short time the revolt in Oriente and Las Villas Province, in which negroes exclusively are taking part." The *Chicago Defender* focused on the tensions between "the Spaniards and the Negroes," noting that much of the unrest was in Oriente, "where an immense majority of the population is [*sic*] blacks." An important concern for the *Defender* was the possibility of US intervention in Cuba. "Uneasiness is caused owing to the press cables from Washington announcing that the United States would interfere."[87]

In July 1912, the *Crisis* published a powerful and sobering article by Arturo Schomburg simply entitled, "General Evaristo Estenoz." In it he explained the revolt from the perspective of the PIC, declaring that many "Negroes curse the dawn of the Republic." Schomburg's powerful and provocative statement referred to the broken promises of a Republic Afro-Cubans had fought so hard to manifest "in time of hardship during the days of revolution." As a key figure in the nineteenth-century exile and migrant revolutionary and independence movement in New York, Schomburg's conclusion that the "Negro had done much for Cuba. Cuba had done nothing for the Negro," reflected the deep disillusionment of those in the United States who had supported independence and racial enfranchisement in Cuba.[88] It also signaled a change in how black Cuban and Puerto Rican migrants approached questions of race, freedom, and equality in the early twentieth century. Independence from colonial powers was no longer seen as a solution for ending racism.

Two years after the revolt the *Chicago Defender* published an article on the changing political dynamics between Cuba and the United States. Entitled "Annexing Cuba," the article questioned the US government's continuing interest in controlling the island, and warned Cubans to not look to the United States to solve its problems. Arguing that the United States is a "labyrinth of prejudice and unchristianlike [*sic*] spirit" the *Defender* advised that, "If Cuba is wise it will shun annexation."[89] The *Chicago Defender's* use of the term annexation was deliberate. The aim was to denote the United States' colonial practices and future intentions in Cuba; a directive that influenced how the *Chicago Defender* covered race in Cuba.

In 1924, a year before Gerardo Machado was elected president, the *Chicago Defender* published an article that blamed the United States for the racism in Cuba, and argued that Afro-Cubans fared better than African Americans. "Colored Cubans are as much Cuban as are the ones with the 'white skin,' and, from the personal experiences of this writer, racial prejudices are hard to find outside of the places operated or mainly patronized by white Americans, a class notorious for their faculty of [*sic*] spreading hate against color." Rejecting the Cuban consul F. B. Caballero's claim that "the whites and Negroes do not exactly mix in Cuba," the *Chicago Defender* reported that Caballero probably did not wish "uninformed white Americans to know that in his home country the people of darker color can go as far as they like." Despite the earlier revolts, ongoing protests, political betrayals, and racism, the *Chicago Defender* considered race relations in Cuba worthy of emulation in the United States. "We may have the same conditions in the United States some day, and along this line Cuba, despite the consul's protest, sets this country a splendid example."[90]

Imperial Migrations: Moving North Under Empire

Imperialism is said to be responsible for a very peculiar mania now prevalent among natives of the West Indies who come to this country—an irresistible desire to pose as Cubans.
Washington Post, 1902[91]

To the stranger expecting to find the typical kennels of the underdog, such as the hovels of poor which disgrace many a European city, the native quarters in South Africa or the old Chinatown in Havana, the colored section of New York is an agreeable revelation.
Bernardo Ruiz Suárez, 1922[92]

In 1902 the *Washington Post* reported on the hundreds of "West Indians, Porto Ricans, Dominicans, and others" who migrated to the United States "after the Spanish war." US occupation facilitated migrations not only from Cuba, but also from other Caribbean nations. According to the *Post*, Caribbean migrants pretended to be Cuban, what the *Post* termed "Bogus Cubans," to take advantage of the current good will toward Cuba and Cubans. "The press, the pulpit, and Congress suddenly built up such a general sympathy for long-suffering Cuba that any Cuban coming to this country was sure of hearty welcome." From the *Post*'s perspective, much of the sympathy was due to the average New Yorker's "lazy conception of geography. To him Cuba is the West Indies and the West Indies is Cuba, and anybody from Cuba is entitled to his sympathy."[93]

While New Yorkers may not care about hemispheric geography, they were, as the *Post* reported, quite aware of the relationship between race and status, noting that New Yorkers understood that a "strain of negro blood in his veins" marked the migrants as being from the "lower classes of Latin America." Claiming that the deception "really harms no one while benefitting a few," the *Post* warned of the possibility of a large number of racialized migrants entering the United States as a result of US imperialism. Citing the case of the Philippines as a possible watershed, the *Post* reported that by the time Filipinos arrive at a sufficient appreciation of the advantage of being Americans, "every South Sea Islander may proclaim himself a Filipino, and that then it will be time to draw the line."[94]

The *Washington Post* delineated what was perhaps the greatest change in migration from the Caribbean to the United States during the early twentieth century: the role of US empire in defining and shaping migrations north. Despite the United States' efforts at stabilizing governments through occupation and control, migrations from the Caribbean to the

United States, including Cuba and Puerto Rico, were on the rise. In 1903 Cuban migration doubled from an estimated 4,711 in 1902 to 8,170 a year later. By 1907, migrations from the Caribbean, including Cuba and Puerto Rico, had quadrupled to 16,689.[95] Cubans who migrated to New York during this period settled primarily in Harlem, Washington Heights, Chelsea, Brooklyn, and the Bronx, areas with a sizeable Cuban and Puerto Rican community. Afro-Cuban migrants moved to Harlem, Washington Heights, and the Bronx.[96] In 1917 the US government passed the Jones Organic Act conferring citizenship on Puerto Ricans. This made it possible for Puerto Ricans to travel and migrate without restrictions, and for the US government to draft Puerto Rican men to fight in World War I. In his memoirs Bernardo Vega painted a vivid picture of Puerto Ricans leaving the island and settling in New York during this period.

> But war or no war, the emigration continued unabated. It was in those years that the Puerto Rican community in Harlem began to swell. The Chelsea area, from 26th Street down to 15th Street, was also inhabited by large numbers of Puerto Rican families, as was the Boro Hall area in Brooklyn. But the largest concentration was situated around 116th Street, which came to be known as the Barrio Latino.[97]

Puerto Ricans established vibrant Spanish-speaking neighborhoods with businesses, political organizations, and social clubs. Some of the earlier businesses were boarding houses, barbershops, and "restaurants like those back home."[98] On June 4, 1918, the Spanish-language newspaper *La Prensa* was first published.[99] By the 1930s the number of Puerto Ricans living in New York was close to 45,000, with the majority living in East Harlem where, according to the Federal Writers Project, Puerto Ricans were "in the overwhelming majority."[100]

The number of Cubans leaving the island did not rival or even match the number of Puerto Ricans. Nonetheless, Cubans migrated. By the late 1920s to the mid-1930s a steady and continuous stream of Cubans, including a significant proportion of Afro-Cubans, arrived in the United States. Some, including José Isabel León, moved to New York in the 1920s to study, while others, like the musician Mario Bauza, traveled to New York in 1926 to play clarinet and record with the orchestra Antonio

María Romeu for RCA. While in New York, Bauza was "overwhelmed by the negro shows at the Lafayette Theater in Harlem . . . the jazz . . . black men and women doing their thing, no interference, no signs of racism." Bauza was so taken by New York, and Harlem in particular, that he decided to move there permanently. On April 28, 1929 (his eighteenth birthday), Bauza got his passport and moved to New York for good.[101] For Bernardo Ruiz Suárez, Harlem was "a revelation." In 1922, his book, *The Color Question in the Two Americas* was published. Ruiz Suárez characterized Harlem as "a city within a city." Noting that while for "white New York, Harlem is reputed to be a good place to keep away from," for him Harlem was "far more attractive than some of the other parts of city. Streets as clean as any are lined with buildings newer and better constructed than the flats and apartment houses in many other sections in the city."

Similar to many Afro-Cubans, Ruiz Suárez lived and worked in Harlem. A lawyer by trade, Ruiz Suárez published pamphlets, was involved in Cuban cultural clubs, and forged links with the African American community, dedicating his book to the Reverend Charles D. Martin, the pastor of Beth-Tphillah Moravian Church in New York. Interested in the multiple readings of blackness in the United States and Cuba, Ruiz Suárez employed a cultural argument for explaining what he considered to be the fundamental differences between the two. At times problematic and simplistic, Ruiz Suárez's work remains a compelling look at how one Afro-Cuban immigrant in the early twentieth century sought to understand the multiple workings of race and its role in shaping diasporic and immigrant communities. A meditation on the impact of historical policies, events, and legacies, Ruiz Suárez references slavery, the politics of independence and racial violence, religion, capitalism, the Morúa Amendment, the Race War of 1912, and the limitations of US democracy, to explain the differences and similarities between the two.

A central theme in the text is whether blackness was enough to bind African Americans and Afro-Cuban migrants. According to Ruiz Suárez, the answer is no. Citing what he considered to be the ignorance "in the Spanish-American countries," where very little is known regarding "the ability and progress of the black man in this country," Ruiz Suárez writes that it was a common thing to hear, "as incontrovertible postulate of racial and intellectual superiority, the statement: I am not an American negro." For Ruiz Suárez such a statement is a "characteristic expression of contempt" commonly made by a select number of Afro-Cubans who "have made themselves the standard bearers of racial aristocracy."[102] Ruiz Suárez's book is one of the few works that examines how the workings of nation, nationalist identities, and culture traveled with Afro-Cubans, influencing their views and positions as migrants in New York.

By the late 1920s, the number of Afro-Cubans arriving to the United States increased. In 1930 alone, more than 18,000 Cubans left the island, surpassing the number of Cubans who left in 1880 during the aftermath of the Ten Years' War.[103] Those arriving included journalists, musicians, students, activists, and artists fleeing the economic depression and the political repression of the Machado government. First elected on May 20, 1925, President Gerardo Machado promised to end political corruption and initiate policies and programs to modernize Cuba. Machado, who was popular at the time, was seen as an advocate of positive change and reform. He called for an end to US influence and publicly challenged the Platt Amendment. By the late 1920s, however, it was clear that Machado was more interested in protecting Cuba's elite, foreign capital, and business interests than instituting reforms. While still president he was accused of illegally changing the Cuban constitution to extend his term from two to six years without the right for reelection. In 1930 he passed a number of decrees limiting civil rights, supporting censorship, and prohibiting all public demonstrations by political parties and groups not registered with the government.[104] That same year on October 12, the *New York Times* reported on the violence that ensued after an estimated three hundred University of Havana students protested the closure of the university until after the presidential election. In response, the police fired directly at the protesters, killing one student and wounding twelve others.[105] The violence continued after the election, with workers, students, labor organizers, and Socialist Party members periodically beaten and imprisoned for challenging Machado and his policies.

The repression led to more demonstrations and calls for an end to Machado's presidency. Cubans formed organizations that directly questioned Machado's policies, including the Federación de Estudiantes de la Universidad de la Habana, La Agrupación Comunista de la Habana, and El Partido Comunista de Cuba, which by the late 1920s merged with La Confederación Nacional Obrera de Cuba (CNOC). Cuba, like most of the Americas, was hit hard by the economic depression, adding fuel to the already unstable political situation. Strikes and work stoppages in lucrative and key industries, including sugar, tobacco, railroads, construction, and manufacturing, made the political and economic situation in Cuba unbearable—so much so that on August 12, 1933, even after Ambassador Sumner Wells' attempts at mediation, President Machado was overthrown, largely as a result of organized labor.[106]

The rise of labor and the Communist Party's efforts at organizing across ethnic and racial lines during and after the Machadato radicalized a large number of Afro-Cubans. Realizing the need to seriously address race if they were to successfully organize, the CNOC devoted their attention to the "black question" and launched a campaign against racial discrimination; economic discrimination against black employment; political discrimination and the social discrimination "practiced in parks, theaters and other public spaces." According to Alejandro de la Fuente, by 1934 "one-third of the militants were black." After the fall of Machado, the communist-controlled CNOC emerged as a "key player in national and local politics."[107]

In 1929, a year after Machado was elected unopposed, Manuel Delgado left Cuba to escape the political chaos and realize his dream of becoming a musician. Only nineteen years old, Delgado arrived in New York City alone and without money. He worked long hours at a local barbershop and in the evenings and weekends played saxophone with an "orquesta" at the various Cuban and Puerto Rican social clubs, including El Club Julio Antonio Mella, where he was a member.[108]

Named after the charismatic student activist, labor organizer, and cofounder of the Cuban Communist Party, El Club Julio Antonio Mella was a racially integrated club located at 1413 Fifth Avenue on the corner of 116th Street in East Harlem. El Club Mella, as it was commonly known, was one of twenty-four different nationwide Spanish-speaking lodges (logias) that made up the Cervantes Fraternal Society (Spanish/Hispanic section) of the International Worker's Order (IWO), a Communist Party–affiliated insurance, mutual aid, and fraternal organization founded on March 30, 1930, following a split from the Workingmen's Circle.[109]

The Cervantes Fraternal Society of the IWO was formed a year later, on March 31, 1931. In the IWO's Fifteenth Anniversary Almanac, Jesús

Primer Baile Aniversario

LOGIA 4763

JULIO A. MELLA

★

PARK PALACE
5-5 West 110th Street
New York City

★

Sábado 20 de Mayo
1 9 3 9

Cover of the program for the "Primer Baile Aniversario Julio Antonio Mella," IWO, 1939. Jesús Colón/Justo Ambrosio Martí: Archives of the Puerto Rican Diaspora, Centro de Estudios Puertorriqueños, Hunter College, City University of New York.

Colón wrote a brief entry on the Cervantes Fraternal Society explaining the aim of the club and why they chose to name it after the sixteenth-century writer, poet, and playwright Miguel de Cervantes.

> We are a society of various nationalities. Puerto Ricans and Mexicans, Spaniards and Cubans; all the multiple types of colorful humanity from the Rio Grande to Patagonia. And we have chosen the name the "Cervantes Fraternal Society" because, while national distinctions do exist, a common language links us together, and Cervantes is regarded as the Father of the Spanish language.[110]

Colón's entry reveals the tendency to emphasize the Spanish language as a site of diasporic unification. By emphasizing "Spanish and Spanish-speaking peoples," Colón and by extension the IWO used the work engendered by nationalist discourses to create a separate community, without adhering to the pitfalls of nationalist exclusivity and distinction.

El Club Julio Antonio Mella soon followed. Organized in February 1932, El Club Mella was like no other.[111] It was organized precisely "at the moment the Cuban people were under the despotic and tyrannical regime of the Machado government." According to a report authored by the National Committee of the Hispanic Section of the IWO, "there were no clubs in the United States for Cuban residents who wanted to protest and challenge the Machadato." Once El Club Mella was formed, "thousands of workers, many of them Cuban," as well as those who "had been exiled for political reasons," joined the club.[112] Among them was the Afro-Cuban migrant Basilio Cueria y Obrit, who was born in Marianao, Cuba in 1895 and began his career as a baseball player for the Cuban armed forces, then professionally with the *All Cubans*, and later the *Cuban Stars*. He toured Cuba and the Southern United States, and in 1923 retired from baseball and moved to Jacksonville, Florida. In 1926 Cueria first moved to Long Island and then to New York City, where he lived and worked among the Cuban community, becoming an early member of El Club Julio Antonio Mella.[113]

In naming the club after Julio Antonio Mella, the members declared their unequivocal support for Mella's communist politics, his views on labor rights, ending poverty, and the need to address racial inequalities. They also registered their disapproval of Machado and the United States' policy in Cuba, especially the despised Platt Amendment. On September 25, 1925, Julio Antonio Mella was expelled from the University of Havana and later imprisoned for committing terrorist acts against the government. After staging a hunger strike in prison, Machado, who had recently won the presidency, appeased opposing factions by freeing Mella in December 1925.

Less than a year later, Mella was forced out of Cuba. He fled to Honduras, Guatemala, and finally Mexico City where he continued to organize against Machado. After leaving a meeting at the Red Aid's headquarters on Isabel la Católica Street, and drafting a telegram to the editor of *La Semana* in Havana, Julio Antonio Mella was shot and killed on January 10, 1929, a few feet away from the Zamora Building. Mella's assassination inspired strikes, riots, and demonstrations in Cuba, parts of Latin America, Europe, and in the United States. In Mexico City alone, a "thousands-strong procession bearing Mella's coffin" marched through the streets, ending at the Dolores cemetery where Mella was laid to rest.[114] Mella's assassination captured the world's attention and renewed efforts to oust President Gerardo Machado, who was blamed for his death.

One of those who demanded an end to the Machado presidency was Luis Alvarado. Warned by a pro-Machado officer to stop protesting or he could find himself "dead in one of those big cane plants," Alvarado left his family behind in Mayarí, Oriente, Cuba and joined his brother-in-law Manuel Delgado in New York. Born in Puerto Rico and raised in Cuba, Alvarado was a naturalized citizen who moved to New York in 1931 with the help of the US consulate. Alvarado had no intention of leaving Cuba for good. Expecting to return when the situation calmed, he worked at odd jobs until finally opening a dry cleaning business at 1359 Fifth Avenue on the corner of 113th Street. The neighborhood that Alvarado moved into had "a lot of Spanish people, mostly Puerto Rican." On the same block as the dry cleaner was the Cafe Bustelo Roasting Company. Next door was the Valencia Bakery, and a few blocks over, the Teatro Hispano. The dry cleaner was located only a few blocks away from El Club Julio Antonio Mella. Members of El Club Mella frequented Alvarado's business to get their clothes dry cleaned and their suits and dresses pressed. Alvarado knew the members well and considered them to be part of an extended community. It was common for them to linger, talk politics, and drink "buches de café" that Alvarado served throughout the day. Although on friendly terms, he never joined El Club Julio Antonio Mella.[115]

Despite the fall of Machado, political conditions in Cuba were slow to improve. Knowing that he would not be able to return to Cuba anytime soon, Alvarado sold his home in Mayarí and sent for his family. On May 19, 1936, his wife Mariana Mejias Alvarado and their six children, including his daughter Melba, arrived at the port of New York on the ship *Santa Elena*. Before the family arrived, Alvarado secured an apartment on the top floor of the building where his dry cleaning business was located. They lived there from 1936 to 1942.[116]

The Most Revolutionary: El Club Julio Antonio Mella and the Radical Imaginary in New York

We are the most revolutionary in New York. We, the Latin American revolutionaries who have emigrated here, forced out of our countries, persecuted by an imperialism that by its own internal contradictions, tolerates us here, where we agitate in meetings, in the revolutionary press, in the clubs, and in societies.
Pablo de la Torriente Brau, 1935[117]

I'll repeat what I have said in previous conferences. Our section [Hispanic Section IWO] was founded by radical elements, and it is therefore necessary and natural that our section be organized in a way that expresses those same opinions and sentiments.
César Fuentes, 1937[118]

The same month that Luis Alvarado's family arrived in New York, Eladio de Paula Bolaños marched down Fifth Avenue with members of El Club Julio Antonio Mella to commemorate the fifty-year anniversary of May Day. Carrying the Cuban flag, Bolaños joined thousands of people, including the Cuban journalist Pablo de la Torriente Brau, who he first met "en un mitin" at El Club Julio Antonio Mella.[119]

That day members of El Club Julio Antonio Mella marched alongside El Comité Hispano-Americanos, a contingent of twelve different organizations and labor unions representing twenty-three Latin American countries. Members of El Comité Hispano-Americanos walked "under their flag" to protest the oppressive conditions in their individual countries, as well as imperialism, fascism, unfair deportations, and racial discrimination in the United States. According to Torriente Brau, the May Day celebration was "one of the biggest demonstrations of unity, power, and protest ever mounted by the Hispanic American residents of New York." He was particularly impressed by the large number of Latin American migrants who protested against "the brutal and tyrannical regimes back home that are maintained and supported by imperialism, as well as the discrimination they face in their social, political, and economic lives in this country."[120]

The march ended at Union Square, or what Torriente Brau called "the red square of New York," at around four in the afternoon. Demonstrators "protested the war and fascism, and it was there, where American workers made their demands. Everyday of the year groups of men and women met to talk about revolution." As the marchers arrived, they exchanged pamphlets and bought copies of El Estampa Libera, El Socialista, the Daily Worker, the Fight, Socialist Call, New Masses, China Today, and Frente Hispanos. They gathered to hear speeches supporting the Republican forces in Spain and calling for a "world-wide proletariat." Torriente Brau remembered how quickly the square filled with organizations raising money for multiple fund-raising campaigns, including one organized by the Industrial Ladies Garment Workers, which raised thousands to assist "heroic Spanish women." He commented on the different languages: German, Italian, Russian, Japanese, Hebrew, and Chinese spoken in unison. But perhaps what moved him the most was witnessing hundreds of women and men clapping and cheering loudly at the speeches given in Spanish. As Torriente Brau later noted, "Nobody understood us, but they all comprehended."[121]

A few months after the May Day demonstrations, Bolaños and Torriente Brau traveled to Spain to fight against General Francisco Franco: Bolaños as a soldier, and Torriente Brau as a war correspondent. Bolaños, who was born to Cuban parents on December 14, 1916 in Tampa, departed for Spain in December 1936 and spent more than two years fighting the war. He traveled with Rodolfo de Armas y Soto and Angel Rufo, fought with ten different fronts, including the Lincoln Brigade, and was wounded five times.[122] Members of El Club Julio Antonio Mella, including Ricardo Gómez Oliva, Isidoro Martínez, and Basilio Cueria y Obrit, were directly involved in supporting the Republican forces in Spain.[123] They, like other members of El Club Mella, fought in the war, recruited soldiers, and helped organize the Cuban section of the First American Battalion/A. Lincoln/Centuria Antonio Guiteras/International Brigade, known simply as the Centuria Antonio Guiteras. Guiteras, who served under Cuban President Ramón Grau San Martín, was founder of Joven Cuba, a movement that called for revolutionary socialism and land reform. The Centuria Antonio Guiteras included about a hundred Cuban soldiers—many who left from the United States. It is estimated that more than one thousand Cubans fought in the Spanish Civil War, with a sizeable number coming from New York.[124] One of the leaders of the section, Rodolfo de Armas y Soto, was a medical student in Cuba who, like countless others, had been exiled to the United States for his anti-Machado activism.[125]

In an oral history conducted by Elizabet Rodríguez and Idania Trujillo, Bolaños recounted how Torriente Brau was so eager to leave that "he sought work as a reporter for a US newspaper so he could go to Spain immediately."[126] On August 18, 1936, Torriente Brau departed New York on the Île de France as a war correspondent for *New Masses*, a socialist magazine based in New York, and *El Machete*, the official newspaper of the Communist Party in Mexico.[127] He arrived in Madrid on September 24, after attending a peace conference in Brussels and making his way through Barcelona. Torriente Brau's book, *Aventuras del soldado desconocido cubano: Crítica artística y literaria*, was published shortly after his death in 1940. The book follows his experiences working closely with a cadre of Cuban and Puerto Rican political allies, and his efforts in forming the Organización Revolucionaria Cubana Antimperialista (ORCA) and El Club Martí, both founded in Harlem in 1935. ORCA was founded on July 22, 1935 in an apartment located at 612 W. 135th Street. El Club Martí, whose aim was "to educate as many people as possible concerning the current political and economic issues in Cuba," operated under the auspices of ORCA and was formed in October 1935. First located at 17 Hamilton Place near 137th Street and Broadway, El Club Martí later moved to 477 W. 144th Street between Amsterdam and Convent. A founding member of ORCA, Torriente-Brau published ORCA's official but short-lived newspaper, *Frente Único*.[128] Torriente Brau was also involved with El Club Julio Antonio Mella. In a letter to the editors of the Mexican publication *Ruta*, he mentioned how he "frequently speaks at El Club Julio Antonio Mella, a club for Latin American workers, and that he frequently writes for the revolutionary press." He goes on to add that it would be easy for him "to establish contact between *Ruta* and El Centro Mutualista de Mexico of New York."[129]

It was no surprise that Torriente Brau was involved with El Club Mella. He knew Julio Antonio Mella well and together, they helped form Ala Izquierda Estudiantil, a militant student organization in Havana. He was also the founder of *Línea*, the official publication of Ala Izquierda Estudiantil.[130] Similar to Mella, Torriente Brau was forced to leave as a result of his political activism. He first left Cuba on May 16, 1933, a day after being released from prison. Once Machado was overthrown, Torriente Brau returned to Cuba in September 1933. By March 1935, citing the "disastrous general strike," Torriente Brau once again moved to New York.[131]

Torriente Brau was skilled at making connections among various political groups in New York and Cuba. He linked members of El Club Mella and ORCA with leaders of the CNOC and the Cuban Communist Party. These networks continued long after Torriente Brau's death. Members of El Club Mella and later El Club Cubano Inter-Americano cultivated long-standing associations with Cuban politicians, labor organizers, journalists, artists, musicians, and associations well into the 1940s. Like many Cuban migrants and fellow activists, Torriente Brau worked odd jobs to make ends meet. He was a watchman, "porter de cabaret," busboy, and a waiter at El Toreador and the Harvard Club, where he lived off the tips. He worried constantly about money and was always short of cash. In a letter addressed to his friend Luis Gómez Wangüermert, editor of *Carteles* in Havana, he complained about his "economic problems" and not having enough time to study English. At the same time, he was proud of the fact that when it came to the Cuban cause, "no other migrant worked as hard."[132]

Remarkably thorough, detailed, and insightful, Torriente Brau's writings document both the migration of Cubans during this period and their involvement in revolutionary political activity, labor unions, and social clubs. Although an important account of the time, Torriente Brau's writings nevertheless failed to discuss race, either in the United States or in Cuba. There is no discussion of the Harlem Race Riot in 1935, of the growing racial tensions in Cuba, the large number of Afro-Cubans migrating as a result of the Machadato, Afro-Cuban membership in El Club Julio Antonio Mella, and the fact that Afro-Cubans, including Angel García and Basilio Cueria y Obrit, fought against Franco. After joining the Communist Party in 1935, Cueria volunteered for the International Brigades in the fall of 1936. He served in the Lincoln Battalion and after five months transferred to the Spanish 46th Division, where he commanded the Machine Gun Company. At the battle of Jarama he "single-handedly wiped out an enemy machine-gun nest." Cueria was promoted to captain and received a citation for distinguished service from General Miaja.[133]

Under-studied and often glossed over, the late 1920s and 1930s are pivotal chapters in Cuban political and migrant history in New York. Cubans who were involved with El Club Mella, El Club Martí, ORCA, and the different labor unions reconfigured Cuban diasporic political activism and thinking during this period. Progressive, socialist, and oriented toward labor and left-wing causes, they rearticulated definitions of labor, migration, race, gender, and the future meanings of Cubanidad in New York. Unlike in the past, this migration was not defined, nor comforted by temporalities. The economic depression, the rise of labor, the persistent racism, and the political chaos and instability in Cuba, convinced Cubans that perhaps it was better to *settle* in New York and be part of a larger immigrant community, than return to Cuba. The Cuban nation was no longer part of a shared diasporic imaginary and returns were no longer cast as a refuge or solution. Under these circumstances, *staying* in the United States was seen as a viable option. In her interviews, Melba Alvarado echoed these sentiments. "We didn't think about going back to Cuba. We kept the Cuban taste, let's say, with the music and the Spanish, and all that in the house." Except for a few bouts of homesickness, she never considered returning to Cuba, at least not for good.

Alvarado did not belong to El Club Mella, but she knew many of the members, some, quite well. While working at her father's dry cleaning businesses, she struck up conversations with club members and spent hours talking about politics, culture, and what she called "lo diario," the everyday. Young and hungry for knowledge, these informal conversations impressed her deeply and proved to be "her education." They shaped her political views and taught her the importance of establishing community "entre los hispanos," a factor that later influenced the founding of El Club Cubano Inter-Americano in 1945. Her father encouraged these discussions, voicing his support for her burgeoning activism, telling everyone that "she's like me." In many respects, she was. Much like her father who was "president of one of the societies in Cuba," Alvarado would also become president of a Cuban society in New York.[134]

As one of the logias organized under the Spanish section of the IWO, El Club Mella offered its members health, employment, and disability insurance regardless of race or occupation. For newly arrived Spanish-speaking migrants with little resources or contacts, the benefits offered by the IWO were invaluable. According to an internal report, by 1940 the IWO had "paid $14,000 in life insurance benefits and nearly $7,700 in disability benefits to our Spanish-speaking members." When first founded the Spanish section counted close to 1,900 members. Ten years later there were more than 3,000 members.[135]

No doubt the logias were part of an ongoing effort by the IWO to recruit Spanish-speaking immigrants. Depending on the membership and activity level, the number of logias fluctuated over the years. There were twelve to nineteen logias during most of the 1930s, with a membership that ranged from 659 to 1,200 adult members. Located throughout New York, the largest numbers of logias were in Harlem with thirteen. Next were Brooklyn and Lower Manhattan, each with three, and the Bronx with one.[136] Committed to representing the interests and rights of the foreign-born, the IWO called for solidarity among all immigrants, promoted the publication of foreign-language newspapers, and disseminated *Fraternal Outlook Magazine*, which was published in several different languages.[137]

Although directly connected to the IWO, the logias were remarkably independent. In fact, members of the National Committee of the Hispanic Section cited in their annual report a "certain detachment between the Spanish sections and the IWO." This, it turns out, was a problem. Although supportive of dances, banquets, and celebrations

CLUB DE DAMAS

Sentadas de izquierda a derecha: Isabel Blanco, Dolores Puñales, Clara Santiago.
Josefina Q. Cepeda, Isabel Radeliffe.—Linea intermedia de izquierda a derecha.
Cristina Knowles, Carmen Velázquez, Dominga Lamont, Alma Blanco, María
O. Fontrodona, María Antonia Polanco, Inocencia Valdés, Angelina Figueroa,
Petra Polanco.—Linea de atrás de izquierda a derecha: Raimunda D'Oyen.
Consuelo Correa, Zenobia Graterón, Margot Ortega, Magdalena Medina y
Gabriela Correa.

DIRECTIVA

Presidenta, JOSEFINA Q. CEPEDA
Vicepresidenta. CLARA SANTIAGO
Secretaría. ISABEL RADELIFFE
Vocal, ISABEL BLANCO
Consejera. DOLORES PUÑALES
Sargento de Armas. APOLONIA MIRANDA

Members of El Club de Damas, Club Julio Antonio Mella, 1939. Jesús Colón/Justo
Ambrosio Martí: Archives of the Puerto Rican Diaspora, Centro de Estudios Puertorriqueños, Hunter College, City University of New York.

that strengthened the bond among members, the Spanish section of the IWO stressed that the clubs needed to be "connected to the radical movement." Cognizant that many of their members were "attracted by the benefits administered by our order," it was the responsibility of those in charge to provide stability by holding regular meetings and exhibiting responsible leadership. Moreover, as the leadership noted several times, the logia's primary responsibility was to the workers and the revolutionary cause.[138] By 1940 the Spanish section had at last entered into the spirit of the IWO. "We are no more Spanish section separate [sic] and aloof, but we are mature enough to understand the importance of the IWO as a whole."[139] The committee's concerns were warranted. It was difficult for the logias to solely follow the IWO's political agenda. The membership fluctuated and the political interests of its members were rarely uniform. Although open to the public, the banquets, speakers, events, and publications were all in Spanish and designed to appeal to the cultural and community interests of the Spanish-speaking migrant community.

One of the areas where the IWO made important strides was in the recruitment and promotion of women. Amparo López, for instance, served on the Organizational Bureau of the National Committee of the Hispanic Section, and Isabel López Moraler was a delegate of the Spanish section to the IWO.[140] Members of El Club Mella also named Josefina Q. Cepeda and Dolores Puñales to leadership and key positions within the club. In addition, the female members of El Club Mella organized El Club de Damas, "to give women the unique opportunity to discuss and find solutions to problems that affect them as well as their partners."[141]

Affiliated with Women's Progressive Council of the IWO, El Club de Damas met every Thursday night to discuss issues important to "la mujer moderna." Admittedly, the club started slowly. Only five women attended the first meeting. However, by 1938 the club recorded twenty-five official members.[142] Josefina Q. Cepeda, the founding member of El Club de Damas, hoped to attract even more members by offering classes for women working in the textile industry and providing assistance with childcare. By offering these services, El Club de Damas reinforced their commitment to working-class immigrant women, and challenged what continued to be a gendered and male-dominated discourse on labor.

El Club de Damas was a departure from past women's clubs. Instead of supporting all male organizations, El Club de Damas was a separate space, apart from men, where members forged a feminist agenda that spoke to "their rights and obligations." Cepeda described the club as a place where women dealt with issues related to children, the cinema, market prices, and "problems of the real world." The combination of the practical and the political "exacted the best results." In Cepeda's words, it allowed women, even the "most shy and reserved, to openly express their opinions and find solutions." Aware of the sexism that permeated El Club Mella and other political arenas, Cepeda wrote that El Club de Damas was formed so that women could organize political and social activities "without having to depend on men. Gone are the petrified looks and gestures of disgust of our male comrades as we attend a particular meeting of interest to us as mothers and wives."

Despite the IWO's efforts, sexism existed both in the IWO and within the different logias. It was a constant problem that Cepeda herself addressed. On the one hand she reassured the male members that in seeking equality, women were not relinquishing their roles as wives and mothers. On the other, she was clear that sexism would not be tolerated and that women needed to be given more power. "We look forward to the day when we can proudly refer to El Club de Damas of our logia as a place where we solve the problems that until recently, were resolved solely and exclusively by our brothers."[143] El Club Mella's reach extended beyond the immigrant and Spanish-speaking community. In 1937 the artist Henry Glintenkamp painted what has been described as a meeting in "a popular assembly hall in New York which served as an assembly hall for Cuban workers." Active in the Communist Party and a teacher at both the New York School of Fine and Industrial Arts and the John Reed Club School of Art, Glintenkamp was an early member of the American Artists' Congress formed in 1936 with Stuart Davis as executive secretary. In 1937 Glintenkamp served as chairman of the exhibition organizing committee and in 1940 he was elected executive secretary. Years earlier he had been involved with the WPA and was a political cartoonist for *The Masses*, the same magazine that hired Torriente Brau to report on the Spanish Civil War.[144]

Employing the club's interior as backdrop, Glintenkamp presented an "uplifting vision of ordinary urbanites of various races and backgrounds," gathered to eat, drink, and talk politics at the end of the working day. The painting, entitled *El Club Julio Antonio Mella* (The Cuban Workers Club), captured the socialist and communist underpinnings of the club as well as its racial and gendered composition. At the center of the painting is a man of color speaking to a white man and a woman of color. The woman of color is featured prominently, emphasizing the important role that women of color played in the club. In the foreground, on the back wall, is a reproduction of Augusto's famous protest poster against Franco's 1936 bombing of Madrid and above the poster is the banner of *El Machete*.[145]

In 1940, three years after Glintenkamp completed his painting, the Hispanic Section of the IWO disbanded El Club Mella. On October 24, members of the Hispanic Section and Ramón Fuentes, who represented El Club Mella, met at the headquarters of the Cervantes Fraternal Society at 80 Fifth Avenue to decide the future of the different logias, and how to best consolidate the remaining members. El Club Mella was not the only one to be disbanded. El Club Obrero Español, El Club Obrero Chileno, Alianza Hispanoamericana, along with several others, were merged into one Spanish-speaking logia.[146]

The loss of Spanish-speaking members coincided with the United States' entry into World War II and the subsequent attacks on the IWO. Shortly after the war, the IWO was at its peak, with almost 200,000 members. However, by 1945 the Special Committee on Un-American Activities of the US House of Representatives, also known as the Dies Committee, publicly attacked the leadership and agenda of the IWO. In 1947, the US Attorney General Tom C. Clark put the IWO on its list of subversive organizations, resulting in the IWO losing its tax-exempt status and insurance charter; putting its members at risk and leading to its eventual demise in 1954.[147]

Archival Disappeared: El Club Cubano Inter-Americano and the Unknowable History of El Club Julio Antonio Mella

In an effort to maintain the fraternity that should exist between the Cuban community and that of other Latin American countries, El Club Cubano Inter-Americano is founded in New York City, which will maintain a distance from all

partisan political or religious tendencies, will carry forth social and cultural activities; will extend bonds of solidarity with similar associations; will maintain the appropriate stance in relationship to the legal authorities, and will be alert to the issues that tend to improve health and human welfare.
Article I, El Club Cubano Inter-Americano, Proyecto de Reglamento, 1945[148]

Some of the founders of the new club (CCI) were members of Julio Antonio Mella. They have that resentment, you know, they were left alone.
Melba Alvarado[149]

On June 18, 1945, future members of the El Club Cubano Inter-Americano celebrated the hundred-year anniversary of Antonio Maceo's birth at Town Hall on West 43rd Street. Sponsored by El Comité Pro-Centenario Del General Antonio Maceo and presided over by the Honorable Cayetano de Quesada, Consul of the Cuban Republic and Julio Cardenal, a soon-to-be founder of the CCI, the event, by all accounts was a great success. The program listed some of the most distinguished names in Cuban literature, arts, and music: Enrique Martí Rosell, Eusebia Cosme, Angel Suárez Rocabruna, who spoke on "Maceo y la actualidad cubana," Rómulo Lachatanere, Carmen M. Pedroso, Alberto Socarras, Trio Servando Díaz, Narciso Figueroa, Luis Humberto Varona, and the Orquesta Marcelino Guerra.

The politicians invited to speak that evening were high-ranking officials from Cuba, and included the Mayor of Havana, Raul G. Menocal; Cuban senator, Salvador García Agüero, who presented on "Maceo, cifra, y carácter de la revolución"; and General Fulgencio Batista, the "Ex-President of Cuba," who concluded the evening with a summary, a "resumen" of the festivities. Also invited to present were Jesús Colón, who spoke on "Maceo y Puerto Rico," and the Reverend Adam Clayton Powell. It was an extraordinary evening devoted to Antonio Maceo. Until then, no event organized by an exile and migrant community in New York had focused solely on the life and influence of Antonio Maceo.[150]

Velada Lírico Literaria

Conmemoración del centenario del natalicio del

GRAL. ANTONIO MACEO

Lunes 18 de Junio,
8 P. M.

Oradores:	*Variedades por:*
GRAL. FULGENCIO BATISTA Ex Presidente de Cuba	**EUSEBIA COSME**
	NARCISO FIGUEROA
DR. RAUL ROA Catedrático de la Universidad de la Habana	**LUIS UMBERTO VARONA**
JESUS COLON Presidente, Soc. Fraternal Cervantes	**TRIO SERVANDO DIAZ**
DR. ANGEL S. ROCABRUNA Comisionado del Ayuntamiento de la Habana	
	Musica por
REV. A. CLAYTON POWELL Congresista de los E. U.	**MARCELINO GUERRA** y su orquesta

TOWN HALL
123 West 43rd Street, New York City

ENTRADA GRATIS

Auspiciada por el COMITE PRO CENTENARIO DEL GENERAL ANTONIO MACEO
357

Flyer promoting the 100-year anniversary of General Antonio Maceo's birth. Town Hall, New York City, June 18, 1945. Jesús Colón/Justo Ambrosio Martí: Archives of the Puerto Rican Diaspora, Centro de Estudios Puertorriqueños, Hunter College, City University of New York.

What was not clear, at least not from the program and the accompanying historical documents, were the struggles, difficulties, and problems associated with organizing the centennial. Not everyone in the Cuban community wanted to celebrate the centennial birth of the Afro-Cuban hero of the Ten Years' War. The organizing committee, which included past members and sympathizers of El Club Mella, reached out to the white Cuban community, who were not interested in working with the organizing committee to honor Maceo.[151] Despite attempts at communications and efforts at establishing an integrated committee, the organization of the centennial was left mostly to Afro-Cuban migrants.

Since the dissolution of El Club Julio Antonio Mella five years earlier, there were no racially integrated Cuban clubs in New York, and the Cuban clubs that existed did not welcome Afro-Cubans as members.[152] On September 17, 1945, the organizers of the Maceo centennial met at the home of Julio and Francisca "Paquita" Cardenal at 135 W. 116th Street. In addition to being a reunion of sorts, it was also Francisca Cardenal's birthday. During the gathering and as a result of much conversation and debate, those in attendance decided that it was time to form a club for "people of color." In a revealing and thoughtful passage written a few months after the meeting, Generoso Pedroso explained that the preliminary clauses that made it possible for him to accept "the presidency of this club" were the same ones that would "break that inexplicable and painful tradition observed by many institutions similar to ours to not accept individuals based on race or nationality." El Club Cubano Inter-Americano, Pedroso added, is a club for "interamericanos," and the only requirement for membership is to "be a decent person."[153]

By November 25, 1945, the founding members of the CCI elected Generoso Pedroso president of an interim managing committee (Comité Gestor), and approved their bylaws (Proyecto de Reglamento). On January 18, 1946 the CCI was a formally incorporated club. Two days later, the members met at the Saavdera Auto School at 139 West 116th Street to verify the election of the club's first governing body. On May 20, 1946, the CCI held its first official meeting at their new headquarters located at 914 Prospect Avenue in the Bronx.[154]

Although never formally acknowledged, the CCI borrowed heavily from the cultural and social directive of El Club Julio Antonio Mella. The CCI offered its members health insurance and unemployment benefits,[155] and used the term "Inter-Americano" to denote inclusivity, expansion, and community, while at the same time privileging "lo cubano," by requiring that the president be Cuban. Nonetheless, the club attracted members from Puerto Rico, the Dominican Republic, Jamaica,

First president of the CCI, Generoso Pedroso (seated behind the table), with the first board of directors, 1946. Photographs and Prints Division, Schomburg Center for Research in Black Culture, New York Public Library, Astor, and Tilden Foundations.

Haiti, Colombia, and Venezuela as well as African Americans. In 1947, the members of the CCI outlined the parameters of the club, declaring that among the "Spanish-speaking community in the city of New York" the CCI is "where Cubans and Hispanic-Americans gather without any racial, gender, political and religious distinction."[156]

The CCI's resistance to being a political club made sense. This was postwar New York, where the combination of radical and leftist politics could easily lead to deportation, loss of jobs, and jail. Members of the CCI witnessed the Red Scare, the virulent attacks on labor unions, the blacklisting of Communist and Socialist Party members, the deportation of immigrant political and labor organizers, and the devastating consequences of the House Un-American Activities Committee. As members noted at the time, "We now live in a period of international inquietude."[157] Perhaps this is why there is no mention of El Club Julio Antonio Mella in the archives; why there is so little to indicate that the

Portraits of Abraham Lincoln, George Washington, Antonio Maceo, José Martí, and Simón Bolívar line the wall of the first CCI club. Jesús Colón/Justo Ambrosio Martí: Archives of the Puerto Rican Diaspora, Centro de Estudios Puertorriqueños, Hunter College, City University of New York.

CCI had any relationship with El Club Mella and its members. There are little to no documents or sources that mention the club or its members, even though past members of El Club Mella helped to found the CCI.

And yet, like a proper haunting, El Club Mella permeates the seemingly innocuous archives; unknowable, yet visible to those willing to see. In a pamphlet that was routinely distributed to new members, there, along with the bylaws and regulations, is a list of the club's founders. Some of the names listed as founders were previous members of El Club Mella. Basilio Cueria y Obrit, Ricardo Gómez, and Isidro Martínez were all official members of El Club Mella who as noted earlier, fought in the Spanish Civil War. Frank Díaz, Eugenio Llimo, Generoso Pedroso, Anacleto Romero, Pablo Soublette, Rómulo Lachatanere, José Valdés, Pedro Millet, Josefina Valdés, and Ernesto and Christina Knowles were in one way or another involved with El Club Mella. It also lists Angel Suárez Rocabruna and Juan Marinello Vidaureta, influential men who had long-standing connections with El Club Mella.[158]

Although committed to *not* being a political organization, the CCI forged alliances with many of the same clubs and organizations that had been involved with El Club Mella, namely the Cervantes Fraternal Society of the IWO, the Comité Coordinator Pro República Española, and the Communist Party. Again, the sources belie the CCI's insistence that they were *not* a political club. In August 1947, *El Boletín Mensual* of the CCI stated that "a large number of CCI members were invited and attended an annual camping trip sponsored by the Cervantes Fraternal Society of the IWO."[159]

This period was also marked by racial tensions and separations among Cubans. No doubt, the CCI's commitment to racial integration and ethnic inclusivity was in direct response to their own exclusion. Afro-Cubans were not only denied membership to clubs like El Ateneo Cubano de New York, but were also excluded from their celebrations, dances, and events. The separations were subtle, unexplained, and effective. In Alvarado's words, "they (El Ateneo Cubano) wanted nothing to do with blacks." It was common for Afro-Cubans to not be invited, informed, or asked to participate in organizing Cuban social and cultural events. Afro-Cubans who arrived at a dance or an event were asked to show proof of membership. Since Afro-Cubans were not allowed or invited to be members, they were denied entry. In her interviews, Alvarado called this practice "la reserva," and recalled how she and other members of the CCI would arrive at the door only to be told that the club "reserved the right to refuse admission." Attempts at an explanation or justification were met with silence.[160]

The exclusions were commonplace. In her important oral history of the Afro-Cuban singer Graciela Pérez Gutiérrez, Miriam Jiménez Román details the everyday racial indignities that Graciela experienced when she moved to New York in 1943. Citing racial separations among Cubans, the difficulties renting an apartment, and getting gigs in the city, Graciela commented that "there were many places like that, and restaurants too, where Blacks, people of my color, could not enter."[161] In one particular passage, Graciela explains in detail what happened when her friends tried to get into one of the local Cuban clubs.

And there was a dance hall on Broadway and 145th Street—the Monte Cristo—where the Cuban owner didn't allow Blacks. One time, friend of ours—a *negrita*, a Puerto Rican and a Spaniard—went to the ticket booth and the Spanish girl asked for three tickets. The man in the booth said, "Two only." "What do you mean, 'two only'? There are three of us." He pointed to the Black girl and said, "Because she can't come in." "What?! If she can't go in, neither can we" and the three of them left."[162]

It was within this context that the CCI established a space where Afro-Cubans could dance, listen to music, enjoy poetry, and hold banquets without risking humiliation or feeling uncomfortable. In her interviews, Alvarado noted that CCI was partly created for those who were "tired of being turned away. It was a place for us." At the same time, she was quick to remind that members of the CCI never used membership as a strategy to exclude others. "If they wanted to come to our dances, they [white Cubans] were welcome to come and hear music and dance like everybody else."[163]

For Alvarado, the cultural separations were the most painful. Despite her personal experiences and those of people she knew well, she remained committed to the idea of a shared Cubanidad that belonged to all Cubans regardless of race. For Alvarado, some events and rituals were so highly identified with being Cuban, so sacred, that it was hard to imagine they could be racially divided. But they were. In addition to "la reserva," she often discussed the events that led up to the separate celebrations of La Caridad del Cobre, the patron saint of Cuba.

According to Alvarado the ritual had always been celebrated in a Catholic church on 114th street. Organized by "una señora de color," the service and ensuing celebration attracted all Cubans from New York City to come to "la Milagrosa." However, when the principal organizer returned to Cuba in the mid-1950s and more white Cubans migrated to New York, the once integrated celebration was now organized on the basis of race. It was the white Cubans, "lo cubanos blancos," who decided that "the real mass" in honor of la Caridad del Cobre would now be held at the church on 156th street. It was at this moment that the once integrated celebration "se dividió" into two racially divided masses. Afro-Cubans were not informed of the change, nor were they invited to participate in the one held on 156th street. They were left out. Afro-

Cubans continued to have their mass in honor of la Caridad de Cobre at the church on 114th street and Seventh Avenue.

In the oral histories and in our many conversations, Alvarado always circled back to one comment that stayed with her for years. In the mid-1950s, "ten or fifteen years after the club was formed," Alvarado heard something so painful that it changed her. On her way home from a dance at the Palm Garden, she ran into a white Cuban newspaper reporter who worked for *El Diario* who casually mentioned that he was on his way to the CCI to attend a party given by "los negritos del Bronx." Alvarado was in shock; "tremendo choque." She had no idea that white Cubans commonly referred to the members of the CCI as "los negritos del Bronx." For Alvarado, it was the diminutive of the word black, "negrito," that bothered her the most. With one word the CCI and its members had been infantalized, dismissed, and ridiculed.[164]

The racism and exclusion that inspired the founding of the CCI and shaped its policies are not always mentioned in the sources. There are hints and references, but no clear delineations. Considering that the club prohibited any discussion of politics and religion, this is not altogether surprising. In her interviews, Alvarado put it this way. In the club, "you could do whatever you wanted except talk about religion and politics. You can, for example, go to the club, be black, be communist and whatever else, but don't speak about racism or political parties, that's not important."[165] It is difficult to imagine that the members of the CCI *never* discussed politics and religion while at the club. The early members who formed the club were quite political and had a history of political involvement in both New York and Cuba. Instead, the regulations, bylaws, and the continual assertions of not being political were most likely used to protect members from past political involvement and actions, such as those organized by El Club Julio Antonio Mella. Again, this is not surprising during a period of intense anti-communism; Afro-Cuban political involvement was scrutinized, questioned, and criticized. In other words, the decision to not be political was in itself quite political.[166]

Perhaps the most visible example of the racism among Cubans was the CCI's tireless commitment to install a monument honoring Antonio Maceo and later, Maceo and Martí in Central Park. The members organized committees, raised funds, held events, and commissioned and paid for a bust of Antonio Maceo and José Martí. The monument was never built. But the busts of both men graced countless photos of banquets, events, and celebrations. I couldn't help noticing that the bust of Maceo was larger than the one of Martí. When I asked why this was the case, and why Maceo was so important to the club, Alvarado simply stated, "He was black."[167]

The CCI would probably not have existed without El Club Julio Antonio Mella. The clubs were connected through a network of alliances, organizations, and transnational connections that shaped the CCI and the Afro-Cuban migrant community for decades. The memories and past experiences of El Club Mella influenced decisions, made policy, and served as a warning to future CCI members of the dangers of becoming too involved in politics, especially with the Communist Party. In many respects, the CCI was organized as a result of broken promises, racial exclusions, and a shared "resentment" at being "left alone." Afro-Cubans had little choice but to create and build their own spaces. Integral to the rebuilding was the need to script silences, diffuse archives, and dwell in the *known*. This was not difficult or new for Afro-Cuban migrants. As Alvarado explained, "we have always known what to do to keep the club and ourselves going."[168]

5

Monumental Desires and Defiant Tributes

Antonio Maceo and the Early History of El Club Cubano Inter-Americano, 1945-1957

This is a story within a story—so slippery at the edges that one wonders when and where it started and whether it will ever end.
Michel Rolph Trouillot[1]

The Story Within the Story

At the corner of 59th Street and the Avenue of the Americas at Central Park South, there is a grand and majestic sculpture of José Martí. Made of bronze, the large and imposing statue depicts Martí on horseback at the very moment he is killed in battle. Sculpted by the renowned artist Anna Vaughn Hyatt Huntington, it was completed in 1959 when she was eighty-two. Hyatt Huntington gifted the statue to the Cuban government for presentation to the people of New York City. In return, the Cuban government donated the monument's dark granite pedestal. Although completed in 1959, the "political climate between pro- and anti-Castro elements in New York necessitated the delay of the monument's unveiling until 1965."[2]

This story, however, is not about the breathtaking monument to José Martí or the reasons why it was unveiled six years after being completed. It is about the other monument, the one that was never built. The archive reveals little about why the monument to Antonio Maceo and later to José Marti *and* Antonio Maceo was never built. There are no answers, only reasons: financial burden, lack of organization, political instability, and little cooperation. There is even less to suggest that the statue of José Martí in Central Park was related to the one the CCI worked so hard to build. But there is talk. And those discussions in people's homes, at events, and over dinner recall painful memories that for some are better left unstirred, while for others beg to be told.[3]

In her oral histories, Melba Alvarado confirmed that the CCI members wanted to erect a monument to Martí and Maceo in Central Park. "The CCI always had the idea of putting the monument in Central Park where we wanted to have a space for Martí and Maceo. But it never came to fruition." When asked why, Alvarado referred to the statue of Martí. "They (white Cubans) were able to put (a statue to) Martí. They put Martí on a horse. Martí was never on a horse. And there is Martí in Central Park, but there is no Maceo."[4] From 1945 to the mid-1950s the CCI tirelessly raised funds, organized events, formed transnational committees, cultivated political connections, and did everything possible to build a monument in honor of Antonio Maceo. Even at its most dismal moments, when it appeared that a monument honoring Maceo would never be built, the CCI continued to organize, write letters, and have meetings. There is no one moment, at least documented, that signaled the end of the CCI's desire to build a monument to Maceo. There are no indications from the archives that members ever stopped discussing, planning, and hoping that it would eventually be built. And yet, something happened.

This chapter examines the "story within the story" of how and why the monument was *never* built. It theorizes the unraveling, the slippery, and the forgotten to get at why Afro-Cuban diasporic visibility and honor were so unthinkable, and in turn, why it was so necessary for the CCI to honor Maceo despite the criticisms leveled against them. As previously discussed, the CCI was formed as a result of the soon-to-be founders and members' experiences organizing a centennial celebration of Maceo in 1945. The refusal of white Cuban clubs to be involved led to the formation of the CCI, deeply influenced the club's purpose, and marked Maceo as a symbol of Afro-Cuban diasporic resistance to white Cuban racism.[5] A revered Afro-Cuban general of the Ten Years' War who was killed in the Cuban War for Independence in 1896, Antonio Maceo represented unrepentant blackness, enfranchisement, power, and the unequivocal belief that Afro-Cubans were equal partners in the making of a Cuban diasporic nationalist imaginary—all elements that informed and were sacred to the CCI.

Before the CCI there were few, if any, events that honored Maceo. Once the CCI was established, the members not only celebrated Maceo's birthday on June 14, they also celebrated the beginning of the Ten Years' War on October 10, and Maceo's death on December 7. It would be this way for decades.[6]

The Short History and Long Memory of the Un-Building

Considering all the work the Committee Pro-Monument has completed, we can be assured that very soon we will see our efforts converted into reality, and for this they (The Cuban Government) congratulate us all.
CCI Board of Directors meeting, March 31, 1949[7]

It was never possible for us to put Maceo anywhere. Nowhere. Don't you see?
Melba Alvarado, 2012[8]

On November 15, 1945, only months after El Club Cubano Inter-Americano had been founded, the consul general of Cuba in New York, Reinaldo Fernández Rebull, wrote to the future president of the CCI, Generoso Menéndez Pedroso, expressing support for placing a bust of Antonio Maceo in "a public place in this city." The idea was not far-fetched. That same year Mayor Fiorello H. La Guardia suggested that Sixth Avenue be renamed the Avenue of the Americas to honor "Pan-American ideals and principles." As part of the plan, La Guardia proposed building a new plaza where the avenue meets Central Park, and where statutes of great men from Latin America would be installed.[9] Enthusiastic about the possibility of including Maceo to the list of great men, Fernández Rebull referenced an earlier conversation with Dr. Angel Suárez Rocabruna, an esteemed scholar and member of the Afro-Cuban club El Club Atenas in Havana. In the letter, Fernández Rebull confirmed that both men would do everything possible to insure that a monument to Maceo be built in New York and provided Pedroso with a list of men "who may prove helpful to his goals."

A week later Pedroso responded to Fernández Rebull and informed him that club members had already organized El Comité Pro-Centenario del General Antonio Maceo, which in addition to honoring Maceo was entrusted to raise funds for the monument to Maceo in Central Park. He further added that his friend and co-founder of the CCI, Julio Cardenal, would serve as president of the committee. Since the club was still in the early stages and had yet to elect a governing body, Pedroso was pleased that Fernández Rebull had offered his assistance with one of "the club's greatest ambitions." Pedroso ended the letter by inviting Fernández Rebull to be a guest of honor at one of their events.[10]

The following year was especially busy for the CCI and El Comité Pro-Centenario del General Antonio Maceo. On January 22, 1946 the CCI invited Dr. Andrés Iduarte, professor at Columbia University and an "expert on the life of José Martí," to give a talk at the first Cena Martiana, a dinner in honor of Martí. A number of people attended the Cena Martiana including the vice secretary of El Ateneo Cubano and a reporter from the Spanish-language newspaper *La Prensa*. A few days later, on January 27, the CCI members invited everyone to a midnight gathering to commemorate Martí's birthday and lay a wreath at his statue located at 155th Street and Riverside Drive.[11]

The Cena Martiana kicked off a year of banquets, events, celebrations, and the inauguration of the CCI held on May 20 at the first "casa-club" located at 914 Prospect Avenue in the South Bronx. After meeting in private homes and businesses for most of the year, the members were ready to celebrate a space of their own, one that included a stage, dance floor, and library.[12] That night there was food, music, dancing, and of course speeches. In his inauguration speech the new president, Generoso Pedroso, called the formation of the CCI "one of the most transcendental acts in the history of the Cuban community in New York." He told the audience gathered that evening that "the unanimous idea" was to create a place where all Cubans from New York, who for "diverse reasons keep ourselves inexplicably apart, could come together, and be in unity with all of our brothers from the different colonias hispana de esta metrópolis." Pedroso was particularly proud of the club's inter-American focus; of seeing "so many people of different nationalities in the audience, in solidarity and happily affiliated with our nascent institution." Expressing the "sentiment of all Cubans," Pedroso called for the "political improvement of our brothers who identify with us on the basis of race, language, and traditions, and who along with us, live in the same neighborhoods and struggle within the same working-class." Pedroso ended his "entrega oficial" by thanking the founding members "for using their precious time off from work, and for abandoning their obligations to home and families to renovate and improve the club."[13]

Pedroso's speech is a remarkable testament not only to the club's burgeoning ideals and goals, but also to its strong identification with workers. Members worked in the garment industry, factories, and businesses that catered to the growing "colonia hispana." Some belonged to labor unions and remained active in the local lodges years after the CCI had been founded. Pedroso himself was a barber who owned "la barbería Pedroso" at 845 Westchester Avenue in the Bronx. Before the official club on Prospect Avenue was rented, Pedroso invited members, mostly men, to the barbershop to speak with him as he cut hair. Pedro Millet, president of the CCI in 1949, was also a barber. His barbershop was located in Harlem at 117 West 116th Street. Members were also welcome to meet with the secretary of the club, Narciso Saavedra, at his home located at 135 West 116th Street.[14]

Pedroso was the perfect person to lead the CCI. Respected, tenacious, patient, and connected, he was a tireless advocate of social causes and committed to unifying and empowering the Afro-diasporic migrant community.[15] Older than most of the members, Pedroso served only one term as president. Yet, for the next decade he remained active in all aspects of the club and was considered a model of integrity, discretion, and kindness. In 1949 the members expressed their gratitude by awarding him a diploma of merit.[16]

Born in Havana on July 17, 1863, Pedroso had a long history of activism in Cuba, where among other things he served as treasurer of the prestigious Sociedad Habanera Unión Fraternal.[17] By the time he was elected president of the CCI, Pedroso had lived in New York for more than thirty years and had a long history of "struggling in support of the colonia hispano-americana." Familiar with El Club Mella and friends with some of its members, notably Jesús Colón, Pedro Millet, Frank Díaz, Ricardo Gómez, Isidro Martínez, Cristina and Ernesto Knowles, Basilio Cueria y Obrit, and his good friend Anacleto Romero,[18] Pedroso deftly adapted Club Mella politics with post–World War II realities. According to Melba Alvarado, it was Pedroso who insisted that the club's bylaws prohibit politics and religion. After years of seeing clubs, organizations, and associations unravel as a result of political disagreements and in-fighting, Pedroso was adamant that the CCI not engage in partisan politics.[19] This proved difficult since most of the founders and members, including Pedroso, had a long and varied history of political involvement and activism.

Although officially apolitical, the club was affiliated with labor unions, political parties, and radical social clubs. This was not unusual given that many of these alliances existed before the CCI was founded. According to Alvarado, "many of those blacks were communist, but they didn't have to go to the club. You can do whatever you wanted in the club, except talk about politics and religion." In other words, it didn't matter if a member was communist as long as the club did not endorse political candidates, causes, movements, or as Alvarado put it, "take sides."[20] It was a delicate balance. The CCI's archive attest to the club's early affiliations, activism, and their expansive definitions of what it meant to *not* be political. The correspondence, invitations, CCI newsletters (*Circular, Acuerdo, y Noticias*),[21] and the many greetings, "saludos," that were paid for and published in the different programs and event flyers, provide invaluable insight into the CCI's extensive network.[22] The greetings are particularly salient in revealing who the CCI considered to be part of their community during this period.[23]

The early CCI programs include greetings from the Communist paper, the *Daily Worker*, as well as the Popular Socialist Party in Cuba, Logia 4832 of the IWO, Logia Amparo Latino No. 10059, and El Club Obrero Español. There are also greetings from congressman and representative of East Harlem, Vito Marcoantonio, the San Juan Social Club, La Sociedad Cultural Puertorriqueña, Borinquen Post, No. 126, as well as from Machito y sus Afro-Cubanos, and the owner of the New York Cubans, Alejandro Pompez.[24] There were also a series of greetings from local businesses, the majority of which catered to the Spanish-speaking community, including Crema Coffee Company, Quintero's Delicatessen and Bar, El Encanto Dressmakers, Domínguez's Furniture Store, González's Funeral Home, and Fuentes' Restaurant, known as "El Restaurante del los Artistas, Boxeadores y Profesionales."[25]

The CCI supported political causes including Puerto Rican independence and sovereignty. On August 28, 1946 Julio Cardenal, the first president of El Comité Pro-Centenario de Maceo, was invited to represent the CCI at the inauguration of Jesus I. Piñero, the first and only native Puerto Rican to be appointed governor of Puerto Rico, in San Juan.[26] A distinctly Cuban club, the CCI was nonetheless committed to the Puerto Rican community and to Puerto Rican causes; what Alvarado called "un sentimiento puertorriqueño."[27] The relationship between the CCI members and Puerto Rican activists and organizers solidified with El Club Julio Antonio Mella, and expanded with the formation of the CCI. Members worked closely with several Puerto Rican organizations including the Borinquen Post 1216 and the Association of Puerto Rican Employees. They bought tickets, attended meetings, and worked with "la colonia Puertorriqueña en Nueva York."[28] Puerto Ricans Francisca Cardenal and Jesús Colón, both founding members of the CCI, had a profound impact on the early political, structural, and ideological direction of the CCI.

In 1954 Francisca Cardenal was the first woman to be elected president of the CCI. She was involved in all aspects of the formation and running of the club. In addition to having the club be founded in her home, she served on the Board of Directors (Junta Directiva), numerous committees, and was a strong advocate for building a monument to Maceo. She raised funds and traveled to Havana repeatedly to meet with supporters at critical moments.[29] Colón had the distinction of being the only member who bridged El Club Mella and the Cervantes Fraternal Society of the IWO with the CCI. He assisted the CCI with creating strong ties with El Club Borinquen, Mutualista Obrera Puertorriqueña logia 4792, Porvenir Puertorriqueño logia 4840, Sociedad Fraternal de Pulidores Puertorriqueños, logia 4821, and the Sociedad Fraternal Ramón Emeterio Betances among others. On January 11, 1947, the club hosted its first of many events celebrating the nineteenth-century Puerto Rican revolutionary, Eugenio María de Hostos. The CCI soon organized similar events in honor of Ramón Emeterio Betances.[30]

The CCI's political leanings were also apparent in who they chose to host and honor. One of the first and by all accounts most successful visit was that of Juan Marinello Vidaurreta, a founder of the Cuban Communist Party, member of the Popular Socialist Party, current vice president of the Cuban Senate, and an honorary founder of the CCI.[31] On January 31, 1946, Pedroso informed Marinello that the CCI wanted to honor him for his work "in favor of democratic and popular causes."[32] Almost a month later, Marinello responded to Pedroso's letter by apologizing for the late reply, stating that he was busy with "politics in the province of Camaguey." Marinello expressed his gratitude and accepted with much satisfaction the club's invitation for a "banquete-homenjae de simpatía." His only request was that the banquet be humble and in keeping with the traditions of "Cubans living abroad."[33]

The members wasted little time in promoting the event. Scheduled to take place on April 10 at La Giralda Restaurant in the Bronx, Narciso

Saavedra invited members of the community, including William Z. Foster, the chairman of the Communist Party. Foster was unable to attend. He informed Saavedra that he was scheduled to meet with Marinello at another banquet and enclosed $18.00 to cover the cost of six tickets for the CCI event. Saavedra also invited the past president of Cuba, Fulgencio Batista, who at the time was supported by the Popular Socialist Party.[34] Saavedra sent two tickets to the Hotel Waldorf Astoria with a note expressing his hope that Batista would attend the tribute to Marinello.[35] Marinello's tour was indeed busy. In addition to traveling to New York he was scheduled to be in Tampa before heading back to Havana on April 17. While in New York, Marinello met with activists, politicians, artists, and members of the Cuban migrant community. He was honored by the Comité Latinoamericano de Acción Cívica, and gave a talk commemorating the anniversary of the Spanish Civil War on April 7 at the Manhattan Center. Sponsored by the Comité Coordinador Pro República Española, Marinello supported anti-Franco elements both within and outside of Spain, and called for a "united international front against Franco."[36]

A few days after the Manhattan Center event, Marinello was honored by the CCI. Marinello accepted the CCI's invitation because, as he noted, it was a club made up of black and white members, "as in the days of Martí and Maceo." He was particularly impressed by the CCI's commitment to unifying all Cubans as well as the entire "colonia hispana in this great city of New York."[37] That Wednesday evening La Giralda restaurant was packed, "numeroso hasta el limíte." The pianist and local notary public Gregorio del Vignau, also known as Goyito, played both the Cuban and US national anthems, Julio Cardenal served as the master of ceremonies, and Pedroso was tasked with introducing Marinello. In his introduction Pedroso provided a possible reason for why Marinello decided to tour the Cuban immigrant community in New York and Tampa. After expressing his gratitude, Pedroso introduced Marinello as the "futuro presidente de nuestra patria." Two years later, Marinello ran unsuccessfully to become president of Cuba.[38]

Before giving his speech, several members of the club and community took turns addressing the crowd. They included Arminda González, vice secretary of the CCI, Jesús Colón, Reinaldo Fernández Rebull, Blas Molina, Carmen Meana, Frank Ibañez, and James Ford, the highest-ranking

African American member and leader of the "Central Committee of the US Communist Party."[39] After acknowledging Colón and Ford by name, Marinello gave a speech in which he addressed several key concerns, notably the future of Cuban society, politics, and economy; the ongoing threat of imperialism; anti-Franco activism; his support for Puerto Rican independence; and the "painful existence of racial discrimination in Cuba, our country, which should be extirpated." Marinello ended his speech by honoring his close friend Ruben Martínez Villegas who had recently died, and reciting a few stanzas from a Walt Whitman poem.[40]

Little more than a month later the members honored Dr. Angel Suárez Rocabruna. At the time, Rocabruna was a visiting professor of Spanish at Howard University, a "corresponsal-asociado" of the CCI in Havana and a current member of the CCI. Rocabruna's position at Howard University was facilitated by Reinaldo Fernández Rebull and sponsored by the State Department's Division for Cultural Cooperation.[41] While at Howard University, Rocabruna hosted visits from CCI members and introduced them to African American scholars, activists, and to Sergio "Henry" Grillo, president of the Cuban-American Good Will Association.[42] The relationship among the CCI, Howard University, and the Cuban-American Good Will Association continued long after Rocabruna's professorship ended. CCI members traveled to Washington, DC to attend informal gatherings and events, including those in 1949 and 1950 to honor the Fourth of July, and Armistice Day, and to celebrate the recent formation of a CCI club in Washington, DC.[43] The relationship between the clubs and the university was so close that Francisca Cardenal suggested to the musician Arsenio Rodríguez that he get in touch with the CCI club in DC "and go to Howard University."[44]

Unlike the others, Rocabruna's banquet was specifically organized by El Comité Pro-Centenario del General Antonio Maceo. This was no coincidence. Rocabruna was a powerful ally of the CCI and El Comité. Similar to Rebull, Rocabruna was the CCI's "Cuban connection" and helped to formalize the committee's vision and reinforce its initial commitment to building a monument in New York and Havana. On May 17, members gathered at El Mundial restaurant on 222 West 116th Street to hear Rocabruna discuss the importance of the monument and to call for the "necessary unity" among all "hispanos americanos" who make up the distinct neighborhoods of this city.[45]

On November 6, the CCI held its last formal banquet of the year. This time the club honored Lazaro Peña, president of the Confederation of Cuban Workers. A respected Afro-Cuban labor and political organizer, Peña traveled frequently to the United States and was known among African American labor organizers. Three years earlier, on August 14, 1943, the State Department denied Peña entry into the United States to attend the fourth annual convention of the CIO National Maritime Union. The National Negro Congress protested the State Department's actions and sent a letter to Secretary of State Cordell Hull requesting that Peña be given permission to enter the United States.[46]

Like Marinello, Peña visited several organizations and spoke with colleagues and supporters, including one held on November 3 at the Manhattan Center and organized by the Coordinating Committee of the Pro-Spanish Republic. Peña shared the stage with José Giral, the president of the Spanish Republic in exile, and Vito Marcantonio, congressman representing East Harlem.[47] Unlike the other two, Peña's banquet was held in the new casa-club. He congratulated the members for so quickly establishing a respectable institution, and publicly recognized the CCI as the "indisputable authority" representing the social concerns of the "legitimate colonia de hispanos-americanos in this great city." He complimented the CCI for its "healthy politics," commitment to social equality, and for eliminating barriers. His speech received a standing ovation.[48]

Peña's declaration that the CCI was a respectable institution with the indisputable authority to represent the *legitimate* claims of "Hispanic Americans in this great city" was bold. In doing so, Peña deliberately empowered the CCI and elevated the club's standing among the Cuban community. His strong advocacy of the club's "healthy politics" and their commitment to social equality was a direct challenge to the racism targeted at the CCI members and the ongoing controversy surrounding a monument to Maceo. Peña, along with Marinello and Rocabruna, were quite aware of the racial tensions among Cubans, and were determined to quell them by openly supporting the CCI and the monument to Maceo.

The relationship between Afro-Cuban and white clubs during this period was complicated, cordial, tense, and distant. It was not uncommon for the clubs to come together to support a particular event or issue, and then separate. On February 24, 1946, Fernández Rebull organized an event celebrating the beginning of the Cuban War for Independence in 1895, known as El Grito de Baire. All Cuban clubs were invited.[49] Less than a month later the "Presidents of all of the Cuban Centers, Clubs, Ateneos and Associations located in New York" signed a letter to the president of Cuba, Ramón Grau San Martín, thanking him for reinstating Reinaldo Fernández Rebull as the consul general of Cuba in New York.[50] At the same time, letters from the CCI went unanswered, invitations were refused, and attempts to collaborate were ignored. According to Melba Alvarado, the CCI had a very difficult and complicated relationship with El Ateneo Cubano, "a white club that was formed a year or so earlier than the CCI." The relationship remained troubled for years and was a source of great frustration and disappointment for CCI members, especially when it came to honoring Maceo.[51]

During the two years that the CCI organized the campaign for a monument to Maceo, there were those outside of the CCI and Afro-Cuban community who considered building a monument *only* to Maceo to be divisive and controversial. The criticism and lack of cooperation prompted CCI members to reconsider their original idea of building a monument solely to Maceo.[52] In 1947, two years after the centennial, El Comité Pro-Centenario del General Antonio Maceo was renamed El Comité Permanente Pro-Monumento Martí y Maceo. The decision was not difficult. Similar to Maceo, the members were devoted to Martí and considered his writings integral to the club's ideological underpinning. Along with the Cena Martiana, which was held every year in late January to honor Martí's birth, Martí's portrait hung on the wall of the CCI next to Maceo, George Washington, Abraham Lincoln, and Simón Bolívar. Members recited Martí's poetry, distributed his writings, and made sure that children from an early age understood Martí's historical significance. The CCI members were also aware that Martí was the one figure that all Cubans openly supported without question. By including Martí, the CCI laid claim to his influence, removed perceived barriers, and insured that Maceo would be represented. This was especially urgent since there was "talk" of a campaign to eliminate Maceo and install a monument *only* to Martí.

El Comité celebrated the change with a spectacular concert held at the Audubon Hall on July 9. Billed as a fund-raiser for the "Monumento Martí y Maceo," the concert was headlined by "el gran babalú" Miguelito Valdés, and included performances by some of the biggest names in

Event in support of El Comité Permanente Pro-Monumento Martí y Maceo. Pablo
Soublette is seated behind the speaker. 1948. Photographs and Prints Division, Schom-
burg Center for Research in Black Culture, New York Public Library, Astor, and Tilden
Foundations.

Members gathered at the CCI club in the South Bronx, approximately 1949. Photographs and Prints Division, Schomburg Center for Research in Black Culture, New York Public Library, Astor, and Tilden Foundations.

Cuban music—Olga Guillot, Chano Pozo, Chapotin, and Frank García and his Orchestra. The concert was a great success and raised the needed funds to begin the process of building. In addition to the performers, there were a number of speakers, including Dr. Gilberto Campo Lizama of the Sociedad Gran Maceo de Santa Clara, and Pedro Portuondo Calá, newspaper reporter and columnist of *El País*, who was both an affiliate and member of El Comité Permanente Pro-Monumento Martí y Maceo. Both were there to assist with "erecting in this city a monument to Martí and Maceo."[53] That evening El Comité Permanente Pro-Monumento Martí y Maceo also gained the support of Vincent Michael Lee, a staff member of Theater Inc., who offered the committee his services free of charge.

In a newsletter detailing the event, committee member Julio Aroza-rena referred to Lee's generous offer and used it to scold those "rabidly patriotic Cubans" who despite much discussion have done little. Singling out the monument as one of the club's most important causes, one that "was entrusted" to the club by the founders, Arozarena demanded that the CCI be more involved with the monument and that it not be left just to El Comité Permanente Pro-Monumento Martí y Maceo.[54] Arozarena's concerns were warranted. Over the years, the CCI left most if not all of the work to a committee whose leadership and direction changed frequently over the years.

On October 1, 1947, a few months after the gala fund-raiser, Narcisco Saavedra wrote to Jesús Colón asking him to name a delegate to the new committee, and he invited Colón to the first meeting on October 8th at the CCI to discuss the logistics of building the monument and fine-tuning the new committee.[55] So far, with the help of Rocabruna and Fernández Rebull, the committee had forged important connections and expanded its appeal to a broader contingent of Cubans. A month later, in November 1947, the CCI's affiliates now included Henry Grillo in Washington, DC; Antonio González in Tampa and Key West; Dr. Pura Olano in Santiago de Cuba; and Pedro Portuondo Calá in Havana. All that was left was for Fernández Rebull to speak with New York City officials to secure a location in Central Park.[56]

In March 1949 the committee, with the help of senators and representatives in Cuba, received a donation of a thousand dollars from the city council of Marianao to help fund the monument. Pedro Portoundo Calá, who was in Havana at the time, was entrusted with depositing the money into the Grand Masonic Lodge's treasury in Cuba, and later into the CCI's bank in New York. The donation spurred a larger conversation about funding the monument. It was agreed that the Comité would be given a separate checking account and a blank check so they could withdraw $288.00 from the CCI account. Several members expressed concerns over the Comité's ongoing debts and finances. Javier de la Paz recommended that the Comité Pro-Monumento provide information concerning their finances, especially since Comité member Apollinar Mendoza told the other members that he could not say, "no se puede decir," what the final cost of the monument would be.[57]

From the onset, the CCI struggled with money. By 1949 the CCI was already experiencing difficulty with getting members to pay their dues, covering their rent,[58] funding mutual aid benefits, supporting the work of other committees, and having enough to pay for events, performers, and banquets. On March 31 members discussed passing a rule that in order to receive mutual aid benefits, members would have had to pay their dues "for no less than five years consecutively." This sparked an intense debate with Saavedra, Lara, de la Paz, and Pedroso arguing against the proposed changes. Pedroso, for one, considered it unfair that "just because a member had stopped paying for a time, they were no longer allowed to receive benefits." Eventually, the costs proved too expensive for the club and within a few years, the CCI eliminated mutual aid benefits.[59]

The financial demands and strains prompted arguments and disagreements. After being denied $175.00 to cover league costs for the CCI's baseball team, Mr. Cuevas asked why there was money for dances, but not for the CCI's baseball team. The treasurer's response was firm. The club, Francisca Cardenal stated, was "in no condition" to fund a baseball team.[60] Dances, however, brought in money and the CCI organized their fair share of performances. Before the meeting ended, members elected Pedroso, Pedro Millet, and Pablo Soublette to the Comité Pro-Monumento Martí y Maceo with the hope that the founding members might quell the ongoing financial unrest and get the committee back on track.[61]

By this time the political tenor of the club had shifted. In the early evening of June 6, 1949, ten members met at the casa-club on Prospect Avenue in the Bronx. As always, the meeting began with general announcements, including reading and accepting invitations. This time, when the secretary general read a notice inviting CCI members to a meeting of the Communist Party—a frequent occurrence—there was open dissension. Francisco de la Paz proposed that club members not attend any meetings or establish affiliations with any organization that contradicted the "the principles or ideals of our club." The motion was seconded and passed by the members.[62] Seemingly indistinguishable from any other club meeting, the CCI's actions that evening marked a turning point in the club's history. The members who attended the meeting, including de la Paz, had embodied a club that in the past had cultivated alliances with the Communist Party and the IWO.[63] Now, they were concerned with protecting the club from any show of alliance or solidarity with communists.

Growing anti-communism in the United States and Cuba did not bode well for the CCI. The attacks on the IWO threatened to expose certain members' past affiliations and possibly confirm the suspicions of those who questioned the club's political direction and alliances. In addition, the election and presidency of Carlos Prío Socarrás in 1948 derailed the CCI's influence among politicians and bureaucrats in Cuba. In 1944 Prío served as the minister of labor under then President Ramón Grau San Martín, who was steadily moving to the right. Influenced by the Cold War, Prío advised President Grau San Martín to move against the Communist Party and the communist-dominated worker's union.[64] By the time he was elected president, Prío, as the historian Julia Sweig has written, had established "one of the most polarized, corrupt, violent, and undemocratic" presidencies in Cuba's Republican history. Prío did not last long. Rightly fearing that Batista would stage a military coup, Prío sought asylum in the Mexican embassy and left the country before Batista could take over. In 1952, Batista once again assumed the presidency, effectively ending constitutional government in Cuba.[65]

The political instability and changes had a direct effect on the CCI's influence in Cuba, especially when it came to garnering support for the monument. It was no surprise that the second announcement read was a letter written by El Comité Pro-Monumento of Havana informing the CCI that they had been left out of the new organizing committee in Cuba. This, it turns out, was good news for the CCI who, according to the minutes, had every intention of distancing themselves from the committee in Havana. It was agreed that a letter would be sent to Havana explaining, in "la mejor manera," in the best way possible, that the CCI not be included in the plans to build a monument in Havana.[66] The members ended the meeting with a brief recap of boxer Kid Gavilán's banquet a few weeks earlier on May 20, and a reminder that the CCI would soon be organizing their yearly celebration of Antonio Maceo's birthday on June 14.[67]

By the end of the year the CCI was losing money, again. Despite being given a thousand dollars, El Comité Pro-Monumento Martí y Maceo still owed $388.00. The situation was so dire that members met a few days before Christmas to discuss the continual and persistent lack of funding for the monument. After some discussion, it was decided that the only solution was for each member to donate $3.00 to the Comité. This money, Francisca Cardenal told the members, "was sacred." Unfortunately for El Comité, there was another problem with building the monument. At the same meeting, members discussed a letter sent by Pedro Portuondo Calá to the CCI. In it, Calá wrote that during his last visit to New York, there were disagreements concerning who should be credited, what the look of the monument should be, and how "things were being done in this city." The criticisms were pointed enough for José Pérez to consider them "very tough," and asked if anyone had responded.[68]

On a recent trip to Havana, the members of El Comité Pro-Monumento Martí y Maceo came across a newspaper article written by César Fages that was critical of the CCI and El Comité Pro-Monumento Martí y Maceo. The members demanded to see a copy of the article. Given that Fages was not a member of the club, they were suspicious of his criticisms. Despite several attempts to contact him, Fages refused to speak with the CCI and El Comité Pro-Monumento, even though Mrs. Pérez-Galos wrote a letter requesting to speak with him about the article. Less than a month later, in January 1950, Fages finally responded to the CCI. He informed them that the article in question was based on an earlier piece published in the Cuban newspaper, *El Mundo*.[69]

The minutes do not list the criticisms in the letter or why Pérez considered them to be so tough. There is no information on what Fages reported and why it made the CCI members so uneasy. A possible explanation is that supporters in Havana had already decided that the monument in New York honor only Martí, effectively leaving CCI out of the process. Perhaps this is what Calá meant when he referred to the disagreements over how the monument "should look," and his concerns over who should be credited. This may also explain why the CCI believed it was urgent for El Comité to travel to Havana to meet with officials in an attempt to change their minds. More than a year later, on March 29, 1951, Calá informed the members that work on the monument had begun in Cuba. Three months later, on June 30, Narciso Saavedra traveled to Cuba to see for himself and report back to the CCI. A year later, in March 1952, Francisca Cardenal went to Havana to check the status of the monument, a project the members noted they "had supported since 1948."[70] During such a precarious period, the CCI reached out to the community, the press, and allies to garner support. On April 12, 1951, Mario Bauza agreed to play for "almost free," to assist the club with raising needed funds.[71] In February 1952 the newspaper, *Diario of Nueva York*, expressed support for the monument. A month later, Saavedra recorded a radio interview at Fordham University with Afro-Cuban journalist Vicente Cubillas, Jr.[72]

Flutist and CCI member Alberto Socarras raising funds and awareness for the monument to Martí-Maceo. José I. Leon and Narciso Saavedra are at the front of the table. Alvarado is seated behind Leon, and Francisca "Paquita" Cardenal is seated in front of Socarras with beret. 1949.

By 1953 it had become abundantly clear that, despite their efforts and hard-earned community support, the CCI's greatest obstacle to building the monument in New York was racism. According to Alvarado, El Ateneo Cubano did not want to work with Afro-Cubans or be involved in any way with honoring Maceo. While the CCI suspected this, it was during a centennial celebration of José Martí's birth, held on January 28, 1953 at Carnegie Hall, that their suspicions were confirmed. With a donation of a hundred dollars from the Cuban consul of New York, the CCI organized a lavish centennial in honor of José Martí's birth at the revered Carnegie Hall on West 57th Street. Everyone was invited: the ambassador of Cuba to the United Nations, Emilio Nuñez Portuondo; the Cuban Consul General, Alfredo Hernández; local politicians; representatives of social and cultural clubs; and even the president of Cuba, Fulgencio Batista. CCI member and renowned flutist Alberto Socarras performed several pieces that evening. According to Alvarado, "it was beautiful." The CCI spared no expense. All of their money was spent "on mounting the Centennial to Martí in Carnegie Hall." Alvarado remembered everyone being there, except the members of El Ateneo Cubano. As organizers had reserved a coveted place on the stage for them, their absence was striking. For the entire evening their seats on stage remained empty. "Not one member showed up." For Alvarado the only explanation for their absence was racism. El Ateneo Cubano did not want to support an event that had been organized by Afro-Cubans or be around so many Afro-Cubans. In her words, "they did not want to be without other whites."[73]

The humiliation was compounded by the fact that the celebration was not for Maceo, but for Martí. Accustomed to being ignored when it came to Maceo, the CCI members were stunned that El Ateneo Cubano would do the same when honoring Martí. If Martí, the ultimate symbol of racial solidarity and an inclusive Cuban nationalism, could not bring these communities together, then nothing and no one could. The irony was that up to that moment the CCI and El Ateneo Cubano had gathered multiple times to honor Martí. It was expected. The departure from protocol made it clear that this absence had meaning. It was, for Alvarado, a deliberate snub, a way of letting the CCI and the greater community know that El Ateneo Cubano was not interested in working with or establishing any common ground with the CCI. This, as Alvarado recalled, was the beginning of the end.

Echando Pleito: Gendered Migrations, El Comité de Damas, and 'Making Trouble'

The women's club made the dinners; they did everything. And I said to myself, but we don't have a vote or a voice in the running of the club. And that's when I started making trouble.
Melba Alvarado[74]

In 1947 the CCI's *Circular, Acuerdos, y Noticias* published a column devoted to women entitled, "Para Ellas: lealo hoy y recuerdalo mañana" (For her: read it now and remember it tomorrow). There are few surviving columns, but those that do exist provide a fascinating look at how women negotiated their power and place within a male-dominated club. The columns, written for and by women, offer advice on a range of topics including finding work, raising children, and handling health issues within the context of a working-class, immigrant framework. In one column dedicated to staying young, the columnist, whose name is not given, does not offer makeup tips or suggest beauty creams. Instead, the columnist explains how "the woman of today, who works, earns her own salary, and is obligated to complete chores can very easily waste her energy." The advice is "to be prudent with one's energy, slow down and find a balance between the physical and spiritual."[75]

The advice was warranted. Women worked exceedingly hard and as a result, made the CCI a success. They helped to found the club, held leadership positions, coordinated events, were responsible for running the CCI, organized El Comité de Damas, and were at the forefront of assisting newly arrived migrants with finding employment, housing, and learning English.[76] They were also committed to creating a feminist intellectual community. One of the first events was a talk by Dr. Ana Echegoyen de Cañizares, the first woman of color to hold a teaching post at the University of Havana, and as Frank Guridy writes, a feminist who was a major force behind the Asociación Cultural Femenina (Women's Cultural Association).[77] Given in September 1946 and coordinated by Otilia Ruibal Sterling and Ana María Vasquez, the talk examined the future of a post–World War II reality, the impact of the Atlantic Charter, and results of the Scottsboro Case of 1931, what Echegoyen called the "painful racial events that recently took place in Alabama." The talk drew a large number of people and initiated a series of academic and political talks organized by and for women.[78]

That same year, three women were elected to serve on the CCI's first board of directors: Josefina Valdés, first vice president; Arminda González, first vice secretary; and Francisca Cardenal, first vice treasurer.[79] Women in the CCI had a long history of activism in political organizations, labor unions, and social clubs, including El Club Mella. El Comité de Damas, which was formed shortly after the founding of the CCI, closely mirrored El Club de Damas, the women's club of El Club Mella. Much like El Club de Damas, El Comité de Damas was not an auxiliary to the CCI, but a separate organizing space where women made decisions, organized events, and when necessary challenged policies that had been voted on by the board of directors. Some women, as Alvarado recalled, avoided the CCI altogether and preferred to attend only the Comité de Damas meetings.

In addition to responding to "women's issues," El Comité de Damas addressed problems and setbacks associated with moving to New York. During this period the majority of women leaving Cuba did so for economic reasons. The most pressing problems were finding work and learning English.[80] In 1949 Mrs. Pérez de Galos offered classes in "cutting and sewing once a week" to help women secure employment in the garment industry. The sewing classes were so popular that a year later the CCI purchased a sewing machine to keep up with the demand. That same year Carmelina (Carmen) Bovi began teaching English classes several times a week. These classes, which were free of charge, were critical in helping women find work in the garment industry.[81] Women raised money to assist with rents and held donation campaigns for food, coats, and shoes. They lobbied the CCI board of directors for funds to help with medical care and costs related to childbearing, and offered childcare services. On Sundays, they cooked and served dinner for members and nonmembers alike.[82]

The need to assist women was great. After World War II the number of Cuban women migrating to the United States increased.[83] According to Alvarado there were "a lot of single women" who migrated to New York after the war and just stayed. She recalled one instance when "some newspaper man," most likely Pedro Portuondo Calá, "organized excursions to New York, and there would be close to forty people traveling with him. When they were supposed to return only twenty went back. Many of them stayed here."[84]

Except for those who had a sponsor willing to be fully responsible for them (i.e., public charge)[85] or those who migrated to the United States on a student visa, there were two major avenues used to gain entry into the United States: B-29 tourist visas, and claiming to be Puerto Rican. The B-29 tourist visas refer to the number of days (29) that tourists were legally allowed to be in the United States. Once in the country, women found work and eventually over-stayed their visas. Seen by the United States as caregivers who would not leave their families behind, it was easier for women than men to be granted B-29 visas. Since women were paid less for their labor, it was also easier for them to find employment in the garment industry. Combined, these factors led to an increase in Cuban women using the B-29 visa to migrate to New York.[86]

By the late 1940s there were so many Caribbean migrants passing as Puerto Rican that the Puerto Rican consul in New York complained that it could not confirm that an applicant "holding a Puerto Rican birth certificate is really a Puerto Rican." In one memorandum, Pablo Vera, supervisor of the Identification Section, notified Joseph Monserrat, director of the New York office, that their section had discovered, in an internal check of all applications "filed prior to 1950, that identification cards issued to applicants born in a foreign country (Cuba and Dominican Republic), claiming citizenship were found to be aliens passing as Puerto Ricans." In another, Vera informed Monserrat that the section has been working in "close cooperation" with the Immigration and Naturalization Service "for the purposes of checking into the identity of individuals who are aliens and have secured through unscrupulous agents, birth certificates from Puerto Rico." By 1953, Vera provided evidence that "a certain individual in this city has a large stock of birth certificates that he is selling to other individuals, possibly aliens at a rate of $10.00 and up." It was so easy to pass as Puerto Rican that many Cubans simply decided to "stay Puerto Rican" and not make the changes necessary to become legal Cuban residents.[87]

In 1957, Alvarado was the second woman elected president of the CCI. Her election was controversial and split the club. Five years earlier, Alvarado had been elected president of El Comité de Damas. A member for only a few years, Alvarado rose quickly through the ranks, becoming one of the most powerful members of the CCI. The reason, Alvarado pointed out, was that "We (the women) organized activities that made money for the club."[88] Outspoken, intelligent, extremely hard-working, and by her own admission "pushy," Alvarado was both admired and feared. Known for not mincing words, she complained about the lack of cooperation from men who were quick to take credit for women's work. "Women were on the directiva (board of directors), on certain committees, but men were the ones who dominated."[89]

Tired of doing most of the work and getting little to no recognition, Alvarado decided that it was time for women to be acknowledged for their contributions and more importantly, be given a vote on the board of directors. At the time, El Comité de Damas did not have a vote or voice on the board. Once Alvarado was elected president of El Comité she was successful in convincing the board of directors to give El Comité de Damas a vote. This meant that Alvarado, as the newly elected leader of El Comité, now had a vote on the board. Alvarado's actions angered Francisca Cardenal, who as past president of El Comité de Damas and member of the board of directors was, up to that moment, the most powerful woman in the club. "She (Cardenal) wanted all of the power, that the Board of Directors do what she wanted. But the person who had made the club big and organized special events was me."[90] Alvarado's actions caused friction within the club. But they also expanded opportunities for women's leadership and power. By demanding that El Comité de Damas have a vote on the board of directors, Alvarado insured that women's contributions were recognized and their voices heard.

Five years later and with the support of Pedro Millet, José I. Leon, Marcos Llerena, and Generoso Pedroso, Alvarado ran for president. "I was very lucky because I had four or five old men who used to be, you know, former co-founders of the club and they really encouraged me a lot. They really fought for me."[91] Alvarado would need their support. Soon after declaring her intentions, Alvarado learned she had made a few enemies, namely, Francisca Cardenal. "That was the first clash I had with 'la Cardenal.' I pushed her off the horse."[92] Cardenal campaigned against her and warned members that if Alvarado was elected she and her husband Julio would leave the club and begin a new one. Francisca Cardenal kept her word. Shortly after Alvarado was elected president of the CCI, Francisca and Julio Cardenal formed El Círculo Cubano with "the same bunch" of her supporters, including their good friend and past president of the CCI, Narciso Saavedra. The split was big news. On April 29, 1957, the columnist for *El Diario de Nueva York*, Bobby Quintero, reported on the split and highlighted Francisca Cardenal's decision to create a similar club, "one that might possibly compete with the former one." Much like the CCI, the first meeting was held at Cardenals' apartment on 135 W. 116th Street. El Círculo Cubano eventually rented a space on 125th street.[93]

Although Alvarado claimed that the split had no effect on the CCI, the loss of certain influential and key figures was undeniable. Past members Julio and Francisca Cardenal and Narciso Saavedra were pivotal to the success of the CCI and El Comité Pro-Monumento Martí y Maceo. The split, the CCI's problems with El Ateneo Cubano, the ongoing financial

Melba Alvarado flanked by supporters after being elected president of the CCI. L to R: Marcos LLerena, Luis Alvarado (father), Melba Alvardo, José Leon, and Pedro Millet. Photographs and Prints Division, Schomburg Center for Research in Black Culture, New York Public Library, Astor, and Tilden Foundations.

issues, and the political chaos in Cuba contributed to a tenuous period for the CCI and El Comité's ambitions for the monument. A year before the split, it was evident that the goal of building a monument to both Martí y Maceo was quickly dissipating. In 1956 *La Prensa* reported that a statue to Martí would be installed in the newly built plaza in Central Park South and gave full credit to El Ateneo Cubano. There was no mention of the CCI or the fact that CCI members had worked diligently for years to install a monument to Martí *and* Maceo.[94] In the late 1950s, after more than a decade of work, El Comité Pro-Monumento Martí-Maceo disbanded. The CCI no longer had a reason to organize or campaign for a monument honoring Martí and Maceo.[95] Despite the deep disappointment and hurt, or perhaps because of it, the CCI remained committed to honoring Maceo. For the CCI it was no less than an act of defiance and resistance. They positioned the bust intended to be part of the monument prominently in the club, highlighted his portrait, celebrated his birth and death, emphasized his role in the Ten Years' War and the Cuban War for Independence, and continued to use the CCI as a site for honoring Afro-Cuban performers, musicians, artists, writers, and politicians.

By the time the statue of Martí was unveiled in 1965, El Ateneo Cubano no longer existed. Four years later, in 1969, the club Francisca Cardenal helped to found, El Círculo Cubano, disbanded. That same year Melba Alvarado was elected president of the CCI for the second time.[96]

"Honoring Our Own": Enacting Afro-Cuban Performance, Space, and Visibility

Taking the performativity of space seriously also means understanding that categories such as gender, race, and sexuality are not only discursively constructed but spatially enacted and created as well.
Mary Pat Brady[97]

We have no reason to be grateful to Cubans. They didn't come to our performance and they had White Cuban social clubs where people of color could not enter.
Graciela Pérez Gutiérrez[98]

Where there were blacks, whites did not want to go.
Melba Alvarado[99]

When asked about her experiences as president of the club in 1957, Alvarado's first response was that *she* was the one to bring Beny Moré and the Orquesta Aragón to the CCI. Because, as she put it, "a la gente le gusta lo bueno."[100] After years of interviewing, speaking, and working with Alvarado, I was not surprised that she referenced music and performance as her defining achievements. In fact, I expected it. Alvarado has always loved music and admired musicians. As a young girl she spent the money she earned working at her father's dry cleaning business to see Cab Calloway perform at the Apollo Theater. She went to every free concert and if need be, snuck into local venues to see her favorite acts. Introduced to music at an early age by her family, she dreamed of becoming a singer. The only problem was that she couldn't sing. But she could dance, and won several prizes. Emboldened by the accolades, she informed her mother that she was going to be a performer. Not easily impressed, her mother responded by telling Alvarado that, "to be an artist, you have to be pretty, and you're too ugly." Unfortunately, Alvarado believed her mother and relinquished her dreams of becoming a professional dancer. Despite her disappointment, Alvarado was passionate about music and brought some of the most talented musicians to perform at the CCI and later, La Fiesta del Mamoncillo, a popular music festival partly founded by Alvarado in 1969.[101]

For Alvarado, bringing the best in Afro-Cuban music to perform at the CCI was exciting, transformative, and defiant. She never got tired of the idea that the best in Cuban music and culture routinely performed at a small Afro-Cuban club in the South Bronx. These relationships, performances, and events shaped the club's direction, purpose, and relevance. By the 1950s they defined the CCI. It was during this period that Alvarado developed important and long-lasting friendships with some of the most renowned Afro-Cuban artists in New York. Mario Bauza, Graciela Pérez Gutiérrez, and Eusebia Cosme were especially close friends.

In conversations and interviews Alvarado often spoke of how Mario Bauza, admired among Afro-Cubans and Puerto Ricans, never received the recognition he deserved from white Cubans in New York. This, she observed, made him "un negro herido," a wounded black man. She called Alberto Soccaras a "great man" and brilliant flutist. She liked Arsenio Rodríguez, but complained that he never paid his club dues. She respected Machito and considered him, and his band, to be the best in New York. But her favorite was Beny Moré. Already a star in Latin America, getting Moré to perform at the club was nothing less than a coup.[102]

The CCI was known as a place where revered Afro-Cuban musicians and artists performed during the golden age of Cuban music.[103] Yet, what is rarely discussed is how spaces, like the CCI, operated as sites of community formation, safety, transgression, empowerment, rebellion, and celebration. When asked about the performances at the CCI, Alvarado's responses typify the closeness and intimacy among the CCI members and the artists who performed there. They were, as she often stated, "lo mismo," part of the same community and "lo nuestro," in

Beny Moré surrounded by CCI members and fans after performing at the CCI, 1957. Photographs and Prints Division, Schomburg Center for Research in Black Culture, New York Public Library, Astor, and Tilden Foundations.

community. Along with politicians, writers, activists, scholars, poets, and a string of former Club Julio Antonio Mella members, musicians Marcelino Guerra and Alberto Socarras are listed as official founders of the CCI.[104] Musicians attended CCI meetings, sat on committees, were dues-paying members, organized events, represented the CCI in Havana, performed at important club events, and helped to raise money for the club.[105] In other words, they were involved in building and shaping the direction of the CCI. Many of the studies that examine the history and careers of musicians who performed at the CCI cast them as devoid of politics and community, separated from club members, events, and the everyday running of the club. Yet, as the CCI records and Alvarado's oral histories confirm, artists such as Mario Bauza, Alberto Socarras, Marcelino Guerra, Eusebia Cosme, and Arsenio Rodríguez supported the construction of a monument to Martí and Maceo, and in the case of

Eusebia Cosme, Julia Mendoza, Celia Cruz, and Melba Alvarado honoring Celia Cruz at the CCI. 1957. Jesús Colón/Justo Ambrosio Martí: Archives of the Puerto Rican Diaspora, Centro de Estudios Puertorriqueños, Hunter College, City University of New York.

Socarras, he traveled to Cuba to represent the interest of the CCI and El Comité Pro-Monumento Martí y Maceo.[106]

Citing the work of spatial theorists Henry Lefebvre, Doreen Massey, and Edward Soja, Mary Pat Brady argues that space and the production of space not only configure social and cultural groups and institutions, but also involve the "processes that shape how these places are understood, envisioned, defined, and variously experienced."[107] Moreover, as Brady contends, the processes of producing space, "however quotidian or grand, hidden or visible," have an enormous effect on "subject formation—on the choices people can make and how they conceptualize themselves, each other and the world." To put it simply, "places are felt and experienced."[108]

The CCI was one of those spaces that was felt and experienced. Continually evolving, it was a critical site for articulating Afro-Cubanidad through community, performance, and Afro-diasporic belonging. Be-

Cuban baseball player Orestes "Minnie" Miñoso honored by the CCI members. Miñoso is seated to the left of CCI President Joaquin Maldonado at the microphone. Generoso Pedroso is seated next to Melba Alvarado. Photographs and Prints Division, Schomburg Center for Research in Black Culture, New York Public Library, Astor, and Tilden Foundations.

cause there were so few places where these artists could perform to a black audience, the shows at the CCI were different. There was no fear of being turned away, disrespected, or mistreated; no separate section, entrance, or room. There was, as Alvarado would say, "no racism." For the performers, it was a rare communal space to meet with friends, have dinner, drink coffee, play dominoes, organize events, practice, and of course, perform.[109] Because they were in community, the performances were legendary. Musicians were not afraid to take risks, perform with other artists, experiment, and play late into the evening.

In addition to being an important site for black performance, the CCI was also one of the few spaces that routinely honored black musicians, artists, athletes, and writers. It was, as Alvarado remarked, a way of "honoring our own."[110] The list of honorees is long and the figures

CCI members Arsenio Rodríguez and Eusebia Cosme honored by the club. Photographs and Prints Division, Schomburg Center for Research in Black Culture, New York Public Library, Astor, and Tilden Foundations.

legendary. They include, but were not limited to: baseball player Orestes 'Minnie" Miñoso; boxers Kid Chocolate, Kid Gavilán, and Niño Valdés,; musicians Mario Bauza, Beny Moré, Celia Cruz, Chano Pozo, Arsenio Rodríguez, Miguelito Valdés, Olga Guillot, Alberto Soccaras, Noro Morales, Marcelino Guerra, Alfredito Valdés, Frank 'Machito' Grillo y sus Afro-Cubanos, Xiomara Alfaro, Jorge Bolet, Domingo Pouble, and Gilberto Valdés; orator Eusebia Cosme; and journalists Carlos Guzman Chamizo, Pedro Portuondo Calá, and Sonia Ellis.[111]

Prized by white audiences for their talent and skill, Afro-Cuban musicians and athletes were rarely singled out for their achievements and contributions. The CCI members understood this, and believed it was their "rightful duty" to honor Afro-Cuban talent. The CCI banquets, diplomas, and honors showcased artists, sports figures, and journalists as multidimensional artists worthy of tribute and recognition. The "homenajes" were used to project worth and merit to a wider community that often dismissed the CCI and its members. To publicly honor black achievement during a period of intense racism was a transgressive act of visibility designed to disrupt the marginalization of Afro-diasporic cultural and knowledge producers and afford them the respect they so richly deserved.

Erasing Maceo: Post-Monument Conclusion on the Eve of Revolution

To remember is a high-stakes project. It does not always result in healing, in uncovering or discovering an empowering subject or narrative, in resolving the past, or making the present more secure.
Deborah Vargas[112]

Thirteen years ago and as a result of the centennial celebration of Major General Antonio Maceo Y Grajales at the Town Hall, a group of men of good faith devoted themselves to founding what we know today as El Club Cubano Inter-Americano, which started in 1945 with Generoso Pedroso as its first president (QEP).
Trece Años, 1958[113]

In 1958, Generoso Menéndez Pedroso died. It was a blow to the CCI. In a one-page hand-out entitled "Trece Años" and distributed to members, the CCI included Pedroso's signature contribution: his determination to build community, promote racial inclusivity, and empower Afro-Cuban migrants. In it, the CCI recounted the one event that led to the founding of the CCI and the role that Antonio Maceo, as symbol and imaginary, played in articulating diasporic Afro-Cubanidades. What makes this especially poignant is that members already knew that Maceo would not be included in the monument soon to be unveiled in Central Park. It is certain that during the last years of his life Pedroso witnessed the unraveling of more than a decade of work to install a monument that at the very least included Maceo. One could only imagine what it must have felt like to experience the literal and figurative erasing of Maceo from public memory and space. To date there are no public monuments to Antonio Maceo in New York.

CCI members posing with busts commissioned (but never used) for the monument to Antonio Maceo and José Martí. Photographs and Prints Division, Schomburg Center for Research in Black Culture, New York Public Library, Astor, and Tilden Foundations.

The erasing of Maceo coincided with the Cuban Revolution, the Red Scare, and the ongoing debate over whether the CCI was communist. Rarely discussed publicly, certain CCI members were targeted as communist sympathizers, including Alvarado. "They accuse you of being communist, and you're not. The worst thing you can be called here is a communist." Being labeled a communist was not surprising, considering the CCI's connection with El Club Julio Antonio Mella and early members' affiliation with socialist and communist organizations and leaders. The problem was that those who accused CCI members of being communist knew very little about the CCI's history, and why it was formed in 1945. Instead, they were, as Alvarado noted, "whites who were fleeing" the Communist Revolution. "They were combative with me and called me a communist, and I have never been a member of the Communist Party."[114] There were times, as Alvarado remembered, when the club was

Sign announcing the soon-to-be-constructed statue of José Martí in Central Park. Jesús Colón/Justo Ambrosio Martí: Archives of the Puerto Rican Diaspora, Centro de Estudios Puertorriqueños, Hunter College, City University of New York.

threatened with being bombed and members' lives were in danger. It was as though the club, one formed before the revolution and *not* shaped by exile politics, was already suspect. For those fleeing the Communist Revolution, it was unthinkable to have a Cuban club that refused to be political, especially one that eschewed anti-communism. This time around, the CCI's bylaws could not protect the members from accusations, ridicule, and attacks. On the contrary, it would be used against them.

As a club defined by El Club Julio Antonio Mella and post–World War II realities, the years after the Cuban Revolution were extremely difficult. The majority of Cubans fleeing the island were white and their politics were at odds with the CCI. The majority of exiles who moved to New York and New Jersey wanted very little to do with the club. Nonetheless, the CCI was determined to do what it did best: create community, honor their own, organize events, mount performances, celebrate

José Martí and Antonio Maceo, and promote their brand of Cubanidad. Claiming their Cubanidad during this period was critical to their very existence as a club and community. As Alvarado often mentioned, the Cubans fleeing the revolution considered themselves to be "more Cuban than anyone." The truth, as she would like to say, is that we were already here when they arrived. We had our club, our people, our desfile, and we never stopped being Cuban.

EPILOGUE

"Telling will take a long, long time," she said softly, "but I can
say a few things now, at least."
Elizabeth Kostova[1]

On September 18, 2015, El Club Cubano Inter-Americano celebrated
its seventieth anniversary at the esteemed American Negro Theater at
the Schomburg Center for Research in Black Culture. Celebrating its
own seventy-fifth anniversary, the American Negro Theater proved a
perfect setting for honoring one of the oldest surviving Cuban clubs in
New York. There was music, food, speeches, interviews, discussions, and
a display of precious photographs of the club and its members. There
was also a well-deserved tribute to Melba Alvarado, who held the club
together during the most trying periods in the CCI's history. For members who attended that evening, the event seemed unfathomable. Few
imagined that El Club Cubano Inter-Americano would last very long,
let alone seventy years.

In addition to being an important and inclusive site for building community, the CCI has been a barometer for the dramatic political and social changes taking place between Cuba and the United States. As one of
the few clubs that bridged pre- and post-revolutionary Cuba, the history
of the CCI and its members expand our understanding of Afro-Cuban diasporic history. In addition to providing evidence of a pre-revolutionary
community, the CCI offers important insights into how Afro-Cubans,
already in the United States, were affected by the revolution, the politics of exile, and the subsequent waves of migration. Although the club
remained officially apolitical (itself a political act), it was nonetheless influenced and drawn in by the politics of the period.

Shortly after the Communist Revolution, thousands of Cubans left
the island, never to return. Those who left were now in exile. The Cuban
Refugee Program (1961) and the Cuban Adjustment Act (1966) assisted

newly arrived Cuban exiles with employment, housing, medical care, education, and residency. While the majority settled in Miami, a number of Cubans moved to New York and New Jersey. The bulk of Cubans who left the island during this period had little interest in joining a racially inclusive club organized close to fifteen years earlier and rumored to be "communist." The fact that the club was founded by and consisted primarily of Afro-Cubans who left the island decades before the revolution was enough for the club to be considered suspect.

No doubt, as this book chronicles, there was a relationship among the founding members and the Communist and Socialist Parties and movements in both New York and Cuba during the 1930s and 1940s. However, by the mid- to late 1950s the CCI, for varied reasons, chief among them the rise of anti-communism, reaffirmed its commitment to being solely a social and cultural club. For the next fifty years it would be Cuban culture, reimagined through a diasporic lens and filtered through memories and nostalgia, that most defined the CCI and its members. Celebrating, creating, and disseminating culture through Cuban music, dance, poetry, and other forms of expression, as well as service to the community, were ways for members to redefine Cubanidad in a manner that incorporated and honored blackness.[2]

The CCI's determination to be seen solely as a cultural and social club, however, did not protect it from racism, exclusion, and accusations that the club was communist. The Cuban Revolution, as Alvarado noted, "changed many things." One event in particular symbolized what Alvarado believed to be one of the biggest problems facing the CCI during this period: violence. In the early 1960s, Alvarado invited Lazaro Ginebra, "a fantastic orator," to speak at the annual "Maceo celebration." Unfortunately, the event had to be canceled due to bomb threats.[3] This was not an isolated event. For the next ten years, the CCI and its members would be harassed, criticized, and publicly maligned.

While the club and its members rarely, if ever, publicly complained about their treatment, in private they wondered if it was worth the trouble to keep the club open. Adding to the frustration were the club's persistent problems with money and financing the different events. Consisting of working-class members who had very little money to spare, it was not uncommon for members to take out loans and for individuals, including Alvarado, to shoulder the costs of maintaining the club.

After the 1970s the CCI faced an altogether different challenge. The increase in Puerto Rican, Dominican, Cuban, and other Latina/o migrations to New York, along with the changing interests and needs of second and third generations, led to the formation of "younger" clubs all vying to attract audiences to their events and venues.[4] The competition hurt the CCI. It was, as Jo-Ana Moreno remembered, "a place you went with your parents to celebrate special occasions."[5] The generational shift changed the dynamics of the club. It was also during this period that CCI members traveled frequently to Cuba to meet with sister organizations, attend conferences, hold meetings, and make pilgrimages to el Cobre in Santiago de Cuba as well as celebrate la fiesta de San Lazaro and Santa Barbara.[6]

Traveling to Cuba during this period was controversial. Although the Antonio Maceo Brigades of 1977 and the ensuing Diálogos were successful in opening the relationship among Cubans and Cuban exiles, travel to Cuba still polarized the community.[7] Those who traveled to Cuba were labeled communist sympathizers by anti-Castro organizations, and many experienced dissension and backlash among families and friends. The Mariel Boatlift of 1980 and the fourth wave of Cuban migration, known as the Balseros (rafters) who arrived roughly around 1990–1994, further changed the dynamic of the club.[8] Unlike in the past, these migrations included a larger number of Afro-Cubans, many of whom moved to New York. Some became members of the CCI, while others preferred to just attend events and dances. Nonetheless, the CCI was seen as an important site for networking and building community. The numbers, however, were not enough to significantly alter the club's membership or direction. Yet, it was enough to keep the club viable for a few more years.

By the late 1990s and 2000s, the club was having a difficult time retaining its membership. The running of the club was left to a handful of aging members. Some retired, while others moved away to be near family. The lack of members and membership dues took its toll on the few members committed to keeping the club open. For all intents and purposes, the club officially closed when Alvarado was forced to move from her apartment on McGraw Avenue in the South Bronx to an assisted living facility. The club's records were packed and put into storage.[9] Although the CCI no longer has a physical location, it still remains a powerful presence in the city. Under the direction of Moreno, there has been a resurgence of CCI activity, ones that both looks to the past and pivots to the future. These activities, which include La Cena Martiana and La Fiesta del Mamoncillo, provide a necessary opening for carving out transnational Afro-Cuban spaces and communities that speak to multiple generations.

After seven decades of challenges and triumphs, the fact that Afro-Cuban spaces continue to exist is a testament to the CCI's long and varied history. Although the connections are at times fragmented and weathered, the CCI's history is nonetheless deeply informed by a history and legacy of club organization and activity that not only included clubs in Cuba, but also ones founded in New York, including La Liga sociedad de instrucción y recreó, El Club de los Independientes, El Partido Revolucionario Cubano, and El Club Julio Antonio Mella. No doubt, the CCI was influenced by a diasporic history shaped by uneasy alliances, racism, deliberate invisibilities, transnationalist political organizing, and yes, suspect freedoms. Yet, much like those who came before them, for the members of the CCI it was imperative to build community, cultivate Afro-diasporic belonging, and redefine a Cubanidad on their terms.

NOTES

LIST OF ABBREVIATIONS

Centro de Estudios Puertorriqueños/Center for Puerto Rican Studies, Hunter College, New York (CPRS)

Jesús Colón Papers (JCP)

El Club Cubano Inter-Americano Papers/Archive (CCI)

Comité Gestor, Minutes of the Meetings (CGMM)

Junta Directiva, Minutes of the Meetings (JDMM)

Oral History, Melba Alvarado (OHMA)

New York Public Library, Manuscripts and Archives Division, Astor, Lenox, and Tilden Foundations, New York (NYPL)

New York Times (*NYT*)

Schomburg Center for Research in Black Culture and Rare Book and Manuscript Collection (SCM)

INTRODUCTION

1 Translated this reads, "Well my daughter, hurry up with this work, with these interviews, because we are getting old, some of us have even died. And (our) history, what can I say, (our) history leaves us. Oral History, Melba Alvarado, (OHMA) (1995).

2 "The Late Reverend Dr. Garnet: Memorial Services in Cooper Union Last Evening." *NYT*, May 11, 1882.

3 "The Negro Race in Cuba: Insular Society Draws No Discriminating Color Line." *NYT*, September 16, 1900. According to Carlos Manuel Trelles y Govín, several poems by Juana Pastor, authored in 1815, did survive. It is believed, however, that most of her work was indeed destroyed. See Trelles, "Bibliografía de autores de la raza de color en Cuba," 30–78. Thank you to Gema Guevara for pointing this out and making the citation available.

4 Avery F. Gordon, *Ghostly Matters: Haunting and the Sociological Imagination* (Minneapolis: University of Minnesota Press), xvi.

5 The early members gathered on September 17, 1945 to discuss the possibility of organizing the club and considered this the founding meeting. According to a Certificate of Incorporation the CCI was incorporated as a club on January 18, 1946. The first *official* club meeting was on May 20, 1946. CCI Records, Box 1, Folder 2, SCM.

6 El Festival del Mamoncillo is no longer held at the Bohemian Club in Astoria. Recently, club members have had to change the venue. Several studies on Afro-Cuban music and musicians in 1940s and 1950s New York have looked at how the CCI provided a space for Afro-Cuban musicians to perform, and be part of larger Afro-diasporic community. Some have cited El Festival del Mamoncillo, Alvarado's role in organizing the festival, and her relationship with Afro-Cuban musicians. See David García, "Contesting that Damned Mambo: Arsenio Rodrí-guez, Authenticity, and the People of El Barrio and the Bronx in the 1950s," *Centro Journal*, 2004; and Pam Sporn's film "Recordando el Mamoncillo."

7 Nicole Guidotti-Hernández, *Unspeakable Violence: Remapping U.S. and Mexican National Imaginaries* (Durham: Duke University Press), 5.

8 OHMA (1995), (2002).

9 Arthur J. Sabin, *Red Scare in Court.*

10 The most exact date of the club's founding is 1932. There are several secondary sources that date the club 1935. In *Escapé de Cuba*, Ana Suárez Díaz writes that the club was founded in the 1920s.

11 According to the International Migrations and Naturalization census data for 1930, 18,493 Cubans entered the United States during this period. To estimate the number of Afro-Cubans I counted those who were identified as "negro" and cross-referenced it with the New York City local census data to get a better estimate of the number of Afro-Cuban migrants in New York. It is important to note that it was during this period that an increase in the number of Afro-Cuban musicians, athletes, writers, activists, and performers arrived in New York. They were not, however, always counted. Names of certain well-known Afro-Cubans do not always appear in the census data. Yet, because of oral histories, photographs, and other paraphernalia, it is clear that they were living in New York during this period.

12 OHMA (1995).

13 Michel Rolph Trouillot, *Silencing the Past*, 70.

14 Jana Evans Braziel and Anita Bannur, eds., *Theorizing Diaspora*, 8.

15 Eloisa Piñiero is mentioned in Rafael Serra, *Ensayos políticos.*

16 Richard Newman, Patrick Rael, and Philip Lapsansky, (eds.), *Pamphlets of Protest: An Anthology of Early African American Protest Literature, 1790–1860* (London: Routledge, 2000). 3. Gerald Poyo, Louis A. Pérez, Nicolás Kanellos, and Rodrigo Lazo have estimated that there were close to 70 different Cuban exile newspapers. Combined, it is possible that Cuban exiles and migrant knowledge and cultural productions were in the hundreds.

17 Martín Morúa Delgado, "La cuestión obrera," 141.

18 *La Verdad*, New York, 1849. Rodrigo Lazo discusses the role of censorship laws in Cuba and how they were used to limit the circulation of revolutionary texts. See *Writing to Cuba*, 17–18.

19 Lillian Guerra, *The Myth of José Martí*, 14–15.

20 Earl Lewis, "'To Turn as on a Pivot," 786; and Brent Hayes Edwards, *The Practice of Diaspora*, 14.

21 Michelle Stephens, *Black Empire*, 13.

22 Avtah Brah, *Cartographies of Diaspora*, 192–193.

23 Ibid., 193. For Brah the politics of location allow for a larger analysis rooted in the "longstanding feminist debate around issues of home, location, displacement and dislocation which are related to the concept of a 'politics of location.'"

24 See the pamphlet "Por Cuba y para Cuba," which include Martí's famous, "With All and for the Good of All" speech given on the steps of La Liga Ignacio Agramonte in Ybor City in November 1891. The pamphlet is referred to in José Martí, *Política de Nuestra América*, 215. See Agnes Lugo-Ortiz, "En un rincón de la Florida: Exile and Nationality in José Martí's Biographical Chronicles in Patria," 9–21; and "El alma cubano: Poética y política del sujeto nacional en las crónicas biográficas de José Martí." "Postmodern Notes/Apuntes Postmoderno," V. 2 (1995) 39–45. The pamphlet is in the Pizzo Collection, Special Collections Department University of South Florida.

25 Antonio Benítez-Rojo, *The Repeating Island*.

26 The reference to Señora Agüero y Ricardo is in "Patriot Sanguily Welcomed," *NYT*, 1895.

27 *La Discusión*, October 10, 1923, La Habana Cuba. This edition chronicled the life and memory of Sotero Figueroa and Inocencia Martínez. Schomburg personal papers, file 0668, reel 11, SCM. Martínez was the founder of El Club Mercedes Varona, the first women's club of the Partido Revolucionario Cubano.

28 Carmen Montejo Arrechea, "*Minerva*: A Magazine for Women (and Men) of Color." Lisa Brock and Digna Castañeda Fuertes, eds., *Between Race and Empire*.

29 Thank you to April Mayes for her insightful comments and thoughts on this topic. See Stephens, *Black Empire*, 15. Stephens explains that the inherently masculine global imaginary was created to "fit the needs of a new and modern black male subject entering onto the stage of world politics," and, in focusing on the "male sovereign it must be understood that these figures were working with the most powerful symbols and definitions of modern political identity available during this period."

30 Juan J. E. Casasús, *La emigración cubana y la independencia de la patria*, 440–441. Agnes Lugo-Ortiz, *Identidades imaginadas*, 155-180, for a thorough and important discussion of Rodríguez's impact on Martí's thinking.

31 Félix Varela, *El Habanero*; and José Antonio Piqueras, *Félix Varela y la prosperidad de la patria criolla*.

32 Scholars who have credited Varela include Gerald Poyo, *With All and for the Good of All*; Nicolás Kanellos and Helvetia Martell, *Hispanic Periodicals in the United States, Origins to 1960*; and Enrique López Mesa, *La comunidad cubana de New York*.

33 Gema Guevara, "Founding Discourses of Cuban Nationalism." In *Señal en la noche*, Carlos Manuel de Céspedes García-Menocal writes that it "would be interesting to verify Father Varela's relationship with the abolitionist movement in the United States, and in particular with the North American Abolitionist Society made-up of mostly Protestants during a period of acute tensions between them

and the Catholics." This is important since so little has been written on Varela's abolitionist activity in the United States. De Céspedes nonetheless has his doubts concerning Varela's participation in the North American abolitionist campaign. "It is not difficult to imagine that the father, in principal, supported the cause of the abolitionists as demonstrated by the actions of the comité de Amistad, but I myself ponder if he [Varela] publicly commented on or actively participated in the defense of the Africans." He ultimately justifies Varela's ambivalence by arguing that he was a "prudent man who did not want to alienate North American supporters, and moreover, he was not a citizen of the United States, but of Spain, complicating matters even further." 179.

34 On July 4, 1827, the New York State legislature abolished slavery. The end of slavery in New York and the growing free people of color community did not end racial discrimination and exclusion.

35 According to David Luis-Brown, two organizations, Young America and Joven Cuba, "violated the principles of equality and liberty by endorsing the Fugitive Slave Act of 1850 and by applauding the US Annexation of 55% of Mexican territory at the conclusion of the Mexican War (1846–48)." See Luis-Brown, "An 1848 for the Americas," 431–453.

36 Thirty years after the legislative act, the Supreme Court ruled in the *Dred Scott v. Sanford Case* (1857) that slave owners had the right to own slaves wherever they traveled, regardless of whether they moved within a free state or not. Essentially, as Leslie M. Harris has argued, "slave owner's property rights in humans held across state lines." The Dred Scott decision threatened an earlier law passed by the state legislature in 1841 that declared free any slaves brought to New York by their owners. Harris, *In the Shadow of the Slavery*, 274–275. In regard to the quote on the large number of free people of color, see ibid., 3.

37 José Antonio Saco, "The Color Line," *Revista bimestre cubana* 3, 7 (1832): 173–231; Saco, "La situación política de Cuba y su remedio," 151–178; and *Contra la anexión Tomo I y II.*

38 *The Frederick Douglass Papers,* March 21, 1859. The early black press made it a point to warn Cubans that annexation to the United States would forever compromise their freedom and sovereignty.

39 *Patria,* December 21, 1898.

40 César Andréu Iglesias, ed., *Memoirs of Bernardo Vega,* 83.

41 In collaboration with Pam Sporn and Diana Lachatanere, we conducted an interview of Melba Alvarado to be archived as part of El Club Cubano Inter-Americano papers located in Manuscripts, Archives, and Rare Books Division, Schomburg Center for Research in Black Culture.

42 Ann Laura Stoler, "Intimidations of Empire: Predicaments of the Tactile and Unseen," 1.

43 Organización Revolucionaria Cubana Anti-imperialista (ORCA) was founded in 1935 in New York.

44 CCI Minutes of the meetings, CCI Records, Box 5, Folder 1, SCM.

45 According to the Schomburg Center's Accession Records, the boxes were received by Diana Lachatanere and Steven Fullwood in May 1998 and December 2007. In regard to problems with keeping the club afloat, see a letter written by Melba Alvarado to Philip Newman and dated April 26, 2000, noting that the club is "almost inactive" and that "responsible" members are doing their best to cover their debts. Alvarado enclosed $100.00 and promised to include more after a planned event to cover the balance. CCI Records, Box 5, Folder 10 (2000–2002), SCM. In several interviews that I conducted with Alvarado, she spoke of her disappointment in having to close the club.

CHAPTER 1. RHETORICAL GEOGRAPHIES

1 *New York Daily Times*, December 3, 1856.

2 "Cuban Affairs: Emancipation in Cuba," *Journal of Commerce*, April 21, 1855. The issue of Chinese workers in Cuba continued to be a problem for US anti-slavery activists years after the Civil War. See "Chinese Coolies in Cuba: The Horrors of Modern Slavery," *NYT*, July 16, 1876.

3 Robert E. May, *The Southern Dream of a Caribbean Empire, 1854–1861*, 16–17.

4 Ira Berlin and Leslie M. Harris, "Introduction: Uncovering, Discovering, and Recovering: Digging in New York's Slave Past Beyond the African Burial Ground," in Berlin and Harris, eds., *Slavery in New York*, 22. Also see Berlin, *Many Thousands Gone*; Harris, *In the Shadow of Slavery*; Rhoda Golden Freeman, *The Free Negro in New York City*; and David N. Gellman and David Quigley, *Jim Crow New York*.

5 Berlin and Harris, "Introduction: Uncovering, Discovering, and Recovering," 22.

6 Lester D. Langley, *Struggle for the American Mediterranean*, 39.

7 Cuban annexationists lobbied the Polk administration to purchase Cuba. They offered to put up a hundred million dollars of their own money to secure the purchase. President Polk refused the offer. See Tom Chaffin, *Fatal Glory*, 41.

8 May, *The Southern Dream of a Caribbean Empire 1854–1861*, 69.

9 *Appleton's American Annual Cyclopaedia: Register of Important Events*, 1870. Vol. X, New York: D. Appleton and Company, 376–77 (1871) and *Expedición Goicuría, Diario de un soldado* (Nassau, 1869).

10 *La Verdad*, March 25, 1857.

11 *Appleton's American Annual Cyclopaedia: Register of Important Events*, 376–377 (1871).

12 Although López attracted a large number of pro-slavery advocates to his cause, he was reticent to reveal his own position on slavery. Chaffin, *Fatal Glory*.

13 General Quitman supported annexation and the expansion of slavery into Cuba. See Thomas David Schoonover, ed., *Mexican Lobby: Matías Romero in Washington, 1861–1867* (Lexington: University of Kentucky Press, 2014); and Brian P. Hamnett, *Juárez: Biography and Autobiography* (Longman Press, 1993). Pedro Santacilia spent a great deal of his time in Mexico, helping to organize Narciso López's campaigns, transporting arms, and even marrying Benito Juárez's daughter. Casasús, *La emigración cubana*, 445.

14 *Appleton's American Annual Cyclopaedia: Register of Important Events*, 376–377.

15 "The Cuban Junta," *NYT*, October 26, 1852, mentions Goicuría's role in "the system of European immigration" to Cuba. Casasús, *La emigración cubana*, 400; Inés Roldán de Montaud, "Origen, evolución, y supresión del grupo negros emancipados en Cuba," 167–168; and Miguel Estorch, "Apuntes para la historia sobre la administración del marques de la Pezuela en la isla de Cuba. On exile annexationist thinking and politics, see "La anexión de Cuba y los peninsulares residentes en ella." (n.d.).

16 Don Lorenzo Allo y Bermúdez, "Domestic Slavery in its Relations with Wealth: An Oration." According to Gerald Poyo, Juan Clemente Zenea was a member of El Club de la Habana and an earlier supporter of annexation. *With All and For the Good of All*, 4.

17 Allo, 13.

18 Ibid., "Domestic Slavery in its Relations with Wealth: An Oration," 8.

19 Quoted in Carlos Manuel de Céspedes García-Menocal, *Señal en la noche*, 179–181.

20 Casasús, *La emigración cubana*, 396.

21 Allo, "Domestic Slavery in its Relations with Wealth: An Oration," 8. According to Casasús, Allo was a student, along with José Antonio Saco and José Luz y Caballero, of Father Félix Varela at the San Carlos Seminary. Casasus, *La emigración cubana*, 395.

22 Dale Tomich, "The Wealth of Empire," 4–5.

23 Cited in Matt Childs, *The 1812 Aponte Rebellion in Cuba and the Struggle Against Atlantic Slavery*, 9; and Ada Ferrer, *Insurgent Cuba, Race, Nation and Revolution, 1868–1898*, 2.

24 Allo, "Domestic Slavery in its Relations with Wealth: An Oration," 5.

25 Ibid., 6.

26 Ibid., 7.

27 Ibid.

28 Free women of color took advantage of the racialized discourse on the "sexually available mulata" to establish beneficial relationships with white men. Luz Mena, "Stretching the Limits of Gendered Spaces: Black and Mulatto Women in 1830s Havana." *Cuban Studies/Estudios Cubanos*, 36, (2005): 87–104; Vera M. Kutzinski, *Sugar's Secrets: Race and the Erotics of Cuban Nationalism*; and Gema Guevara, "Inexacting Whiteness," 105–128.

29 At certain points in his speech, Allo references the discourse of the US free-soil party, an anti-slavery political party primarily based in the North. In 1844, free-soilers held their founding convention. The free-soil party was committed to ending slavery and insuring that no new US territories be slave territories. Allo, "Domestic Slavery in its Relations with Wealth: An Oration," 10.

30 Ibid., 11.

31 *El Mulato*, March 25, 1854. According to *El Mulato*, Allo's urn was draped with the flag of Cuba Libre, the US flag, and the flag of universal democracy.

32 Cited in Leopoldo Horrego Estuch, *Emilia Casanova*, 19–20; and "The Cuban Junta," *NYT*, October 26, 1852.

33 Basil Rauch, *American Interests in Cuba, 1848–1855* (New York: Octagon Books, 1974); Poyo, *With All and for the Good of All*; and Chaffin, *Fatal Glory*. Also see Lazo, *Writing to Cuba*; Richard Bureleigh Kimball and Cristóbal Madan, *Cuba and the Cubans; Compromising a History of the Island of Cuba, Its Present, Social, Political and Domestic Condition*; J. C. Thrasher, *A preliminary essay on the purchase of Cuba*; and the Miguel de Aldama collection in Special Collections, University of Miami.

34 There are several versions concerning the making of the Cuban flag in New York. Most credit Narciso López with the design of the flag and agree that it was flown on May 11, 1850. Others argue that Miguel Teurbe Tolón assisted López with the design. With regard to who stitched the flag, so far three different women have been named. They include the wife of Narciso López, the wife of Cirilo Villaverde (Emilia Casanova de Villaverde), and the wife of Miguel Teurbe Tolón. Some versions, especially those who examine the history of Masonry, contend that the five-pointed star of the Texas flag was used as a model because it represented the Masonic five points of fellowship. Basing the flag of Cuba Libre on the flag of the Texas Republic not only reflected Freemasonry, but also the pro-slavery and pro-annexationist politics that gave rise to the Texas Republic. See Eugene E. Atkinson, "Miscellanea: History of the Cuban Flag," *American Lodge of Research Transaction* 13, 3 (January 29, 1962): 449–452; Charles A. Brockaway, "Masonic Symbolism in the Cuba Flag," *Masonic Outlook* (March 1931); Antonio Rafael De la Cova, "Filibusters and Freemasons: The Sworn Obligation," *Journal of Early Republic* 17 (Spring 1997): 105–106; Francisco J. Ponte Domínguez, "Historia y simbolismo de la bandera cubana." *Revista de la Biblioteca Nacional* 1, 4 (La Habana: Agosto, 1950): 12; and Enrique López Mesa, *La comunidad cubana de New York*, 17.

35 Atkinson, "Miscellanea: History of the Cuban Flag," 449–452.

36 Chaffin also mentions the impact of La Escalera in organizing El Club de la Habana and its role in hastening the annexationist cause. *Fatal Glory*, 12.

37 Sibylle Fischer, *Modernity Disavowed*, 82. Also see Robert Paquette, *Sugar Is Made with Blood*.

38 Ifeoma Kiddoe Nwankwo, *Black Cosmopolitanism*, 48.

39 Robert Levine, *Martin Delany, Frederick Douglass*, 175.

40 Nwankwo, *Black Cosmopolitanism*, 59.

41 Fischer, *Modernity Disavowed*, 77.

42 *La Verdad*, April 8, 1849.

43 *La Verdad*, 1848.

44 For whites in the United States, Cubans, despite their strong alliances, exhibited what Alejandro de la Fuente refers to as a "dubious whiteness." Rodrigo Lazo also notes that US slaveholders and allies considered Cubans "a distinct hybrid race." So why did Creole Cuban exiles and migrants establish alliances based on whiteness with their US counterparts who racialized their whiteness? Lazo and David Luis Brown argue that it was based on a shared notion of white republican

Americanism within the hemisphere. See de la Fuente, *A Nation for All*, 177; Lazo, *Writing to Cuba*, 145, and Brown, "An 1848 for the Americas."

45 "Series of Articles on the Cuban Question." *La Verdad*, 1849, 1.

46 Ibid., 5.

47 Ibid.

48 Ibid., 16.

49 Ibid., 4.

50 Ibid., 2.

51 Ibid., 10.

52 Ibid., 10–11.

53 Ibid., 4.

54 Cited in Levine, *Martin Delany, Frederick Douglass*, 202.

55 "Facts of Slavery," *Frederick Douglass' Paper*, March 16, 1855.

56 *The Black New Yorkers: Schomburg Illustrated Chronology*. Howard Dodson et al., 60. Newspapers include *Ram's Horn*, *North Star*, *Frederick Douglass' Papers*, *Douglass' Monthly*, and the *National Era*. Frankie Hutton, *The Early Black Press in America, 1827–1860*.

57 *Colored American*, June 3, 1837. There were several black newspapers that devoted columns and articles on slavery in Cuba. See "Slavery in Cuba," *Freedom's Journal*, November 30, 1827, and the *Provincial Freeman* based in Chatham, Canada, September 29, 1855. The *Provincial Freeman* was a Canadian black newspaper made up of black emigrants who left the United States. In February 1856, the *Provincial Freeman* welcomed Martin Delany, who used the newspaper to challenge Douglass' position on black emigration out of the United States.

58 "A Caution to Travelers in General," *Colored American*, October 21, 1837.

59 "Slavery in Cuba," *Colored American*, April 18, 1840.

60 "Rumored Insurrection," *Colored American*, April 10, 1841.

61 Harris, *In the Shadow of Slavery*, 221 and 206; Hutton, *The Early Black Press in America, 1827–1860*, and Gellman and Quigley, *Jim Crow New York*.

62 "Notice of Colored Emigrants to the British Island of Trinidad," *Colored American*, March 14, 1840. Notices were signed by S. R. Buchanan, a government agent for Trinidad.

63 "The Immigration Question," *Colored American*, May 2, 1840.

64 Samuel Cornish resumed editorship and renamed the newspaper *The Rights of All*. John Brown Russwurm was born a slave in Port Antonio, Jamaica and was a graduate of Bowdoin College in Maine. Russwurm's experience as a slave as well as his migration, education, and mobility within North America most likely influenced his support of emigration as a necessary strategy for empowerment. Harris, *In the Shadow of Slavery*, 141, and *The Black New Yorkers: Schomburg Illustrated Chronology*, 61.

65 Joel Schor, *Henry Highland Garnet: A Voice of Black Radicalism in the Nineteenth Century*, 91.

66 "Slavery in Cuba," *Colored American*, April 18, 1840. "Annexation of Cuba" quoted in Levine, *Martin Delany, Frederick Douglass*, 201.

67 *Frederick Douglass' Paper*, November 23, 1855.

68 *Freedman's Journal*, 1827.

69 "Late From Cuba," *Frederick Douglass' Paper*, September 3, 1852, Rochester, New York. The entire quote reads: "*The New York Courier* and *Enquirer* states that it has perused letters from Madrid which state that "The Government is now convinced that Cuba is lost forever to the Spanish crown, but that the Queen will sooner part with the negroes than that the creoles should possess the islands."

70 "The Africanization of Cuba," *Frederick Douglass' Paper*, November 23, 1853.

71 "El Mulatto," *Frederick Douglass' Paper*, March 31, 1854.

72 Hutton, *The Early Black Press in America, 1827–1860*, 28. James W.C. Pennington was one of the founders of the Brooklyn Temperance Association. In 1855, Samuel Ringgold Ward published *The Autobiography of A Fugitive Slave: His Anti-Slavery Labours in the United States, Canada and England*. See *The Black New Yorker*, 78.

73 *El Mulato*, April 25, 1854. A possible explanation for Delany's protest is *El Mulato*'s emphasis on racial mixture as a basis for establishing Cuban identity, thereby diluting blackness. The letter is also mentioned in Lazo's *Writing to Cuba*, 157.

74 My analysis of *El Mulato* is based on editions 4–10/12–17 and dated roughly from March 11, 1854 to June 17, 1854. Although Carlos de Colins edited most of the newspapers, Ricardo Gainfort edited numbers 13–17. Edition no. 12 lists no editor. I am deeply indebted to Gema Guevara for generously sharing her copies of *El Mulato* with me.

75 *El Mulato*, March 18, 1854. The seemingly sudden change among the past members of El Club de la Habana has been attributed to several factors: the large number of free people of color who were now becoming increasingly important to the revolutionary cause; the growing anxiety over US hegemony on the island; and the belief that slavery was antithetical to modernity.

76 Using *El Filbustero*, February 1854, as source, Gerald Poyo writes of a mass meeting that was called to condemn the newspaper and pass a resolution declaring that *El Mulato* did not represent the ideals of the exile community. See Poyo, *With All and for the Good of All*, 17; and Lazo, *Writing to Cuba*, 146.

77 "The Nebraska Bill," *El Mulato*, no. 10, April 25, 1854.

78 "Nebraska," *El Mulato*, May 29, 1854.

79 Brown, "An 1848 for the Americas," 432. In reference to the Black Warrior Affair see "Case of the Black Warrior and other Violations of the Rights of American Citizens by Spanish Authorities," Washington, DC, June 26, 1854, House Document 86.

80 Ibid., 431.

81 Kutzinski, *Sugar's Secrets: Race and the Erotics of Cuban Nationalism*, 5.

82 *El Mulato*, April 17, 1854. My gratitude to Maria Cetto for her assistance in translating this passage.

83 *La Revolución*, 1869. Cited in Poyo, *With All and for the Good of All*, 37.
84 "Grand Banquet Speech of a Cuban Patriot and Reply of the American Consul-Cuba Libre,." *NYT*, November 10, 1869.

CHAPTER 2. "WITH PAINFUL INTEREST"

1 "Slavery in Cuba. A Report of the Proceedings of the Meeting held at Cooper Institute." The report was written and distributed to publicize the founding and activities of the Cuban Anti-Slavery Society. The report includes excerpts of speeches, letters to the editors, communications from New York and international newspapers, including *La Siecle*, and the *Anglo-American Times*. I located this copy at the Library of Congress, Washington, DC, in 2008. A copy is also available at the Schomburg Center for Research in Black Culture. The Cuban Anti-Slavery Society and/or Samuel Scottron have been mentioned and discussed in Philip Foner, *History of Cuba, II*; Lisa Brock, "Back to the Future: African-Americans and Cuba in the Times(s) of Race"; Craig Wilder, *In the Company of Black Men*, and *A Covenant with Color: Race and Social Power in Brooklyn*; Earl Ofari Hutchinson, *Let Your Motto be Resistance*; Paul Ortiz, "'Washington, Toussaint, and Bolívar, The Glorious Advocates of Liberty': Black Internationalism and Reimagining Emancipation," 187–216. In *Rethinking American Emancipation: Legacies of Slavery and the Quest for Black Freedom*, eds. William A. Link and James J. Broomall, Cambridge; Cambridge University Press, 2016; and Susan Alexis Thomas Holder, "Henry Highland Garnet: His Life."

2 "Slavery in Cuba: A Report of the Proceedings of the Meeting held at Cooper Institute," New York City, December 13, 1872, 16.

3 Ibid.

4 "The Cuban Negroes—An Enthusiastic Meeting of the Cubans Last Night," *NYT*, December 14, 1872.

5 Ibid.

6 "Slavery in Cuba: A Report of the Proceedings of the Meeting held at Cooper Institute."

7 "Report on the Proceedings of the Meeting." On December 23, over a week after the meeting in New York, Pindell set up a meeting to establish the Boston chapter of the Cuban Anti-Slavery Society and was elected president. Soon Pindell sent a call inviting the public to attend a meeting at the racially inclusive and pro-abolitionist Menonian Hall in Boston. Led by James M. Trotter, vice president, and Peter H. Nott, secretary, of the Boston Chapter of Society, the meeting began with a prayer offered by Mr. John W. Williams, a student from Andover. More than 40 members attended the meeting in Boston and signed the proclamation calling the meeting to order.

8 "Slavery in Cuba: A Report of the Proceedings of the Meeting held at Cooper Institute," New York City, December 13, 1872, 5.

9 Ibid.

10 "The Cuban Negroes-An Enthusiastic Meeting of the Cubans Last Night," *NYT* December 14, 1872.

11 "Slavery in Cuba: A Report of the Proceedings of the Meeting held at Cooper Institute," 9–12. There is no reference, at least in the published and archived sources, to free people of color in Cuba, or if any free Afro-Cuban migrants attended the meeting that evening.

12 The full quote reads, "Indeed we look back but a very brief period to the time when it was necessary for other men to hold conventions, appoint committees and form societies, having in view the liberation of four million among whom were ourselves; but thanks to the genius of free government, free schools and liberal ideas, all the outgrown of an enlightened and Christian age, we are enabled in the brief period of ten years to stand, not only as freemen ourselves, but with voices and with power to demand the liberation of five hundred thousand of our brethren, who are afflicted with the curse of human slavery." "Slavery in Cuba: A Report of the Proceedings of the Meeting held at Cooper Institute," 6–7.

13 Ibid., 15–16.

14 "The Colored Men and Cuba: Meeting in Washington, Speeches by Sella Martin, Honorable N.P. Banks and Others." March 10, 1873, "The Colored People of the District of Columbia," November 18, 1873. Both in the *NYT.*

15 "Slavery in Cuba: A Report of the Proceedings of the Meeting held at Cooper Institute," 9–10.

16 Stephens, *Black Empire*, 15.

17 Maurice O. Wallace, *Constructing the Black Masculine.* 56.

18 Ibid., 85.

19 "Free and Equal. Our Colored Citizens Jubilee-Celebration in Honor of the Fifteenth Amendment-Procession-Demonstration at Cooper Institute," *NYT* (n.d.), and "The Fifteenth Amendment: The Coming Celebration by Our Colored Citizens-Great Preparation–The Procession-Line of March-Public Meeting, *NYT* (March 25, 1871). Also see Gellman and Quigley, *Jim Crow New York*, 296–297.

20 "Free and Equal. Celebration at the Cooper Institute," *NYT*, April 9, 1870. See the *National Anti-Slavery Standard*, New York, January 29, 1870.Wendell Phillips was a Massachusetts-based abolitionist, lawyer, and president of the Anti-Slavery Society.

21 "Toussaint L'Ouverture." Lecture delivered by Wendell Phillips, December 1861, New York. In regard to Betances see Arroyo, *Writing Secrecy: Technologies in Caribbean Freemasonry.*

22 Harris, *In the Shadow of Slavery*, 280.

23 Burrows and Wallace, *Gotham: A History of New York City to 1898*, 890.

24 Harris, *In the Shadow of Slavery*, 284–286. Harris details a chilling example of Abraham Franklin, who was taken from his apartment and hanged from a lamppost. His lifeless body was then pulled from the lamppost and dragged through the streets by his genitals.

25 Ibid., 288.

26 Brock, "Back to the Future: African-Americans and Cuba in the Time(s) of Race," 17.

27 "Slavery in Cuba: A Report of the Proceedings of the Meeting held at Cooper Institute," New York City, December 13, 1872, 7.

28 Ibid., 8. "The Cuban Cause: Mass Meeting in Brooklyn," *NYT*, July 8, 1870.

29 Ferrer, *Insurgent Cuba*, 22.

30 Ibid., 9.

31 "Slavery in Cuba: A Report of the Proceedings of the Meeting held at Cooper Institute," 7–9.

32 "Walker's Appeal with a Brief Sketch of his life By Henry Highland Garnet and Garnet's Address to the Slaves of the United States of America," New York. Printed by J. H. Torbitt, 9 Spruce Street. 1848. David Walker and Henry Highland Garnet, *Walker's Appeal and Garnet's Address to the Slaves*. By looking toward the West Indies, Trinidad, Jamaica, and Cuba, Garnet privileged African Americans as anti-slavery activists. While he welcomed the leadership of white northern abolitionists, he wanted African Americans to be empowered by the movement. This appeared to be the impetus for the founding of the American and Foreign Anti Slavery Societies, which were organized by those disenchanted by William Lloyd Garrison's leadership. Interestingly enough, the majority of black abolitionists took Garrison's side, while Garnet and a handful of black abolitionists, including Charles B. Ray, an editor of the *Colored American*, joined the American and Foreign Anti Slavery Societies.

33 Both Garnet and Walker were Freemasons. Few if any records connect Garnet and Walker on the basis of Freemasonry. Yet, it is possible that this was one of the reasons why Garnet sought to preserve Walker's legacy and use it to inform his own politics.

34 Henry Highland Garnet, "The Past and the Present Condition, and the Destiny of The Colored Race: A Discourse. Delivered at the Fifteenth Anniversary of the Female Benevolent Society of Troy, New York, February 14, 1848," (Troy, NY: Steam Press, of J.C. Kneeland and Co. 1848), 16–18.

35 "Slavery in Cuba: A Report of the Proceedings of the Meeting held at Cooper Institute," 17. According to Joel Schor, little is known about Garnet's travels to Cuba. What is known is that Garnet made two trips to Cuba in 1828. It is not clear from this speech if he is referring to these trips or others he may have made later in life. Shor, *Henry Highland Garnet*.

36 Ibid., 17.

37 "Slavery in Cuba: A Report of the Proceedings of the Meeting held at Cooper Institute," 5.

38 Ofari Hutchinson, *Let your Motto be Resistance*, and Susan Alexis Thomas Holder, "Henry Highland Garnet: His Life."

39 "Slavery in Cuba: A Report of the Proceedings of the Meeting held at Cooper Institute," 17–18. Garnet's discussion and use of Plácido was not new. He had a long history of speaking to and writing about Plácido. In one of his earlier speeches, Garnet noted how Plácido, "a mulatto," was a "true Poet, and of course a Patriot." He goes on to recall how Plácido was executed. "The next day they led Plácido forth to execution, and from the mouths of bristling musketry a shower of lead was poured upon his quivering heart." "The Past and the Present Condition, and the Destiny of The Colored Race," 17.

40 "The Cuban Negroes—An Enthusiastic Meeting of the Cubans Last Night," *NYT*, December 14, 1872. In addition to Fuentes, the article refers to speeches given by the soon-to-be-elected president of the Boston Chapter of the Cuban Anti-Slavery Society, Charles E. Pindell, which was included in the proceedings. The article misspelled Fuente's last name and referred to him as a "Señor' Félix Fumentis." After conducting extensive research, primarily census data and club records, there are no records of Cuban men in New York during this period with the name Félix Fumentis. Félix Fuentes, however, appears in a number of sources, mostly club records, which place him in New York during this time. He was part of the Afro-Cuban revolutionary community and active in exile and migrant Cuban politics.

41 In regard to Fuentes's involvement in clubs see Enrique Trujillo, *Apuntes históricos*, 12–13, and Teófilo Domínguez, *Figuras y Figuritas*, 22. Another source that refers to the existence of Félix Fuentes and his relationship to Rafael Serra is in Serra's *Patriota y revolucionario, fraternal amigo de Martí*. It includes a letter to Rafael Serra dated September 22, 1888 in New York that is signed by José Martí, Rafael de C. Palomino, Dr. M. Parraga, and Félix Fuentes.

42 See document from the Offices of the American Foreign Anti-Slavery Society dated October 12, 1877. The note is written to J. M. Mestre Esq. at 35 Broadway and signed by Samuel Scottron, secretary of the Society. Ignacio Rodríguez Papers, container #64, Library of Congress, Washington, DC.

43 Booker T. Washington, *The Negro in Business*, 156. Washington devotes an entire chapter to Samuel Scottron's inventions and political activism. It is in this chapter that Washington mentions the reorganization of the Cuban Anti-Slavery Society and cites Scottron's reasons for the change. Despite the change in organization many of the founding members of the Cuban Anti-Slavery Society were founders and members of the American Foreign Anti-Slavery Society. These included John J. Zuille, Dr. Peter Ray, and Peter W. Downing. Ignacio Rodríguez Papers, container #64, Library of Congress, Washington, DC. Early in his career, Garnet was interested in expanding the question of slavery and freedom to the hemisphere. Garnet, "The Past and the Present Condition, and the Destiny of The Colored Race."

44 Nell Painter, *Standing at Armageddon: A Grassroots History of the Progressive Era*, 4–5.

45 See José Ignacio Rodríguez Papers, container #64, Library of Congress, Washington, DC, for a receipt signed by Samuel Scottron for $10 from J. M. Mestre on October 17, 1877. According to Casasús, Morales Lemus died on June 23, 1870. He also writes that Mestre earned a law degree from Columbia University. Casasús, *La emigración cubana*, 430. In the José Ignacio Rodríguez Papers, container #61, there are sources that indicate that Mestre knew José Antonio Saco and exchanged letters with him while Saco was in Paris during the 1860s. In addition, Mestre spent much of his career assisting wealthy Cubans to gain US citizenship so they could protect and/or recover lost property that had been taken or damaged as a result of the Ten Years' War. With regard to La Junta Revolucionaria de Cuba y Puerto Rico, see the Moses Taylor Papers, NYPL.

46 In addition to Mestre, Scottron also forged relationships with Colonel Fernando López de Queralta, a member of the Cuban Junta, and General Ramón Leocadio Boanchea. S. R. Scottron, "Slavery in Cuba. Its Abolition Depending on the Overthrow of Spanish Rule." *New York Globe*, August 11, 1883.

47 *Apuntes biográficos de Emilia Casanova de Villaverde*, 93.

48 Ibid.; Casasús, *La emigración cubana*, 385; Leopold Horrego Estuch, *Emilia Casanova*; and Ana Cairo, "Emilia Casanova y la dignidad de la mujer cubana." 231–241.

49 Plutarco González, "The Cuban Question and American Policy in the Light of Common Sense." González's name does not appear on the pamphlet. Yet, according to Gerald Poyo, he was indeed the author and the pamphlet was financed and supported by the Junta Central. Poyo, *With All and for the Good of All*, 26. In 1869, González is listed as an "agente general" in the Junta Central papers, confirming his leadership position within the Junta. Moses Taylor Papers, Special Collections, NYPL.

50 The issue of property rights in Cuba was an ongoing dilemma for landholding Cubans who migrated to the United States. Much of José Manuel Mestre's legal career in Washington, DC and New York was devoted to assisting Cubans with becoming US citizens so they could recoup their property and assets in Cuba. See papers on Mestre in the José Ignacio Rodríguez Papers, Library of Congress, Container #64.

51 Letter was published in the *NYT*. "Meeting in Favor of Cuban Independence," *NYT*, March 23, 1869. The full list of signatories includes: W. C. Bryant, Henry Ward Beecher, A. W. Greeblkaf, Joseph H. Van Allen, Simon Leland, J. Edgar, John D. Sherwood, George Wilkes, C. P. Lowrey, George W. Curtis, John K. Porter, Charles A. Dana, Henry Clews, James Gordon Bennet, Fletcher Harper Jr., P. H. Du Chaillu, William P. Tomlinson, Silas M. Stillwell, William C. Church.

52 Emilia Casanova de Villaverde, La Liga de las Hijas de Cuba, "A los cubanos," 1872. I am grateful to Maria Cetto for her invaluable assistance in translating this quote.

53 Casanova de Villaverde, La Liga de las Hijas de Cuba, "A los cubanos," 1872.

54 Ibid., 3.

55 Several letters written by and about Casanova de Villaverde mention her unwillingness to cooperate. There are also a few passages that describe Casanova de Villaverde's penchant for forming organizations and then leaving them when disgruntled with the membership. Moses Taylor Papers, NYPL.

56 *Apuntes biográficos*, 139. Also see Ana Cairo, who cites this same quote, 237. At the same time, Casanova de Villaverde expressed her frustration with the patriotas who according to her were satisfied with only raising funds and nothing more. Casanova de Villaverde was also known for dismantling organizations and starting others, often without informing previous members. At the same time, she found it difficult to work with the men, who often excluded her from meetings and events.

57 *Apuntes biográficos*, 139.

58 "The Daughters of Cuba," *NYT*, February 5, 1871. Zenea was killed in August 1871. For more on the different readings of Juan Clemente Zenea and the Zenea Affair, see Enrique Pineyro, Vida y escritos de Juan Clemente Zenea, (Garnier Hermanos, Libreros-Editores, 6, Rue des Saints-Peres, 6, 1901); and Cintio Vitier, *Rescate de Zenea* (Habana: Ediciónes Union, 1987).

59 *Apuntes biográficos*, 7.

60 Lazo, *Writing to Cuba*, 216; see footnote 84, where Lazo names Villaverde as the author of *Apuntes biográficos*.

61 Papers of La Liga de las Hijas de Cuba and the Junta Revolucionario. Moses Taylor Collection at NYPL.

62 Cirilo Villaverde associates Casanova Villaverde with Madame Roland, a supporter of the French Revolution who fell out of favor during the Reign of Terror and was guillotined. *Apuntes biográficos*, 35.

63 Scott E. Casper, *Constructing American Lives*.

64 Roland Barthes, *New Critical Essays* and *The Semiotic Challenge*; and Michel de Certeau, *The Writing of History*.

65 The dating of the book is unclear. According to Ana Cairo the book was actually published in 1884. See Ana Cairo, "Emilia Casanova y la dignidad de la mujer Cubana."

66 *Apuntes biográficos*, 37.

67 Casper, *Constructing American Lives*.

68 Cirilo Villaverde, *Prologue to Cecilia Valdés*. Iván Schulman, ed. (Caracas, Venezuela: Biblioteca Ayacucho, 1981); *Homenaje a Cirilo Villaverde* (Havana UNESCO, 1964); Kutzinski, *Sugar's Secrets*; and Lazo, *Writing to Cuba*.

69 José Ignacio Rodríguez Papers, Library of Congress, Container #64.

70 "What the Cubans of New York Are Doing," *NYT*, February 26, 1869.

71 "Local Miscellany. The Late Gerrit Smith," *NYT*, December 30, 1874. Smith died on December 28, 1874. Octavius Brooks Frothingham, *Gerrit Smith: A Biography*. New York: G.P. Putnam's Sons. 1878, 364. For more on Charles B. Ray, see M. N. Work, "The Life of Charles B. Ray," *Journal of Negro History* 4, 4 (1919): 361–371.

72 Frothingham, *Gerrit Smith: A Biography*, 364.

73 Gerrit Smith, "Let crushed Cuba arise!" July 4th, 1873. Syracuse, New York. Ephemera Collection, Portfolio 128, Folder 26. Library of Congress.

74 "A Letter from the Honorable Gerrit Smith to the Cuban Anti-Slavery Society," New York: Peterboro, 1873. S. R. Scottron, Henry Highland Garnet. Ephemera Collection, Portfolio 128, Folder 26. Library of Congress.

75 Gerrit Smith, "Let crushed Cuba arise!".

76 "The Freedom of Cuba," *NYT*, October 25, 1877.

77 The alliance between Smith and the Cuban Junta speaks to a possibility of shared interests in the future of a post–US Civil War annexation of Cuba to the United States. It also provides insight into why members of the Cuban Junta attended his funeral and considered him to be so critical to the Cuban cause.

78 "The Freedom of Cuba," *NYT*, October 25, 1877. A year earlier, on January 28, 1876, House Representative from Illinois, William Springer introduced a bill to prevent American citizens from holding slaves in foreign countries. The bill, HR 1603, provided that US citizens temporarily residing and doing business in foreign countries be prohibited from owning, leasing, buying, selling or trafficking slaves. See HR 1603, 44th Congress, 1st session. January 28, 1876. Collections of the Manuscript Division, Library of Congress.

79 "The Freedom of Cuba," *NYT*, October 25, 1877.

80 This version of *La Verdad* was published from 1876 to 1878 and directed by Diego V. Tejera. See Casasús, *La emigración cubana*, 455. Quoted in Philip Foner, *A History of Cuba and its Relations with the United States: From Annexation to the Second War for Independence, 1845–1895*.

81 Antonio Maceo and his allies formerly denounced the Pact of Zanjón in the "Protest of Baraguá." Despite his protest there were few, if any, resources to continue fighting. Attempts to reignite an insurrection were soon crushed by the Spanish. Maceo left Cuba to regroup in Jamaica and Central America in an effort to rekindle the fight. Rebecca Scott, *Degrees of Freedom*, 104.

82 In reference to Martí, see his essay (euology) on Henry Highland Garnet, Obras completas 13, 235. Many thanks to Kevin Meehan for helping me locate this reference. Also see Kevin Meehan and Paul B. Miller, "Martí, Schomburg y la cuestión racial en las Américas," 73–88. Edward Blyden preached the funeral sermon in Liberia. Schor, *Henry Highland Garnet*; Ofari Hutchinson, *Let Your Motto Be Resistance*; Alexander Crummell, "Eulogium on Henry Highland Garnet DD," *Africa and America*. (Springfield, MA: Wiley and Company, 1891). Eulogy was given at the Union Literary and Historical Association on May 4, 1882 in Washington, DC.

83 "The Late Reverend Dr. Garnet: Memorial Services in Cooper Union Last Evening," *NYT*, May 11, 1882.

84 Richard T. Greener and S. R. Scottron, "The American Foreign Anti-Slavery Society," *New York Globe*, December 1, 1883. Thank you to Shawn Leigh Alexander and David Goldberg for providing me with this citation, and to JuLondre Karlveon Brown for locating it. The members in attendance included: Richard T. Greener, Reverend A. N. Freeman, Reverend William T. Dixon, Charles A. Dorsey, and Samuel Scottron.

85 According to Scott, the Moret Law "did not free significant numbers of slaves of working age, but by multiplying regulations and establishing the Juntas, it did create an additional lever—a small fragile, and awkward one—that some slaves could use to bring about their own emancipation." At the same time, as Scott explains, the government's reluctance to enforce the law and the opposition of masters to changes in the slave structure, appeals for freedom were difficult to file and "even more difficult to win." Rebecca Scott, "Gradual Abolition and the Dynamics of Slave Emancipation in Cuba, 1868–86," 449–477.

86 S. R. Scottron, "Slavery in Cuba. Its Abolition Depending on the Overthrow of Spanish Rule," *New York Globe*, August 11, 1883.

87 Greener and Scottron, "The American Foreign Anti-Slavery Society."

88 Samuel Scottron, "Mr. Scottron's Views: On the Advantages of the Proposed Negro Colonization in South America: An Interesting Discussion." *Brooklyn Eagle,* September 19, 1899.

89 In 1894 Scottron was appointed to the Brooklyn board of education, first by Mayor Charles A. Scieren and then reappointed by Mayor F. W. Wurster and then again by Mayor Van Wyck. Booker T. Washington, *The Negro in Business,* 155. However, as Craig Wilder has written, Scottron's time on the school board was filled with controversy and problems. He was not reappointed and his writings on education and the role of public schools were racist and elitist. Wilder, *A Covenant with Color,* 114–115.

90 "A Reception at the Henry Highland Garnet Colored Club." *Brooklyn Eagle,* October 6, 1900.

91 Ibid.

92 "Mr. Scottron's Views: On the Advantages of the Proposed Negro Colonization in South America: An Interesting Discussion." The article is separated into three sections: Newly Acquired Territory Presents a New Problem to the American People; Dewey's Work; Chinese Versus Negroes. *Brooklyn Eagle,* September 19, 1899.

93 Wilder, *A Covenant with Color,* 114. Wilder cites an article written by Scottron, "Little Prejudice in New York City." *New York Age,* August 10, 1905. Wilder writes that Scottron called these migrants "red-eyed, rum drinking Neg[r]oes, full-bloods, Negro-Indians and half-castes." He considered them to be the lowest specimen of human-kind, and assured his readers that Southern migrants would "assimilate or die off."

94 There is confusion concerning where exactly Scottron was born. Almost all secondary sources claim it was in Philadelphia. Yet, according to Lumet Buckley in *The Hornes,* Scottron was born free in New England. He owned a number of patents, but the one that made him rich was a "leather hand strap device" for trolley car passengers. He also owned a prosperous furniture store that specialized in more of his patented devices (adjustable cornices, window cornices, pole tips, curtain rods, and supporting brackets). Scottron died in 1905 and left two of his sons, Cyrus and Oscar, with good jobs. Lumet, 66.

95 Scottron's good fortune did not last long. Within a few years, Thomas Richmond bought Pitkin's interest in the business. Soon thereafter, Richmond lost almost all of his property in the Great Chicago Fire of October 1871, which also had a devastating impact on the mirror business. One of his last inventions, a process to make glass look like onyx (porcelain onyx), was invented in 1894. The process, however, was never patented. "Manufacturing Household Articles," *Colored American Magazine,* October 1904. Schomburg Center for Black Culture. Regarding Scottron's business affairs and experiences also see Booker T. Washington, *The Negro in Business,* 153–154.

96 Washington, *The Negro in Business,* 156–157.

97 Lumet, 63. Washington mentions Scottron's education and states that he graduated from the Cooper Institute with a degree from the Scientific Department in 1878. He also studied English and Spanish, "under one teacher." *The Negro in Business*, 157–158.

98 Lumet, 63. Scottron wrote several essays that discussed his involvement in Freemasonry published in the *Colored American Magazine*. See "Introductory to the Masonic Department," 7, 10 (1904); "The Works of Brother Clark Considered (Freemasonry)," 7, 11 (1904); "Masonic Department," 9:6 (1905); and "Scottish Rite Masonry," 13, 3 (1907).

99 Joanna Brooks, *American Lazarus*, 148. Brooks writes that the "literature of nineteenth-century black nationalism is laced with references to and borrowings from Prince Hall Freemasonry."

100 Serra, *Para blancos y negros*, 168–171. The entry was written by R.O.C. Benjamin and translated by Serra. In it, Benjamin writes that Scottron profoundly knew his race and their conditions. He characterizes Scottron as mixed-race, "mestizo," who could easily pass for Italian or Spanish if so desired. For an important historical analysis of Masonry among nineteenth-century Puerto Rican and Cuban revolutionaries, see Jossiana Arroyo, *Writing Secrecy*.

101 Washington, *The Negro in Business*, 150.

102 "Mr. Scottron's Views: On the Advantages of the Proposed Negro Colonization in South America: An Interesting Discussion," *Brooklyn Eagle*, September 19, 1899.

103 Ibid.

104 Ibid.

CHAPTER 3. IN DARKEST ANONYMITY

1 Josefina Toledo, *Sotero Figueroa, Dditor de Patria: Apuntes para una biografía*, 11.

2 *La República*, New York, 1884. Martín Morúa Delgado, *Obras Completas*, III, 131. Cited in Poyo, "The Anarchist Challenge to the Cuban Independence Movement, 1885–1890." *Cuban Studies/Estudios Cubanos* 15:1 (Winter, 1985): 32.

3 "Tributes to Karl Marx, who has died." March 29, 1883. *La Nación* (Buenos Aires), May 13 and 16, 1883. *José Martí: Selected Writings*. Edited and Translated by Esther Allen. (Penguin Books, 2002).

4 "Cigars," *NYT*, November 5, 1871.

5 "Cuban Patriots in Council," *NYT*, August 6, 1883 and "The Cuban Revolutionists," *NYT*, August 20, 1883. In addition to Pouble, the members elected Francisco Fernández vice president; Francisco Varona secretary; Juan Arnao treasurer; and Ramón Rubiera auditor. "The Cuban Refugees: Address to the Cubans of this City—This Evening's Mass Meetings," *NYT*, February 14, 1875 (Leandro Rodríguez was one of the men who called this meeting to order), and "Cubans in this City," *NYT*, February 21, 1875. Both articles refer to Cubans as refugees. See Enrique Trujillo, *Apuntes históricos*, 8–10. Clarendon Hall was located at 114–116 East Thirteenth Street in New York City. On January 27, 1902

it burned down. See "Old Clarendon Hall Burns," *NYT*, January 28, 1902. In regard to Morúa Delgado see López Mesa, *La comunidad cubana de New York*, 41. According to Deschamps Chapeaux, Serra and Morúa Delgado left Cuba in 1880, spent time in Key West organizing and were part of the Club San Carlos, and then moved to New York. *Rafael Serra y Montalvo: Obrero incansable de nuestra independencia*, 41–42. Also see Serra, *Patriota y revolucionario, fraternal amigo de Martí*, 15–16.

6   "Favoring a Cuban Revolution: Enthusiastic Meeting in Philadelphia," *NYT*, July 19, 1883. Less than a month earlier General Bonachea traveled to Philadelphia to speak with Cubans at a meeting held at No. 317 South Fifth Street. Here too, he met with about "35 Cubans including a half dozen negroes" to ask for financial support from the increasingly powerful exile and migrant community.

According to Casasús, Bonachea arrived in New York City on July 11, 1883 and left in December. See Casasús, *La emigración cubana*, 190–191; and Enrique Trujillo, *Apuntes históricos*, 8–10.

7   Casasús, *La emigración cubana*, 222, 226. Regarding El Club Hijas de Martí, see Serra, *Patriota y revolucionario, fraternal amigo de Martí*, 16–17.

8   "Favoring a Cuban Revolution: Enthusiastic Meeting in Philadelphia," *NYT*, July 19, 1883 and "Cuban Patriots in Council," *NYT*, August 6, 1883. Regarding Bonachea and Pouble, see Casasús, *La emigración cubana*, 381, 437. For information on Serra as an honorary member of El Club Bartolome Masó, see Serra, *Patriota y revolucionario, fraternal amigo de Martí*, 16. For details on Sotero Figueroa's involvement with the club, see Josefina Toledo, *Sotero Figueroa: Editor de Patria*, 44.

9   "About the Cubans," *NYT*, November 13, 1873.

10   Deschamps Chapeaux, *Rafael Serra y Montalvo*,. 42. According to Deschamps Chapeaux, Serra boarded the *San Jacinto*, which left New York and traveled throughout "the Americas." In *Figuras y Figuritas*, Teófilo Domínguez also mentions Serra's time in Panama (Estados Unidos de Colombia) and his time in Jamaica. He also states that Serra was a member of a contingent of Cuban revolutionaries committed to promoting the plan, 16–17. For more on El Plan Gómez-Maceo see Carmen Almodóvar, *Máximo Gómez, Diario de campaña, 1868–1898*. Although it is difficult to gauge the exact number of Afro-Cuban men who traveled during this period, there was a surge in the number of articles and essays tracing Afro-Cuban mobility. A few examples include F. V. Domínguez, "Deuda sagrada" (Sacred Debt), *Patria*, May 25, 1898; Juan Gualberto Gómez, "Martí y yo," *Revista bimestere cubana*, enero–febrero 1933; and Toledo, *Sotero Figueroa: Editor de Patria*, 37.

11   Morúa Delgado, *Obras completas*, III, and Manuel Deulofeu y Lleonaut, *Héroes del destierro. La emigración. Notas históricas* (Cienfuegos, Cuba Imprenta de M. Mestre, 1904), 32.

12   Domínguez, *Figuras y Figuritas*, 16–18; and Serra, *Patriota y revolucionario, fraternal amigo de Martí*, 16–17.

13 F. V. Domínguez, "Deuda sagrada" (Sacred Debt), *Patria*, May 25, 1898. Cited in Deschamps Chapeaux, *Rafael Serra y Montalvo*. 42.

14 Guerra, *The Myth of José Martí*, 26.

15 Speech by José Martí cited in Trujillo, *Apuntes históricos*, 34–35; and Deschamps Chapeaux, *Rafael Serra y Montalvo*, 45.

16 Poyo, *With All and for the Good of All*, 97. See "Cuban Patriots in Council," *NYT*, August 6, 1883; and "The Cuban Revolutionists," *NYT*, August 20, 1883, which discuss the membership and identify Juan Arnao as treasurer.

17 According to Joan Casanovas, the Treaty of Zanjón (1878) allowed working-class Cubans to return home to Cuba. The peace treaty stipulated freedom for all those imprisoned or deported. Casanovas, *Bread or Bullets*, 124–125. Also see Juan Gualberto Gómez, *La cuestión de Cuba en 1884, Historia y soluciones de los partidos cubanos* (Madrid: Impresa de A.J. Alaria, 1885).

18 Domínguez, *Figuras y Figuritas*, 45. According to Domínguez, Gutiérrez was a member of the "Union Internacional de Trabajadores de América." He was a member of a committee that fought against the Foster Treaty in 1884 and represented cigar workers at a mass meeting in New York that subsequently presented a petition challenging the sanctions to the US Senate.

19 Poyo, "The Anarchist Challenge to the Cuban Independence Movement, 1885–1890," 30.

20 Ibid., 30–31.

21 Casanovas, *Bread or Bullets*, 125. The strikes in New York were followed by strikes in Key West. Workers in Key West organized a union and walked out to protest wage cuts. They did not fare well. When they requested support from the separatist leadership, the Aldamista-led junta in New York "did nothing" and the strike collapsed in a month.

22 Ibid., 112.

23 Morúa Delgado, "La cuestión obrera," *Obras completas*, Tomo III, 141–144.

24 Morúa Delgado, "Señores Directores de la Oportunidad," *Obras Completas*, Tomo III, "Integración cubana," 144–145.

25 Casanovas, *Bread, or Bullets*, 168.

26 Ibid., 168–169.

27 Ibid., 169.

28 Poyo, "The Anarchist Challenge to the Cuban Independence Movement, 1885–1890," 29–41.

29 Casanovas, *Bread, or Bullets*, 169.

30 José Martí, "Class War in Chicago: A Terrible Drama," *José Martí: Selected Writings*, 195. According to Esther Allen, it changed his views on the rights of workers and the role of labor in the United States.

31 Ibid., 207, 219.

32 "Cigars," *NYT*, November 5, 1871.

33 Ibid.

34 "Directory of the Tobacco Industry of the United States and Havana Cuba," published by *Tobacco Leaf*, 1885–1887. Also see *New York Directory of Cigar Factories*, 1894; and the *United States Tobacco Journal Business Directory*, 1898, 1899, 1900. The *U.S. Tobacco Journal* was headquartered at 119 Maiden Lane. Another reason for the increase in the New York cigar industry was the devastating Chicago fire of 1871.

35 Ibid.

36 "Will you dine here, señor? Among the gourmet cigareros down in Maiden Lane." *NYT*, February 25, 1894.

37 "Cigars," *NYT*, November 5, 1871.

38 Ibid.

39 Ibid.

40 Ibid.

41 Deschamps Chapeaux, *Rafael Serra y Montalvo*.

42 Louis A. Pérez, Jr., "Reminiscences of a Lector: Cuban Cigar Workers in Tampa, *Florida Historical Quarterly Review*, 53:4 (April, 1975): 443–449; Deschamps Chapeaux, *Rafael Serra y Montalvo: Obrero Incansable De Nuestra Independencia*; and Gary Mormino and George E. Pozzetta, *The Immigrant World of Ybor City: Italians and their Latin Neighbors in Tampa, 1885–1985* (Urbana: University of Illinois Press, 1987).

43 See Morúa Delgado, "Señores Directores de la Oportunidad," 1883, (Edición de la comisión nacional del centenario de Martín Morúa Delgado, La Habana, Cuba 1957), 145–146, where he mentions the existence of a women's labor union, "un gremio de despalilladoras," who demanded more pay for their work.

44 According to the Ninth and Tenth Census of the United States, State and County of New York data for 1870, there were 43 "negro" and 7 "mulatto" women from Cuba who migrated to New York City. In 1880 those numbers jumped to 204 "negro" and 236 "mulatto" women from Cuba who migrated to New York City. In 1870 there were a total of 1,004 Cubans, including 176 who identified as "negro" and 104 "mulatto" who migrated to New York. In 1880 there were 7,318 Cubans in New York City with 556 who identified as "negro" and 595 "mulatto." The majority of jobs listed for women included laundresses, boarding house keeper, servants, dressmakers, and cigar workers. As with all census data, these numbers are imprecise. It is not clear if Cubans identified themselves as "negro" and/or "mulatto," or instead, were identified as such by the census taker. What they do reveal, however, is an increased number of Cubans arriving to New York in 1880, during the height of the cigar industry.

45 Eighth Census of the United States, State and County of New York, Borough of Manhattan, July, 1860.

46 Irma Watkins Owens, *Blood Relations*. Teófilo Domínguez also mentions the relationship between West Indians and Afro-Cubans. He notes how Margarito Gutiérrez, for one, translated important documents from Spanish to English,

which, according to Domínguez, were published in the *West Indian Abrout*. *Figuras y Figuritas*, 43.

47 "Will you dine here, señor? Among the gourmet cigareros down in Maiden Lane." *NYT*, February 25, 1894.

48 Ibid.

49 Deschamps Chapeaux, *Rafael Serra y Montalvo*, 147–148.

50 Serra, "La anexión," *La Doctrina de Martí*, July 16, 1899, *Fraternal amigo de Martí*, 136, and *Ensayos políticos*, 214–218. Serra also notes that annexation to the United States would pit African Americans against Afro-Cubans and vice versa. Also see Deschamps Chapeaux, *Rafael Serra y Montalvo*, 147–148.

51 Deschamps Chapeaux, *Rafael Serra y Montalvo*, 62–63.

52 Serra, *Ensayos políticos*, 172. It is important to note that Serra wrote this in 1899 and was most likely speaking to past experiences as well as to the future independent Cuba. Also see Deschamps Chapeaux, *Rafael Serra y Montalvo*, 80.

53 Serra, *Ensayos políticos*, 145.

54 Serra led the club La Armonía in 1879 while still in Cuba. The club was an educational center that also fostered "socio-political ideas." *Patriota y revolucionario*, 15.

55 Deschamps Chapeaux, *Rafael Serra y Montalvo*, 45.

56 Cited in ibid., 53–54. See Serra, *Para blancos y negros*.

57 Serra, *Ensayos políticos*, 146. Throughout much of his writings, Serra used the words "to elevate" men of color. In doing so, he echoed the familiar and controversial discourse on racial uplift, one that he subscribed to for most of his career.

58 Deschamps Chapeaux, *Rafael Serra y Montalvo*, 45.

59 Serra, *Ensayos políticos*, 167.

60 Manuel De J. González, "Una clase en 'La Liga.'" Serra, *Ensayos políticos*, 180.

61 *Minerva*, "Sumario." December 30, 1888.

62 Deschamps Chapeaux, *Rafael Serra y Montalvo*, 52. Serra, *Patriota y revolucionario, fraternal amigo de Martí*, 16.

63 Teófilo Domínguez, *Figuras y Figuritas*, 17.

64 Deschamps Chapeaux, *Rafael Serra y Montalvo*, 52–53.

65 Serra, *Ensayos políticos*, 145–147 and 180, *Patriota y revolucionario, fraternal amigo de Martí*, 16–17. The membership consisted of regular and irregular members. Regular members, known as "socios," were founders, teachers, full-time members, and those who organized the club. Irregular members were affiliated with the club and invited to events and fund-raisers. They were not, however, intimately involved with running the club. Also see Deschamps Chapeaux, *Rafael Serra y Montalvo*, 52–53.

66 Names appear in *Ensayos políticos*. There is an additional list of names, which appears in *Figuras y Figuritas*, 17, and is not included in *Ensayos políticos*. These are: Manuel Caballero, Manuel Montejo, Ventura Portuondo, Modesto Tirado, Frederico Sánchez, Plácido Díaz, Gregorio Graupera, Silvestre Pivaló, Juan F. Beato, Adriano Portuondo, Antonio González, Julio Castro, Ramón Román.

67 Serra, *Ensayos políticos*, 145.

68 Ibid., 146–147.

69 Ibid., 111–112. Several editions of *Patria* list the Directiva del Club Guerilla de Antonio Maceo and Las Dos Antillas as part of the PRC's New York clubs. In a brief article published in the October 12, 1895 edition of *Patria*, it states that "Serra spoke on behalf of the Guerilla de Maceo." In regard to Las Dos Antillas, see "Reglamento Del Club Politicó, Las Dos Antillas," April 16, 1891 and Minutes of the Meetings, 1892–1895, SC Micro. R2251 Schomburg Center for Research in Black Culture. At the same time, there were a number of racially integrated clubs that represented the interests of Cuba and Puerto Rico that were either founded or involved black Cuban and Puerto Rican migrants in New York. These included: El Club José Martí, El Club Borinquen, El Club Los Independiente, El Club Pinos Nuevos, and the all-women club, El Club Mercedes Varona.

70 Serra, *Ensayos políticos*, 181. "Los lunes de 'La Liga,'" *Patria*, March 26, 1892.

71 González, "Una clase en 'La Liga,'" *Ensayos políticos*, 180.

72 Ibid.

73 "En La Liga," *Patria*, November 1, 1892.

74 González, "Una clase en 'La Liga,'" 180.

75 Deschamps Chapeaux, *Rafael Serra y Montalvo*, 50.

76 Domínguez, *Figuras y Figuritas*, 17.

77 "En La Liga," *Patria*, July 1, 1893.

78 González, "Una clase en 'La Liga,'" 181.

79 "En La Liga," *Patria*, July 1, 1893.

80 Martí, *Obras completas*, Vol. 5–8. In casting Fernández as primarily Arturo Beneche's companion, Martí, as the author of this source, attempts to legitimize her via Beneche's membership in La Liga. In doing so, Martí cast membership as a masculinist privilege and reifies Fernández, and by extension all women, as secondary to male membership and activism. Also see Deschamps Chapeaux, *Rafael Serra y Montalvo*, 58. Although not formally recorded, it is most likely that Mariana Calderín was related to Pedro Calderín, the third president of La Liga. "Beneche's companion" refers to Arturo Beneche, a member of La Liga. There is mention of América Fernández singing at an event at La Liga on July 1, 1893. See "En La Liga," *Patria*, July 1, 1893.

81 For more on Carmen Miyares and her relationship with José Martí, see Nydia Sarabia, *La patriota del silencio*: Carmen Miyares.

82 Despite repeated and constant attempts, it was extremely difficult to locate sources on these women: where they worked, lived, and affiliation with other clubs. There is some indication the some of these women were involved in the Club Mercedes Varona, which was the auxiliary club of the Partido Revolucionario Cubano. See Serra, *Ensayos políticos*, 173, for an image and listing of the Señoras de La Liga.

83 Montejo Arrechea, "*Minerva*: A Magazine for Women (and Men) of Color," 34. Gema Guevara, *The Sound and Silence of Race: Contesting Cuba's Racial Paradigm*,

1833–1930 (Manuscript in progress). I am deeply grateful to Gema Guevara for making this collection available to me and for noting key points.

84 *Minerva*, May 30, 1889, no. 16. Also see Montejo Arrechea, "*Minerva*: A Magazine for Women (and Men) of Color," 35–36. In Montejo Arrechea's account she lists the agent from Kingston as Isolino Renifo. However, in the May 30th edition of *Minerva* the agent is identified as a woman by the name of Señorita Isolina Rengifo in Kingston. Thank you to Gema Guevara for pointing this out to me.

85 See Sección poetica, "De la niña Juanita Febles," by Joaquin Granados, *Minerva*, January 28, 1889; "A las ilustradas señoras y señoritas, colaboradoras protectoras y simpatizadoras de 'Minerva,'" by Joaquin Granados; "La mujer fea" (New York, 1883) and "El baile," (Kingston, 1885), by Rafael Serra, all in *Minerva*, February 7, 1889. The February 28, 1889 edition of *Minerva* names Granados's wife Señora Aurora Coca.

86 Montejo Arrechea, "*Minerva*: A Magazine for Women (and Men) of Color," 36.

87 "La mujer-Sus derechos." This column appeared in a number of editions of *Minerva*.

88 Africa Céspedes, "A Cuba," *Minerva*, March 16, 1889.

89 Ibid.

90 For the article on the history of the women's movement in Europe, see "La mujer–Sus derechos," *Minerva*, July 19, 1889.

91 *Minerva*, January 26, 1889.

92 For an example, see "A L. . . ." *Minerva*, December 15, 1888.

93 See Montejo Arrechea, "Minerva: A Magazine for Women (and Men) of Color," 41. *Minerva* reappeared on September 15, 1910 and was published until April 1915. After 1915 editions were irregular. The name of the magazine changed to *Minerva Illustrated Magazine: Sciences Art, Literature and Sport: The Expression of the Colored Race*, and the contents from 1910 to 1915 also differed. According to Arrechea, although there was a section called "Feminist Pages," the magazine emphasized "issues of importance to the black race as a whole."

94 "Cubans Preparing to Revolt. Clubs in American Cities Collecting Arms for the Effort at Freedom," *Chicago Daily Tribune*, July 22, 1892.

95 "For Cuban Independence: A Vast Meeting in Commemoration of the Uprising of 1868, Patriots Fired with Enthusiasm," *NYT*, October 11, 1895.

96 Ibid.

97 María Caridad Pacheco, *Juan Fraga: Su obra en la pupila de Martí*, 6. Casasús states that Fraga was president of Cuerpo de Consejos, 404; Toledo, *Sotero Figueroa: Editor de Patria*, discusses Fraga's impact and Club Los Independientes as a precursor to the PRC. 37–42.

98 "Diez de Octubre en Chickering Hall," *Patria*, October 12, 1895, no. 186. Fraga's name and his activities appeared more frequently in *Patria* before Martí's death on May 19, 1895.

99 Pacheco, *Juan Fraga: Su obra en la pupila de Martí*, 29–30. Pacheco cites a letter written by Fraga to Serra located in the Archivo Nacional Fondo Fonativos y Remisiónes, Caja 470, no. 53.

100 Pacheco, *Juan Fraga: Su obra en la pupila de Martí*, 3. According to Pacheco, it is likely that Fraga migrated in 1868. She cites a letter to General Julio Sanguily dated April 14, 1877 that places Fraga in Brooklyn. In addition, the newspaper *Patria*, dated April 22, 1893, states that Fraga had been a migrant for 25 years.

101 Editions of *Patria* (1892–1895) list his tobacco shop at this address.

102 *Patria*, February 14, 1893. The cigar factories listed include J. M. Agüero at 50 Fulton Street; F. Bentacourt at 29 Fulton Street; and R. C. Galindo at 20 Fulton Street.

103 Pacheco, *Juan Fraga: Su obra en la pupila de Martí*, 4–6.

104 Trujillo, *Apuntes históricos*, 30–32; Casasús, *La emigración cubana*, 202; Pacheco, *Juan Fraga: Su obra en la pupila de Martí*, 8–9. Poyo also notes that El Club de los Independiente was focused on propaganda and raising funds.

105 "La reunión en Nueva York," *Patria*, April 22, 1893.

106 Ibid.

107 Casasús, *La emigración cubana*, 403–404. Pacheco, *Juan Fraga: Su obra en la pupila de Martí*, 11.

108 Orlando Castañeda, "Martí, los tabaqueros y la Revolución de 1895," 16.

109 Pacheco, *Juan Fraga: Su obra en la pupila de Martí*, 28

110 Toledo, *Sotero Figueroa, Editor de Patria*, 37.

111 Ibid., 38–39. Gonzalo de Quesada, who was Cuban, served as treasurer of El Club Borinquen. According to Bernardo Vega, not everyone was in support of La Sección Puerto Rico. The founding of La Sección Puerto Rico was met with an "icy reception" among the working class, especially the cigar workers. Although Figueroa attempted to "remedy the situation," the problem, according to Vega, was that for many workers the PRC and La Seccíon Puerto Rico did not focus enough attention on the needs of workers and was, in the opinion of many, subservient to the interests of the PRC. *Memoirs of Bernardo Vega*, 76–77.

112 "Cuba's Independence Day, Celebrated by a Gathering of Her Sons and Daughters," *NYT*, October 11, 1891.

113 Poyo, *With All and for the Good of All*, 101.

114 Castañeda, "Martí, los tabaqueros y la Revolución de 1895," 26.

115 Using the listing of clubs published in the edition of *Patria* dated July 22, 1893, it is clear that the number of clubs, albeit associated with the PRC, in Tampa and Key West far outnumber those in New York. Cited in the Minutes of the Meeting, Las Dos Antillas, May 21, 1895. Arturo Schomburg Papers, Schomburg Center for Research in Black Culture. This is noted in a number of texts and monographs, including Poyo.

116 Greenbaum, *More than Black*, 72.

117 There are several different dates associated with the founding of La Liga in Tampa. Deschamps Chapeaux claims the club was founded on November 27, 1892. See

Greenbaum, *More than Black*, 72–74, for more details on the role of La Liga in Tampa. In addition to the one in Tampa, there were branches of La Liga in Havana and Santiago de Cuba. La Liga was not the first Afro-Cuban club in Tampa or Key West. There were Afro-Cuban and racially integrated clubs that existed years before La Liga was founded in New York. One in particular, La Sociedad el Progreso in Key West, counted Rafael Serra a member years before he moved to New York. Serra remained in contact and worked closely with Tampa-based Afro-Cuban revolutionaries Guillermo Sorondo, Joaquin and Manuel Granados, Bruno Roig, and Francisco Segura.

118 Greenbaum, *More than Black*, 74–76; Nancy Hewitt, "Paulina Pedroso and Las Patriotas de Tampa," in Ann Henderson and Gary Mormino eds., *Spanish Pathways in Florida, 1492–1992* (Sarasota: Pineapple Press), 258–279.

119 Pacheco, *Juan Fraga: Su obra en la pupila de Martí*, 11–12.

120 *NYT*, "Promoting a Revolution," March 7, 1892. The meeting is referenced in different sources. Horatio Rubens, *Liberty: The Story of Cuba*, 24; Enrique Collazo, *Cuba Heroica* (Habana: Imprenta, La Mercantil, 1912), 159; Casasús, *La emigración cubana*; Pacheco, *Juan Fraga: Su obra en la pupila de Martí*, 12–14; and Poyo, *With All and for the Good of All*, 115.

121 *NYT*, "Promoting a Revolution," March 7, 1892. Notes that members of the "Cuban Ladies Club" were not invited to this meeting. The article also mentions that the women's club was for the wives of the "many Porto Rican and South American merchants." No doubt this led to the drafting of a PRC platform where women's rights are nonexistent.

122 Poyo, *With All and for the Good of All*, 101–102. Martí declared that "all Cubans, Puerto Ricans and Spaniards interested in the freedom of Cuba and Puerto Rico" were welcomed into the PRC, further expanding its scope,

123 Pacheco, *Juan Fraga: Su obra en la pupila de Martí*, 15; and Poyo, *With All and for the Good of All*, 102.

124 Poyo, *With All and for the Good of All*, 101.

125 "Preparing for a Revolt: Señor Martí in South America Organizing Cuban Patriots," *NYT*, September 20, 1892.

126 "De Haiti, La visita del delegado," *Patria*, November 1, 1892. Martí was in Haiti from September 24th to the 26th.

127 "The Cuban Revolutionists," *NYT*, October 20, 1892. Alejandro González was a delegado to the PRC. See notice of Martí's visit to Jamaica "En Jamaica," and a letter written by González under the heading "Un buen cubano," both published in *Patria*, November 7, 1892.

128 In regard to Martí's visits abroad, see "De Haiti, La visita del delegado," *Patria*, November 1, 1892; "Los cubanos de Mexico," *Patria*, January 28, 1893.

129 "A War Fund for Cuba," *NYT*, July 26, 1892. "El delgado en viaje," *Patria*, November 12, 1892.

130 "Revolutionists will Assist," *NYT*, May 2, 1893.

131 Guerra, *The Myth of José Martí*, 27; and Toledo, *Sotero Figueroa, Editor de Patria*, 47.

132 Deschamps Chapeaux, *Rafael Serra y Montalvo*, 106.

133 In regard to Varona, see Toledo, *Sotero Figueroa, Editor de Patria*, 160. For quote and more information on methods of organizing, see Toledo, ibid., 125–126.

134 *Patria*, February 17, March 6, and March 31, 1897. The all-women's club was based in San Pedro de Macoris, Dominican Republic. There were also clubs in the United States formed in honor of Maceo, including "Vengadores de Antonio Maceo," established in Tampa in early 1897.

135 "Club Morelos y Maceo," *Patria*, July 31, 1897.

136 "El negro en Cuba," *Patria*, January 1, 1896. Figueroa served as editor during 1895 and 1896. On the same page there is an advertisement for Figueroa's translation services and printing press.

137 Deschamps Chapeaux dates the first edition of *La Doctrina de Martí* "around July 9, 1896." He lists Manuel de Jesús, Sotero Figueroa, Juan Bonilla, Domingo Collazo, Pedro Calderín, Francisco Gonzalo Marín, "and others." *Rafael Serra y Montalvo*, 115, 119.

138 Poyo, *With All and for the Good of All*, 128.

139 Deschamps Chapeaux, *Rafael Serra y Montalvo*, 119–120.

140 Cited in Poyo, *With All and for the Good of All*, 128.

141 Guerra, *The Myth of Martí*, 119.

142 Domínguez, *Figuras y Figuritas*, 53.

143 Ibid., 73.

144 Pedro Duarte, "Carta abierta," *Figuras y Figuritas*, 8.

145 Ibid., 10–11.

146 Domínguez, *Figuras y Figuritas*, 26.

147 Ibid., 26–27.

148 Ibid., 33.

149 Ibid., 36.

150 La Union Martí-Maceo records, minutes of the meetings, October 26, 1900. Special Collections, University of South Florida. Also see Nancy Raquel Mirabal, "Telling Silences and Making Community," for more details on the separation.

CHAPTER 4. ORPHAN POLITICS

1 *NYT*, July 29, 1898. Cited in Louis A. Pérez, Jr., *Cuba Between Empires, 1878–1902*, 204.

2 "The Race Question in Cuba: La Lucha Says Supremacy of the Whites Must Be Guaranteed, Although Negroes Are in the Majority," *NYT*, September 15, 1899.

3 "The Negro in Cuba: In the Eyes of the Law He Stands on an Equal Footing with the White Man—A Suggestion to Bar Him from the First Artillery Resented." *New York Tribune*, August 26, 1901.

4 "Reception tendered by the Cuban Orphan Society to Brigadier-General William Ludlow, Governor of Havana," November 16, 1899, published by the Cuban Orphan Society (New York Public Library, 1901).

5 Ibid., 21–22. In 1899 the society, which by then raised close to $37,000, sent twelve women to Cuba on behalf of the Cuban Orphan Society to work in asylums and

hospitals in Remedios and Cienfuegos. They formed a kindergarten, and taught classes in agricultural training at Santa Maria de Rosario in the "most modern methods, of young Cuban women to be teachers."

6 Ibid., 2–3.

7 Ibid., 13.

8 Ibid., 14.

9 Ibid., 16.

10 Ibid., 10.

11 Ibid., 4.

12 Ibid., 13.

13 Román de la Campa, "Latin, Latino American: Split States and Global Imaginaries," in Nancy Raquel Mirabal and Agustin Laó, eds., *Technofuturos: Critical Interventions in Latina/o Studies* (Lanham: Rowman and Littlefield, 2007), 32.

14 Ludlow, "Reception tendered by the Cuban Orphan Society to Brigadier-General William Ludlow, Governor of Havana," 11–14. Although Ludlow refrained from using blackness as a central trope, he asserts that Cubans are "not Anglo-Saxon in any sense," and although "we find people saying that they are a race of rats," he instead argues that it is because Cubans are "Latin-American" that they are unfit.

15 *New York Herald*, January 30, 1898, cited in "Ni Española, Ni Yankee," Rafael Serra, *Fraternal amigo de Martí*, 125.

16 "Cuba May Be Another Haiti," *NYT*, August 7, 1899. The racialization and gendering of Cuba and Cubans in the mainstream press was constant. US newspapers published countless articles, editorials, and cartoons depicting Cubans as completely ill-equipped to self-govern. The more rebellious elements were depicted as black, unruly children in need of discipline. Those considered more subservient were characterized as young, white Cuban women ready and willing to accept US dominance. See Michael Hunt, *Ideology and U.S. Foreign Policy*; and Louis A. Pérez, Jr., *Cuba in the American Imagination*.

17 "The Negro in Cuba," *New York Tribune*, August 26, 1901.

18 "Change of Sentiment in Cuba: Little Is Said About Independence, and the Annexationists Are Growing Bolder Daily," *NYT*, August 29, 1899.

19 Hunt, *Ideology and U.S. Foreign Policy*, 38.

20 "The Platt Amendment," National Archives & Records Administration. US National Archives, Washington, DC.

21 Cuban women were finally given the vote in 1933 under the 100-day presidency of Ramón Grau San Martin. For more on the impact of the 1901 Cuban Constitution on women's rights in Cuba, see Lynn Stoner, *From the House to the Streets*.

22 Pérez, Jr., *Cuba Between Empires*, 181.

23 Pérez, Jr., *On Becoming Cuban*, 109. By 1905 approximately 13,000 North Americans purchased land in Cuba.

24 Figures cited in de la Fuente, "Two Dangers, One Solution," 34.

25 Pérez, Jr., *On Becoming Cuban*.

26 "Many Americans in Cuba," *NYT*, May 6, 1900.
27 Ibid.
28 Cited in Aline Helg, *Our Rightful Share*, 102.
29 "The Negro Race in Cuba," *NYT*, September 16, 1900.
30 "Many Americans in Cuba," *NYT*, May 6, 1900.
31 "The Negro Race in Cuba," *NYT*, September 16, 1900. Stanhope also examines the plight of poor women in Cuba and the exportation of their labor, primarily needlework, in "Sells the Work of Poor Cuban Women," *NYT*, March 22, 1903.
32 "The Negro Race in Cuba," *NYT*, September 16, 1900.
33 Ibid.
34 Quoted in Williard B. Gatewood Jr., *Black Americans and the White Man's Burden*, 161.
35 Frank Andre Guridy, *Forging Diaspora*, 23.
36 "What If War Comes?," *Cleveland Gazette*, March 5, 1895.
37 "Restrained Patriotism," *Kansas City American Citizen*, April 7, 1898.
38 *Indianapolis Freeman*, March 19, 1898.
39 *Richmond Planet*, August 20, 1898. For more on the newspapers that favored annexation, see George Marks III, ed., *The Black Press Views American Imperialism*.
40 "Restrained Patriotism," *Kansas City American Citizen*, April 7, 1898.
41 *Cleveland Gazette*, October 8, 1898.
42 Serra, "La anexión," 135–136.
43 Ibid., 135.
44 Ibid., 136–137.
45 Ibid., 136.
46 Gatewood, Jr., *Black Americans and the White Man's Burden*, 170.
47 David Helwig, "The African-American Press and the United States Involvement in Cuba, 1902–1912," in Brock and Castañeda Fuertes, eds., *Between Race and Empire: African-Americans and Cubans before the Cuban Revolution*, 71.
48 "The Color Line in Cuba: Efforts of the Negroes to Secure Recognition in Public Affairs—Will President Palma Invite Them to the Reception?" *New York Tribune*, November 4, 1902.
49 Cited in Helg, *Our Rightful Share*, 129; and Serra, "Prospecto de El Nuevo Criollo," *Para blancos y negros*, 52–55. Serra continued to travel and publish in New York after returning to Cuba. See Serra "Carta abierta: Al director del 'Pueblo Libre,'" New York City, January 26, 1901.
50 Helg, *Our Rightful Share*, 68.
51 Ibid., 120–121.
52 "Sotero Figueroa," *La Discusión*, October 10, 1923, 5. Memorial to Figueroa upon his death on October 5, 1923. Document was translated into English by his son, Pace Figueroa. Arturo Schomburg Papers, File 0668, Reel 11, SCM.
53 "Sotero Figueroa," *La Discusión*, October 10, 1923, 6.
54 In New York and Cuba, Serra both worked with and questioned Estrada Palma. This was a common and oft-used strategy among Afro-Cubans in exile and within

the Partido Revolucionario Cubano. The issue was whether this strategy was ultimately effective. See Descamps Chapeaux, *Rafael Serra y Montalvo*, where he outlines this debate. 161.

55 Serra, *Para blancos y negros*, 142–144. Also see section entitled "La escuela de Tuskegee," 147–149. Helg also references Serra and *El Nuevo Criollo*, 134.

56 Miguel Gualba, "Consuelo Serra y Heredia," in Serra, *Para blancos y negros*, 120–121.

57 Serra, *La república posible*, 10.

58 Guerra, *The Myth of Martí*, 154.

59 Ibid., 155–156.

60 Ibid., 165.

61 Pappedemos, *Black Political Activism and the Cuban Republic*, 77, 149.

62 Ibid., 61.

63 "The Color-Line in Cuba," *New York Tribune*, November 4, 1902.

64 Pappedemos, *Black Political Activism and the Cuban Republic*, 65; and Helg, *Our Rightful Share*, 124.

65 Pappedemos, 67.

66 Ibid.

67 "El censo," *Diario de la Marina*, April 22, 1900. Cited in de la Fuente, "Two Dangers, One Solution," 30–49.

68 Between 1902 and 1907, 128,000 Spaniards, mostly young men, migrated to Cuba, with a population of 2 million, to work. According to Helg, 60,000 were here on a permanent basis. As Helg writes, new legislation prohibited the migration of "races of color," but promoted Spanish immigration. Helg, *Our Rightful Share*, 99. For more on the impact of Jamaican migration, see de la Fuente, "Two Dangers, One Solution."

69 Helg, *Our Rightful Share*, 6.

70 "The Color Line in Cuba." *New York Tribune*, November 4, 1901.

71 de la Fuente, *A Nation for All*, 33.

72 "Negro in Cuban Cabinet: Delgado, ex-President of the Senate, First to Get Portfolio from Gómez," *NYT*, April 17, 1910.

73 de la Fuente, *A Nation for All*; Helg, *Our Rightful Share*; and Pappedemos, *Black Political Activism and the Cuban Republic*.

74 "Rafael Serra Montalvo," *Minerva Revista Universal Ilustrada*, no. IV–V, October 1910. In reference to the procession, see de la Fuente, *A Nation for All*, 71.

75 Serra, "La república posible," 8.

76 Ibid., 14.

77 Helg, *Our Rightful Share*, 129.

78 "A la memoria de un patriota: Martín Morúa Delgado, El 28 de abril de 1910," *Minerva*, April 1911.

79 Pappedemos, *Black Political Activism and the Cuban Republic*. 149.

80 Gema Guevara, *The Sound and Silence of Race: Contesting Cuba's Racial Paradigm* (Unpublished manuscript, cited with author's consent), 27–28.

81 "¿Existe en Cuba la clasificación official de razas?" *Minerva*, January 15, 1911; "Europeizemonos," *Minerva*, October, 1911; "El peligro blanco," *Minerva*, July 1913; and "Una carta de Campos Marquetti," *Minerva*, January 1913.

82 Except for an excerpt of *Au fil de la vie* entitled "El feminismo" and written by La Infanta Eulalia of Spain, Duchess of Galliera, there were almost no articles on the role of feminism. First published in Paris in 1911, the excerpt is a radical treatise on women's rights and harkens back to *Minerva*'s earlier period. In it, La Infanta Eulalia writes that a "woman's life is the same as that of a man's," and argues against current conditions of marriage, which cast women as "property," the lack of women's rights, and the scientific and philosophical discourses used to oppress women, including the works of Schopenhauer. The book caused a sensation in Europe and the United States, where it was translated into *The Thread of Life* in 1912. It is not clear why *Minerva* published the works of a controversial Spanish duchess, as opposed to Afro-Cuban women, and does so three months before the Race War of 1912.

83 Guevara, *The Sound and Silence of Race*, 29.

84 "Club feminista 'Minerva,'" *Minerva*, January 31, 1911.

85 *Minerva*, June 12, 1912. A year later, in June 1913, *Minerva* reported on the passing of Paulina Pedroso, a respected patriota who was a central figure in the Cuban revolutionary movement in Ybor City and Tampa.

86 Helg, *Our Rightful Share*, 2.

87 "Gomez Sees End of Cuba Revolt," *NYT*, May 23, 1912. Also see "President of Cuba Expresses Regrets," *NYT*, September 6, 1912.

88 Arthur A. Schomburg, "General Evaristo Estenoz," *Crisis*, July 1912.

89 "Annexing Cuba," *Chicago Defender*, February 17, 1914.

90 "Cuba Free From Race Prejudice," *Chicago Defender*, May 24, 1924.

91 "Bogus Cubans the Latest," *Washington Post*, August 24, 1902.

92 Bernardo Ruiz Suárez, *The Color Question in the Two Americas*, 69.

93 "Bogus Cubans the Latest," *Washington Post*, August 24, 1902.

94 Ibid.

95 Adapted from International Migration and Naturalization, Series C-85–110 Immigrants by Country, 1820–1970. US Bureau of the Census.

96 "Manhattan: The Harlems," *WPA Guide to New York City. Federal Writers' Project Guide to 1930s New York*. New York: Pantheon Books, 1982, 266. Early membership records of El Club Julio Antonio Mella list the addresses in Washington Heights, West Harlem, Hamilton Heights, East Harlem, and Chelsea, JCP. Suárez Díaz notes that Cubans, including Torriente Brau, moved to neighborhoods where Cubans were already living. *Escapé de Cuba.*, 16, 243.

97 César Andréu Iglesias, ed., *Memoirs of Bernardo Vega*, 98. See Ruiz Suárez, *The Color Question in the Two Americas*, for more details on Harlem during this period.

98 Andreu Iglesias, ed., *Memoirs of Bernardo Vega* 102.

99 Ibid., 99.

100 "Manhattan: The Harlems," *WPA Guide to New York City. Federal Writers' Project Guide to 1930s New York*, 266. In his memoirs, Bernardo Vega pointed out that landlords in Harlem were "making good money by charging Puerto Ricans high rents." *Memoirs of Bernardo Vega*, 102.

101 OHMA (1995). León was a founding member of the CCI. Lista de Fundadores, 17 de septiembre, 1945. CCI Records, SCM Box 1, Folder 8. For more on Mario Bauza, see *Cubop: The Life and Music of Maestro Mario Bauza*. Caribbean Cultural Center, in Association with Con Edison and the Friends of the Davis Center, Inc./Aaron Davis Hall Presents, 1993, 6–7.

102 Ruiz Suárez, *The Color Question in the Two Americas*, 16, 69.

103 The census lists the exact number for 1930 as 18,493. It lists 23,256 Cubans who left for the United States in 1890. This number is imprecise since, according to the notes included in the census records (C-110–114 Immigration from America, 1820–1970) in 1890, Cubans were counted along with other populations from the West Indies. Suárez Díaz lists the years from 1928 to 1933 as the most active in terms of Cuban political migration to the United States, no doubt correlating to the Machadato. *Escapé de Cuba*, 9.

104 For many in Cuba, Machado's policies resulted in a constitutional dictatorship. The modifications, which were overwhelmingly approved by the Chamber of Representatives, 94 to 8, included adding the Isle of Pines as territory of Cuba, extending the vote to women, acknowledging the right of minority parties to be represented in the Senate, strengthening rules for future modifications of the Cuban constitution, augmenting the number of senators from 4 to 6 for each province elected for a term of 9 years, eliminating the office of the vice presidency, electing the president for a 6-year term without the right of reelection, prolonging the term of the present president for 2 years, and holding an election for a Constituent Assembly to consider the revision of the Constitution. See Aguilar, *Cuba 1933: Prologue to Revolution*, 64–65.

105 Raymond Leslie Buell, Research Director, Foreign Policy Association, "Cuba's Political Crisis Sharpens as Her Election Draws Near," *NYT*, October 12, 1930.

106 Aguilar, *Cuba 1933: Prologue to Revolution*; Pérez, Jr., *Between Reform and Revolution*; de la Fuente, *A Nation for All*; and Suárez Díaz, *Escapé de Cuba*.

107 de la Fuente, *A Nation for All*, 192–193.

108 OHMA (1996), (2002). In his memoirs, Bernardo Vega makes a connection between musicians and barbershops. *Memoirs of Bernardo Vega*, 98.

109 These included lodges in New York City, Los Angeles, San Francisco, Denver, and Chicago. JCP, Box 1, Folder 1. The IWO was organized into 15 different sections, including the Jewish Section (Jewish People's Fraternal Order); Mutualista Obrera Puertorriqueña; the Italian Section (Garibaldi American Fraternal Society), etc. See Eric Arneson, ed., *Encyclopedia of US Labor and Working Class History*. (London: Taylor and Francis, 2006), 694–695. Over the years, this number changed. In New York, the logias were consolidated or phased out. See "Reporte de la Segunda Conferencia Annual," IWO, April 25, 1937 JCP, Box 18, Folder 5,

and "Report," JCP, Box 18, Folder 7. El Club Mella also attracted local members, including those from La Alianza Obrera Puertorriqueña and the Ateneo Obrero Hispano de Nueva York, both founded in the 1920s. JCP, Box 1, Folder 5. Primary sources list La Alianza Obrera Puertorriqueña as being founded in 1923 and El Ateneo Obrero Hispano de Nueva York in 1926. It also lists the address of El Ateneo Obrero as 62 East 106th Street. See Box 3, Folder 9 for related information on both clubs.

110 *Fifteenth Anniversary Almanac: International workers Order, 1930–1945*. Box 1, Folder 5: Guide to the IWO Records 1930–1956 (Bulk 1940–1951).

111 This is the most exact date for El Club Julio Antonio Mella's founding. The date is listed on a banner in a photograph of El Club de Damas. The banner reads "Branch 4763 Julio A. Mella, Org. February 1932, New York City." The photograph is included in "Primer Baile Aniversario Logia 4763, Julio A. Mella, Sábado 20 de Mayo, 1939." JCP, Box 17, File 3. The early dating is confirmed by both Suárez Díaz in *Escapé de Cuba*, who dates the club's founding to the late 1920s; and in a report drafted by Jesús Colón that dates the founding of the Spanish section of the IWO as March 31, 1931. JCP, Box 18, File 7. As one of many lodges that were part of the Spanish section, El Club Julio Antonio Mella could not have been organized before March 31, 1931.

112 "Reporte de la Segunda Conferencia Annual," presentado por César Fuentes Srio, Comité Nacional Sección Hispana, IWO, April 25, 1937, New York City. JCP, Box 18, Folder 5. Quote in the OHMA (1995). La Liga Puertorriqueña Inc. also supported the protest against the Machado administration. See flyer for talk given by Edgardo Buttari, "La Nueva Generación Cubana y el Regimen de Machado," (n.d.) JCP, Box 16, Folder 8.

113 Abraham Lincoln Brigade Archive. IWO Records, Taimement/Robert F. Wagner Labor Archives.

114 Hooks, *Tina Modotti: Photographer and Revolutionary*, 172–177. Modotti and Mella were in a relationship and lived together in Mexico City. According to Hooks, Mella bled to death in Modotti's arms. Modotti was interrogated and initially implicated in his death. The Mexican police entered the apartment she shared with Mella and confiscated photos of Mella, letters, and all personal papers and documents.

115 OHMA (1995), (2002), (2012). According to Alvarado, her father arrived at the US Consulate in Cuba and told them he was a Puerto Rican national who was being threatened by the Cuban government. The US Consulate put Alvarado on the next boat and paid for his passage from Havana to New York. The Cafe Bustelo Roasting Company was located at 1364 Fifth Avenue and the Valencia Bakery was next door at 1365 Fifth Avenue. See advertisements for businesses in the CCI Boletin Oficial, December 1947. CCI Records, SCM.

116 Passenger and Crew Lists of Vessels Arriving at New York, New York, 1897–1957; (National Archives Microfilm, Publication T715, 8892 Rolls) records of the Immigration and Naturalization Service; National Archives, Washington, DC. I am

grateful to Miriam Jiménez Román for generously providing me with this document. Certificate of Identity and Registration for Mariana Mejias Alvarado, May 28, 1936; American Consular Services (copy provided to me by Melba Alvarado); OHMA (1995), (2002). Luis Alvarado was born in Puerto Rico and then moved to Cuba when he was five. Because he was Puerto Rican, his family members are all listed as naturalized citizens. The address of the dry-cleaning business at 1359 Fifth Avenue was provided by Melba Alvarado and cross-referenced with local directory records located at the New York Public Library.

117 Suárez Díaz, Escapé de Cuba, 206.

118 Cited in "Reporte de la Segunda Conferencía Anual," presented by César Fuentes, member of the National Committee of the Hispanic Section of the International Workers' Order, April 25th, 1937 in New York City. El Club Mella was one of the lodges, "logias," under the Hispanic Section. JCP, Box 18, Folder 5.

119 Elizabet Rodríguez and Idania Trujillo, "Voluntarios de la libertad: Las voces de la memoria" (Alicante, Biblioteca Virtual, Miguel de Cervantes, 2005), Edición digital a partir de la literature COU y la cultura del exilio republicano español de 1937, 7. In Suárez Díaz's Escapé de Cuba, there is a photo of Bolaños carrying the Cuban flag, 532.

120 Suárez Díaz, Escapé de Cuba, 455–458. According to Torriente Brau, marchers included those from Puerto Rico, Mexico, Cuba, Spain, Venezuela, Chile, Argentina, Dominican Republic, Colombia, Ecuador, Peru, El Salvador, Honduras, Guatemala, Brazil, Nicaragua, Haiti, Costa Rica, Paraguay, Uruguay, Bolivia, Portugal, and Panama. Organizations that marched included: Club Martí, Joven Trinitaria, Club Mella, Comité Pro-Puerto Rico, Club Obrero Español, Club Tampa, Consejo de Desempleados, Local No. 1, Sección del Partido Comunista, Circulo Cubano, Asociación Patriótica Venezolano, Perla del Sur Social Club Inc., and Mutualista Obrera Mejico.

121 Suárez Díaz, Escapé de Cuba, 533–534.

122 Bolaños left for Spain with Rodolfo de Armas, Angel Ruffo, and Rodolfo Rodríguez. He mentioned that Cubans fought alongside US troops. He was in combat in February 1937 under James W. Ford, who later headed the Harlem Communist Party and was one of the highest ranking African Americans in the Communist Party. See Rodríguez and Trujillo, "Voluntarios de la libertad: Las voces de la memoria," 7. For more on the Cuban Section (Centuria Antonio Guiteras), see Fernando Vera Jiménez, "Cubanos en la Guerra Civil Española. La presencia de voluntarios en las Brigadas Internacionales y el Ejército Popular de la República," Revista Complutense de Historia de América, 1999, 25: 295–321.

123 Names were cross-referenced with those listed in la Sección Cubana (Centuria Antonio Guiteras) of El Club Julio Antonio Mella in Vera Jiménez's "Cubanos en la Guerra Civil Española, 306, with the list of founders of El Club Cubano Inter-Americano, "Lista de Fundadores, 17, Septiembre de 1945," CCI Records, SCM Box 5, Folder 1, and JCP Box 17, Folder 3. For instance, Ricardo Gómez Oliva was

the treasurer of El Club Mella. I further referenced these names with those in the Abraham Lincoln Brigade Archives (ALBA).

124 Antonio Guiteras was one of Mella's allies, a proponent of revolutionary social-ism, and participant in the radical government installed after the overthrow of Gerardo Machado. Guiteras was named Minister of the Interior under President Ramón Grau San Martín. After the "government of 100 days," Guiteras became even more radical and founded Joven Cuba in 1934, an organization inspired by anti-capitalism and anti-imperialism. Guiteras was a US citizen born in 1906 to a Cuban father and English mother in Pennsylvania. He was killed on May 8, 1935 in Matanzas. Richard Gott, *Cuba: A New History* (New Haven: Yale University Press, 2004), 135–141.

125 "Plan de Trabajo Para El Segundo Medio del 1936," especially the section "Apuntes Para La Campaña Por Miembros" for more on how the Sección Hispana, which included El Club Mella, organized around the Spanish Civil War. JCP, Box 18, Folder 5. Suárez Díaz also references Rodolfo de Armas.

126 Rodríguez and Trujillo, "Voluntarios de la libertad: Las voces de la memoria," 7.

127 *New Masses* (1926–1948) was the premier Marxist magazine associated with the Communist Party in the United States. *El Machete Criollo* was published in New York during the late 1920s.

128 Pablo de la Torriente Brau, *Aventuras del soldado desconocido cubano*, has since been reprinted by the Centro Cultural Pablo de la Torriente Brau, in 2000. Those in attendance at the founding of ORCA included Raúl Roa, Carlos Martinez, Alberto Samvell, Álvaro Soto, and Pablo de la Torriente Brau, who was secretary of the club. *Frente Único* lasted from October 1935 to February 1936. Suárez Díaz, *Escapé de Cuba*, 208–209 and 322.

129 Suárez Díaz, *Escapé de Cuba*, 176. Suárez Díaz notes that Torriente Brau gave a speech on July 1, 1935 at El Club Mella entitled, "The Triumph and Defeat of Cuban Revolutions," 57.

130 Ibid., 27, 37.

131 Ibid., 1–6. Since Torriente Brau was born in Puerto Rico, it was easy for him to migrate back and forth. He would not return to Cuba. He left for Spain in August 1936 and was killed on December 19, 1936.

132 Suárez Díaz, *Escapé de Cuba*, 140.

133 For information on Angel Garcia and Basilio Cueria y Obrit, see Abraham Lincoln Brigade Archives (ALBA). James D. Fernández and Sebastian Faber, *The Volunteer*, Founded by the Veterans of Abraham Lincoln Brigade, "Mystery Photo: Gift to Obama puts ALBA in the Spotlight," March 26, 2010. In this piece the authors discuss the Afro-Cuban members of El Club Julio Antonio Mella who fought in the Spanish Civil War. The article centers on one particular photo as-sumed to be of an African American male, but whom, it turns out, is Afro-Cuban.

134 OHMA (2002).

135 "Report," JCP, Box 18, Folder 7.

136 The "Plan de Trabajo para el segundo medio del 1936" outlines the aim of the IWO to recruit Spanish-speaking immigrants using lodges organized under the Spanish section. "Reporte de la Segunda Conferencia," 1–2. The report counted from 200 to 500 members who belonged to youth logias. I did not include the number of children in the overall membership. Both documents in the JCP, Box 18, Folder 5.

137 For copies of the *Fraternal Outlook Magazines Guide*, see IWO Records 1930–1956 (Bulk 1940–1951). Tamiment Library/Robert Wagner Labor Archives.

138 In "Reporte de la Segunda Conferencia," on the first page of a letter dated February 16, 1938, New York City, the leaders of the Hispanic Section of the IWO (César Fuentes, Jesús Colón and Amparo López), list the five major problems with the logias: acute sectarianism; the lack of an expansive cultural life; the lack of political incentives outside of the political conferences; the lack of effective participation in the immediate problems of our members and of workers in general; the lack of stability among the mass membership. Box 18, Folder 5, JCP.

139 "Report," Box 18, Folder 7, JCP, p. 4; and "Plan de Trabajo para el segundo medio del 1936," Box 18, Folder 5, JCP.

140 Reporte de la Segunda Conferencia, February 16, 1938 NYC. López served along with César Fuentes and Jesús Colón. Morales was one of five delegates listed as Spanish out of 400 who went to the IWO convention in 1938. She was an outspoken critic of Franco and is featured in "Women at the Convention," where she provided a "heroic account of the Spanish women in their fight against fascism." *The New Order: Official Organ: International Worker's Order*, January 1938. IWO Records, 1930–1956, Tamiment Library/Robert Wagner Labor Archives.

141 "Nuestro Club de Damas," (1938). Box 18, Folder 5, JCP.

142 Josefina Q. Cepeda, "Nuestro Club de Damas," (1938). Box 18, Folder 5, JCP.

143 Ibid. It is important to note that in a document entitled "Convención de la Sección Hispana de la IWO," dated June 8–13, 1940, there is a brief reference to a column written by Colón in *Fraternal Outlook* where he requests that "white women cooperate more with black women." There is also a statement by López confirming her difficulty with organizing women, noting that there are "impassable barriers" to getting women to attend meetings and be more involved in the club and IWO. López's concerns are refuted by "brother Coca" who argues that the lack of participation has more to with female members being older and having too many obligations." Box 4, Folder 5, JCP.

144 Henry Glintenkamp, 1887–1946, *Ash Can Years to Expressionism: Paintings and Drawings, 1908–1939* (March 25–May 16, 1981), Special Collections, NYPL. Glintenkamp traveled to Mexico in 1917 and from 1919–1920 was the editor of the English section of *El Heraldo de Mexico*. He moved to England in 1922–23, traveled throughout Europe, and returned to the United States in the early 1930s. He died in New York in 1946.

145 Dennis Henderson, *Three Hundred Years of American Art in Chrysler Museum*, Exhibit Catalog, Norfolk VA, 1975, 192.

146 According to a hand-written letter by Jesús Colón dated October 24, El Club Mella (lodge number 4763) was consolidated with other logias under the "Hispanic section" of the IWO. There is another document dated July 15, 1940 that refers to the pending dissolution of several lodges, including El Club Mella. In "Libretas para las Actas del Comite de la Cuidad," it states that "Isabel López informed members that El Club Obrero Español had been dissolved and consolidated with lodges 4788, 4763 (El Club Mella), 4798, 4827, 4830, 4831, and 4832." Box 4, Folder 7, JCP. Finally, in a document entitled "Conferencia Distrial de la Sección Hispana de IWO en la cuidad de Nueva York dated February 24–25, 1940," lodge 4763 is mentioned confirming that it existed in 1940. However, by 1941 lodge 4763 does not appear in the records. Box 4, Folder 5, JCP.

147 Sabin, *Red Scare in Court*. On April 3, 1947, the US Attorney General's List of Subversive Organizations was drawn up at the request of US Attorney General Tom C. Clark. It greatly expanded the list first compiled by US Attorney General Francis Biddle. Under Clark the list of organizations increased to 90.

148 CCI, "Proyecto de Reglamento," Capitulo I De la Institucíon, Articulo I. CCI Records, Box 1, Folder 1, SCM. There is another copy in Box 15, Folder 7, JCP. The Proyecto de Reglamento was approved by the CCI on November 11, 1945 and finalized on November 25, 1945. Thank you to Gema Guevara for her assistance in translating.

149 OHMA (2012). According to Alvarado many of the white members of El Club Mella returned to Cuba, leaving behind Afro-Cubans in New York.

150 Program for "Centenario del Natalico del General Antonio Maceo, 1845–1945," June 18, 1945. SCM 97-7, SCM 07-37, MG 608. Box 5, Folder 14. SCM, Manuscripts, Archives, and Rare Books Division. Also see "Velada Lirico Literaria," Box 15, Folder 7, JCP.

151 CCI *Circular, Acuerdos, y Noticias*, March 12, 1946. Box 15, Folder 7, JCP. The organizing committee, known as the "Consejeros," consisted of 27 members, including Jesús Colón, Rómulo Lachatanere, Anacleto Romero, Lalita Zamora Parodi, Generoso and Carmen Pedroso, and Jesus Solis. In addition to the "Consejeros," there were two presidents, three vice presidents, a secretary, a vice secretary, treasurer, vice treasurer, and correspondent. Almost all of the names are listed as founders of the CCI, and some have direct connections to El Club Mella. See "Centenario del Natalico del General Antonio Maceo, 1845–1945." June 18, 1945. Box 5, Folder 14, SCM. In her interviews, Alvarado confirmed that the CCI was organized as a direct result of white Cubans refusing to work with Afro-Cubans in organizing the Cenntenial. OHMA (2002), (2012).

152 CCI *Circular, Acuerdos, y Noticias*, March 12, 1946. Box 15, Folder 7, JCP. "Meeting Notices, 1946," Box 1, Folder 3. CCI Records, SCM. In her oral histories Melba Alvarado cited El Club Ateneo Cubano de New York located at 2824 Broadway as an example of a club that did not offer formal membership to Afro-Cubans. OHMA, (1995), (2002), (2012).

153 CCI *Circular, Acuerdos, y Noticias*, March 12, 1946. Box 15, Folder 7, JCP and "Meeting Notices, 1946," CCI Records, SCM, Box 1, Folder 3. The address listed on the *Circular, Acuerdos, y Noticias*, March 12, 1946, matches Julio and Francisca Cardenal's address listed on the CCI membership list dated February 22, 1946. Box 3, Folder 3. This confirms that the first meeting on September 17th was at the home of Julio and Francisca Cardenal. Moreover, according to Melba Alvarado, September 17th was the birthday of Francisca Cardenal, which further explains why the members were at their home. OHMA (2012).

154 "Proyecto de Reglamento, Box 1, Folder 1; "Junta General de Elecciónes, Citación," December 27, 1945; "Certificate of Incorporation, 1946," Box 1, Folder 2; "Meeting Notice, 1946, Box 1 Folder 3; "Minutes, 1949–1952," Box 3, Folder 3. All located in the CCI Records, SCM.

155 JDMM, March 31, 1949. JDMM, discuss funding benefits for members. Also see "Articulos del Socorro Mutuos." Box 1A, Folder 2. CCI Records, SCM.

156 "Saludo," Programa de Gala, Baile Final. 1946–47, CCI Records, Box 5, Folder 14, SCM.

157 "Document introducing the club and celebrating Columbus Day." Box 15, Folder 7, JCP.

158 "Lista de Fundadores," "Relaciones de Socios Fundadores" and CCI "Tesoreria" (February 22, 1946). CCI Records, Box 1, Folder 8, SCM.

159 CCI, "Viajando," *El Boletin Mensual*, August, 1947, 7. CCI Records, Box 5, Folder 14, SCM.

160 OHMA (2012).

161 Miriam Jiménez Román, "¡Graciela Eso Es Tremendo!: An Afro-Cuban Musician Remembers." Miriam Jiménez Román and Juan Flores, eds., *The AfroLatin@ Reader*, 151.

162 Román and Flores, eds., *The AfroLatin@ Reader*, 150–152.

163 OHMA (1995), (2002), (2012). See Mirabal, "Melba Alvarado, El Club Cubano Inter-Americano and the Creation of Afro-Cubanidades in New York City."

164 OHMA (1995), (2002). Also see Mirabal, "Ser de Aquí: Beyond the Cuban Exile Model," 366–382.

165 OHMA (2012).

166 In regard to religion, it was primarily Santeria that could not be discussed or practiced openly. There were members of the CCI who practiced Santeria, but were not allowed to discuss or disclose it. In an interview given in 1995, Alvarado offers a rare mention of Santeria. "You can have your politics at home, but in the club there are no politics. You can have the religion that you like, like being a member of la Caridad, but here you do not discuss the oddun. And the president had to be Cuban." Catholicism, on the other hand, was considered a unifying marker of Cubanidad and members appeared to have had no problem publicly attending Catholic masses, processions, and celebrations of Catholic saints. OHMA (1995).

167 OHMA (2012).

168 Interview/personal discussion, Melba Alvarado, 2013.

CHAPTER 5. MONUMENTAL DESIRES AND DEFIANT TRIBUTES

1 Michel Rolph Trouillot, *Silencing the Past: Power and the Production of History*, 1.
2 Central Park: José Julian Martí, Official Website of the New York City Department of Parks and Recreation. www.nycgovparks.orgs/parks/central-park/monuments.
3 During my scholar in residency at the Schomburg Center for Research in Black Culture (2012), I had several conversations concerning the monument with members of El Club Cubano Inter-Americano. Some were willing to engage and talk, others preferred to leave it in the past.
4 OHMA (2012).
5 "Trece Años," 1958. CCI Records, Box 5, Folder 13, SCM.
6 The first event honoring Maceo's death was on December 7, 1946. See the Invitational Card from Generoso Pedroso inviting "you and your distinguished family to a commemoration of the death of Antonio Maceo and other martyrs of the Cuban War for Independence." December 7, 1946. In addition to the CCI, El Consul General de la Republica de Cuba celebrated the anniversary of El Grito de Yara at Studio 8-H National Broadcasting Co., 30 Rockefeller Plaza, on October 9, 1946. CCI Records, Box 5, Folder 1, SCM. The CCI celebrated events honoring Maceo for close to 70 years. See CCI Records, SCM, for information concerning the different events over time.
7 CCI JDMM, March 31, 1949, CCI Records, Box 1A, Folder 2, SCM.
8 OHMA (2012).
9 Simón Bolívar Monument, Central Park, New York City Parks, Official website of the New York City Department of Parks and Recreation. www.nycgovparks.orgs/parks/central-park/monuments.
10 Pedroso kept his promise and the CCI organized a banquet in honor of Fernández Rebull. CCI Records, Box 5, Folder 1, Correspondence 1945–1947, SCM. From earlier letters it appears that there was a great interest in building monuments to Maceo in both Havana and New York City.
11 CGMM, *Circular, Acuerdo y Noticias*, January 22, 1946 and February 1, 1946. CCI Records, SCM. According to the *Circular* dated February 1, 1946, The Cena Martiana was held at the Restaurant El Mundial. The name of the vice secretary of El Club Atenas was not printed. JCP, Box 15, Folder 7. According to Melba Alvarado, El Club Atenas was formed by white men a year before the CCI. OHMA (2012).
12 Earlier in the year the club received a number of books for their budding library, including several volumes on the life of Maceo, donated by Suárez Rocabruna. CCI *Circular, Acuerdos y Noticias*, February 1, 1946, JCP, Box 15, Folder 7.
13 CCI, "La Nueva casa-club," *Circular, Acuerdos y Noticias*, May 30, 1946.JCP, Box 15, Folder 7. Also CCI Records, SCM, Box 5, Folder 12.
14 It was customary for barbershops to be seen as meeting places. However, it is important to note that barbershops were distinctly male spaces. CCI "Nueva Direccíon," *Circular, Acuerdos y Noticias*, May 30, 1946. JCP, Box 15, Folder 7. See

Programa de Gala, Baile Final, 1946 for more information on they type of businesses that supported the CCI. CCI Records, Box 5 Folder 14, SCM.

15 "Trece Años" (1958). This brief page documents Pedroso's role as president and his impact on the club. Its title refers to the thirteen years from when he assumed the presidency in 1945 until his death in 1958. CCI Records, Box 5, Folder 13, SCM.

16 JDMM, April 25, 1949. CCI Records, SCM.

17 "Perfiles del Club Cubano Inter-Americano," *Programa de Gala, Baile Final.* 1946. CCI Records, Box 5 Folder 14, SCM.

18 JDMM, April 25, 1949. CCI Records, SCM According to the Minutes of the Meetings, Pedroso attended Romero's funeral and requested that he be recognized for his role as a founding member and acknowledged his close relationship with Romero, who was a past member of El Club Mella.

19 OHMA (2002). The question of religion and the role it played in the club were not discussed or present in the archival sources. Outside of the bylaws and oral histories of Melba Alvarado, it remained a very private part of the CCI.

20 Quote is from OHMA (2012). Alvarado speaks of the club's bylaws and their determination to remain neutral in oral histories conducted in 1995, 2002, 2012. She also briefly discussed religion, stating that they prohibited religion because "it didn't matter if you were Catholic or Protestant, they only cared that you were an upstanding person you could be in the club." When pressed about whether the prohibition of religion had to do with Santería, Alvarado responded to the effect that Santería was not practiced back then.

21 A letter dated November 7, 1945 mentions how the CCI is working with other organizations. One example of the CCI working with labor unions is in the CCI's newsletter dated February 1, 1946, which states that CCI member Enrique Martí will be in charge of S.B. Union, Local 16. CCI *Circular, Acuerdos y Noticias,* February 1, 1946, Box 15, Folder 7, JCP.

22 In the *Programa de Gala, Baile Final,* there are notations detailing who has paid for their "saludos," confirming their role as a source of fund-raising.

23 Since club members were the ones who initiated and accepted the requests, it was unlikely that greetings from an unknown or unfavorable organization, party, or individual would be published in the programs, flyers, and notices.

24 *Programa de Gala, Baile Final,* 1946. CCI Records, Box 5, Folder 14, SCM. According to notations on the program, Pompez had not paid his dues. For more on Pompez, please see Adrian Burgos, *Cuban Star.*

25 *Programa de Gala, Baile Final,* 1946. CCI Records, Box 5, Folder 14, SCM.

26 CCI member Roberto Serrano was also invited. Julio Cardenal CCI, *Circular, Acuerdos, y Noticias,* "Sección de Prensa y Propaganda," September 1946. Box 15, Folder 7, JCP.

27 In her oral history, Alvarado noted that they had, as she put it, a Puerto Rican sentiment. Cited in OHMA (2012). She also refers to the CCI and her close relationship with the Puerto Rican community in OHMA (1995), (2002). In 1962 the

CCI was given a certificate of honor for their work with children in Puerto Rico. CCI Records, Box 1, Folder 14, SCM.

28 JDMM, February 9, 1950. CCI Records, Box 1, Folder 11, SCM. In addition, the CCI assisted with a conference on health in the Puerto Rican community and donated to the Bronx Tuberculosis and Health Committees.

29 Cardenal traveled to Cuba on several occasions. It is likely that there were other trips to Havana that were not noted in the minutes.

30 *Circular*, January 11, 1947, Box 1, Folder 7, JCP. Minutes of the meetings and newsletters mention collaborations with Puerto Ricans and events organized in honor of Betances and Hostos throughout the years. See CCI JDMM, February 9, 1950 and March 31, 1952. CCI Records, SCM. In 1962 the CCI was awarded a certificate of honor by El comité pro-ayuda á niños Lisiados de Puerto Rico. CCI Records, Box 5, Folder 1, SCM.

31 Lista de Fundadores, 17 de septiembre de 1945. CCI Records, Box 1, Folder 8, SCM.

32 CCI *Circular, Acuerdos y Noticias*, March 23, 1946, Box 15, Folder 7, JCP. Letter to Juan Marinello Vidaurreta from Generoso Menendez Pedroso dated January 31, 1946. CCI Records, Box 5, Folder 1, SCM.

33 Letter to Generoso Pedroso from Juan Marinello, February 20, 1946 CCI Records, Box 5, Folder 1, SCM.

34 In 1944, the Communist Party reorganized and changed its name to the Popular Socialist Party. After being rejected by the newly elected president of Cuba, Ramón Grau San Martín, the Communist Party turned to Batista and made a deal with him. If Batista allowed them to organize, they would offer him the political support he needed. Batista accepted the deal. Marinello was at the center of these negotiations See Pérez, Jr., *Cuba: Between Reform and Revolution*, 288; and Gott, *Cuba: A New History*, 143–144.

35 Letter from Jesús Colón to members of the Cervantes Fraternal Society, IWO, April 19, 1946. Box 15, Folder 7, JCP. Letter from Narciso Saavedra to Fulgencio Batista Zaldivar, March 27, 1946 (It appears that Batista did not attend the Marinello event). Letter from Narciso Saavedra to William Z. Foster, (n.d.). Letter from William Z. Foster to Narciso Saavedra, April 2, 1946, CCI Records, Box 5, Folder 1.

36 CCI *Circular, Acuerdos, y Noticias*, August 17, 1946. Box 15, Folder 7 and "Voz de Marinello" por José Ferrer, May 31, 1946, Box 15, Folder 7, JCP. The event sponsored by the Comité Latinoamericano de Acción Cívica took place on April 12, at the Tom Mooney Hall of the Local 65. Letter to Jesús Colón from Juan Marinello, March 2, 1946. Box 3, Folder 3, JCP.

37 "Voz de Marinello" por José Ferrer, May 31, 1946, Box 15, Folder 7, JCP. CCI Sección de Prensa y Propaganda, *Circular, Acuerdos, y Noticias*, April 14, 1946, 2. Box 15, Folder 7, JCP.

38 CCI Sección de Prensa y Propaganda, *Circular, Acuerdos, y Noticias*, April 14, 1946, 2. Box 15, Folder 7, JCP. After his visit, Marinello sent the CCI a folder of photos and newspaper clippings of his visit to New York, a copy of his speech

given at the Manhattan Center, and a copy of "Acta Histórica de la Invasión," which detailed the history of Cuba from 1896 to 1946. The folders have not been recovered and are not part of the CCI Archives. Cited in CCI, "Sección de Prensa y Propaganda," *Circular, Acuerdos y Noticias*, August 17, 1946. Box 15, Folder 7, JCP.

39 In 1944 the Communist Party was dissolved and renamed the Communist Political Association. Ford served as the previous leader of the Communist Party in Harlem, past vice presidential candidate for the Communist Party, and past central committee of the Communist Party. He ran several times for president on the Communist ticket. The last was in 1940. For more on the Communist Party in Harlem during this period, see Naison, *Communists in Harlem During the Depression*.

40 CCI Sección de Prensa y Propaganda, *Circular, Acuerdos, y Noticias*, April 14, 1946, p. 2. Box 15, Folder 7, JCP.

41 Rocabruna is listed as a dues-paying member in the CCI's Treasurer's Report, July 1947. Also see CCI Boletín Mensual, 1947. CCI Records, Box 3, Folder 3, SCM. According to Frank Guridy, it was during this period that Howard University hosted an exhibition of sculptor Teodoro Ramos Blanco, who provided Howard University with a bust of Antonio Maceo. Guridy, *Forging Diaspora*, 180.

42 In addition to extending invitations to CCI members to meet his colleagues at Howard University, Rocabruna also invited the members to meet with the International Committee of the National Council of Negro Women. CCI *Circular, Acuerdos y Noticias*, March 12, 1946. Box 15, Folder 7, JCP.

43 CCI JDMM, July 13, 1950. The members read a letter from the CCI in Washington, DC, and shared photos that the DC members sent honoring the creation and incorporation of the CCI club in Washington, DC. They also shared photos of the members visiting the murals in the city. CCI Records, Box 1, Folder 11, SCM.

44 CCI JDMM, May 12, 1950. There are several references to a CCI club in Washington, DC. See Minutes for June 26, 1949, July 13, 1950, and August 7, 1950, Box 1, Folder 11, SCM. The CCI in DC was different from the Cuban-American Good Will Association. Although they worked closely together, it appears that the CCI in DC had been formally incorporated as early as 1949 and no later than 1950. Sergio "Henry" Grillo was Evelio Grillo and Sylvia Griñan Grillo's older brother. Evelio Grillo is best known for his memoir *Black Cuban, Black American*. See Guridy, *Forging Diasporas*, 184.

45 CCI Sección the Prensa y Propaganda, *Circular, Acuerdos y Noticias*, May 30, 1946. CCI Records, Box 3, Folder 3, SCM. Rocabruna was well-known among the African American community for forging positive relationships between African Americans and Cubans. He had close relationships with African American scholars, activists, and politicians. In the CCI's *Circular, Acuerdos y Noticias*, March 12, 1946, makes mention of Rocabruna being honored at the Blair House by the Division of Cultural Cooperation at the State Department on February 27, 1946. In attendance were the President and Dean of Liberal Arts of Howard University, Box 15, Folder 7, JCP.

46 "Barring of Cuban Negro by State Department Assailed, *Chicago Defender,* August 14, 1943. As the article indicates there was a relationship between African American and Afro-Cuban communists and labor organizers. The National Negro Congress was formed in 1935 at Howard University and was an outgrowth of the Joint Committee on National Recovery Conference in May 1935. For more details see Naison, *Communists in Harlem During the Depression.*

47 Flyer, "Defensa de Madrid: Decimo Aniversario. CCI Records, Box 3. Folder 3, SCM.

48 CCI Sección de Prensa y Propaganda, Boletín Oficial," November 1946. Box 15, Folder 7, JCP.

49 CCI *Circular,* March 12, 1946, CCI Records, Box 15, Folder 7, JCP. Also see Mirabal, "Scripting Race, Finding Place."

50 Letter to Dr. Ramón Grau San Martín, President of the Cuban Republic. CCI Records, March 11, 1946. Box 5, Folder 1, SCM.

51 OHMA (1995). In past articles and book chapters, I discuss the racial tensions and separations among US Cuban migrants. Mirabal, "Scripting Race, Finding Place."

52 CCI CGMM, December 22, 1945 mentions that members will be organizing a committee "Pro-Monumento Maceo" to build a monument to Antonio Maceo. CCI Records, Box 1, Folder 1, SCM. In her oral histories, Melba Alvarado discussed the racism within the Cuban community and toward building a monument to Maceo. OHMA (1995), (2002), (2012).

53 CCI *Circular,* "A proposito de la función del día." July 1947, Box 15, Folder 7, JCP. According to minutes of the meeting, Calá was member of El Comité Pro-monumento Martí y Maceo. According to Melba Alvarado, "talk" of Maceo being eliminated from the monument was evident early in the process and was one of the main reasons that CCI members worked so hard to ensure that Maceo be included. Informal discussions with Mirabal (2012, 2013).

54 CCI *Boletín Mensual* "Viajando," August 1947. CCI Records, Box 3, Folder 3. SCM.

55 In addition to signaling the inclusion of Martí, the use of the word "permanent" in the name change conveyed the committee's resolve that a monument would eventually be built. Letter to Jesús Colón from Narciso Saavedra, October 1, 1947. Box 2, Folder 7, JCP. The letter was addressed to Colón and the Cervantes Fraternal Society of the IWO.

56 Boletín, November 1947. CCI Records, Box 3, Folder 3, Box 1, Folder 7, JCP. In a letter to Pedroso dated November 15, 1945, Fernández Rebull had already promised to do everything in his power to assist with building the monument. In the minutes of the meetings, members of El Comité Permanente Pro-Monumento a Martí y Maceo mention that they had asked Fernández Rebull to speak with officials concerning a specific location in Central Park. CCI Records, Box 5, Folder 1, SCM.

57 CCI JDMM, March 7, 1949. Box 1, Folder 11, SCM.

58 The members were concerned that their rent would increase from $100.00 to $125 a month. The CCI signed a new lease for three years for $125.00 a month (from

June 1, 1949 to May 30, 1952). JDMM, March 31, 1949, April 25, 1949, and May 2, 1949. Box 1, Folder 11, SCM.

59 JDMM, March 31, 1949. CCI Records, Box, 1, Folder 11, SCM. Mutual Aid benefits appeared to have been phased out by the mid-1950s.

60 JDMM, March 14, 1949. CCI Records, Box 1, Folder 11, SCM.

61 JDMM, March 31, 1949. CCI Records, Box 1, Folder 11, SCM. In the JDMM, August 7, 1950, there is mention of throwing a party to support the Comité Pro-monumento. It was suggested that Tito Rodríguez perform. Box 1, Folder 11, SCM.

62 JDMM, June 6, 1949. CCI Records, Box 1, Folder 11, SCM. There is nothing in the minutes that explains why the members decided to use the bylaws to refuse the Communist Party's invitation or if any members present disagreed with de la Paz's motion. What is clear is that from all accounts, it appears to have been a unanimous decision.

63 In the *Programa de Gala*, Francisco J. de la Paz is listed as part of the CCI board of directors of 1946. Interestingly enough, he was named president of the Moral Section. CCI Records, Box 5, Folder 14, SCM.

64 Gott, *Cuba: A New History*, p. 145.

65 Sweig, *Inside the Cuban Revolution*, 5. Also quoted in Gott, *Cuba: A New History*, 145, and Pérez, Jr., *Between Reform and Revolution*, 420.

66 JDMM, June 6, 1949. CCI Records, Box 1, Folder 11, SCM. In the minutes of the meetings the members refer to someone known as "Besa la Mano" (kiss the hand), in Cuba. It is clear that the members do not want those outside of the CCI to know who or what they are referring to in the minutes.

67 JDMM, June 6, 1949. The banquet for Kid Gavilán was almost canceled due to a boxing match. See JDMM, April 18 and April 25, 1949 for more on Gavilán. CCI Records Box 1, Folder 11, SCM.

68 CCI JDMM, December 12, 1949. Since the CCI had already purchased a bust of Martí and Maceo, they wanted it to be part of the proposed monument. CCI Records, Box 1, Folder 11, SCM.

69 CCI JDMM, December 12, 1949; January 5, 1950. CCI Records, Box 1, Folder 11, SCM.

70 CCI JDMM, March 29, 1951; June 30, 1951; March 31, 1952. CCI Records, Box 1A, Folder 2. SCM.

71 CCI JDMM, April 12, 1951, Box 1, Folder 11, SCM.

72 CCI JDMM, February 14, 1952 and March 14, 1952, respectively. There are also indications that the Comité Hispano Bronx and President Batista had expressed support for the monument to Martí and Maceo. CCI JDMM, June 30, 1951. Box 1, Folder 11. SCM.

73 OHMA (1995), (2012). The cost of mounting the Centenario to Martí impacted the club's finances for months. In the JDMM dated July 1, 1953, the members note that there are "no funds," and discuss ways to raise money. There also appears to be another reason for the lack of funds. There is talk that the current treasurer had stolen and gambled away all of their money. The treasurer was "thrown out

into the street." JDMM, July 1, 1953. CCI Records, Box 1, Folder 11, SCM. Souvenir: Comité Pro-Centenario del Natalico de Apóstol José Martí, Carnegie Hall, West 57th Street, New York City, January 28, 1853–January 28, 1953. Box 5, Folder 2. CCI 50 Aniversario Program, 1945–1995 (in author's possession).

74 OHMA (1995). Quoted in Mirabal, "Melba Alvarado, El Club Cubano Inter-Americano, and the Creation of Afro Cubanidades in New York City." Jiménez Román and Flores, eds., *The Afro-Latina/o Reader*. Thank you to Miriam Jiménez Román for translating this passage.

75 "Como Conservarse Joven," *Para Ellas, Lealo Hoy y Recuerdelo Mañana. Circular* November 1947, Box 15, Folder 7, JCP.

76 Thirty women are listed as founders of the CCI. There are a total of 134 names listed. El Comité de Damas is the term used in archival records. In her oral history Alvarado referred to it as El Club de Damas. The terms were used interchangeably.

77 Guridy, *Forging Diasporas*, 183.

78 CCI Sección de Prensa y Propaganda, *Circular, Acuerdos y Noticias*, September 1946. Box 15, Folder 7, JCP.

79 Valdés and Cardenal are listed as founders of the club. Lista de Fundadores. CCI Records, Box 1, Folder 8, SCM.

80 Alvarado noted that many of the women who left did so for economic reasons and as such the club had to respond to issues relating to getting a job. OHMA (2002), (2012).

81 CCI JDMM, March 31, 1949. Close to a year later the CCI purchased a sewing machine. CCI JDMM, Meeting, March 26, 1950. Box 1, Folder 11, CCI Records, SCM.

82 CCI JDMM, March 31, 1949 and CCI Boletín Mensual, February and March 1950. CCI Records, Box 1, Folder 11, SCM. These classes were available throughout most of the 1950s.

83 Census data show an overall increase in migration from the Caribbean to New York after World War II. Because these were considered temporary visas, data concerning the specific migration of Cuban women using B-29 visas during this period are imprecise. Historical Census Statistics on the Foreign Born Population in the United States, 1850–2000, NYPL.

84 OHMA (2002).

85 A sponsor refers to individuals who are willing to take full responsibility for a migrant who may be liable to be a public charge to the United States. First introduced in the Immigration Act of 1882, anyone considered a "public charge" to the US government could be deported. Several monographs speak to the politics and realities of public charge. See Mai Ngai, *Impossible Subjects: Illegal Aliens and the Making of Modern America* (Princeton: Princeton University Press, 2005) and Natalia Molina, *Fit to Be Citizens?: Public Health and Race in Los Angeles, 1879–1939* (Berkeley: University of California Press, 2006).

86 According to Alvarado, it was not difficult to get your residency as long as you had someone who was willing to sponsor you and/or provide you with employment. She also refers to the politics of public charge. OHMA (1995), (2002), (2012).

and Oral History of Lydia 'Tata" Caraballosa (2000). Caraballosa worked in the garment industry in New York and noted the high rate of Cuban women hired to work in the factories. See Mirabal, "Scripting Race and Finding Place," for more on Cuban women migration and B-29 visas.

87 Memos dated January 3, 1950; August 13, 1952; August 27, 1953; and September 4, 1953 respectively. "Puerto Ricans in New York: Preserving Identity," Reel 115, Box 244, Folder 1–7 (January, 1950–1955), CPRS

88 OHMA (2012). On April 26, 1957 the Comité de Damas celebrated her presidency with a party.

89 OHMA (1995).

90 OHMA (2012). As noted earlier, Francisca Cardenal was the CCI's first female president, having been elected in 1954.

91 OHMA (2002).

92 OHMA (2012). Mirabal, "Melba Alvarado, El Club Cubano Inter-Americano, and the Creation of Afro Cubanidades in New York City."

93 *El Diario de Nueva York*, April 29, 1957. CCI Records, Box 5, Folder 14, SCM. OHMA (1995), (2012). Mirabal, "Melba Alvarado, El Club Cubano Inter-Americano, and the Creation of Afro Cubanidades in New York City."

94 Alvarado referenced the shift to Martí in her oral history 2012. In regard to newspapers, see *La Prensa*, April 30, 1956. CPRS.

95 There is no one exact date when El Comité disbanded. By 1956–57, the CCI JDMM no longer references El Comité Pro-Monumento Martí y Maceo.

96 From the 1970s onward more women were elected president of the club. Ana González, for instance, was elected in 1977. CCI Records, Box 1, Folder 2; Box 5, Folder 16.

97 Brady, *Extinct Lands, Temporal Geographies: Chicana Literature and the Urgency of Space*, 8.

98 Jiménez Román, "¡Graciela Eso Es Tremendo!: An Afro-Cuban Musician Remembers," 150–152.

99 OHMA (2012).

100 Ibid. That same year Alvarado brought Celia Cruz to El Teatro Puerto Rico. *El Diario de Nueva York* reported on the upcoming concert and Alvarado's "romance amoroso . . . con el Club." *El Diario de Nueva York*, April 29, 1957. CCI Records, Box 5, Folder, 14. SCM.

101 OHMA (1995), (2012).

102 Personal conversation with Melba Alvarado. Also see Mirabal, "Melba Alvarado, El Club Cubano Inter-Americano, and the Creation of Afro Cubanidades in New York City." In the CCI Records, JDMM, March 31, 1952, members discuss that it was not only difficult to get Rodríguez to pay his dues, but he also owed the club members money. Pedro Soublette was tasked with getting Rodríguez to pay. Apparently, Rodríguez told CCI member Joaquin Maldonado not to bother. It appears that they were not able to get Rodríguez to pay his dues. Instead, they opted to have him play at the club. See CCI Minutes of the Meeting, May 14, 1952.

103 David García, *Arsenio Rodríguez and the Transnational Flows of Latin Popular Music* (Philadelphia: Temple University Press, 2006), and Christina Abreu, *Rhythms of Race: Cuban Musicians and the Making of Latino New York City and Miami, 1940–1960* (Chapel Hill: University of North Carolina Press, 2015).

104 These include politician Juan Marinello Vidaureta, consul general Reinaldo Fernández Rebull, poet Enrique Martí Rossell, writer Rómulo Lachatanere, and scholar Angel Suárez Rocabruna. Past members of El Club Mella include Jesús Colón, Basilio Cueria y Obrit, Frank Díaz, Ricardo Gómez, Isidro Martínez, Anacleto Romero, and Cristina and Ernesto Knowles. The list includes 134 names and is a snapshot of the different figures and communities that influenced the founding of the CCI.

105 CCI JDMM, January 25, 1951 and April 12, 1951. Box 1, Folder 11. CCI Records, SCM.

106 In regard to Socarras, see JDMM, Box 1 Folder 11. SCM.

107 Brady, *Extinct Lands, Temporal Geographies*, 7.

108 Ibid., 7–8.

109 The CCI records list a number of such examples. For instance, Rodríguez often rehearsed at the club. JDMM, April 14, 1952 CCI Records, Box 1, Folder 11, SCM.

110 OHMA (2012).

111 The CCI recognized César Romero. He was made an honorary member of the CCI in 1950. CCI, JDMM, March 26, 1950, Box 1, Folder 11, SCM. For more information on those that were honored, see CCI Records, primarily boxes 1, 3, 5, 6 SCM.

112 Deborah R. Vargas, *Dissonant Divas: The Limits of La Onda in Chicana Music* (Minneapolis: University of Minnesota Press, 2012), 1.

113 CCI Records, Box 5, Folder 13, SCM.

114 OHMA (2012).

EPILOGUE

1 Elizabeth Kostova, *The Historian* (New York: Back Bay Books, Little Brown and Company, 2005),660..

2 A good example was La Fiesta del Mamoncillo or Recordando el Mamoncillo, which Alvarado partly founded in 1969 and was inspired by the Cuban radio shows she listened to as a young girl in New York. The music shows would be broadcast from different salons and venues known as El Mamoncillo, la Tropical. Years later when she traveled to Havana, she had someone take her to one of those venues to dance and listen to music. OHMA (2012).

3 OHMA (2012). Interestingly enough, Alvarado mentions that Ginebra's wife was "furious" with her and refused to speak to her for cancelling the event. There were several other incidents where members and the club were threatened, slandered in local newspapers, and excluded from cultural events.

4 OHMA (2012).

5 Conversation with Jo-Ana Moreno, September 18, 2015. New York City.

6 OHMA (2012).

7 On December 22, 1977, 55 members of the first brigade returned to Cuba and were welcomed by the Cuban Institute of Friendship (ICAP). This was known as the Antonio Maceo Brigades.

8 Scholars have separated the Cuban exile migration into four distinct waves: (1959–1962, Cuba's elite); (1965–1974, reunification); (1980, Mariel Boatlift); and (1991–1994, Balseros). See Silvia Pedraza, "Cuba's Revolution and Exile," *Journal of International Institute* 5, 1 (Winter 1998). Also see works by Alejandro Portes, Maria de los Angeles Torres, Marifeli Pérez Stable, Lisandro Pérez, Guillermo Grenier, Lillian Guerra, Robert Bach, and Iraida López.

9 Many of these documents were later donated to the Schomburg Center for Research in Black Culture and are now part of the CCI Collection.

BIBLIOGRAPHY

PRIMARY SOURCES

Manuscript and Special Collections

NEW YORK PUBLIC LIBRARY, SCHOMBURG CENTER FOR RESEARCH IN BLACK
CULTURE AND RARE BOOK AND MANUSCRIPT COLLECTION
Arturo Schomburg Collection
El Club Cubano Inter-Americano Papers/Archive
Eusebia Cosme Collection
Henry Highland Garnet Collection
New York Public Library, Manuscripts and Archives Division, Astor, Lenox and Tilden
    Foundations, New York, NY
Moses Taylor Papers
New York City Census Data
Directory of Cigar Factories of New York City: The Cigar Makers and Packers Unions
    of New York (under the Jurisdiction of the Cigar Makers' International Union of
    America, New York, 1894)
Fiorello La Guardia Papers
Vito Marcoantonio Papers

NEW YORK HISTORICAL SOCIETY, MANUSCRIPT COLLECTIONS
Inventario general del archivo de la delegación del Partido Revolucionario Cubano en
    Nueva York (1892–1898) Tomo 1.
Association for the Benefit of Colored Orphans Records, 1836–1972 (MS24)
Association for the Relief of Respectable, Aged, Indigent Females in New York City,
    1813–1883 (MS 801)
Ladies Christian Union Records, 1850–1910
New York African Free School Records, 1817–1832 (MS 747)
New York Exchange for Women's Work, 1878–1950 (MS 446)
New York Manumission Society Records, 1785–1849 (MS 1465)
Manuscripts, Lectures, and Addresses, 1809–1957 (NYHS-RG10)
Celebratory and Memorial Events Records, 1854–1954 (NYHS-RG12)
Publications, Editorial Records, 1939–1960 (NYHS-RG17)
Slavery Collection, 1709–1864 (MS 569)

ROBERT F. WAGNER LABOR ARCHIVES, TAMIMENT LIBRARY, NEW YORK
UNIVERSITY, NEW YORK, NY
International Workers Order Papers 1930–1956
The Abraham Lincoln Brigade Papers/Archives
Oral History of the American Left
New York City Immigrant Labor History Project

CENTRO DE ESTUDIOS PUERTORRIQUEÑOS/CENTER FOR PUERTO RICAN
STUDIES, HUNTER COLLEGE, NEW YORK, NY
Jesús Colón Papers
Joaquín Colón Papers
Oscar Rivera Papers
R. Castilla Collection
Labadie Collection, University of Michigan Special Collections, Ann Arbor, MI

US LIBRARY OF CONGRESS, MANUSCRIPTS DIVISION, WASHINGTON, DC
José Ignacio Rodríguez Collection, Division of Documents
Leonard Wood Papers
Booker T. Washington Papers

CUBAN HERITAGE COLLECTION, UNIVERSITY OF MIAMI
Tomás Estrada Palma Collection
Gonzalo de Quesada Collection

UNIVERSITY OF SOUTH FLORIDA
George E. Pizzo Collection

ARCHIVO NACIONAL DE CUBA, HAVANA
Fondo Academia de la Historia de Cuba
Fondo Máximo Gómez
Fondo Partido Revolucionario Cubano (PRC)
Registro de Asociaciónes

Pamphlets, Speeches, Government Publications, and Other Primary Sources
Appleton's American Annual Cyclopaedia: Register of Important Events, 1870. Vol. 10.
    (New York: D. Appleton and Company, 1871), 376–377.
Juan Bellido de Luna. *La anexión de Cuba a los Estados Unidos*. (New York: El Prove-
    nir, 1892).
Emilia Casanova de Villaverde. La Liga de las Hijas de Cuba, "A los cubanos." (1872).
Angel De Loño y Pérez. "Vindicación de los patriotas cubanos mal juzgados por la
    revolución." (del 8 de Febrero de 1870).

Martín Morúa Delgado. "La cuestión obrera," Martín Morúa Delgado, *Obras completas*, III. (La Habana: Edición de la Comisión Nacional Del Centenario de Martín Morúa Delgado, 1957).

Miguel Estorch y Siqués. "Apuntes para la historia sobre la administración del marques de la Pezuela en la isla de Cuba: desde 3 de deciembre hasta 24 de septeimbre de 1854." (Madrid: Imprenta de Manuel Galliano, 1856).

Expedicion Goicouría, Diario de un soldado. (Nassau, 1869).

Henry Highland Garnet. "A Memorial Discourse: Delivered in the Hall of the House of Representatives," Washington, DC, February 12, 1865. With an Introduction by James McCune Smith. (Philadelphia: Joseph M. Wilson, 1865).

"Facts about Cuba, published under the authority of the New York Cuban Junta." (1870).

Sotero Figueroa. "¡Inmortal!: 19 de Mayo del año 1895." *Patria* (June 25, 1895).

Octavius Brooks Frothingham. *Gerrit Smith: A Biography.* (New York: G.P. Putnam's Sons, 1878).

Juan Gualberto Gómez. *La cuestión de Cuba en 1884: Historia y soluciones de los partidos cubanos.* (Madrid: Impresa de A. J. Alaria, 1885).

Juan Gualberto Gómez. "Martí y yo." *Revista cubana. Homenaje a José Martí en el centenario de su nacimiento: "Los que conocieron a Martí."* (La Habana, 1951–52).

Plutarco González. "The Cuban Question and American Policy in the Light of Common Sense." (New York, 1869).

Murat Halstead. *The Story of Cuba: Her Struggles for Liberty; the Causes, Crisis and Destiny of the Pearl of Antilles.* (Chicago: Cuba Libre, 1896).

"Independencia de Cuba. 1821–1869." *Paralelos.* (Nueva York, 1869).

Richard Bureleigh Kimball and Cristóbal Madan. *Cuba and the Cubans; Compromising a History of the Island of Cuba, Its Present, Social, Political and Domestic Condition; Also its Relation to England and the United States.* (New York: Samuel Hueston, George P. Putnam, 1850).

"La anexión de Cuba y los peninsulares residentes en ella." Por un cubano. (New York: Imprenta de J. Mesa, 1853).

Don Lorenzo Allo y Bermúdez. "Domestic Slavery in its Relations with Wealth: An Oration." Pronounced in the Cuban Democratic Athenaeum of New York. January 1, 1854. (New York: W.H. Tinson, Printer and Stereotyper, 24 Beekman Street, 1855).

Memoria de los trabajos realizados por la Sección Puerto Rico del Partido Revolucionaria Cubano, 1895–1898. (New York City, n.d.).

New constitution establishing self-government in the islands of Cuba and Porto Rico: Authorized translation of the preamble and royal decree of November 25th, 1897, pub. in the Official gazette of Madrid (New York: Published at the office of "Cuba," 1898).

Notes about Cuba: Slavery. I. African slave trade. II. Abolition of slavery. III. Inferences from the last presidential message. The revolution. IV. Forces employed by Spain against Cuba V. Condition of the revolution. VI. Spanish anarchy in Cuba. VII. Conclusion. (New York: s.n., 1872).

Gonzalo de Quesada. *Free Cuba: Her Oppression, Struggle for Liberty, History and Condition with Causes and Justifications of the Present War for Independence.* (New York Publishers' Union, 1897).

"Reglamento de la Junta Patriótica de Cubanos de Nueva York." (1870).

"Reglamento de la Sociedad Cubana de Beneficía de Nueva York." (1870).

"Reglamente de la Junta Patriótica de Cubanos de Nueva York." (1870).

"Reglamento de la Sociedad Cubana de Beneficía de Nueva York." (1870).

"Slavery in Cuba: A Report of the Proceedings of the Meetings held at the Cooper Institute, New York City, December 13, 1872," Cuban Anti-Slavery Committee: S. R. Scottron, Chairman; Henry Highland Garnet, Secretary. No. 62 Bowery Room 2 & 3. (New York, 1873).

"Spain, Cuba and the United States. Recognition and the Monroe Doctrine by Americas." (New York, 1870).

J. C. Thrasher. *A preliminary essay on the purchase of Cuba.* (New York: Derby & Jackson, 119 Nassau St. 1859).

Translation of the Law of civil procedure for Cuba and Porto Rico, with annotations, explanatory notes, and amendments made since the American occupation. (Washington, DC: Government Printing Office, 1901).

Enríque José Verona. *Martí y su obra política.* (New York, 1896).

Juan Clemente Zenea. *La revolución en Cuba.* (1868).

Newspapers/Periodicals

US CUBAN MIGRANT PRESSES

La América, New York, 1871

El Avisador Cubano, New York, 1885–1888

El Avisador Hispano-Americano, 1888, 1889

El Boletín de la Revolución, New York, 1868–1869

El Cometa, New York, 1855

El Correo de Nueva York, 1874–1875

Cuba, New York, 1893–1898

Cuba Weekly Herald, New York, 1872

Cuba y América, 1896–1899

El Cuidadano, New York, 1880

Diario Cubano, New York, 1870

La Doctina de Martí, New York, 1896–1898

El Esclavo, Tampa, 1891–1894

El Mulato, New York, 1854

El Oriente, Tampa, 1897

Patria, New York, 1892–1898

El Porvenir, New York 1890–1896

La Prensa, New York, 1918–1960

Revista de Cayo Hueso, Key West, 1897–1898
La Revista de la Florida, Tampa, 1887
El Vigia, Key West, 1897
La Voz, Tampa, 1930s
El Yara, 1878–1898

CUBAN PRESS
Boletín, 1902
La Discusión, 1902–1911
El Figaro, 1898–1912
Juventud, 1924
La Lucha, 1895–1930
Minerva, 1887–1888; 1910–1915
El Nuevo Criollo, 1904
El Productor, 1887–1890

BLACK PRESS
Anti-Slavery Examiner (American Anti-Slavery Society), New York, 1836–1840
Anti-Slavery Reporter (British and Foreign Anti-Slavery Society), London, 1874–1875;
    1896
Chicago Defender, Chicago, 1910–1940
Colored American, New York, 1837–1841
Crisis, New York, 1910–1935
Douglass Monthly, Rochester, NY, 1859–1860
Frederick Douglass' Papers, Rochester, NY, 1851–1859
Freedman's Advocate, Albany, NY, 1842
Freedom's Journal, New York, 1827–1829
Liberator, Boston, 1831–1865
New York Age, New York, 1887–1953
New York Amsterdam News, New York 1909–1940
North Star, Rochester, NY, 1847–1851
Weekly Advocate, New York, 1837
Weekly Anglo-African, New York, 1859

UNITED STATES PRESS
Brooklyn Daily Eagle, Brooklyn, 1841–1940
New York Daily Tribune, New York, 1842–1866
New York Herald, New York, 1840–1920
New York Sun, New York, 1833–1895
New York Times, New York, 1851–1957
San Francisco Chronicle, San Francisco, 1865–1910
Washington Post, Washington, DC, 1877–1910

Oral History/Interviews Conducted by Nancy Raquel Mirabal
Melba Alvarado, 1995, 2002, 2012
Lydia "Tata" Caraballosa, 2001

INTERVIEWS/DISCUSSIONS WITH NANCY RAQUEL MIRABAL
Club Cubano Inter-Americano
Pablo Foster, 2012, 2013
Gabriel Guardarramas 2015
Diana Lachatanere, 2012, 2013
Guillermo López Alan, 2015
Jo-Ana Moreno, 2012, 2013
Juan Rivera, 2015
Nilda Ruiz, 2012

Secondary Interviews
José Alvarez, interviewed by Paul Buhle, 1983
Robert Wagner Oral Histories

SECONDARY SOURCES
Aguilar, Luis E. *Cuba 1933: Prologue to Revolution*. Ithaca: Cornell University Press, 1972.
Almodóvar, Carmen. *Máximo Gómez, Diario de campaña, 1868–1898*, Estudios Preliminar: Universidad de Oviedo, 1998.
Anderson, Benedict. *Imagined Communities: Reflections and the Origins and Spread of Nationalism*. London: Verso, 1983.
Andréu, Iglesias, César, ed. *Memoirs of Benardo Vega: A Contribution to the History of the Puerto Rican Community in New York*. New York: Monthly Review Press, 1984.
Andrews, George Reid. *Afro Latin-America, 1800–2000*. New York: Oxford University Press, 2004.
Arredondo, Alberto. *El negro en Cuba*. Havana: Editorial Alfa, 1939.
Arroyo, Jossiana. *Writing Secrecy: Technologies in Caribbean Freemasonry*. New York: Palgrave Press, 2013.
———. "Technologies: Transculturations of Race, Gender, and Ethnicity in Arturo A. Schomburg's Masonic Writings." In *Technofuturos: Critical Interventions in Latina/o Studies*, eds. Nancy Raquel Mirabal and Agustin Laó-Montes. Lanham: Rowman and Littlefield, 2007.
Barthes, Roland. *The Semiotic Challenge*. Berkeley: University of California Press, 1994.
———. *New Critical Essays*. Berkeley: University of California Press, 1990.
Benítez-Rojo, Antonio. *The Repeating Island: The Caribbean and the Postmodern Perspective*. Durham: Duke University Press, 1992.
Berlin, Ira. *Many Thousands Gone: The First Two Centuries of Slavery in North America*. Cambridge, MA: Harvard University Press, 1998.

Berlin Ira, and Leslie M. Harris, eds. *Slavery in New York*, published in conjunction with the New York Historical Society. New York: New Press, 2005.

Bhabha, Homi K. *The Location of Culture*. London: Routledge, 1994.

Brady, Mary Pat. *Extinct Lands, Temporal Geographies: Chicana Literature and the Urgency of Space*. Durham: Duke University Press, 2001.

Brah, Avtar. *Cartographies of Diaspora: Contesting Identities*. London: Routledge, 1996.

Braziel, Evans Jana, and Anita Bannur, eds. *Theorizing Diaspora*. Oxford: Blackwell Publishing, 2003.

Brock, Lisa. "Back to the Future: African-Americans and Cuba in the Time(s) of Race." *Contributions in Black Studies* (Ethnicity, Gender, Culture, and Cuba, Special Section). 12, 3 (1994): 9–32.

Brock, Lisa, and Digna Castañeda Fuertes, eds. *Between Race and Empire: African-Americans and Cubans Before the Cuban Revolution*. Philadelphia: Temple University Press, 1998.

Bronfman, Alejandra. *Measures of Equality: Social Sciences, Citizenship and Race in Cuba, 1902–1940*. Chapel Hill: University of North Carolina Press, 2004.

Brooks, Joanna. *American Lazarus: Religion and the Rise of African-American and Native-American Literature*. New York: Oxford University Press, 2007.

Brown, David Luis. "An 1848 for the Americas: The Black Atlantic, 'El negro mártir,' and Cuban Exile Anticolonialism in New York City," *American Literary History* 21, 3 (Fall 2009): 431–463.

———. *Waves of Decolonization: Discourses of Race and Hemispheric Citizenship in Cuba, Mexico, and the United States*. Durham: Duke University Press, 2008.

Burgos, Adrian, Jr. *Cuban Star: How One Negro League Owner Changed the Face of Baseball*. New York: Hill and Wang, 2012.

———. *Playing America's Game: Baseball, Latinos and the Color Line*. Berkeley: University of California Press, 2007.

Burrows, Edwin G. and Mike Wallace. *Gotham: A History of New York City to 1898*. New York: Oxford University Press, 1999.

Cabrera, Raimundo. *Cuba and the Cubans*. Philadelphia: The Levytype Co. 1896.

Cairo, Ana. "Emilia Casanova y la dignidad de la mujer cubana." In *Mujeres Latinoamericanas: Historia y Cultura, Siglos XVI al XIX*, ed. Luisa Campuzano, I: 231–41. Havana and Mexico City: Casa de las Américas and University Autónoma Metropolitana Iztalapa, 1997.

Candelario, Ginetta E. B. *Black Behind the Ears: Dominican Racial Identity from Museums to Beauty Shops*. Durham: Duke University Press, 2007.

Cantón, Navarro José, ed. *El Partido Revolucionario Cubano de José Martí*. Havana: Editorial Política, 1982.

Casanovas, Joan. *Bread or Bullets: Urban Labor and Spanish Colonialism in Cuba, 1850–1898*. Pittsburgh: University of Pittsburgh Press, 1998.

Casasús, Juan J. E. *La emigración cubana y la independencia de la patria*. Havana: Editorial Lex, 1953.

Casper, Scott E. *Constructing American Lives: Biography and Culture in Nineteenth Century America*. Chapel Hill: University of North Carolina Press, 1999.

Castañeda, Escarra Orlando. *Martí, los tabaqueros y la Revolución de 1895*. Havana: Comisión de Propaganda y Defensa del Tobaco Habanero, 1946.

Chaffin, Tom. *Fatal Glory: Narciso López and the First Clandestine U.S. War against Cuba*. Charlottesville: University Press of Virginia, 1996.

Chao, Raúl Eduardo. *Baraguá: Insurgents and Exiles in Cuba and New York During the Ten Years War of Cuban Independence, (1868–1878)*. Dupont Circle Editions, 2009.

Childs, Matt. *The 1812 Aponte Rebellion in Cuba and the Struggle Against Atlantic Slavery*. Chapel Hill: University of North Carolina Press, 2006.

Cohen, Robin. *Global Diasporas: An Introduction*. Seattle: University of Washington Press, 1997.

Coronado, Raúl. *A World Not to Come: A History of Latino Writings and Print Culture*. Cambridge, MA: Harvard University Press, 2013.

Cruz, Malavé Arnaldo. "Under the Skirt of Liberty: Giannina Braschi Rewrites Empire." *American Quarterly* 66, 3 (2014): 801–818.

Curry, Leonard. *The Free Black in Urban America*. Chicago: University of Chicago Press, 1981.

Cuyas, Arturo. *Estudio sobre la inmigración en los Estados Unidos*. New York: Thompson y Moreau, 1881.

Dana, Jr., Richard Henry. *To Cuba and Back*. Carbondale: Southern Illinois University Press, 1966.

Delany, Martin. *Blake; or, The Huts of America*. Floyd Miller, ed. Boston: Beacon, 1970.

———. *The Condition, Elevation, Emigration, and Destiny of the Colored People*. New York: Arno, 1968.

de Certeau, Michel. *The Writing of History*. New York: Columbia University Press, 1992.

de la Fuente, Alejandro. *A Nation for All: Race, Equality and Politics in Twentieth Century Cuba*. Chapel Hill: University of North Carolina Press, 2001.

———. "Cuban Myths of Racial Democracy: 1900–1912." *Latin American Research Review* 34, 3 (1999): 39–47.

———. "Two Dangers, One Solution: Immigration, Race, and Labor in Cuba, 1900–1930. *International Labor and Working-Class History* 51 (Spring 1997): 30–49.

Derby, Lauren. *The Dictator's Seduction: Politics and the Popular Imagination in the End of Trujillo*. Durham: Duke University Press, 2009.

Deschamps Chapeaux, Pedro. *Rafael Serra y Montalvo: Obrero incansable de nuestra independencia*. La Habana: Unión Escritores y Artistas de Cuba, 1975.

Deulofeu, Manuel. *Héroes del destierro. La emigración. Notas históricas*. Cienfuegos, Cuba: Imprenta de M. Mestre, 1904.

Domínguez, Teófilo. *Ensayos biográficos: Figuras y Figuritas:* Primera Serie, INP Lafayette Street, 105. Tampa, FL, 1899.

Dubois, Laurent, and John D. Garrigus. *Slave Revolution in the Caribbean, 1789–1804: A Brief History with Documents*. New York: Bedford Cultural Edition Series, 2006.

Dzidzienyo, Anani, and Suzanne Oboler, eds. *Neither Enemies Nor Friends: Latinos, Blacks, Afro-Latinos*. New York: Palgrave Press, 2005.

Edwards, Hayes Brent. *The Practice of Diaspora: Literature, Translation and the Rise of Black Internationalism*. Cambridge, MA: Harvard University Press, 2003.

Estrade, Paul. "Los clubes femeninos en el Partido Revolucionario Cubano." *Anuario de Estudios Martianos* 10 (1987): 175–192.

Fernández Robaina, Tomás. *El negro en Cuba, 1902–1958: Apuntes para la historia de la lucha contra discriminación racial*. La Habana, Cuba: Editorial de Ciencias Sociales, 1990.

Ferrer, Ada. *Insurgent Cuba: Race, Nation and Revolution, 1868–1898*. Chapel Hill: University of North Carolina Press, 1999.

———. "The Silence of Patriots." in *José Martí's Our America: From National to Hemispheric Cultural Studies*, ed. Jeffrey Belnap and Raúl Fernández. Durham: Duke University Press, 1998.

Fischer, Sibylle. *Modernity Disavowed: Haiti and the Cultures of Slavery in the Age of Revolution*. Durham: Duke University Press, 2004.

Foner, Philip. *Antonio Maceo: The "Bronze Titan" of Cuba's Struggle for Independence*. London: Monthly Review Press, 1977.

———. *A History of Cuba and its relations with the United States*. 2 Vols. New York: International Publishers, 1963.

———. *A History of Cuba and Its Relations with the United States*. Vol. 1, *1492–1845: From the Conquest of Cuba to La Escalera*. New York: International Publishers, 1962.

Freeman, Rhoda Golden. *The Free Negro in New York City in the Era Before the Civil War*. New York: Garland Publishing, 1994.

Gaines, Kevin K. *Uplifting the Race: Black Leadership, Politics, and Culture in the Twentieth Century*. Chapel Hill: University of North Carolina Press, 1997.

García-Menocal, Manuel de Céspedes Carlos. *Señal en la noche: Aproximación biográfica al padre Félix Varela*. Santiago de Cuba: Editorial Oriente, 2003.

Garskof-Hoffnung, Jesse. "The Migrations of Arturo Schomburg: On Being Antillano, Negro and Puerto Rican in New York." *Journal of American Ethnic History* 21, 1 (Fall 2001): 3–49.

Gatewood, Williard B. *Black Americans and the White Man's Burden, 1898–1903*. Urbana: University of Illinois Press, 1975.

Gellman, David N., and David Quigley. *Jim Crow New York: A Documentary History of Race and Citizenship, 1777–1877*. New York: New York University Press, 2003.

Gilroy, Paul. *The Black Atlantic: Modernity and Double Consciousness*. Cambridge, MA: Harvard University Press, 1993.

Greenbaum, Susan. *More than Black: Afro-Cubans in Tampa*. Gainesville: University of Florida Press, 2002.

Greenberg, Cheryl. *Or Does It Explode: Black Harlem in the Great Depression*. New York: Houghton Mifflin, 1991.

Griffin, Farah Jasmine. *Who Set You Flowin': The African American Migration Narrative*. New York: Oxford University Press, 1995.

Grillo, Evelio. *Black Cuban, Black American: A Memoir.* Houston: Arte Publico Press, 2000.

Gruesz, Kirsten Silva. *Ambassadors of Culture: The Transamerican Orgins of Latin Writing.* Princeton: Princeton University Press, 2002.

Guerra, Lillian. *The Myth of José Martí: Conflicting Nationalisms in Early Twentieth-Century Cuba.* Chapel Hill: University of North Carolina Press, 2005.

Guevara, Gema. "Inexacting Whiteness: Blanqueamiento as a Gender-Specific Trope in the Nineteenth Century." *Cuban Studies/Estudios Cubanos* 36 (2005): 105–128.

——. "Founding Discourses of Cuban Nationalism: La patria, blanqueamiento and La raza de Color." PhD dissertation, University of California, San Diego, 2000.

Guglielmo, Jennifer. *Living the Revolution: Italian Women's Resistance and Radicalism in New York City, 1880–1945.* Chapel Hill: University of North Carolina Press, 2010.

Guridy, Frank Andre. *Forging Diasporas: Afro-Cubans and African-Americans in a World of Empire and Jim Crow.* Chapel Hill: University of North Carolina Press, 2010.

——. "From Solidarity to Cross-Fertilization: Afro-Cuban and African-American Interaction during the 1930s and 1940s." *Radical History Review* 87 (Fall 2003): 19–48.

Harris, Leslie M. *In the Shadow of Slavery: African American in New York City, 1626–1863.* Chicago: University of Chicago Press, 2003.

Helg, Aline. "La Mejorana Revisited: The Unresolved Debate between Antonio Maceo and José Martí." *Colonial Latin American Historical Review* (Winter 2001): 61–89.

——. *Our Rightful Share: The AfroCuban Struggle for Equality, 1886–1912.* Chapel Hill: University of North Carolina Press, 1995.

Hewitt, Nancy A. *Southern Discomfort: Women's Activism in Tampa, Florida, 1880s–1920s.* Urbana: University of Illinois Press, 2001.

Hietala, Thomas. *Manifest Design: Anxious Aggrandizement in Late Jacksonian America.* Ithaca: Cornell University Press, 1985.

Higginbotham, Evelyn Brooks. "African-American Women's History and the Metalanguage of Race." *Signs* 17, 2 (1992): 251–274.

Holder, Thomas Alexis Susan. "Henry Highland Garnet: His Life. Times and an Afrocentric Analysis of his Writings." PhD dissertation. Temple University, 1995.

Hooks, Margaret. *Tina Modotti: Photographer and Revolutionary.* London: Harper Collins, 1993.

Horne, Gerald. *Race to Revolution: The U.S. and Cuba During Slavery and Jim Crow.* New York: Monthly Review Press, 2014.

——. *Black and Brown: African Americans and the Mexican Revolution, 1910–1920.* New York: New York University Press, 2005.

Horrego, Estuch, Leopoldo. *Martín Morúa Delgado: Vida y mensaje.* La Habana: Editorial Sánchez, S.A. 1957.

——. *Emilia Casanova: La vehemencia del separatismo.* La Habana: September 16, 1951.

Howard, Philip. *Changing History: Afro-Cuban Cabildos and Societies of Color in the Nineteenth Century*. Baton Rouge: Louisiana State University Press, 1998.

Howe, Ward Julia. *A Trip to Cuba*. Boston: Ticknor and Fields, 1860.

Hunter, Tera W. *To 'Joy My Freedom: Southern Black Women's Lives and Labors after the Civil War*. Cambridge, MA: Harvard University Press, 1997.

Hutchinson, Ofari Earl. *Let Your Motto Be Resistance: The Life and Thought of Henry Highland Garnet*. Boston: Beacon University Press, 1971.

Hutton, Frankie. *The Early Black Press in America, 1827 to 1860*. Westport, CT: Greenwood Press, 1993.

Iglesias, Andreu César, ed. *Memoirs of Benardo Vega: A Contribution to the History of the Puerto Rican Community in New York*. New York: Monthly Review Press, 1984.

Jacobsen, Matthew Frye. *Whiteness of a Different Color: European Immigrants and the Alchemy of Race*. Cambridge, MA: Harvard University Press, 1998.

James, Winston. *Holding Aloft the Banner of Ethiopia: Caribbean Radicalism in Early Twentieth Century America*. London: Verso, 1998.

Jiménez Román, Miriam, and Juan Flores, eds. *The Afro-Latina/o Reader*. Durham: Duke University Press, 2010.

Kanellos, Nicolás, and Helvetia Martell, eds. *Hispanic Periodicals in the United States, Origins to 1960: A Brief History and Comprehensive Bibliography*. Houston: Arte Publico Press, 2000.

Kaplan, Amy. *The Anarchy of Empire in the Making of U.S. Culture*. Cambridge, MA: Harvard University Press, 2005.

Kazanjian, David. *Colonizing Trick: National Culture and Imperial Citizenship in Early America*. Minneapolis: University of Minnesota Press, 2003.

Kelley, Robin D. G. "How the West Was One: The African Diaspora and the Remapping of U.S. History." In *Rethinking American History in a Global Age*, ed. Thomas Bender. Berkeley: University of California Press, 2002.

———. " 'But a Local Phase of a World Problem': Black History's Global Vision, 1883–1950." *Journal of American History* 86, 3 (December 1999): 1045–1077.

———. *Hammer and Hoe: Alabama Communists during the Great Depression*. Chapel Hill: University of North Carolina Press, 1990.

Kirk, John. *José Martí: Mentor of the Cuban Nation*. Tampa: University Press of Florida, 1983.

Knight, Franklin W. *Slave Society in Cuba during the Nineteenth Century*. Madison: University of Wisconsin Press, 1970.

Kutzinski, Vera M. *Sugar's Secrets: Race and the Erotics of Cuban Nationalism*. Richmond: University Press of Virginia, 1993.

Lamas, Carmen E. "The Black Lector and Martín Morúa Delagado's Sofia (1891) and La Familia Unzúazu (1901)." *Latino Studies Journal* 13 (Spring 2015): 113–130.

Langley, Lester D. *Struggle for the American Mediterranean: United States- European Rivalry in the Gulf Caribbean, 1776–1904*. Athens: University of Georgia Press, 1976.

Lazo, Rodrigo. *Writing to Cuba: Filibustering and Cuban Exiles in the United States.* Chapel Hill: University of North Carolina Press, 2005.

Levine, Robert S. *Martin Delany, Frederick Douglass: And the Politics of Representative Identity.* Chapel Hill: University of North Carolina Press, 1997.

Lewis, Earl. "To Turn as on a Pivot: Writing African-Americans into a History of Overlapping Diasporas." *American Historical Review* 100, 3 (June 1995): 765–787.

———. *In Their Own Interests: Race, Class and Power in Twentieth Century Norfolk, Virginia.* Berkeley: University of California Press, 1991.

Lomas, Laura. *Translating Empire: José Martí, Migrant Latino Subjects and American Modernities.* Durham: Duke University Press, 2009.

López, Antonio. *Unbecoming Blackness: The Diaspora Cultures of Afro-Cuban America.* New York: New York University Press, 2012.

López, Iraida. *Impossible Returns: Narratives of the Cuban Diaspora.* Gainesville: University Press of Florida, 2015.

López Mesa, Enrique. *La Comunidad cubana de New York: Siglo XIX.* La Habana, Cuba: Centro de Estudios Martianos, 2002.

Lugo Ortiz, Agnes. *Identidades imaginadas: Biografía y nacionalidad en el horizonte de la Guerra,* (Cuba 1860-1898). Rio Piedras: Editorial de la UPR, 1999.

———. "En un rincón de la Florida: Exile and Nationality in José Martí's Biographical Chronicles in Patria," Louis A. Pérez, ed. *José Martí in the United States: The Florida Experience* Tempe: University of Arizona Press, 1995.

Lynk, Miles V. *The Negro Soldiers in the Spanish American War.* New York: AMS Press, 1899, reprinted 1971.

Marks, George III (ed.). *The Black Press Views American Imperialism, 1898-1900.* Ayer Co., 1973.

Martí, José. *Selected Writings.* Edited and Translated by Esther Allen. New York: Penguin, 2002.

———. *Nuevas cartas de Nueva York.* Mexico: Siglo Veintiuno, 1980.

———. *Política de Nuestra América.* Mexico: Siglo Veintiuno, 1977.

———. *Obras completas.* 27 vols. Havana: Editorial de Ciencias Sociales 1975.

———. *Cuba, Nuestra América y los Estados Unidos.* Mexico: Siglo Veintiuno, 1973.

———. *En los Estados Unidos.* Editorial S.A. Madrid, 1968.

———. *Obras completas.* 21 vols. Havana: Editorial Nacional, 1963.

———. *La cuestión racial.* La Habana: Editorial Lex, 1959.

———. *Cartas á Manuel Mercado.* Ediciónes de la Universidad Nacional Autónoma de México, 1946.

Martínez Alier, Verena. *Marriage, Class and Colour in Nineteenth Century Cuba.* Ann Arbor: University of Michigan Press, 1974.

May, Robert E. *The Southern Dream of a Caribbean Empire, 1854-1861.* Baton Rouge: Louisiana State University Press, 1973.

Meehan, Kevin, and Paul B. Miller. "Martí, Schomburg y la cuestión racial en las Américas." *Afra-Hispanic Review* 25, 2 (Fall 2006): 73–88.

Mena, Luz. "Stretching the Limits of Gendered Spaces: Black and Mulatto Women in 1830s Havana." *Cuban Studies/Estudios Cubanos* 26 (2005): 87–104.

Milian, Claudia. *Latining American: Black-Brown Passages and the Coloring of Latino/a Studies*. Athens: University of Georgia Press, 2013.

Mirabal, Nancy Raquel. "Melba Alvarado, El Club Cubano Inter-Americano, and the Creation of Afro Cubanidades in New York City." In *The Afro-Latina/o Reader*, eds. Miriam Jiménez Román and Juan Flores. Durham: Duke University Press, 2010.

———."Scripting Race, Finding Place: African-Americans, AfroCubans and the Diasporic Imaginary in the United States." In *Neither Friends Nor Enemies: Latinos, Blacks, Afro-Latinos*, eds. Anani Dzidzienyo and Suzanne Oboler. London: Palgrave Press, 2005.

———. "'Ser de Aquí': Beyond the Cuban Exile Model," *Latino Studies Journal* 17 (November 2003): 366–382.

———. "'No Country, but the One We Must Fight For': The Emergence of an 'Antillean' Nation and Community in New York City, 1860–1901." In *Mambo Montage: The Latinization of New York*, eds. Agustin Láo and Arlene Dávila. New York: Columbia University Press, 2001.

———. "Telling Silences and Making Community: Afro-Cubans and African-Americans in Ybor City and Tampa, Florida, 1899–1917." In *Between Race and Empire: Cubans and African-Americans Before the Cuban Revolution*, eds. Lisa Brock and Digna Castañeda Fuertes. Philadelphia: Temple University Press, 1998.

———."'Más Que Negro': José Martí and the Politics of Unity." In *José Martí in the United States: The Florida Experience*, ed. Louis A. Pérez, Jr. Tempe: Arizona State University Press, 1995.

Mirabal, Nancy Raquel, and Agustin Laó Montes, eds. *Technofuturos: Critical Interventions in Latina/o Studies*. Lanham: Rowman and Littlefield, 2007.

Montaud, Roldán de Inés. "Origen, evolución, y supresión del grupo negros emancipados en Cuba (1817–1870)." *Revista de Indias* 42 (1982): 167–168.

Montejo Arrechea, Carmen. "*Minerva*: A Magazine for Women (and Men) of Color." In *Between Race and Empire: African-Americans and Cubans before the Cuban Revolution*, eds. Lisa Brock and Digna Castañeda Fuertes. Philadelphia: Temple University Press, 1998.

Montes-Huidobro, Matías, ed. *El laúd del desterrado*. Houston: Arte Público Press, 1995.

Naison, Mark. *Communists in Harlem During the Depression*. Urbana: University of Illinois Press, 2005.

Nwankwo, Ifeoma Kiddoe. *Black Cosmopolitanism: Racial Consciousness and Transnational Identity in the Nineteenth-Century Americas*. Philadelphia: University of Pennsylvania Press, 2005.

Ortiz, Ricardo. *Cultural Erotics in Cuban America*. Minneapolis: University of Minnesota Press, 2007.

Pacheco, María Caridad. *Juan Fraga: Su obra en la pupila de Martí*. La Habana: Editoral Politica, 1982.

Painter, Nell. *Standing at Armageddon: A Grassroots History of the Progressive Era.* New York: W.W. Norton, 2008.

Pappademos, Melina. *Black Political Activism and the Cuban Republic.* Chapel Hill: University of North Carolina Press, 2011.

Paquette, Robert. *Sugar Is Made with Blood: The Conspiracy of La Escalera and the Conflict between Empires over Slavery in Cuba.* Middletown, CT: Wesleyan University Press, 1988.

Patterson, Tiffany Ruby, and Robin D. G. Kelley. "Unfinished Migrations: Reflections on the African Diaspora and the Making of the Modern World." *African Studies Review* 43, 1 (April 2000): 11–45.

Pérez, Louis A., Jr. *Cuba in the American Imagination: Metaphor and the Imperial Ethos.* Chapel Hill: University of North Carolina Press, 2008.

———. *On Becoming Cuban: Identity, Nationality, and Culture.* Chapel Hill: University of North Carolina Press, 1999.

———. *The War of 1898: The United States and Cuba in History and Historiography.* Chapel Hill: University of North Carolina Press, 1998.

———. *Cuba: Between Reform and Revolution.* New York: Oxford University Press, 1995.

———. *Cuba and the United States: Ties of Singular Intimacy.* Athens: University of Georgia Press, 1990.

———. "Politics, Peasants, and People of Color: The 1912 'Race War' in Cuba Reconsidered." *Hispanic American Historical Review* 66, 3 (August 1986): 509–539.

———. *Cuba Between Empires, 1878–1902.* Pittsburgh: University of Pittsburgh Press, 1983.

Piqueras, José Antonio. *Félix Varela ye la prosperidad de la patria criolla.* Prisma Historico, Viejos Documentos, Nuevas Lecturas, Ediciónes Calles, 2007.

Poyo, Gerald E. *With All and for the Good of All: The Emergence of Popular Nationalism in the Cuban Communities of the United States, 1848–1898.* Durham: Duke University Press, 1989.

———. "José Martí: Architect of Social Unity in the Emigré Communities of the United States." In *José Martí: Revolutionary Democrat,* eds. Christopher Abel and Nissa Torrents. Durham: University of North Carolina Press, 1986.

———. "The Anarchist Challenge to the Cuban Independence Movement, 1885–1890." *Cuban Studies/Estudios Cubanos* 15, 1 (Winter 1985): 29–41.

Pratt, Mary Louise. *Imperial Eyes: Travel Writing and Transculturation.* New York: Routledge, 1992.

Radhakrishnan, Rajagopalan. *Diasporic Meditations: Between Home and Location.* Minneapolis: University of Minnesota Press, 1996.

Ramos, Julio. *Amor y Anarquía: Los escritos de Luisa Capetillo.* Puerto Rico: Ediciónes Huracán, 1992.

Rowe, John Carlos. "Nineteenth-Century U.S Literary Culture and Transnationality." *Publications of the Modern Language Association* 118 (January 2003): 78–89.

Rubens, Horatio S. *Liberty: The Story of Cuba.* New York: Brewer, Warren & Putnam, 1932.

Ruíz Suárez, Bernardo. *The Color Question in the Two Americas.* New York: Hunt Publishing, 1922.

Sabin, Arthur J. *Red Scare in Court: New York Versus the International Worker's Order.* Philadelphia: University of Pennsylvania Press, 1999.

Saco, José Antonio. *Papeles sobre Cuba Tomo I.* Division General de Cultura, *Ministerio de Educación,* La Habana, 1960.

———. *Papeles sobre Cuba Tomo III* (Division General de Cultura, *Ministerio de Educación,* La Habana, 1960.

———. *Contra La anexión Tomo I.* La Habana, 1928.

———. *Contra La anexión Tomo II.* La Habana, 1928.

———. *La situación política de Cuba y su remedio* (1851), *Folletos* Escritos por Don José Antonio Saco, contra la Anexión de la Isla de Cuba a los Estados Unidos de América, 151–178. New York: Lockwood, 1856.

Sánchez, Korrol, Virginia E. *From Colonia to Community: The History of Puerto Ricans in New York City.* Berkeley: University of California Press, 1983.

Sarabia, Nydia. *La patriota del silencio:* Carmen Miyares. La Habana: Editorial Ciencias Sociales, 1990.

Sarduy, Pérez Pedro, and Jean Stubbs, eds. *AfroCuba: An Anthology of Cuban Writing on Race, Politics and Culture.* Minneapolis: Ocean Press, 1993.

Sartorius, David. *Ever Faithful: Race, Loyalty, and the Ends of Empire in Spanish Cuba.* Durham: Duke University Press, 2014.

Schor, Joel. *Henry Highland Garnet: A Voice of Black Radicalism in the Nineteenth Century.* Westport, CT: Greenwood Press, 1977.

Scott, Rebecca. *Degrees of Freedom: Louisiana and Cuba After Slavery.* Cambridge, MA: Harvard University Press, 2005.

———. *Slave Emancipation in Cuba: The Transition to Free Labor, 1860–1899.* Princeton: Princeton University Press, 1985.

———. "Gradual Abolition and the Dynamics of Slave Emancipation in Cuba, 1868–86." *Hispanic American Historical Review* 63, 3 (August 1983): 449–477.

Serra, Rafael. *Patriota y revolucionario, fraternal amigo de Martí.* La Habana: Oficina del historiador de la cuidad de La Habana: 1959.

———. *Republica possible* (obra postuma), Habana: Venta y papeleria de Rambla y Bouza, 1909.

———. *Para blancos y negros: Ensayos políticos, sociales, y económicos.* Habana: Imprenta, "el score" Aguila 117, Cuarta Serie, 1907.

———. *Ensayos políticos, sociales y económicos.* New York, 1899.

Smadar, Lavie, and Ted Swedenburg, eds. *Displacement, Diaspora, and Geographies of Identities.* Durham: Duke University Press, 1996.

Stephens, Michelle Ann. *Black Empire: The Masculine Global Imaginary of Caribbean Intellectuals in the United States, 1914–1962.* Durham: Duke University Press, 2005.

Stoler, Ann Laura. "Intimidations of Empire: Predicaments of the Tactile and Unseen," In *Haunted by Empire: Geographies of Intimacy in North American History,* ed. Stoler. Durham: Duke University Press, 2006.

Stoner, Lynn. *From the House to the Streets: The Cuban Women's Movement for Legal Reform, 1898–1940.* Durham: University of North Carolina Press, 1991.

Suárez, Díaz Ana. *Escapé de Cuba: El exilio neoyorquino de Pable de la Torriente-Brau* (marzo 1935–agosto 1936). La Habana: Ciencias Sociales, 2008.

Sweig, Julie E. *Inside the Cuban Revolution: Fidel Castro and the Urban Underground.* Cambridge, MA: Harvard University Press, 2004.

Thomas, Lorrin. *Puerto Rican Citizen: History and Political Identity in Twentieth-Century New York City.* Chicago: University of Chicago Press, 2010.

Toledo, Josefina. *Sotero Figueroa, Editor de Patria: Apuntes para un biografía.* La Habana: Editorial, Letras Cubana, 1985.

Tomich, Dale. "The Wealth of Empire: Francisco Arango y Parreño, Political Economy, and the Second Slavery in Cuba." *Society for Comparative Study of Society and History* 45, 1 (2003): 4–28.

Trelles, Carlos M. "Bibliografía de autores de la raza de color." *Cuba Contemporánea* 43 (1927): 30–78. Trouillot, Michel Rolph. *Silencing the Past: Power and the Production of History.* Boston: Beacon Press, 1995.

Trujillo, Enrique. *Apuntes históricos: Propaganda y movimientos revolucionarios cubanos en los Estados Unidos desde enero de 1880 hasta febrero de 1895.* New York: El Porvenir, 1896.

Varela, Félix. *El Habanero: Papel político, científico, y literario.* Miami: Ediciónes Universal, 1997.

———. *Escritos políticos.* La Habana: Editorial Ciencias Sociales, 1997.

———. *Jicoténcal,* Luis Leal and Rodolfo J. Cortina, eds. Houston: Arte Publico Press, 1995.

Villaverde, Cirilo. *Cecilia Valdés o la loma del ángel.* New York: Oxford University Press, 2005.

———. [Un Contemporaneo, pseudo.]. *Apuntes biográficos de Emilia Casanova de Villaverde.* New York, 1874.

Walker, David. *Appeal: To the Coloured Citizens of the World.* Edited with an Introduction and Annotations by Peter P. Hinks. University Park: Pennsylvania State University Press, 2003.

Walker, David, and Henry Highland Garnet. *Walker's Appeal and Garnet's Address to the Slaves of the United States of America, 1848.* Reprint. Nashville: James C. Winston Publishing, 1994.

Walker, William. *The War in Nicaragua.* Mobile, AL: Goetzel, 1860.

Wallace, Maurice O. *Constructing the Black Masculine: Identity and Ideality in African American Men's Literature and Culture, 1775–1995.* Durham: Duke University Press, 2002.

Washington, Booker T. *The Negro in Business.* Boston: Hertel Jenkins and Company, 1907.

Watkins, Owens Irma. *Caribbean Immigrants and the Harlem Community, 1900–1930.* Bloomington: Indiana University Press, 1996.

Wilder, Craig Steven. *In the Company of Black Men: The African Influence on African American Culture in New York City.* New York: New York University Press, 2001.

———. *A Covenant with Color: Race and Social Power in Brooklyn.* New York: Columbia University Press, 2000.

INDEX

abolitionism: African American, 71, 72, 242n32; black press and, 49, 51; British, 40, 41, 42, 46; labor and, 102; in New York, 15, 70, 234n34; US, 40, 42, 70–71; Varela y Morales and, 13–14, 233n33. *See also* anti-slavery; emancipation

Ación y Naranjo, Facundo, 163

African American abolitionism, 71, 72, 242n32

African American leaders, 17; on black emigration out of US, 51–52; Ten Years' War and, 16

African American men, 68; black masculinity and, 65–66; Cuban slavery and, 63

African Americans: Afro-Cuban migrants and, 168–69, 202, 273n46; Chinese compared to, 94–95; citizenship of, 95; civil rights of, 65; Cuban Anti-Slavery Society and, 62, 63, 72; Fifteenth Amendment parade of, 67; hemispheric concerns of, 58–59; as migrants from South, 92, 247n93; post-US emancipation difficulties and violence for, 67–68; reporters on race in Cuba, 149; Spanish-American War and, 149–50; US racism and, 150–51. *See also* blacks; race

African American women, 50, 68; *Minerva* and, 119

Africans: diasporic political reality of, 96; previously enslaved, 27, 46

Afro-Cuban clubs, 2, 115, 255n117; white clubs and, 202–3. *See also* El Club Cubano Inter-Americano; *specific clubs*

Afro-Cuban diaspora, in New York, 73, 115, 117

Afro-Cuban exiles and migrants, 100; leaders and Cuban independence from Spain, 19

Afro-Cuban independistas, 8, 128

Afro-Cuban men: La Liga and, 18, 112–15; *Minerva* and, 119; New York Cuban revolutionary club members, 99, 249n10; postwar male imaginaries of, 135–38; Ten Years' War and, 69

Afro-Cuban migrants, 6, 18, 21, 138; African Americans and, 168–69, 202, 273n46; Cuban quarter and, 108–9; discrimination and segregation, 109–10; La Liga and, 112–15, 117; in New York, 108–10, 112, 167–69, 229, 251n46, 261n96; racism and, 109–10, 117; texts of, 99; in US, 169, 227; women, 108, 251n44. *See also* Cuban cigar workers

Afro-Cuban music and performance, 217–23, 277n2

Afro-Cuban musicians, 22, 217–22, 219, 220, 232n6, 232n11, 276n100, 276n102

Afro-Cuban revolutionaries, 18; return to early Cuban Republic, 153

Afro-Cubans: activism, 100, 115; civil rights of, 65, 133–34; in Cuban Anti-Slavery Society, 73; Cuban independence and, 113; Cuban Republic and, 153, 157–64, 170; Cuban whites and, 100, 113, 115; expelled from El Club Nacional Cubano, 137–38; jobs of, 147; labor movement and, 100, 101; membership and exclusion from New York clubs, 186, 189–91, 194, 267n152; *Minerva Revista* and, 162; PIC and, 159, 161–64; PRC and, 131–34; Race War of 1912 and, 163–65, 261n82; respectability of, 154; Spanish Civil War and, 265n133; US racism and, 150–51; veterans of Cuban wars for independence, 157–59

Cuban separatists: Afro-Cubans and white, 100, 113; Cuban exile separatist movement, 17, 101–5, 250n21

Cuban slavery, 25, 34, 72; African American men, 63; black press on, 50, 53, 54, 238n57; expansion of, 35–36; pro-annexationist Cubans, independence and, 40; slave revolts, 41–44, 50, 53; slave trade, 71; Spanish control and, 40; US and, 87, 246n78; US slavery and, 48, 65. *See also* Cuban Anti-Slavery Society; Cuban emancipation

Cuban sovereignty, and Teller Amendment, 145

Cuban War for Independence, 7, 17; US intervention in, 18, 135

Cuban wars for independence: Afro-Cuban veterans of, 157–59. *See also* Cuban insurgency

Cuban whites, 25; Afro-Cubans and, 100, 113, 115; Cuban migrant, 110, 112; La Liga and, 112–14; as outnumbered, 46. *See also* race

Cuban women: as cigar workers, 108, 251n43; enslaved, 36–37; migration to US by, 213–14, 275n80, 275n83, 275n86; rights and justice for, 119, 121, 258n21

Cuban women of color: free, 36–38, 236n28. See also *Minerva: The Biweekly Magazine for the Woman of Color*

Cuban working class, 102, 250n17. *See also* labor

Cuba postwar, 141–47, 158; Afro-Cuban male imaginaries, 135–38; Fraga and, 123–24; Stanhope on, 146–48. *See also* Cuban Republic

Cueria y Obrit, Basilio, 172, 178

Cuerpo de Consejos, 128, 129, 131

Day Book, 26, 27

de la Fuente, Alejandro, 159

Delany, Martin, 16, 42, 43, 52, 239n73

de la Paz, Francisco, 207, 274n62–63

Delgado, Manuel, 2, 170, 173

Deschamps Chapeaux, Pedro, 112, 117, 255n117, 257n137

diaspora: African diasporic political reality, 96; politics of whiteness and practices of, 15

diasporic blanqueamiento (politics of whiteness), 15–16

Dilar, Wen, 133

La Discusión, 11, 153, 233n27

La Doctrina de Martí, 134, 151, 257n137

"Domestic Slavery in Its Relations with Wealth: An Oration" (Allo y Bermúdez), 33–39, 236n29

Domínguez, F. V., 100

Domínguez, Teófilo, 18, 73, 114, 117, 249n10, 250n18; *Ensayos biográficos: Figuras y Figuritas* and, 135–38

Dorsey, Charles, 89, 91

Douglass, Frederick, 16, 53–54, 65, 71, 93, 238n57, 239n69; black press and, 48, 49

Downing, George, 65

Draft Riots of 1863, 68, 241n24

Dred Scott v. Sanford Case, 15, 234n36

Duarte, Pedro, 136

Echegoyen de Cañizares, Ana, 212

emancipation: blackness and, 45; Haiti, 45–46; Jamaica, 45. *See also* abolitionism; anti-slavery; Cuban emancipation; US emancipation

Ensayos biográficos: Figuras y Figuritas, 135–38

La Escalera, 14, 42, 43, 46

Estenoz, Evaristo, 159, 164

Estrada Palma, Tomás, 109, 131; as Cuban Republic president, 19, 135, 152–54, 156, 157, 159, 161, 260n54; as PRC president, 134; Serra and, 109, 134, 152–54, 156, 157, 159, 160, 260n54

exile politics, and Cuban Republic, 154, 156

exiles, Cuban. *See* Cuban exiles

ABOUT THE AUTHOR

Nancy Raquel Mirabal is Associate Professor in the American Studies Department and US Latina/o Studies Program at the University of Maryland, College Park. She currently directs the US Latina/o Studies Program, and serves on the Advisory Board for the Center for Global Migration Studies at the University of Maryland, College Park.